Introduction to THEATRE ARTS

VOLUME TWO / SECOND EDITION

TEACHER'S GUIDE

Suzi Zimmerman

MERIWETHER PUBLISHING
A division of Pioneer Drama Service, Inc.
Denver, Colorado

Meriwether Publishing
A division of Pioneer Drama Service, Inc.
PO Box 4267
Englewood, CO 80155

www.pioneerdrama.com

Executive Editor: Debra Fendrich
Project Manager and text design: Lori Conary
Cover design: Melissa Nethery

© Copyright 2021 Meriwether Publishing
Printed in the United States of America
Second Edition

ISBN 978-1-56608-268-6

Library of Congress Control Number: 2021940017

"The little foolery that wise men have makes a great show."
—William Shakespeare
As You Like It, Act I, Scene ii

DEDICATION

To all the teachers, professionals, students, family, and friends who contributed to this project; and to my own children, my nieces and nephews, and my students—past and present—who inspire me.

A super huge hug to my father for his hours of editing. I hope we did well!

A very special thanks to Kip for his coaching and care packages.

SPECIAL THANKS TO:

Megan Duckett

Diane Matson

Adam Blatner

Lindsay Price, Theatrefolk

Kip Petroff

Len Radin

Greg Arp

Bud Lang

Levi Curtis

Jack French

Aumna Iqbal

Dan Morrow

Richard Engling

Richard Miyasaki

George Nelson, Brigham Young University

Nicholas Zimmerman

Cam Culham, University of Victoria

Amy Langton, Dramatic Publishing, Inc.

Angela V. Farrand, Gallaudet University

Leila Rahimi, A Prairie Home Companion

Kenneth Dingledine, Samuel French, Inc.

Art Zapel, Contemporary Drama Service

David Zak, Bailiwick Repertory, Chicago

Jane Fraser, president, Stuttering Foundation of America

Dr. Paul Winters, president, National Theatre of the Deaf

George Ashiotis, co-artistic director, Theater by the Blind

Monona Rossol, M.S., M.F.A., Arts, Crafts, & Theatre Safety, Inc.

CONTENTS

CHAPTER 4 — SKILL BUILDING ACTIVITIES—THEATRE PROJECTS, MINI-UNITS, AND SELF-GUIDED LESSONS

CHAPTER 5 — UNDERSTANDING AND WRITING SCRIPTS

CHAPTER 6 — THEATRE BEHIND THE SCENES

CHAPTER 7 — PRODUCTION 101: A PRIMER FOR LARGE-SCALE STUDENT-DIRECTED AND STUDENT-PRODUCED SCENES AND PLAYS

INTRODUCTION

For the most successful, being "good enough" is not good enough. The idea of being average, acceptable, or sufficient is synonymous with failure; therefore, many people for whom success is important strive for excellence, greatness, and the "outstanding." They seek to impact, influence, move, impress, and innovate.

For a teacher, the acceptance of "good enough" probably means that education is a chore rather than a passion, a job rather than a calling. For students, it means learning is little more than a requirement, and that the only promise they see in their futures is having jobs they do not enjoy and continuing to live in mediocrity.

In October of 2012, Malala Yousafzai was a 15-year-old Pakistani student who simply wanted the same opportunity and freedom to learn as the boys in her community. At that time, her government had one set of laws, but religious zealots were imposing their own laws, creating chaos in more remote areas. Despite religious restrictions, she continued to go to school. On the ninth day of the month, gunmen boarded her school bus and shot her and two of her young, female classmates for the "crime" of education. Thankfully, all survived. Finally the world seemed to take notice, and the fight, which had seemed so insignificant before, suddenly became a global movement. Everyone deserves the right to learn. The classroom is a sacred place, and a safe, supportive, and creative classroom is a fundamental right.

As this second edition is in development, a world pandemic is ravaging countries everywhere, shutting down schools and forcing classrooms to be replaced with distance learning. Students are missing connections with teachers and with friends. They are forced to learn material without the benefit of one-on-one assistance, without the reassuring pat on the back to keep on trying.

From global fights for a right to an education to the local challenges of making sure students get the proper education even if restrictions keep them out of a classroom, how can teaching and learning ever settle to be just good enough? But if "good enough" isn't good enough, what is? What role does the art of theatre play in this drama and in normalcy?

First of all, every teacher and scholar of the art must know why theatre is important. What is its value in your life? If you have any doubts in your mind of its place in the hierarchy of important things, you will not make it a priority in your own life. Did you know that acting—and all the arts, for that matter—can be healing, therapeutic, and renewing? Take, for example, the innocent civilian victims of terrorism, like Malala. They have experienced a horrible tragedy. Often, art is destroyed—even priceless, historical relics. Homelessness becomes the norm, and children learn to look for emergency shelter in every playful situation—if play even exists. Perhaps worst of all, their once invulnerable, invincible parents, aunts, uncles, and friends become helpless, ill, or destabilized.

Some will seek comfort by writing poetry. Others will take touching photographs. Painters will find relief in putting the pictures that haunt their minds' eyes onto canvases, and singers will harmonize with a passion and understanding that didn't exist in their voices prior to their horrific experiences. Dancers will sweat, reach, stretch, leap, and sway like never before, and they will all slowly begin to mend.

Each artist has their place and means of healing. For actors, the stage is the first place to come to mind, but the classroom will do just as well. As they move from pain and suffering to their familiar pre-tragedy place of comfort, actors will make us feel the wind, the grime, the loneliness, the hunger, the hopelessness, the hope, and the rebirth. While theatre teachers are not therapists and should approach these emotional hurdles with extreme caution, they can still be valuable stepping stones in their students' journeys to wellness.

CREATING THE VALUABLE THEATRE PROGRAM

There are many factors that affect the value of a theatre program. These include how much money a school district has for the arts, how the members of the community value the arts, what role fine arts play in a community's development, and the participation of the teachers and students within the program. Some may interpret this to mean that poorer schools have poorer programs, and vice versa, but this is not necessarily true.

Theatre was born of necessity. In prehistoric times, it is believed that stories of great hunts and battles were passed on when those who were there re-enacted the events for those who were not. This served a number of important purposes. First, it aided with the flow of information. You might think of it as the evening news for cave dwellers. Second, it was a form of entertainment, believed to be followed quickly by music and dance. Tribes probably enjoyed feasting on the kill even as the hunters draped themselves in skins and told how the meal was brought to the hungry. It is even plausible that the stories were inflated a bit to excite the audience and to make the heroes seem even greater.

These re-enactments were almost certainly educational. Young men who would one day be hunters learned the ins and outs of the older, more experienced hunters, and it is highly probable that these early dramas aided in the development of language and the passing down of history.

During the Dark Ages, religious folk used plays to teach the uneducated about religion. A couple of centuries passed, and theatre and song evolved and merged to create opera, which eventually brought us musicals. Today, one of the most common pastimes, watching TV, brings the world of theatre into almost every home. Even televised sports have taken on a theatrical quality. Spectacular lighting, fireworks, special effects, and dramatic commentary have helped to catapult the sports industry to unforeseen heights. There is no arguing that what started as storytelling around a fire has become one of the world's most influential careers, hobbies, pastimes, and passions.

So, what makes a theatre program great? There must be a balanced chemistry of effective teaching, committed learning, and solid support. The continued resistance of any of these factors will kill any good program. The existence of all three is the foundation upon which an incredible program can be built!

First of all, an effective theatre program starts with an effective teacher. The teacher must be approachable, passionate, informed, and driven.

It is said that elementary school teachers teach children, and secondary teachers teach the subject matter. That implies that teachers of older children are less interested in the student and more interested in the curriculum. But a teacher must connect with their students regardless of their ages, and it would be impossible to do that without first really getting to know them.

Imagine standing on a high diving board, much higher than that with which you are comfortable. You are wearing a tiny, clingy swimsuit, and with all eyes on you, you wish you were in something much less revealing. Far below you is the icy pool, and standing on dry, solid ground is your fully clothed diving coach. "Dive," the coach yells. "Come on. You'll be fine. I promise."

Suddenly it hits you. You've never seen your dive coach in the pool or on the diving board. "Hey, Coach! Have you dived from here before?" You want reassurance that it is as safe as the coach says.

"Heavens, no!" the coach replies. "I'd break my neck!"

Being onstage can be a lot like being in a tiny, skin-tight Speedo poised high above an icy pool. For a young person who has not yet discovered the joy of acting or performing, it can be lonely and sickening. An outstanding theatre teacher makes a heartfelt connection with students. Such teachers share their own experiences and find joy in hearing those of their students. They comfort students, address their fears, and reinvent the activity, if needed, to a level more within the players' grasps. Outstanding teachers discover how to ease students' anxieties, draw out their talents, and summon their courage, and slowly the students expand their comfort zones to include the stage. If need be, such teachers take the stage with students to prove to them that it is as safe as the teachers say it is. Outstanding teachers never ask students to do anything they are not willing to do themselves. This does not mean that good teachers must model every performance for their students, nor does it mean every student needs this specialized nurturing. However, should the need arise, the outstanding theatre teacher will patiently and willingly accept the calling.

There is a fine line between caring for one's students and becoming too involved. A good teacher is an educational professiona first. Students and professionals alike must remember that the director is the decision-maker and the students are the learners. In most cases, students are still children, and as such, they still need guidance. It is good teaching to let them learn by discovery, but until each student has demonstrated the ability to make effective, mature choices, there must always be a firm adult presence. Likewise, each young person will take comfort in knowing exactly what is expected and what is considered unacceptable, and having a mature director who demonstrates these expectations consistently (again, the diving board scenario) will offer additional reassurance.

The idea that secondary teachers don't or can't care for their students the same way that the teachers of young children do is absurd. Do elementary teachers not love mathematics, language arts, science, and social studies? They probably do; otherwise, work would be torturous. The drive to teach a certain age of students has little to do with liking or not liking kids. It is much more likely that the choice is about personal preferences and simple logic. Jane loves theatre, but theatre is rarely taught below middle school. Likewise, Jeff loves education as a whole, and he wants to teach it all. At the same time, he finds that he deals with fewer discipline issues in the younger grades. Jane handles discipline more easily and is more at home in higher grades; Jeff is more at home with the lower grades.

But it doesn't stop there. Those who teach theatre probably answered a calling as young people. It is likely that a teacher helped them discover their passion for the subject, and it is just as likely that a love for the educational process began developing at about the same time. Theatre teachers do love their curricula, but they must care for kids too. Just as an effective speaker can move listeners to change or strengthen their beliefs, a theatre teacher's passion for their art can be contagious.

But not always. Some teachers simply lack the deep, intrinsic love of theatre, but that doesn't mean they are theatrically doomed. This book is designed especially for the non-theatre teacher, the young teacher, perhaps the less experienced teacher. Because theatre is, in many (actually most) areas, not a priority, it is often taught by those with room in their schedules. No one wants to be a bad teacher, so this book seeks to guide all teachers to reach all students.

For those who do not ache for the smell of a makeup kit or musty costume shop, there is still the potential to appreciate and understand theatre's draw. Almost all theatre teachers will tell you that reluctant performers are common. These students didn't want to take the class; they have stage fright; they can't act. Passion for the stage, for these few, is highly unlikely. Soon they learn to appreciate and then understand. For some, the interest stops there. However, many reluctant students of the stage begin to enjoy it. From that, love, passion, and even a very healthy addiction may develop. The common thread that turns a theatre skeptic into an appreciator or perhaps even a fanatic is, more often than not, a gifted and passionate teacher.

Maybe a troubled teen will feel attracted to a sketch because the teacher shared the story behind it, allowing the teen to make a personal connection to the art. Likewise, a shy young person may beg not to have to perform. A teacher gently coaxes the shy person to perform, perhaps by allowing modified performances and by understanding why the student has the anxiety and how to cope with it. The stage fright melts away and is replaced with a connection to the stage when the young person realizes that the bright spotlights make it impossible to see individual faces in the audience. The student feels powerful and important for the first time in life, and a love for performing is born.

Everyone is drawn to something, and every attraction has a backstory. Good teachers know enough about theatre, and enough about their students, to help each child discover an appreciation within. Good teachers will broaden each child's theatrical horizons slowly, securely, and comfortably, alleviating pressures and allowing for respect and passion for the art form to develop. Together they will learn as much as they can. This desire to learn, create, improve, and share performances will drive both the educator and the performer to build a better-than-average theatre program.

Besides having a strong theatre teacher, a budding program must also have a talented, enthusiastic, willing, and hardworking pool of students—and not just actors! It helps when there are many students from which to choose, so building a large program is certainly an option. However, many strong, successful programs are small. Quantity is not nearly as important as quality.

In a production, students play so many important roles that most directors (when your program is successful, you can retire the "teacher" title and take on that of "director") find they can't do the job without them. These tight-knit communities of actors, technicians, and crew members complete tasks ranging from repairing lighting instruments to taking calls at the box office, to selling ad space off-campus (where allowed), to directing, and more. They become very much like a professional company.

In these companies, actors learn that good theatre is challenging and that tucked away in those daunting challenges are even greater rewards. Most of these students do not have paying jobs. Their involvement in their school's theatre program keeps them far too busy, so they exist on less income than their money-making, non-theatre peers. Like most artists, actors are often jokingly referred to as "starving" for this very reason. They spend long hours with the company doing jobs most teens and adolescents don't know how to do—that many adults don't know how to do. They sew costumes, build sets, hang lights, program cues, run cables, patch, prompt, clean, paint, and emote.

Producing a high-quality show requires a great deal of sacrifice from everyone involved. Many theatre teachers take costumes home to sew, spend hours outside the workday completing needed tasks, and work weekends buying props and other items. Often these purchases are made out of their own pockets. Oftentimes they can be reimbursed, but only after weeks, or even months, of waiting. Why would teachers put so much of themselves into a job with a reputation for being low-paying? Simply put, the rewards are great.

The same goes for student actors and crew members. Many actors purchase props, costumes, and building materials either for their shows or for their classroom projects. Often, these are not required items, but pride in their work drives them to want to create things of quality. They look upon the purchases as investments in their educations. Each moment of time spent producing a play is compounded learning time. Some believe that producing plays teaches independence better than most extracurricular activities due to the student-to-teacher ratio and the high level of accountability required of each participant.

Parents are also called upon to make a sacrifice. They are often the next key ingredient in successful

I started teaching at a poor high school in 1997. It had a large auditorium with over one thousand seats, and from those seats, the stage appeared to be spacious. However, once onstage, it didn't take long to realize there was nothing but cinderblock behind the curtains. There was absolutely no backstage, no shop, no fly loft, no sound system, and the lighting system was simply frightening. It was a huge, gray station with three broom handles (literally broom handles!) duct-taped to mechanisms that operated rows of colored lights. Rarely did it work, and when it did, it smoked, sparked, and made hissing sounds. The kids nicknamed it the "Big Gray Elephant."

Above this monstrosity was a storage loft with old set pieces. There was a ladder leading straight up the wall to the ten-foot platform, but the ladder was missing bolts, and when the climber would get to the top rung, it would pull slightly away from the wall. The loft itself had no safety railing, and getting set pieces in and out was dangerous.

The stage had been used to store broken desks because there was no room at the district's warehouse. My assistant principal said I had to leave the two hundred-plus desks there, move them before every show, and put them back after. I was also told I'd never get a different lighting system because even though the one I had seemed old and faulty, it worked "great" (their perception, not mine, and they were wrong).

Sadly, I made an enemy when I went over my assistant principal's head and convinced the new head principal (whose son was a theatre major at my old college) to have the desks removed. By mid-year I had a new lighting system, and by the end of my second year I had convinced the school board to match my $5,000 (saved from play profits) to buy a portable sound system, microphones, and more. During my third year the district voted to build a new fine arts complex, complete with a new stage and theatre classroom (up to this point, I had taught in a small, regular classroom next door to a history class). We did the impossible simply by proving ourselves worthy, working hard, and refusing to take "no" for an answer. Had I allowed the inadequate facilities or the uncooperative assistant principal to impede my progress, it is likely those two hundred desks and the Big Gray Elephant would still be there.

theatre programs. Parents will run booster clubs, which have been known to make thousands of dollars for the company, and help the director with some of the more basic tasks. In some schools, parents are solely responsible for publicizing the shows, selling tickets, and running the box office and house. Very often, the one thing teachers will say can make or break a program is the involvement of the students' families.

One area that can either stop a growing program in its tracks or catapult an average program to greatness is the school's administrative team. They have difficult jobs, serving the students, teachers, the community, and the district—all at the same time. When one group has a different agenda from the others, the administrators must guide the stray group onto the right track. According to the hierarchical order of things, this usually means getting the teacher and students to do things according to the district's vision, which is formed around the vision of the voting majority—the parents. All of this must be done within the scope of the state's board of education. The administration is trying to serve various differing parties with as many agendas.

This will rarely mean the difference between having a theatre department and not having a theatre department. Instead, this may mean not getting to do a certain show or a particular type of show. In religious communities, it may mean staying away from controversial subject matter. In religiously diverse communities, it may mean staying away from topics that promote a certain religious belief or that may offend. Even when the religious temperature of a community is insignificant, many administrators will not give their stamps of approval to plays with heavy emotional or controversial historical themes.

Oftentimes, thriving theatre programs run into problems because of their facilities. Perhaps they become so successful that they outgrow their space. This is often the case in small towns that experience rapid growth, and it can also happen when a new teacher comes in and pushes a lagging program to new heights. In older schools, a common problem occurs when the stage and equipment begin to fall apart or become outdated. It may take months or even years to get back up to speed after such an interruption.

Sadly, more often than not, many stages are not built with theatre in mind; rather, their original intention is to house assemblies, PTA meetings, recitals, and graduations. To the unfamiliar, these dinosaurs of technology are state of the art—or at least acceptable. Requests for improvements fall on deaf ears because those in charge do not see a problem. This will often mean that there is no backstage space, no fly loft, inadequate lighting and sound equipment, no workshop or tools, and, most unfortunate, no safety equipment.

Even worse are the schools with no stage or performance facility. The only place to put on plays is the gym floor. Many are forced to pay top dollar to rent performance spaces, but even then, they rarely get to rehearse on the borrowed stages.

For teachers with poor or no facilities, not doing theatre may seem like the only option. However, remember theatre's history. If cavemen could do scenes around campfires, if passion plays could be done on wagons, and if the early American rebel actors could sneak plays in barns, schools certainly can still do good theatre in bad facilities. No one will agree to build a new stage for a teacher who waits to do shows until things are better. However, the people with money will pay attention to a teacher who proves the need by continuing to produce shows in parks or turns the gym into a beautiful Victorian parlor.

Your program will also get your administration's attention if you can demonstrate cross-curricular learning. Some of the most successful theatre programs are in schools where the drama department ventures outside its boundaries and into other parts of the school. When the theatre teacher can establish cooperative, effective relationships with others within her building, something great happens. Interdisciplinary education (or cross-curricular learning) is when two or more disciplines work together for the sake of broadening interest and understanding.

The play *I Never Saw Another Butterfly* by Celeste Raspanti (Dramatic Publishing, 1980) is based on Hana Volavkova's eponymous book (Schocken Books, revised edition; March 15, 1994), a collection of poems and artwork left behind in the children's ward of the Terezin concentration camp. While the play itself is not a true story, it is based on historically accurate "conjecture" about what realistically might have happened, giving it historical merit and making it a good example of cross-curricular learning.

With enough advance notice for the teachers to plan their lessons, a director could produce this show, the English teachers could fully explore the text, write poetry of their own, and discuss the value of diaries in literature, and the history teachers could incorporate it into their study of the Holocaust. The art teacher could teach how emotion, desperation, history, and circumstance affect art and could do a unit on art with minimal supplies. The art teacher could also do an art show in the lobby of the auditorium and use a projection screen to flash images of students' artwork onstage before, during, and after the show. Some of the more touching artwork could be selected for the program covers and publicity posters. The choir teacher could teach an a cappella song that could start the play, and the orchestra and band could do songs from the time period to transition from scene to scene or even to play as background music to some of the poetry.

How does interdisciplinary education affect the success of the theatre department? For one, educators are always seeking better ways to reach their students. Not every student learns the same way, so offering a number of perspectives ensures that more students comprehend and that the learning is more deeply ingrained. The other teachers will appreciate a break from the usual day-to-day teaching, and having a play performance to cap the unit will be an enjoyable experience for all. The students, themselves, will find the experience more refreshing and useful than the usual note-taking and passing of information. You will have a greater number of students participating, which will lead to more parents and family members buying tickets. Your principal will see your impact on the school's performance, the students' learning, and the teachers' teamwork. The principal will become your advocate.

You can even reach outside your campus by inviting other campuses to participate. Why not create black-and-white "coloring page"-type publicity posters and then have younger students from other schools color them for you? You can then have dozens or even hundreds of unique, hand-colored posters that parents will eagerly seek out in search of their children's artwork. You can do the same thing with program covers by printing the cover art in black and white with the cast and crew already listed on the reverse side. Send these to area elementary schools for the younger students to color and return to you. If you have additional pages to be inserted, return the programs to the printer for completion. If not, fold them and enjoy hundreds of unique, meaningful programs.

Besides a great teacher, talented and committed students, and a supportive administrative team, your community can also impact your department's success. Made up largely of your students' parents, neighbors, and relatives, the community wants to see you be successful. Community members want to see all of the activities with which their young people are involved flourish. You must work cooperatively with all the extracurricular and co-curricular activities because many of your actors will be involved in more than just acting.

At the same time, it is wise to keep your finger on your community's moral and ethical pulse. The artist in you will want to create your art at all costs, challenging the unspoken "norms" of the area. But this is one battle where a win could be a loss. You might fare better to work with the community rather than against it. Do not fight them. You accepted a job in their home. You are their guest. They will support you as long as you abide by their house rules. Just as you would never go into a person's home and challenge their morals (that is, you mind your manners), you should not offend your community by challenging theirs.

That doesn't mean you can't do good or even edgy theatre. It simply means that you must test the waters before you get in over your head. Rather than jumping in and doing a controversial play with all the sordid elements that make a thriller thrilling, prove yourself first. Once you have established yourself as someone the community can trust, then you can start experimenting with turning up the heat a bit. Listen to your audiences. If they stop coming or start complaining, you may have to back off some. Also, have faith in your students' parents and in your principal to help guide you. You will eventually find a temperature at which all of you can be comfortable. Your patrons and supporters are also the businesses and individuals who will be there for you financially, and you never want to bite the hand that feeds you.

In larger districts with many schools, it is always a good idea to work across campuses. If your district-wide theatre teachers are not already doing so, have meetings to coordinate performance dates so you aren't competing against one another. If you have schools that feed into yours or if you feed into another school, it's especially important that your schedules do not conflict.

Furthermore, you may find that you and another school have the same play slated for the same season. By cooperating with one another, you can come up with alternative titles, or perhaps one school will agree to hold off for a year.

Perhaps the various directors can coordinate prop sharing. For example, a school may do a show with large, expensive props like *Alice in Wonderland* or *Little Shop of Horrors*. If another school plans to do the same show, it can buy, rent, or borrow the props from the previous school. Perhaps the directors can make an arrangement to trade. Cooperation and sharing rather than competitiveness will benefit both parties.

Production nights are busy enough without having to worry about selling concessions, but these are great moneymakers. What if you sold concessions at another school's show (keeping the profits), and they sold them at your show? Not only are you showing support for one another's performances and getting to see their shows, but you are also making money in the process!

Perhaps the most valuable relationship a teacher can forge is with area colleges and universities. This can be done in all the ways mentioned above, plus many, many more. For example, college students are always looking for extra income, and your students might be interested in acting lessons. There are so many college kids who will jump at the chance to tutor a younger actor to help prepare for an audition or an exam—or just to help hone the young actor's skills.

If allowed, become FaceTime or Skype buddies with college students across the country. Your students can then work out scenes with these more experienced actors, and you can sign off on their volunteer hours or mentorship hours. Because of age-of-consent concerns, you will probably want to do this with both parent and administrative involvement.

Take your students to see the university-produced shows or volunteer for a Saturday set day on their campus so your students can learn from college theatre majors. Attend the college students' workshops or invite them to your campus to present a special lesson. Most importantly, if the college's theatre program is a good one, encourage your actors to apply. Having already established a working relationship with the college, scholarships will likely be plentiful! Even if your students choose to go to school elsewhere, your new contact may be able to help pave the way, get a foot in the door, or shed light on the dos and don'ts of the student's target school.

Growing a budding, healthy theatre program at your school will take more than a strong will and a large budget. There are relationships to be nurtured, obstacles to overcome, and even some occasional politics to navigate. Success will not come to those who sit back and wait for theatre to happen or to those who wait for an ideal environment. Schools with successful theatre programs will attribute their achievements to having a united, proactive team of teachers, students, and parents, and a supportive and involved administration and community. View obstacles as challenges rather than stop signs, and create allies rather than enemies. Also understand, however, that you cannot please everyone, and your "customers" are the students and their parents.

GOAL SETTING

Students, parents, and teachers must work together to build a thriving and valued theatre program. You might want to start by having a meeting or asking your students and their parents to complete a questionnaire about what needs to happen to make the program more successful. Add your own ideas. Now it's time to put those ideas into action!

Try this: what are three things you can do this year to make your theatre program more successful? On page 10, list them in order of importance, with goal 1 being most important.

Put these goals in your daily planner and write in occasional reminders to help keep yourself on track. In your planner, one year from today's date, make a note to ask yourself if you have achieved these goals. If you haven't, define why and create a plan to accomplish them quickly before too much additional time passes. Goal setting is an excellent way to make progress in all areas of our lives!

GOAL 1:

How do you plan to achieve this goal?

When is a realistic date for achieving this goal?

GOAL 2:

How do you plan to achieve this goal?

When is a realistic date for achieving this goal?

GOAL 3:

How do you plan to achieve this goal?

When is a realistic date for achieving this goal?

THEATRE FOR UNIQUE LEARNERS

INTRODUCTION

With most curricula, varying needs offer such a challenge to the teacher that the students are divided into groups and sent to separate rooms. The gifted students study a curriculum at a faster pace, special education students are placed into smaller classes where they are taught more slowly and with more one-on-one teacher time, and the rest attend regular education classes.

Theatre is different in that it offers so many varieties of activities. Not all theatre students have to be on the same path. One student may try a hand at acting but may decide that set construction is more attractive. Another student may love theatre and think that acting is the right outlet, but then may fall in love with directing. Because there are so many different jobs under the theatre umbrella, there is something for everyone—from the most challenged student to the most gifted.

There have been many studies on repetition and learning differences. Some very gifted people can hear new information once or twice and remember it easily. However, typical learners need to hear challenging, new information about six times in order to remember it. Some learners need to hear it even more. Most learners can master information after having heard it between six and thirteen times.

Does this mean that people who need less repetition are more intelligent than those who need more? Absolutely not. As a matter of fact, there are some very intelligent people who must hear facts more often than average, and there are some with severe learning challenges who can play songs on the piano after hearing them just one time. Each student has a unique learning style. Learning styles are so distinct to the individual that they are like a fingerprint of the mind.

This can add a great deal of stress to a teacher's job. How do you teach a student who cannot read while at the same time teaching a child who seems to know the answers before you do? Teachers must learn the styles of dozens of learners, and then they must figure out a way to teach each student without favoring, neglecting, or intimidating any one person.

What does all of this have to do with theatre? Producing a play is a team effort, and in educational theatre, giving equal opportunity to all actors, including those with disabilities and learning obstacles, is the law. But while it is a legal responsibility, meeting the unique challenges of a diverse group presents a lot of opportunities.

Take Shane, for example. Shane was a seventh grader with severe cerebral palsy who was confined to a wheelchair. He had no use of his hands and legs, and actually they tended to get in his way and frustrate him because they would often jerk out of control when he least expected it. He tilted his head to power his wheelchair, pressing pads on the right, left, and back to command direction. Unfortunately, his chair didn't always work properly, and he was often at the mercy of others to assist him.

Relying on others was made even more difficult because Shane couldn't speak. A small reflective laser dot on his forehead served as a cursor. With great difficulty, he would aim the reflection from the dot at a computer that was attached to his chair above his lap. After a second, the computer would attempt to understand his will, and between Shane, his computer, and the people around him, small bits of uncertain conversation would evolve. His computer, however, was also unreliable, and over the years he had developed his own style of communication by using eye contact, subtle shifts of his head, smiles, and wobbly nods to get his points across. To the onlooker, his every moment was filled with chaos and unpredictability. To Shane, this was life, and he handled it all with amusing "humdrum" patience.

Shane selected drama as his elective, so you can imagine his teacher's surprise that first day when this young actor who could not walk or speak rolled into her classroom. Perhaps some would have reacted with fear or astonishment, requesting that he take a class with which his limited skills were more on-level. But this teacher was pleasantly surprised. The teacher saw this as a personal opportunity to learn something new. Together, the teacher and Shane would find a way to both teach and learn about theatre from a variety of new angles.

The class began by learning the basics, and the young actor and his note-taking peer assistant had no problems. When the class did warm-ups and improvisations, both the assistant and Shane participated fully. During a game where each member does a sound and movement and the others mimic (See "Energy Circle" in *More Theatre Games for Young Performers* by Suzi Zimmerman), the class hesitated for fear they would hurt his feelings if they mimicked his uncontrollably thrashing arms and legs. On the contrary—he was so excited that they were doing what he wanted them to that he let out the most amazing giggle. He wasn't just teaching the teacher; Shane was taking the entire class on a great new adventure.

With each performance, Shane, his assistant, the special education department, and the teacher worked together to make sure he was always learning and was regularly performing. Sometimes students would ask him to be in their groups, and sometimes he would perform with his assistant, and there were even some solo performances. The consensus was that he was a natural-born performer with greasepaint in his veins.

One day he came to class early and witnessed the younger students working on lip-syncs (See Chapter 2) to "Hakuna Matata" from the soundtrack to *The Lion King*. After the sixth graders left, he communicated to the teacher that he wanted to try lip-syncing. During the five-minute passing period while the other students changed classes, Shane sang (made vocal sounds) and danced (manipulated his wheelchair around the room) to "Hakuna Matata." As his peers came into the classroom, they began singing too. He loved the company, and spending the passing period performing for the arriving students became his daily ritual. The teacher and many of the incoming students would join in, energizing and preparing the entire class for an hour of theatre. It was, perhaps, the only passing period in the history of the school in which students were actively and willingly engaged in learning!

Every student has a right to learn, and every teacher has a duty to teach, regardless of how much additional time or energy may be required. Shane's teacher did extra work, discovering new ways to involve a non-speaking, less mobile child. Without that extra expenditure of time and attention, Shane would have been neglected or simply told to take another elective, and the rest of the students would never have learned a valuable lesson in patience and compassion. However, by meeting the needs of an extraordinary learner, everyone benefited.

What kinds of learners do you have in your classes? What kind of learner or teacher are you? Most experts agree that there are three basic types of learners. Hands-on (or kinesthetic) learners like

to get up and walk around, get their hands dirty, experiment, and discover. Auditory learners get their information by using their ears, learning best by listening. Visual learners need to see information in order to grasp it. Most people will not be one specific type, but rather a combination of all three.

What makes an individual unique is how important each of the three learning styles is in how they retain information. Visual learners seem to get more out of a lesson when pictures, charts, diagrams, PowerPoint, Flash, and videos are used. If you tend to seek out pictures or visual aids to check your understanding, then you are probably heavily visual. Auditory or verbal learners like hearing information, so they seek out seminars and presentations. They tend to easily rephrase information and get a kick out of passing it on to others. Kinesthetic learners feel the need to get physically involved. They learn best by writing directly in their books or notes or recording information as it is being shared (rather than counting on recall), making models, and self-discovery.

There is more to learning than knowing your style or the styles of the students in the classroom. There are other learning differences, including everything from being gifted to being mentally, physically, socially, or emotionally challenged. Theatre must be available to all, and the news gets even better. Theatre has proven health benefits. So, you see, it's not just fun... it's good for you!

Section 504 of the Rehabilitation Act of 1973 says that if a program or activity receives federal financial assistance, it must grant equal access to people with disabilities. This would apply to all public schools and many private ones as well. But in case that doesn't seem to cover everything, Title II of the Americans with Disabilities Act of 1990 prohibits disability-based discrimination in public entities. This ensures that all students have equal access to education and educational choices.

A lot of non-theatre onlookers might ponder, "What's the big deal? It's not like a sport where someone could get hurt." This is not true. Acting is a very physical pastime, and the physical structure itself can pose dangers (and has in the past) if certain precautions are not taken. Most stages are raised with a sudden drop-off at the apron. Sets will often include even more levels of height, and, unlike public buildings, many are built without longevity in mind. In other words, they may not have safety rails or ramps, there may be some rough edges, the floors may not be perfectly level, or the configuration may change slightly from one rehearsal to the next if the set must be moved frequently. These are issues even with a cast of able-bodied actors; but they become serious issues with a blind actor or an actor in a wheelchair. Consideration must also be given to the safety of other actors and onlookers, as well as the teacher's and school's liability. By taking a little time to think about what might happen and working to reduce the possibility of potential dangers, everyone benefits.

For the most part, educating all students despite their learning styles or differences simply requires the teacher and the class to think creatively. Rely on what you know, or if you have no experience with a particular disability, use your many resources to ask for assistance. The following are some very basic suggestions for making the wonderful world of drama available to all learners n your class.

IN GENERAL

Start by talking to your school's special education advocate about any student who comes into your room with needs that are out of the ordinary. This expert should have a file of information gathered from the student, the parents, and a whole array of doctors, therapists, experts, and previous teachers. This will begin to paint a picture of your learner's needs and limitations. It may go as far as to dictate what you can and cannot do, what resources to use, which volunteers to call, and so on. However, if a student's need has not been ident fied, it will be up to you to start the referral process immediately. The sooner something is determined, the sooner you will be able to customize your process to fit the learner's unique requirements.

In the meantime, take a safety inventory of your classroom and any other areas (such as the stage, shop, costume lab, makeup rooms, and so on) where you plan to teach. Write down everything you find that may pose a hazard to any student. In particular, keep the unique limitations of your student in mind. For example:

- Is the floor level? Unevenness, sudden dips and rises, thresholds that are too severe, and items protruding from the floor can be dangerous to a blind student and can pose challenges to a student in a wheelchair. Consider taking up unnecessary rugs.

- Do all electrical sockets and switches have safety plates? Ensuring that electrical elements are securely hidden is a good idea for all students.

- Are the set pieces in storage stable? Again, this is important to all students, but a handicapped student will be at greater risk if common sense is not used when items are stored. Props piled too high or too deep can create undue risk. Shelving units should be attached to walls, and be especially aware of allowing items to protrude from any direction, any height, or to dangle from the ceiling.

- Consider putting safety cages around makeup lights. This will prevent serious burns.

There are several organizations that work specifically with disabled actors, and they can all be excellent resources for you or for your students who want to learn more. It would be impossible to list them all here, as there are literally thousands. However, the following few have withstood the test of time.

U. S. DEPARTMENT OF EDUCATION
400 Maryland Ave., SW
Washington, DC 20202
1-800-USA-LEARN (1-800-872-5327)
www.ed.gov

THEATER BREAKING THROUGH BARRIERS
(A professional, off-Broadway company of both vision-impaired and seeing actors)

400 West 43rd St., #43R
New York, NY 10036
(212) 243-4337
www.tbtb.org

THE NATIONAL THEATRE OF THE DEAF
Acting company comprised of deaf and hearing actors that tours the nation and the world. Each performance unfolds simultaneously in two languages: for the eye, American Sign Language, and for the ear, the Spoken Word.

139 North Main St.
West Hartford, CT 06107
(860)574-9063
www.ntd.org

NATIONAL DISABILITY THEATRE
Exclusively disabled staff seeking to change social policy on disability inclusion

www.nationaldisabilitytheatre.org

ARTICLE
"The accessible theatre classroom," by Shelley Nowacek, EdTA,
https://www.schooltheatre.org/about/news/the-accessible-theatre-classroom

- Check the temperature of your water heater; it should be set at a temperature that cannot scald but can still effectively heat the water.

- Is there an access ramp, lift, or elevator to the stage or to any area with student access? There must be safe equal access to students in wheelchairs.

- If you have an orchestra pit—especially one on hydraulics or which is especially deep—take every precaution necessary to ensure safety, especially if you have students with vision impairments, who are in wheelchairs, who are otherwise mobility limited, or students with mental impairments.

- Educate your non-disabled students on theatre safety and on working with whatever disabilities are present on your team or in your class.

It is also important to find a level of comfort early in the learning process between your disabled and non-disabled learners. Talk to the special education advocate to discuss how comfortable the disabled student is with talking about their uniqueness. Parents will also be understanding if you contact them and say, "I want to make your child's experience in my class as comfortable as possible, so I'd like to find out what will make them at ease and what might cause them embarrassment before they come tomorrow." Ask if there is anything you should say to the other students, what the disabled student might need done for them, and how to approach their needs in class without humiliation. In most cases, you will probably learn that the student has adapted to the point where any learning difference is practically unnoticeable.

VISUALLY IMPAIRED

George Ashiotis, blind actor and former co-artistic director of Theater by the Blind, has been acting most of his adult life. At eighteen, he joined The Lighthouse Players, a theatre company sponsored by the New York Lighthouse (the original Lighthouse for the Blind in the United States). He advises directors with disabled actors to avoid plays in which the characters are also disabled. "In so many plays that employ characters with disabilities, it is used as a metaphor." Instead, Ashiotis suggests that all actors need to experience mainstream roles in order to grow.

A visually impaired actor will be able to participate in both your class and your production fully. The only obstacles are getting written information to a student who cannot see, and ensuring the student's safety.

First, see if your district has the Student Workbook for this textbook recorded or in Braille. If it does not, have your district's disability advocate try to find it for you. If they cannot, your advocate should have resources available to transcribe it, but this could take a long time. You may find that the job is completed faster with you at the helm.

There are a number of ways to handle transcription (print to voice or print to Braille). First, if the job is small, the teacher or a peer of the student can make the recording. In the same sense that you would not give a sighted student a book that is too damaged to read, your recording must also be clean. There should be limited background noise, the voices should be easily audible and understandable, and the reader should read at a coherent pace with enthusiasm, precision, and skill. This will take both time and technology; your school or district is responsible for covering costs, not your department. The school or district is also responsible for the manpower required to complete the job in a reasonable timetable that keeps your visually impaired student working at the same pace as your other students.

THINGS TO CONSIDER WHEN WORKING WITH A BLIND ACTOR

1. Avoid casting your disabled actor strictly in plays about disabilities; instead allow them to grow by casting them in non-disabled roles in which the handicap will not be an issue (you obviously do not want to cast a blind actor as a photographer).

2. Many blind actors have Braille printers; contact your play's publisher and request a text copy of the script so that your actor can make a Braille copy to read.

3. If an actor has been blind from birth, they may need help with facial expressions, which are learned.

4. In class, games in which actors must mimic what they see will not work. Modify these games for your entire class if you have a student who is visually impaired.

5. When writing, remind students to reference props; instead of saying, "What are you doing with that?" have them say, "What are you doing with that knife?"

Contributed by George Ashiotis, former co-artistic director of Theater by the Blind

At some point you will need to seek out additional resources, as you probably lack the time to record entire plays or chapters from textbooks. Your special education department should have access to assistance on behalf of the student, but the process can be slow. If they cannot get your visually impaired learner's scripts, notes, books, and other materials converted to Braille or voice-recorded in a timely manner, find a volunteer to do the job. Many students need service points for volunteer work, and elderly retirees in your school's neighborhood would probably love the chance to help. Remember that this student's parents may be thrilled to become involved or would be able to refer you to a volunteer. Parents are frequently great resources who are overlooked in situations such as this.

Just as your class is able to use the index or glossary to locate information easily, use technology that also allows your visually impaired learner to use shortcuts. Record audio digitally and organize it into searchable sections.

There are many transcribing companies that will transcribe your textbook or sections from the text into Braille. The cost varies depending on the type of material. Regardless, it will be costly, partly because one page of print becomes three pages of Braille. At the same time, your school or the school district probably already employs the resource, or you may be able to find a certified volunteer to do the job. The National Federation of the Blind keeps a list of Braille transcribers and other resources including a vast library of materials that have already been transcribed in one or another media at https://www.nfb.org/resources/braille-resources/braille-transcription-resources.

As for scripts, contact your publisher. Most will email the text version so that it can be printed on a Braille printer—if they have it available to them. You will still have to pay for the cost of a script. If they do not have the text version, try contacting the playwright or the playwright's agent. Playwright and agent information is often found on the copyright page in a paragraph that includes: "All other inquiries…"

The activities teachers use to engage their students in theatre discovery must take each individual student's needs into consideration. This is even more important when an activity may be impossible for a young person to follow because it involves a particular limitation of the student's disability. For example, if a game involves mimicking the silent movements of an actor onstage, it would be impossible for visually impaired actors to participate or to feel equally included.

The following are suggestions to take into consideration when selecting activities and games for your theatre classroom. Because there are so many activities and a limited amount of space, listen to your students too. They have very likely attended camps and classes where the activities were designed to cater to their strengths and exercise their limitations, so they may be able to teach you a game or two. Jot these down for future reference.

TIPS FOR WORKING WITH VISUALLY IMPAIRED ACTORS

- In classes with mostly seeing actors, blind and visually impaired actors will be able to do the same scene work as their seeing peers.

- Allow actors to write and perform their own scenes.

- Avoid games and activities in which visual mimicry is the focus.

- Select activities in which sound and the physical environment are the focus.

- When participating in activities that are highly visual, allow another student to quietly explain to the blind student important details that can only be seen.

- Keep in mind that many activities that work for blind actors will be counter-effective for deaf actors.

DOG AND BONE

This is a listening game that will encourage movement strategies. Special thanks to the students at Plano Senior High School in Plano, Texas, for providing this activity.

Students will sit in a circle on the floor with one student in the middle, blindfolded. This student is the "dog." Place a set of keys with at least two keys on the ring (for noise) in front of the dog. This is the dog's "bone." Give each student a colored index card or a card with a large colored dot. (Keep one card of each color for yourself.) There should be no more than three or four of any particular color. As you announce a color, only those with cards with the matching color may attempt to steal the dog's bone as quietly as possible. The dog will point to each sound heard. If the dog points directly to one of the thieves, that person must sit down. Any person who can steal the bone and return to their seat without being caught will become the dog.

TIPS:

- Remind students that even sounds they cannot help (like ankles popping) will count against them.

- Allow students to be creative; if shoes squeak and they want to remove them, they may.

- The teacher may need to referee; sounds from students not attempting to steal the bone should not end a player's turn.

- The dog should not be allowed to point non-stop; only when there is actually a sound.

- This is also a great rehearsal activity to teach actors about being quiet backstage.

OLD-FASHIONED RADIO SHOW

Try this activity for creating and interpreting sound.

Have students sit in a circle. You may want to provide them with a variety of props that can be used to make sounds. If these are not readily available, instruct students to make sounds using their hands, feet, mouths, clothing, and the area immediately surrounding them.

Read a fairy tale or other story. As you tell the story, allow the students to add sound effects. You may find that too many students want to participate simultaneously, making it hard to hear the individual sounds. If this is the case, tell students they may only contribute three times and that the sound effect goes to the first person who volunteers.

Another way to play is to write a lot of sounds on cards and pass them out to your class. Have the players place the cards face up so everyone can see. Each time it becomes appropriate for a sound, whoever has the card matching it must make the effect. This version has endless possibilities because your students will never receive the exact cards again.

TIPS:

- Consider throwing in a few optional cards that allow players to "steal" sounds from other players, "pass" to another player if they are too self-conscious to make a particular sound, or even an "action" card for adding a little energy to a scene.

- Have seeing students close their eyes so that they may become both actor and listener in the activity.

- If you find a story in which the sound effects seem particularly effective, rehearse and record it and have students study their creation.

- Experiment with a variety of ways to make sounds. Encourage students to explore how texture, density, and other elements affect sound. Liquid and volume are also fun ways to affect sound.

- If your students enjoy creating sound effects, plan to produce a radio theatre show. (See Radio Theatre in Chapter 3.)

RHYTHMS

Work as a team to create rhythms spontaneously.

Instruct students to sit in a circle with everything they brought to class. Using these items and their clothing, mouths, bodies, and the area immediately around them, students will experiment with sound.

One person starts by creating a simple, repetitious beat or series of repeating sounds. Starting with the person to their right and continuing around the circle, students will add to the existing sound by adding their own one at a time. Each addition should improve the rhythm. Students who have not yet participated can object to any student's sound by raising their hands, at which point the sound-maker can volunteer to drop out. When it is the originator's turn again, they will drop out, as will the others in unison, leaving the very last person to contribute to finish the "song."

TIPS:

- This works best in groups of about seven to ten.
- For advanced groups, allow students to come in spontaneously rather than going in a certain order.
- For advanced groups, work within a theme such as country, hip-hop, or jazz.
- Study the musical *Stomp* to see how a similar activity incorporated dance to become an international phenomenon.

FIND ME!

Develop sensory recall in a hide-and-seek game using feeling rather than seeing.

Have students remove rings, watches, and bracelets and get into pairs. Assign one member of each pair to be A and one to be B. Using a timer, give player A one minute to explore player B's hands. Remember, this is to be done by touch only, so sighted players' eyes should be closed. At the end of one minute, switch and allow player B to explore player A's hands for one minute. At the end of that minute, have players quietly (no speaking is ever allowed in this game) mix up; you may need to help them. Then tell them they must find each other based only on touch. Tell them that if you catch them looking or speaking, they will have to freeze for fifteen seconds while you spin them around a couple of times to disorient them. Remind them that this is a hands-only game.

TIPS:

- Set new teams and try the game again feeling only the partners' faces.
- Play partner Marco Polo in which A's say "Marco" simultaneously, then B's say "Polo" simultaneously. Can you find your partner's voice amidst all the voices in your class?

GEORGE IS LATE AGAIN!

Listen as other actors improvise to create your character, then try to incorporate everything you heard into the scene.

Select several students to play George's friends and one to play George. While George sits on the side of the stage taking mental notes, the players onstage use the fact that he is late to talk about him, giving him peculiar characteristics during their dialogue.

For example, one might say that George is probably late because he is seeing a doctor about his chronic hiccups, and another might say that he has never heard anyone else hiccup a musical scale. George notes that his character has a horrible case of musical hiccups.

Allow the gossipers to talk about George for two to three minutes, then have George enter in character. He must interact with his friends, displaying as many of the characteristics as he can. The others can assist in prompting (in character, of course) any traits he omits or forgets.

Each gossiper must find and clearly improvise his reason to leave until only George and one other player remain. The remaining two must find a clever end to the scene.

HEARING IMPAIRED

It is important to note that deaf people in general do not consider themselves disabled any more than an English-speaking person in a foreign country would consider themself disabled. Angela Farrand of Gallaudet University stresses that deaf people simply speak a different language, American Sign Language. "Other than the fact that they can't hear," she says, "they function just like hearing people."

Because they cannot hear, the hearing-impaired have a difficult time reproducing sound. Not every sound in a word has a visible movement to accompany it, so it is difficult for a deaf person to mimic. Speech therapists spend years working with the hearing-impaired to help make their speech as clear as possible, but clarity is only part of the solution. Becoming comfortable with how one's voice is perceived by others is also a concern. Farrand says there is no decisive ability or skill level that makes a deaf person comfortable with speaking. Some people just prefer to have an interpreter speak for them. "It's a personal choice," she adds.

She continues by saying that teachers often want to learn more about how to teach a deaf student, but they are afraid to ask that student for help. Instead, they go to the principal or other teachers. "Ask the student how best to communicate with them. Everyone is different, so there isn't one answer that will work for everyone." You will want to work closely with the student's advocate on your campus to ensure that you stay within the scope of the educational plan created to ensure success. At the same time, remember that your students know themselves better than anyone else and will tell you how to communicate with them, what they're comfortable with, and what they cannot do.

Farrand estimates that there are three million deaf Americans, and that is just one reason why organizations for deaf actors seem to outnumber those for actors with other differences. Another explanation, however, is that there is a culture that is unique to the deaf community.

They speak a different language, have their own slang, and tell jokes that hearing people frequently wouldn't understand. This seemed to be a theme that was repeated with each interview conducted in completion of this section. The deaf do not consider themselves impaired. They are simply "of a different culture."

Imagine a hearing actor attending auditions, seeking the "big break" that all actors desire to launch their careers. It is a long, tedious, and often heartbreaking venture. "Now imagine being deaf and trying to start an acting career," Farrand says. "This may be a deaf actor's greatest challenge."

In real life, the deaf, the blind, and folks with other differences are everywhere doing all kinds of

THINGS TO CONSIDER WHEN WORKING WITH A DEAF ACTOR

1. Other than the fact that they cannot hear, keep in mind that your deaf actor functions just like everyone else.

2. Avoid working overhead while any deaf student is onstage. In hearing theatre, the words, "Heads up," warn actors that there is movement and potential danger overhead. This might be the only difference between your hearing and non-hearing students, in regard to theatre safety.

3. Deaf actors who are signing need to cheat out toward the audience slightly more than normal, especially if someone is speaking for them and needs to see their signing or if there are deaf audience members. It may not look natural at first, but with practice, naturalness can be achieved.

4. It would be nice if the person speaking for the deaf actor appeared to be in the scene rather than perched to one side, but this is a matter of style and director's choice.

In class, avoid games in which sound, or even mouth movement, is involved. Focus instead on anything visual; pantomime is always a great option.

Contributed by Angela Farrand, former professor at Gallaudet University jobs. They are funny, experience dramatic events and romance, offer support, and so on, so why can they not have principal roles in plays, movies, and TV shows without the storyline revolving around their uniqueness? Why must a deaf actress be in a show about deafness rather than just being the bright private investigator who happens to be deaf?

The trend is changing. Deanne Bray won the title role on *Sue Thomas: F.B. Eye*, a character who was not originally intended to be deaf. Bray, who is mostly deaf but can hear some voices with the help of a hearing aid, won her role over a number of unimpaired actresses. Her deafness has since been minimally incorporated into the story (her character can read the lips of suspects under surveillance, and so on), but it is not central to the story.

TIPS FOR WORKING WITH DEAF ACTORS

- In classes with mostly hearing actors, deaf actors will be able to do all of the scene work their hearing peers do; be flexible with grading, as an interpreter may translate signing to speaking but may not be a trained actor.
- Train hearing actors to watch and listen to the actor, not the interpreter.
- Allow actors to write and perform their own scenes.
- Avoid games and activities in which spoken words are the focus.
- Use games and activities with a great deal of visual imagery, such as pantomime.
- Keep in mind that activities that work with hearing-impaired actors may be counter-effective for visually impaired actors.

WHAT A MESS!

This highly visual, improvised pantomime is effective with both hearing and non-hearing students.

One at a time, students will create an imaginary room or area full of objects. These objects may be furniture or something else. However, a good scene will revolve around and stick to a theme.

After writing the title of the scene on the board, a student will enter the area, identify a problem, and fix it. In fixing the problem, the actor will have to move in and around a series of obstacles in an overly crowded room. The actor must react to each item they encounter in such a way as to allow the audience to know what it is without speaking or signing. These objects may hang from the ceiling, stick out of walls, or be piled on top of one another. They may be stationary, on rollers, or motorized. They may be left in place (in which case the actor will have to remember to crawl over or under them each time they encounter them), or they may be moved (in which case the actor will show size, weight, shape, texture, and mobility).

After the problem has been fixed, the student will wrap up the scene with a solic ending.

Example: Antonia takes the stage after having written her scene title on the board. When she lifts her head, she is very quiet, like one who does not want to be found. She slinks along an invisible wall, rounds a corner mysteriously, and slips into a dark room. She closes the door behind her, locks it, secures the deadbolt, and searches frantically for the light. She finds it, looks around, and when she is sure it is safe, she takes something from her pocket and places it in a safe spot up high. She then takes a number of measures to further secure the door including pushing something large and heavy up against it, nailing it shut, and running tape across it. When she feels completely safe, she returns to the item she had placed up high and takes a moment to appreciate it. She rubs it against her face, smells it, feels it, and hugs it. She then removes its imaginary wrapper, takes a chewy bite, and sinks lovingly to the floor to enjoy the rest of her cardy bar. She drops her head, ending the scene. She then lifts her head, stands, and returns to her seat.

THINGS TO CONSIDER

- How large is the area?
- How does it smell, what is the air like, and how clean is it?

- What is in the area?
- Might there be any surprises in the mess?
- What is the problem?
- What is the solution?
- Why is the problem fixed?
- How difficult is the resolution?
- What is the payoff?

FOR THE TEACHER

- Rather than having the scene be completely improvised, distribute the *What a Mess Planning Guide* (see pages 24-26) and allow students to plan their scenes in advance.
- Add another dimension and have students pair up for the scene.
- Giving an introduction for the scene may replace writing the title on the board.
- If a student does not clearly identify an object, send in another student (in character and within the context of the scene) to silently inquire about the object until it has been clarified.
- Make the activity even more challenging by having students add an obstacle they are not likely to encounter. For example, have them do their scenes as though wading through thick Jell-O, in slow motion, as though weightless, or with a swarm of bees buzzing about.

SAMPLE SCENES

- Change the light bulb in a dark barn full of live animals.
- Enter and exit through opposite sides of a room full of lab spiders in tanks; some of the tanks are blocking the exit.
- Clean up after a party you were not supposed to have before your parents return home.
- Build an igloo in a blizzard.
- Rearrange the furniture in your apartment to make it look more impressive.

NAME ____ PERIOD _______ DATE ______________

WHAT A MESS! PLANNING GUIDE

1. You will create an imaginary space full of things. These things may be furniture or something else. However, a good scene will revolve around and stick to a theme.

2. You will be creating a pantomime in which you will enter the area, identify a problem, and fix it. In fixing the problem, you will have to move in and around a series of obstacles in an overly crowded room. Things can hang from the ceiling, stick out of walls, or be piled on top of one another. They can be stationary, on rollers, or motorized. They can be left in place (in which case you will have to remember to crawl over or under them each time you encounter them) or they can be moved (in which case you will show size, weight, shape, texture, and mobility).

3. After the problem has been fixed, you will need to wrap up the pantomime scene with a solid ending.

You will have _______ minutes to plan this activity.

SOME EXAMPLES OF SCENES YOU MAY CHOOSE TO DO:
- Change the light bulb in a dark barn full of live animals.
- Enter and exit through opposite sides of a room full of lab spiders in tanks; some of the tanks are blocking the exit.
- Clean up after a party you were not supposed to have before your parents return home.
- Build an igloo in a blizzard.
- Rearrange the furniture in your apartment to make it look more impressive.

You may come up with your own scene, but get your teacher's approval first.

What are some messy places you think the class might find interesting? List at least four. Circle your final choice.

____

____

____

____

1. How large is the area? ____

2. How does it smell, what is the air like, and how messy is it? ____________________________

____

____

3. What is in the area to make it messy? ____

____

____

4. What is the problem? ____

____

5. What is the solution? ____

____

6. Why are you fixing the problem?

____

7. How difficult is the resolution?

____

8. What is the payoff?

____

Draw a floor plan of your messy area. Include the things in the space that contribute to it being messy. Using colored pencils or markers, make a key, and color code the obstructions.

Use a dotted line to show your path through the mess. If you go under an item, mark it with a "U." If you go over an item, mark it with an "O."

Give your scene a title: ____

Write a creative intro for your scene:

____

____

____

____

____

Before you perform:

- Is the scene interesting? If not, make it more interesting before going any further.
- Remember not to speak in your scene; use plenty of pantomimed detail to clearly express the items with which you are working.
- When you are ready, practice your scene until you are comfortable with it.

After you perform:

How do you think you did?

What were some of the comments your peers made?

What can you do to improve before next time?

SAMURAI WARRIOR

This highly visual improvisation focuses on controlled movement and facial expressions, following directions, trust, and teamwork.

Two students play at a time. Instruct students that the back sides of both forearms are weapons. They are the only invulnerable parts of their bodies.

In pairs, students will engage in a slow-motion martial arts battle, but any time a student touches their partner with a forearm, the other must respond as though struck by a weapon. Actors may also use their legs, but again, it must be in slow motion. Both must be able to see all "attacks" coming so that each may safely react without risking injury to himself or the attacker.

They may both attack and block with their forearms. The goal is to perform the battle in slow motion keeping all motion fluid; the goal is not to win the battle. If teamwork is used, students will create an interesting visual and both will be successful.

TIPS:

* Add this to any improv scene without prior notice or drop it into the middle of rehearsal when movement is suffering.

* Give bonus points to students who use stage combat movements you have taught them in class—but only if they have used them correctly and with the proper safety measures in place.

* Encourage displays of pain and suffering when a student is "struck" with another's weapon. (After all, this is acting!)

* Encourage students to compete, not to see who can "win," but to see who can best follow the directions.

* Limit players to three strikes; a player receiving three strikes against them must die a dramatic death.

* Remind actors that falling in slow motion will be the true test of their self-control.

* Set this game to Japanese music and have students create a Samurai Warrior scene with a beginning, rising action, climax, and clear ending.

* Study Kabuki and use this game as both a reward for studying and to teach larger-than-life movement.

MYSTERY CATCH

Silently explore weight, size, texture, scent, taste, and emotional reaction.

One person starts by pantomiming holding something, such as a coin. We know it is a coin because the student reaches into a pocket to get it, thinks about spending it, then flips and catches it several times. The student then decides to throw it in a fountain for a wish. The student makes eye contact with the fountain, which is really another player, then makes a wish and tosses the coin.

The player with whom the student made eye contact must now catch the coin and keep it as a coin for a few seconds, Then, the second player changes it into something else. Encourage students to express every detail of the change. The onlookers should be able to watch as the object assumes its new shape—a 200-pound barbell, for example. After a short workout, the actor passes the object to someone who catches it as a barbell but soon changes it to something else.

The item will be passed around the circle until everyone has had a chance to catch it and pass it on.

TIPS:

* After an actor passes their item, have them sit so that only those who have not received the object remain standing.

* Encourage students to explore a wide range of size and weights, textures, temperatures, and more. Each should have an emotional or physical reaction to the object, such as sneezing after receiving a cat, playfully bouncing a ball after catching it, or crying after being given a freshly sliced onion.

* Remind students that in pantomime, anything is possible. They may possess almost any object (so long as it would not be offensive to others), and they may exceed human limitations as long as their efforts can be clearly pantomimed.

PANTOMIME RACE

Teams race to accurately pantomime everyday words.

Divide your students into even teams of about five or six players each. Players will line up behind one another with the first member on each team close to the center of the room and all others behind the first member, fanning out toward the corners.

Give the last player in each line a thick black marker and a stack of index cards. All students in each line will turn their backs to the first player; all first players should be able to see each other and the teacher, who will stand in the center. All other players should have their backs to the center of the room.

The teacher will write one word (either a verb or a noun) on a card and show it to the first students in each line. The teacher will then signal the teams to start at the same time. The first student in each line will tap the second student in line, who will turn and watch as the first student attempts to act out the card. When the second student thinks they know the word, the second student taps the next student in line on the shoulder and acts out the word. This continues without any talking until the last person in line thinks they know the word. The last student writes the word on an index card along with their name and passes it to the teacher. After all teams have handed in their cards, the teacher will read the results.

TIPS:

- Discuss how similarities in words may have caused confusion, how pantomiming more slowly or clearly could help clarify the confusion, and how different participants interpreted the words with their own style.

- Do not allow students to use charades tactics (like "sounds like"), speaking, or signing.

- After each word, have the player who was first for that round go to the end of the line. This will give every actor an opportunity to play in all positions on the team. How does each student's job change as the students change positions in the line?

- Because of the simplicity of the words, require the exact word to be guessed. For example, if the word is "book," do not allow "magazine" or "read" to suffice.

- Play for points by assigning more difficult words double points or play to see who has the most points after a predetermined amount of time.

- You may find it helpful to prepare a stack of cards in advance.

MOBILITY IMPAIRED

As long as mobility or athleticism isn't mandated in the script, what's to prevent your physically impaired actor from playing just about any part? In a time when a Black actor and a Latina actress play the parents of a fair-skinned, fair-haired child, why can't Anne Frank be in a wheelchair? Remember, you are not asking your audience to believe that Anne Frank *was* in a wheelchair; you are asking them to not care because it will have no impact on the story. We ask our audience to suspend their belief long enough to accept that someone who is fifteen years old and wearing a wig becomes a man who is seventy-five years old, so it is time that we also bring mobility impaired actors into lead roles.

Your set will obviously be one of the first things you will need to consider. If you use any kind of unit set with pre-built ramps, those ramps were not built with wheelchairs in mind. The slope will very likely be too great, putting your actor at risk of injury. The common acceptable ratio for the slope of a wheelchair ramp is 1:12, meaning for every one inch of rise, you should have twelve inches of length. Most unit sets have a rise ratio of 3:12 which means they slope too severely. A ratio of 1:8 (eight-foot ramp required for one-foot rise) would likely be acceptable if your actor has average upper body strength. A ratio of 1:6 (six feet of ramp for each one foot of rise) would be acceptable if your actor's chair has a strong motor, if they have an assistant to help maneuver them up the ramp, or if they possess exceptional upper body strength. For more information on ramps and slopes, see the Americans with Disabilities Act at www.ada.gov.

- Actors with physical disabilities will be able to do all scene work.
- Allow actors to write and perform their own scenes.
- Explain physical activities to your disabled actor; if they are mature, they will likely tell you point-blank whether they feel they can or cannot participate. They may even be able to suggest modifications. Monitor younger actors who may sacrifice their own safety.
- Take into consideration your actors' individual strengths when choosing physical activities.

It will also be very important that all areas in which the wheelchair will need to travel be at least thirty-six inches wide, that areas in which turns must be made must be sixty inches square, and that all surfaces (including backstage) are free and clear of rises and obstacles. This may mean purchasing an industrial cable cover—a heavy-duty mini-ramp with a casing for the cords. They work better than taping cables because they are sloped on both sides. They will also increase the lifespan of your cables as they will not be exposed to heavy traffic and will not get covered in the tacky residue left by tape.

THE ABC GAME

A mentally challenging improvisation that combines timing, humor, and creativity.

This game is played in pairs. The audience will give each student a character, then the pair will be given a situation, a location, and a letter of the alphabet to start.

The younger player goes first. That player must start the improvised scene with the first word of their dialogue beginning with the letter the audience selected for them. That player may speak as long as desired. Then that player's partner must begin their dialogue with the next letter of the alphabet. The two take turns improvising their scene in alphabetical order until they return full circle to the letter with which they started.

TIPS:
- Remind students that the scene must make sense.
- Actors should remember to use the characters, situation, and setting assigned to them by the audience.

- It may help to write the alphabet on the board; even though both probably know it very well, it's easy to forget one's place while acting.

- Challenge actors to end the scene solidly and humorously on the letter with which they started.

THE QUESTION GAME

The Question Game is also played in pairs. The audience will give each student a character, then the pair will be given a situation and a location. Every line must be phrased as a question.

The youngest player starts by asking a question. Then the youngest player's partner must respond with another question, but it must be sensible. The two will go on like this for as long as both can ask questions and not make statements. Because this game is so difficult, it encourages a slow, thoughtful pace.

TIPS:
- Buzz students out who make statements; send in a new student to replace an eliminated student.

- Buzz out any student who repeats their partner's question (or asks a very similar question).

- When a student is buzzed out, the person who asked the last question will repeat it, giving the two players a starting point for their leg of the game.

- Play in teams: Divide the class into two teams and line them up facing each other. As a player is buzzed out, they go to the end of their line and the player behind them takes their place. For those who are not buzzed out, limit them to five questions and then send them to the back of their line so that all may play. The team to get their starting player "on deck" again first wins.

A MEETING OF THE MINDS

Have fun with this observation and character interpretation game.

Create a stack of cards naming famous and familiar people, one name on each card. Include several distinctive personalities from your school and even a few from the class. You should have at least twice as many names as you have students in the room (or more if you plan to play the game more than once).

Pass out all the cards to your students so that they all have the same number of cards. You need two small boxes on hand. Have students select one character to act out in the activity and put that card in one box and have them retire the one they do not plan to use in the other. You may need to refer to the character names students selected at the end of the game.

Instruct students to mingle with each other and speak in character. They cannot use their own character's name nor may they ask another actor about their character's name. Instead, they should carry on small talk, just as though they were meeting for the first time at a party. As they guess who an actor is portraying, they should write their guess on a piece of scratch paper. As the party starts winding down, call time and have the students introduce themselves in character.

For a twist on the game, pass out new cards. Have each student bring a chair to the acting area; arrange the chairs into two rows facing each other. Seat half the students in one row of chairs while the others stand behind theirs. Explain that they are now "speed dating," and only the students who started out standing will rotate (to their right). They get thirty seconds to try to get to know the other character in character and to allow the other character to know them. Gender isn't a factor; this is just a fun game about listening, self-marketing, and the chemistry between characters and/or actors. Set your timer and watch as they try to make the best use of their short time allotment.

SPEECH IMPAIRED

Justin stuttered... severely. He had a difficult time communicating, taking much longer to get his message across than the students who did not stutter. This would frustrate him, and he found himself becoming withdrawn, often not speaking to avoid embarrassment.

He was so full of information, emotion, and personality. He wanted so badly to express everything inside himself, but this thing—this stuttering thing—kept smacking him in the face like a gardening rake left hiding in the grass. In his mind, Justin could formulate the thoughts so clearly that he felt certain he could say them; but as soon as he opened his mouth, the old "rake to the face" thing happened.

When he was in tenth grade, he signed up for drama class at his new high school. Drama hadn't been offered at his junior high. His mother worried he would lose what little confidence he had left, and his friends just knew that he would be bullied. After all, there were a lot of kids at this school who didn't know him.

The first assignment was a one-minute monologue. It was due at the end of the first week of school. Most of the students complained that this wasn't enough time to prepare, but Justin was relieved. He said very little that first week, but he worked hard. When it came time to perform, he volunteered to be first. His classmates were awestruck by his performance, praising everything about it and complaining that he had placed the bar too high. They didn't think they would be able to do as well. When the teacher asked him what he thought, he spoke out-of-character for the first time. The students who did not know him before that year learned for the first time that Justin stuttered when he gave his short, difficult response. You see, he had managed to deliver his entire monologue without stuttering even once.

Justin became the person to beat at auditions. He was in every play, received many awards for his acting, and went on to study educational theatre in college. He overcame his stuttering almost completely, thanks in large part to his involvement in theatre. He hopes that, as a drama teacher, he will be able to help others like himself.

Unlike other disabilities, many speech impairments are correctable or improvable with time, speech therapy, or new technology. Theatre seems to be a great avenue for these improvements. Jane Fraser, president of the Stuttering Foundation of America, says that when an actor memorizes lines, they no longer have to search for the word. Sometimes the process of word retrieval, or finding words, is what exacerbates the stuttering. She adds that this may be why people like James Earl Jones can successfully and smoothly deliver a speech in character but still stutter when speaking spontaneously.

You will find that many students, even those without hearing impairments, take your class because of the therapeutic value. Those with shyness hope to learn to cope with it and become more outgoing, and many who are not comfortable with their speech become involved with theatre as a means of surmounting the annoying problem. Many actors attend speech therapy for years to get help for their stuttering. Some find the therapy helpful, but many say that the true cure is theatre. Even if your actor cannot beat their impediment, acting still offers an opportunity to communicate freely to an approving audience. Your job as teacher and audience will be to always express your appreciation for the actor's effort and accomplishments.

TIPS FOR WORKING WITH ACTORS WITH SPEECH IMPEDIMENTS

- Because speech impediments are all unique, there is no one activity or set of guidelines that will work for all; teachers must address each student's needs with a personalized plan.

- In most circumstances, speech-impaired actors will be able to do scene work.

- Use vocal warm-ups before rehearsals.

- Teach your non-speech-impaired actors to be patient, supportive, and understanding, and never to mimic or torment speech-impaired actors.

Work with the student's advocate to discover which techniques work, what the immediate and long-term goals might be, and what role you can play in the process. This may require some modification of the assignment or the grading rubric. In the end, you will probably find the positives far outweigh any negatives. Giving a talented but impaired actor the momentum they need to cope with or even overcome their disability makes up for any additional time or effort needed to effectively teach them.

PACING PRACTICE

This series of simple activities helps create a flowing rate of smooth speech for students who stutter or speak too quickly.

Begin with a memorized sentence or paragraph, perhaps a speech from a scene. Dim the lights and have students lie on their backs on the floor with plenty of space between them. With arms outstretched to their sides so that the body resembles a cross, students will recite the memorized piece quietly in their heads. With each silent word (it is important that the movement happen only with words, not syllables, to achieve fluid speech), students will smoothly raise their arms above their bodies to meet soundlessly above them, then lower them smoothly to the ground on the next word. For example, the line "To be or not to be" would look like this: To (arms meet above body with fingers pointing toward sky) be (arms outstretched with backs of hands flat against ground, cross-like) or (arms above body, fingers toward sky) not (arms cross-like) to (arms above body, fingers toward sky) be (arms cross-like).

After the entire piece has been successfully paced silently, challenge students to do it again in a whisper as slowly as they can, repeating the arm movements and relaxing the rest of the body. Watch to make sure they are not fidgeting, worrying about whether others are watching them, tensing their bodies, or moving their arms with syllables rather than whole words. Calmly redirect anything that is taking them off course. If they are having any difficulty, tell the students it may be helpful to say the word in their heads before saying it out loud.

Next, have them repeat the piece again, using a normal speaking voice but a slower-than-normal pace. Instead of lowering their arms to the ground, instruct students to lower just their elbows but to fully extend their arms toward the sky, still repeating the movements with every other word.

Finally, have students repeat the piece once more. This time they will project with a strong voice that can be heard easily across the room. They will still lower their elbows to the ground for half the words, and for the other half, they will still extend their fingers toward the sky, only now they will also lift their shoulders one or two inches off the ground during the extension. This will force them to push slightly with their diaphragms while still pacing themselves.

If your students do not have room to lie down or you are not comfortable with this, have them walk out the pacing, stepping once with each word (again, not each syllable), and tapping their hands first in front of them, then in back. Walking in a circle ensures that they have plenty of space and will not hit each other. Again, start slow and quiet and work toward a louder voice and more normal pace.

Thinking carefully about what one is going to say before speaking is one of the most effective remedies for stuttering. The pacing forces speakers to take the time to think, but it can't force them to think. Remind your actors to use the time between words to think of what comes next and to say it in their heads.

You can also do the *Pacing Practice* by having students pace themselves with non-memorized material, by working in pairs and carrying on paced conversations, and by using material from plays and scene work.

DEVELOPMENTALLY DELAYED

Because there are so many levels of ability and such a variety of disorders, this may be a more challenging area for theatre arts success. Cognitive delays affect a student's ability to comprehend the material, to retain it, and to apply what they have learned. In many cases, the student's ability to socialize and work alongside non-delayed peers becomes another obstacle for the theatre teacher. While most of the other actors with disabilities will merge into neurotypical groups successfully, oftentimes your students with mid- to high levels of cognitive delay will not.

As always, talk to a student's advocate to find out what the student can do. Perhaps the student can read, but memorization is out of the question. Modify your assignment to allow the student to use a script onstage. If the student is not a reader but communicates well, work with having the student listen to recordings, improvising, and doing pantomime. If the student is severely disabled, allow the student to perform using a type of self-discovery. This means allowing the student to create a performance based only on what they can do and having nothing to do with the other students' goals. This may mean singing nursery rhymes, dancing, experimenting with rhythms, a loose form of pantomime, telling a story, or whatever allows the student to express themself in front of an audience.

Jaron was severely developmentally delayed. He could write his name, but it required a great deal of encouragement and an entire sheet of paper. His speech was mostly clear, and he loved to talk and tell anyone who would listen about his most recent vacation and his love for rock and roll music. He could not read or memorize, but he could sing and dance, and he could have held a workshop on facial expressions.

Jaron was in a theatre class with a number of regular education students. His teacher knew of his love for music, and when it became apparent that he would not be able to fully complete the same assignments the other students would, she quickly modified his assignments. While the others

rehearsed duets, monologues, and other mainstream acting events, Jaron created lip-syncs to songs from a Disney CD or his favorite rock songs. While they were blocking, he was decorating a box with strips of brightly colored paper and a glue stick. While they were polishing, he was making a mask or a hat.

Jaron loved seeing the others perform, and he became an appreciative audience member and critic. His classmates returned the favor when Jaron performed, clapping wildly afterward. He glowed and smiled from ear to ear as he took his elaborate bows. If the performances were stretched out over several days, he performed his as often as he wanted, and often his special education team of teachers would come to watch.

> **THINGS TO CONSIDER WHEN WORKING WITH A DEVELOPMENTALLY DELAYED ACTOR**
>
> - When possible, use music to motivate students, especially non-readers.
> - Invest in several elementary-level drama supplements.
> - Use visual art as a means of allowing students to express themselves.
> - Allow students to play dress up and to play with props as a means of exploring character and expression.

His teacher later confessed that working with Jaron was the hardest thing she had ever done as a teacher. She was constantly on her toes keeping him on task with something that she hoped would hold his attention for longer than a few minutes. It was worthwhile, she recounted, when she received a note from his parents saying that he never talked about a class as much as he did his theatre class and that it had replaced his Disney World vacation as the main topic at dinner each night.

THE MIRROR

This slow-paced mimicking activity requires focus and attention to detail.

There are many ways to play this classic theatre game. The most basic is to have all students face the teacher, who very slowly leads the class. The class must mirror the teacher's movements and facial expressions. If the teacher moves their right arm, the students mimic the movement with their left arms, just as they would appear if they were watching their reflections in a mirror.

The key is to move slowly. Any sudden movement will cause a delay for the one doing the copying, so since the objective isn't to try to beat anyone or "lose them," the leader should move at a slow, comfortable pace. Also, use a variety of levels so that those following are challenged to reach above their heads and use the space on the floor, the area behind them, and the space between them as they mimic the image.

One way to keep this activity fun and challenging for all is to have students mimic an actual activity such as getting ready for school, applying makeup, or seeing their reflection as a "mime" in a mirror.

Reward students who are following well by allowing them to come to the front of the room and lead the others. This is an exceptional way of reinforcing the good work of your developmentally delayed actors and of giving your students an opportunity to teach. Also, as the class catches on, break them into groups of two and allow them to take turns leading each other. As a final challenge, have your groups of two stand facing each other so that one can clearly see the teacher at the front of the room and the other cannot. The teacher will lead, the student facing the teacher will follow the teacher, and the partner who cannot see the teacher will follow the student who can.

TIPS FOR WORKING WITH DEVELOPMENTALLY DELAYED ACTORS

- Because there are so many levels of impairment, you will want to consider each student individually when selecting activities. Many will be able to participate in all of the classroom's games and exercises. At the same time, you will have some students who will find even the simplest games an extreme challenge.

- Activities that focus on mimicry are probably your most suitable choices.

WHO'S WHO?

There are many very famous, highly successful members of the theatre and film communities who did not let their disabilities stop them.

- Marlee Matlin got her big break playing a deaf student in *Children of a Lesser God*. She has gone on to play numerous other roles having nothing to do with her deafness. Also, if you watched *Sesame Street* as a child, you may remember Linda Bove. She brought hearing impairment and sign language into our homes and gave countless disabled children hope. Nanette Fabray did the same for adults, singing while signing on prime-time TV. Lou Ferrigno, who played the original Incredible Hulk, is deaf. Other famous deaf actors include Deanne Bray, Amy Ecklund, Anthony Natale, Phyllis Frelich, and Howie Seago, to name just a few.

- Kitty O'Neil proved deafness was not a blockade when she became both a successful TV stunt woman and the fastest woman on Earth after driving a rocket car.

- Marion Davies, Marilyn Monroe, Dudley Moore, Madeline Kahn, and Charles Nelson Reilly all battled speech impairments, yet their careers soared. Is it possible that one of the world's most recognizable voices, that of James Earl Jones, became what it did because he fought to become triumphant over stuttering? And who would have thought that tough guy Bruce Willis stuttered as a child?

- Susan Nussbaum, author of *Staring Back*, became a quadriplegic after being hit by a car when she was in college, where she studied drama. She did not allow it to interfere with her plans, and she continues to have a successful career writing and directing.

- Michael J. Fox was already quite successful in his acting career when he was diagnosed with Parkinson's disease. For several years, he continued to act even though the effects of the disease were quite noticeable. His fighting attitude is an encouragement to others with disabilities.

- Bud Abbott of Abbott and Costello fame and the skit "Who's on First?" had epilepsy, as did Richard Burton.

- RJ Mitte began exploring acting as a way of making friends, but despite his cerebral palsy, he was cast on *Hannah Montana* and then became a regular on *Breaking Bad*.

- Chris Burke, born with Down syndrome, starred in *Life Goes On*, a show about a boy with his condition.

- Stacy Keach Jr. was born with a cleft lip.

- Harold Russell lost both hands in World War II. He then starred in *The Best Years of Our Lives* in 1946 and subsequently became the only actor ever to win two Oscars for the same role: Best Supporting Actor and a special award for bringing hope to other soldiers.

- Many actors struggle with learning disabilities including Danny Glover, Cher, Tom Cruise, Whoopi Goldberg, Suzanne Somers, Sylvester Stallone, and Tracey Gold. Henry Winkler managed his attention deficit disorder to become another huge name in the entertainment industry.

- Rex Harrison, Hume Cronyn, and Sammy Davis Jr. were all blind in one eye. Sandy Duncan starred as Peter in the stage version of *Peter Pan* for many years despite having one glass eye. Peter Falk, the detective on *Columbo*, also had a glass eye.

- Geri Jewell draws some criticism for her comedy routine, which often includes jokes about her cerebral palsy, but the praise outweighs the negative. Many actors use their disabilities to their advantage, and while some consider this a type of exploitation, it serves to educate society and to provide a positive outlook to others who may feel trapped by their own uniqueness.

SECTION 2 NOTES:

INTRODUCTION

Several years ago, two students who had been best friends for years decided that drama might help them learn English. They were both in seventh grade and had been enrolled in English as a Second Language classes since elementary school, but with Spanish being their primary language at home, they had issues with confidence when it came to natural-sounding English. Neither was willing to take the class alone, so they spoke to their counselor who assured them that they would be kept together as long as they took the class seriously. This was an unusual move on the counselor's part, but the students were convincing in their desire to become more confident speakers, and their advocate knew they would have a better experience if they had each other's support. The counselor even placed them in a smaller class and personally informed the teacher that the duo received special consideration and should be held to the highest standards.

Several weeks into the course, the two shy students bonded with the comfortable, family-like class. They became friendly with the other students, were invited to join larger groups, and showed an interest in their work. However, the first performance, despite being low-key, was not a huge success.

They were to write introductions, memorize them, and perform them for the class. In writing introductions, it is important to know what happens before, during, and after the scene. However, sharing those events with the audience is a lot like telling a friend how a movie ends before the friend sees it. Instead, it is the performer's job to pique the audience's interest by making it relevant to them. This is often done by focusing on the abstract notion of theme, the underlying message behind the scene.

When a student is learning a new language, it's hard enough to translate the scene and follow the events. However, knowing the moral or theme requires the reader and performer to be able to detect subtle nuances within the story. They must be able to find hidden meaning, understand characters' relationships, and sift through layers and layers of subtext. Even after the student figures out what the theme is, they must use it to craft an introduction that bridges the audience to the scene without giving away the story. It is easy to understand how such a task drove the two performers to frustration.

The drama teacher worked with the two students' ESOL (English to Speakers of Other Languages) teacher, and between them, they eventually developed a simple strategy for teaching theme and building the introduction around it. Step one: find one word to describe what the play is about; the word should be something that cannot be seen. Step two: find a joke, story, question, saying, lyric, poem, or other bit of literature not from the play to talk about the theme (or one word). It should be something that will either interest the audience or at least feel familiar to them. Step three: connect this to the plot somehow.

Realizing the value of teaching and learning abstract concepts to increase the understanding of the language, the ESOL teacher also reinforced the one-word theme concept in language arts classes. The final result: everyone in both the theatre and ESOL language arts classes benefited from a little detour in the lesson that was intended to help the two shy students.

Still, having the ability to write the intro was just the beginning. Imagine being asked to deliver an eloquently written, memorized piece in Japanese, Italian, French, or Chinese in front of natives of that country. This involves many layers of intimidation—not just mastering a new language, recalling memorized material, or public speaking, but a combination of the three. No matter how well-memorized, the speaker will second-guess the accuracy of each word, wonder whether or not they are using the right inflection, forget to gesture, nervously watch the ceiling, and so on.

At the same time, almost all challenging tasks become easier with practice. The teacher refused the shy students' nervous requests not to perform, to perform in front of the teacher only, or to perform another day. The teacher made them take the stage according to schedule and complimented all of their successes, no matter how seemingly insignificant. Sensing that any criticism at all would be disastrous, the teacher avoided negativity. In the end, the teacher suggested one change each (not a criticism, but an alternative way of doing something) and had them try again until they mastered the item, encouraging and supporting the entire way and accepting only supportive comments from the class.

The two shy students had a difficult time with introductions, but with perseverance, mastered the task. Over eighteen or so weeks they were gradually introduced to reading concepts that may have been overlooked in their language classes where the focus tended to be on vocabulary. They learned to attach emotion to words, to understand context clues, to become better listeners, to react and respond appropriately, to read body language and to better understand how their body language is read by others, not just to understand the words that they were reading but to understand the story and all of its interrelated parts.

The class ended the semester with readers theatre (see Chapter 4). Students were given a Dr. Seuss story, *How the Grinch Stole Christmas*, and told to perform it as creatively as possible, scripts in hand, no props or costumes, and using only one chair each. One of the things that make readers theatre such an amazing learning tool is the focus on how single words and phrases carry special meaning within the larger piece. Consequently, it becomes an excellent apparatus for understanding literature and exercising creativity.

The two ESOL students joined a larger group, performed quite successfully, and finished their semester with impressive grades. Their joint desire and quest to improve their English-speaking skills proved to be a great triumph. In their farewell to their drama teacher, the two students confided that they didn't really care to learn to act but that they took the class to improve their language and speaking skills. They proudly told the teacher that learning to act was more about learning to read than physically taking the stage. They also agreed that simple vocabulary without the ability and training to say words with the right tone, emotion, body language, eye contact, and so on, was inadequate. In the end, they declared that readers theatre, the one assignment they both found to be most beneficial, ought to be required in all ESOL classes. "You sometimes don't really understand a word until you have to use it," one of the students said. "When you practice a scene over and over again, the words become natural." At the same time, not having to

There are many words, phrases, and sayings that do not translate well from one language to another. For example, Americans use the word "broke" to mean poor or lacking money. However, to a student learning English, saying someone is broke makes it sound as though they are "broken." The words are used so commonly in daily speech that those who use them—and those who teach them—forget that newcomers to the language struggle to remember one meaning for a word, much less literal and figurative translations.

memorize a script makes it a less stressful and more enjoyable activity, allowing the ESOL actor to have fun focusing on the words and their meanings rather than toil over the memorization.

Upon doing further research, the drama teacher found that many ESOL learners and English-speaking learners with poor reading skills refuse to speak if they do not have 100% confidence that they will be successful. Their fear of being judged a poor reader or speaker causes them to both read and speak less, reducing their oral reading skills and creating a vicious cycle. However, scene work—especially readers theatre—requires a great deal of rehearsal (rehearsal equals confidence) and a more in-depth understanding of the literature. It is also fun, so it doesn't feel like studying, and it involves a group, so there is a sense of teamwork. With both the internal (fun) factor and the external (teamwork) factor, the effort put into practicing readers theatre feels more like playing and less like working, and the results are even more impressive. Actors and speakers of any language background feel a greater sense of comfort in their delivery and pride in the overall quality of their performance.

The teacher was convinced that the key had been found to improving language understanding, not just for those learning English, but for any student trying to improve any language. But there seemed to be a need to set aside time in the rehearsal process for teaching vocabulary. Again, the teacher returned to the ESOL teacher and explained the theory: start with a project in the performers' native language and gradually have them translate the script into the language they are attempting to learn. Then the group will rehearse their slowly changing piece, perhaps even enough to commit it to memory. Furthermore, by performing the piece they are translating, they begin associating the newly learned vocabulary with emotion, body language, action, reaction, and so on, and they slowly start using context clues to decipher the parts of the literature they have not taken the time to translate. The result is a more in-depth understanding of a language and a performance piece.

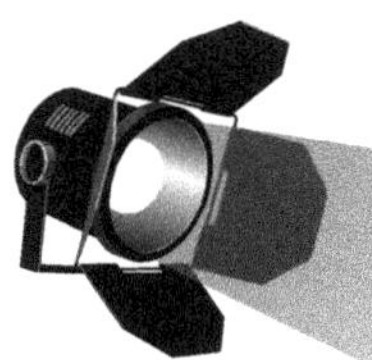

WHAT IS READERS THEATRE?

Almost any piece of literature can become a readers theatre piece. Poetry, song lyrics, short stories, fairy tales, and even historical passages can be interpreted by more than one person with enough creativity to make it truly entertaining. Readers theatre is usually done in groups of three or more. Take any unit of study and combine two or three pieces of different literature creatively to produce a provocative new piece. For example, have students prepare for Cinco de Mayo by combining a time line of Mexican history with the lyrics to a song of their choosing, so long as it fits the overall theme of the holiday. Depending on where they are in their study of English, determine how much of their piece must be in English and how much in Spanish. As they progress, have them increase the English vocabulary a little each day.

Another option is to have the teacher take a piece that is already written in the target language, translate it into the students' native language, and then work with them to gradually translate it back into the target language. This works only when the ESOL class has students of a common first language, such as all Spanish speakers seeking to learn English. It also works only when the teacher is confident as a translator or has access to someone who can translate in gradual steps and oversee the accuracy of the students' work. If this is the method you and your students select, avoid books like those of Dr. Seuss in which words are made up for the sake of rhyme. This may only confuse students who must now focus on fictitious vocabulary with no real meaning. At the same time, rhyme is an excellent device for learning anything new, so a piece that has a simple rhyme scheme may prove to be an excellent learning tool.

How is readers theatre different from other types of theatre? Most theatre is memorized, but readers theatre is just that: theatre read from the script. This is a huge relief to students learning a new language because they have the comfort of having that script nearby in case of nerves. Many students purchase a small (5½ x 8 inches) black binder for their scripts because they need to be able to hold the script with one hand, and larger binders are much too large. To format a script for a small binder, have then set a page up as "landscape," and set up two columns of text with 1½-inch spacing. Double spacing scripts is a good idea for easier readability. Have them cut printed pages in half, use a single-hole punch to line the page holes up with those in a small binder, and the script will be ready to go!

Small binders are available at almost all office supply stores, but even at $4 each, it is an expense many parents would prefer to avoid. Another option is to make lightweight folders for scripts using black construction paper. Use the directions above for formatting your script, put your pages in the correct order, and staple them into a folded piece of black construction paper.

The binder/folder helps students control their pages. They will be using their scripts as props during performance, and you don't want their pages falling out or for them to lose their places. Also, the audience shouldn't be distracted by writing on the script, by the sounds of pages being turned, or by students becoming impatient with difficult scripts. Students have also found that they keep up with their scripts better when they have invested time in preparing them.

If you are using a copyrighted book, have your librarian get you multiple copies and allow students to use them instead of binders. Since the book is copyrighted, it cannot be reproduced.

WHY READERS THEATRE?

Readers theatre, unlike many other types of theater, uses a script in hand during the performance. However, it is not just a play. It can be one of many types of theatre like poetry, storytelling (or prose), or any type of speaking in which actors are allowed to express themselves emotionally. Eventually your ESOL actors will become more confident, and they will be ready for greater challenges. When this time comes, gradually wean them away from using scripts in hand.

Remember, if this tool is useful to those learning English, readers theatre will also be helpful for English speakers learning a foreign language. Suggest scripts to your foreign-language teachers and teach them how to direct a scene. They will appreciate the activity, and you will find that you have once again networked your program outside of the fine arts wing.

READERS THEATRE CHALLENGE: NEW LANGUAGE

Challenge your students to find a poem, short story, or song from their native language (older pieces may be in public domain, and thus copyright-free; well-known folk tales can be retold in students' own words without fear of copyright infringement) and create a readers theatre script that will teach at least fifty new vocabulary words from that language to those who speak English. If the student's native language is English, your readers theatre script will introduce fifty words from a second language common in your region.

KEEP IN MIND

- Type scripts using size 12 font, and keep the font simple (Arial, Times New Roman, etc.). Do not use a font that is distracting or busy.

- Double-space scripts; this will allow for translations and notes to be written right above the words and phrases.

- Write scripts in English except for the fifty vocabulary words and phrases; keep those in the native language or the language students are teaching.

- Make the fifty vocabulary words stand out from the rest of the script by making them bold or highlighting them.

- Stories are the easiest to make into a readers theatre because each character may be played by a different actor; however, creative students can craft wonderful scripts for various actors by simply using echoes and other interesting readers theatre elements. For more information on readers theatre scripts, see Chapter 4.

- Include as few as three characters/actors or as many as six.

- Balance parts so that everyone participates throughout.

- Keep scripts energetic so that actors remain energetic.

Prompt students with these questions:

- What are some poems, songs, or stories you think might make a good readers theatre script for your challenge?

- Are there other students whose language is similar to yours with whom you can become partners so you can benefit from teamwork?

- How might you use props, costumes, movements, or other visual aids to help reinforce the new vocabulary?

- How might using readers theatre in your other classes assist you and others in understanding and retaining the knowledge?

READERS THEATRE SCRIPTS

The readers theatre script at the end of this section was written at the request of an ESOL teacher whose students were mostly Spanish-to-English learners. However, there are probably many stories either in your students' native languages or in your school's library that would make suitable scripts.

READERS THEATRE PROJECT

For students learning English or Spanish

> **OBJECTIVE** You will increase your understanding of English by creating a readers theatre performance of the *Cinco de Mayo* script using the guidelines provided in this lesson.

There is no limit to the amount of creativity allowed in readers theatre! It is not a realistic style; rather, it is almost "vaudevillian" in its nature. Keep movement large and exaggerated, and, because there are many voices, project loudly and articulate clearly.

Another trick to any good performance is to make your voice tell as much of the story as you can. It must be energetic, clear, easy to understand, loud, and confident. If your character is not just like you, your voice should also be different. Become a unique character!

Why is all this extra work important when your goal is to increase your understanding of the language? Because you want to break the habit of "reading" the language and instead become an interpreter of the language. Interpretation has to do with a lot more than just understanding the words. You must express them. If you can put yourself in your characters' shoes, you will know why they do what they do and say what they say. If you understand your characters' goals, you will know the purpose of their dialogue. All of this comes together to make you an expert on the language and the words you will be speaking.

Also, the more fun you have preparing your performance, the more likely it is you will practice, and practice comes before perfection.

Use the following tips to make your performance more fun and successful. Also refer to the lesson in Chapter 4 for additional information about readers theatre.

READERS THEATRE TIPS

- Learn the vocabulary of your script; get clarification on anything that doesn't make sense, especially sayings and expressions that may not translate well from English to your language.

- While the ideal group size is five or six speakers, you can do readers theatre with as few as three or as many as are needed to complete your cast. Keep in mind, though, that actors with only a few lines may be able to play multiple parts, or if you have too many performers, try breaking the large parts (such as the narrator) into parts for several speakers.

- Characters should be unique, especially when it comes to comic pieces; use clues within the script to give each character you play a different personality including voice, posture, style, dialect, mannerisms, and personality.

- Normally, props are kept to a minimum in readers theatre because it's hard to handle both a binder and a prop. For this particular assignment, however, that decision is up to your teacher. Because your goal is to learn a language, props and even costumes may reinforce the learning.

RECOMMENDED READERS THEATRE STORIES

Several of these stories have already been written into children's plays and are the appropriate length for readers theatre. Research fables, short stories, and folktales online.

- Dr. Seuss's *How the Grinch Stole Christmas*
- *Turtle, Frog, and Rat* (Vietnam)
- *One Thousand and One Nights* (Middle East)
- *Who's in Rabbit's House?* (Africa)
- *The Story of the Hard Nut* (Germany)
- *Outwitting a Crocodile* (Malaysia)
- *The Crane Wife* (Japan)
- *Tiger Shoes* (China)

- Each actor may have a chair, if desired; use chairs to create interesting stage pictures by standing on them, crawling under them, or forming them into various set pieces.

- Binders may also be used as props—e.g., as "pizza dough" tossed in the air—but the more you use them, the more you'll need to repair or replace them.

- Introduce as many vocal and sound effects as possible.
    - ◊ A slamming binder might be a gunshot.
    - ◊ Drumming fingers on binders could be rain.

- ◇ Tapping the metal part of a chair could be someone tapping on a window.
- ◇ Humming or singing TV theme songs can add humor.
- ◇ Making sound effects with your mouth, feet, hands, and so on can add personality (like an old radio show) to the performance.

- Experiment with ad-lib, but don't allow it to become overbearing or change the playwright's intent.

- Experiment with "echo effects," in which one actor says a line, and the others echo the last word; using "freezes," when some of the actors freeze in position while the others continue acting; saying lines in unison, when two or more actors say a word, phrase, or line together; or even splitting sentences into individual words or phrases, where several actors take turns saying part of a line such as "and they lived" "happily" "ever" "after" said by four actors instead of one.

- Be careful not to become rhythmic, a common side effect of ensemble reading; also avoid getting into a sing-song cadence or dropping off the ends of lines.

- Even though this is not memorized, you should be very familiar with it; by the performance, actors should be looking up 95% of the time.

- Actors who are "offstage" should still be visible but in a position that takes them out of the scene such as heads dropped, frozen, as set pieces, backs turned, etc.

- Actors who are "onstage" should be in the scene 100%; because it is readers theatre, some will be inclined to read as the others act, but with practice, you will learn to memorize page turns and look down only as a line is needed.

- It is very important that all actors listen and respond when in the scene, unless it has been staged otherwise. For example, the director may stage a poem with all eyes forward and expressionless faces, except when the actor is speaking.

NAME _______________________________________ PERIOD _________ DATE _______________

READERS THEATRE VOCABULARY

WORD OR PHRASE	SPEAKER	TRANSLATION

READERS THEATRE GROUP EVALUATION
FOR LEARNING A NEW LANGUAGE

ACTORS:

____

____

____

____

____

____

1. Students followed the rules set forth by the teacher and the guidelines of the assignment.

   1 2 3 4 5 6 7 8 9 10

   NOTES:

2. Performers appeared comfortable with the language, using proper pronunciation and emphasis.

   1 2 3 4 5 6 7 8 9 10

   NOTES:

3. The group used planned, confident movement to aid in their expression; movement was energetic and lively; movement showed good teamwork.

   1 2 3 4 5 6 7 8 9 10

   NOTES:

4. Teamwork was apparent and aided the group in an overall entertaining performance.

   1 2 3 4 5 6 7 8 9 10

   NOTES:

GROUP SCORE

Record the total group score from this page (out of a possible 40) in the box to the left. Transfer this to each actor's group score on the next page. Finish rating each individual speaker's performance (out of a possible 60 points). Add any applicable bonus points. The total of the group, individual, and bonus points will give you a grade for that actor.

READERS THEATRE GROUP EVALUATION FOR LEARNING A NEW LANGUAGE, CONT.

Actor:

Facial expressions

1 2 3 4 5

Focus/Performance commitment

1 2 3 4 5

Preparation

1 2 3 4 5 6 7 8 9 10

Confidence

1 2 3 4 5 6 7 8 9 10

Characterization/Expression

1 2 3 4 5 6 7 8 9 10

Energy

1 2 3 4 5 6 7 8 9 10

Familiarization

1 2 3 4 5 6 7 8 9 10

Group Score	Individual Score	Bonus Points	TOTAL

Actor:

Facial expressions

1 2 3 4 5

Focus/Performance commitment

1 2 3 4 5

Preparation

1 2 3 4 5 6 7 8 9 10

Confidence

1 2 3 4 5 6 7 8 9 10

Characterization/Expression

1 2 3 4 5 6 7 8 9 10

Energy

1 2 3 4 5 6 7 8 9 10

Familiarization

1 2 3 4 5 6 7 8 9 10

Group Score	Individual Score	Bonus Points	TOTAL

Actor:

Facial expressions

1 2 3 4 5

Focus/Performance commitment

1 2 3 4 5

Preparation

1 2 3 4 5 6 7 8 9 10

Confidence

1 2 3 4 5 6 7 8 9 10

Characterization/Expression

1 2 3 4 5 6 7 8 9 10

Energy

1 2 3 4 5 6 7 8 9 10

Familiarization

1 2 3 4 5 6 7 8 9 10

Group Score	Individual Score	Bonus Points	TOTAL

Actor:

Facial expressions

1 2 3 4 5

Focus/Performance commitment

1 2 3 4 5

Preparation

1 2 3 4 5 6 7 8 9 10

Confidence

1 2 3 4 5 6 7 8 9 10

Characterization/Expression

1 2 3 4 5 6 7 8 9 10

Energy

1 2 3 4 5 6 7 8 9 10

Familiarization

1 2 3 4 5 6 7 8 9 10

Group Score	Individual Score	Bonus Points	TOTAL

Actor:

Facial expressions

1 2 3 4 5

Focus/Performance commitment

1 2 3 4 5

Preparation

1 2 3 4 5 6 7 8 9 10

Confidence

1 2 3 4 5 6 7 8 9 10

Characterization/Expression

1 2 3 4 5 6 7 8 9 10

Energy

1 2 3 4 5 6 7 8 9 10

Familiarization

1 2 3 4 5 6 7 8 9 10

Group Score	Individual Score	Bonus Points	TOTAL

Actor:

Facial expressions

1 2 3 4 5

Focus/Performance commitment

1 2 3 4 5

Preparation

1 2 3 4 5 6 7 8 9 10

Confidence

1 2 3 4 5 6 7 8 9 10

Characterization/Expression

1 2 3 4 5 6 7 8 9 10

Energy

1 2 3 4 5 6 7 8 9 10

Familiarization

1 2 3 4 5 6 7 8 9 10

Group Score	Individual Score	Bonus Points	TOTAL

CINCO DE MAYO
READERS THEATRE

This readers theatre is for eight people, any mixture of boys and girls. Groups may need to alter gender references (pronouns like "he" and "she") to fit their actors appropriately.

1 through 7: *(Yell.)* Happy Cinco de Mayo! Viva la México! *(Other cheers, etc.)*

8: What's all the noise?

4: We're celebrating!

5: That's right, it's Cinco de Mayo! *(1 through 7 cheer again.)*

8: What's that?

1: *(Can't hear over the noise.)* What?

8: I said, what's Cinco de Mayo? *(Sudden silence from 1 through 7.)*

1: The holiday of Cinco de Mayo, The Fifth of May, is a celebration for remembering the victory of the Mexicans over the French army at the Battle of Puebla in 1862.

2: It's mostly celebrated in Mexico, but it's also celebrated in other places with large Mexican populations.

8: So, it's like July Fourth?

1: Kind of. Mexico's Independence Day is actually September sixteenth.

8: So what makes this day, May 5th, so special?

3: Come here. Sit down. Let me tell you a little story about courage.

OTHERS except 8: Courage!

4: Bloodshed!

OTHERS except 8: Bloodshed!

5: Perseverance!

OTHERS except 8: Perseverance!

6: And victory!

OTHERS except 8: Victory!

7: And defeat.

OTHERS except 8: De—

1: Did he—?

3: He did.

8: Defeat? You celebrate defeat?

2: Not exactly. Here. Let's clear things up. You see, the Battle at Puebla in 1862 happened at a violent and confusing time in Mexico's history.

4: Mexico had finally gained independence from Spain in 1821. There were takeovers and wars—

5: Like the Mexican-American War and the Mexican Civil War.

4: That's right. After all that, most Mexicans and their government were out of money.

1: Not just out of money, they were in debt! Mexico owed money to Spain, England, and France, and they were all demanding payment.

8: What about the U.S.?

3: The U.S. cleared Mexico's debt after the Mexican-American War.

4: But France was greedy. They wanted to build their empire.

6: No kidding. France used the debt excuse to establish its own leadership in Mexico.

5: This really made Spain and England mad, and they withdrew their support.

6: When Mexico finally stopped making any loan payments, France sent Napoleon's relative, Archduke Maximilian of Austria, to be the new ruler of Mexico.

7: Then the French invaded. Although American president Abraham Lincoln wanted to help the Mexicans, the U.S. was involved in its own Civil War at the time.

8: You mean they didn't help?

7: They couldn't.

6: So, you see, the invading French army thought it was going to be an easy fight. But they were surprised by how strong the resistance was at Forts Loreto and Guadalupe.

2: But that was nothing compared to the Battle of Puebla!

8: What happened there?

7: It was amazing! This small, poorly armed militia of about 45,000 Mexican men led by General Ignacio Zaragoza Seguin was able to stop and defeat the bigger, better-equipped French army of 65,000 soldiers.

1: And on May 5th, Cinco de Mayo, the French invasion of Mexico was defeated! *(ALL yell in celebration.)*

6: The victory was a glorious moment for Mexican patriots, so you can see why we celebrate!

1: Unfortunately, the victory was short-lived.

2: When he heard the bad news, Napoleon found an excuse to send more troops overseas to try and invade Mexico again, even though most French were against it.

8: What happened?

3: Sadly, 30,000 more troops and a full year later, the French were eventually able to defeat the Mexican army, take over Mexico City, and install Maximilian as the ruler of Mexico.

8: Man! That stinks!

4: Don't worry. He didn't last!

5: That's right. The American Civil War was now over, and the U.S. could help their Mexican neighbors. They sent those Frenchmen packing!

8: What happened to Maximilian?

6: Well, let's just say the Mexicans weren't real happy with him, if you know what I mean.

7: So even though the French did occupy Mexico City, Cinco de Mayo honors the bravery and victory of General Zaragoza's small, outnumbered militia at the Battle of Puebla in 1862.

8: So why celebrate a battle that happened so long ago?

1: Because it's an important piece of Mexican history.

2: Because it reminds us how valuable freedom is.

3: Because it reminds us that we can achieve a lot, even though the odds don't favor us.

4: Because it reminds us that each of us has something to contribute, and it reminds us that when you believe deeply in something, you don't give up.

5: Cinco de Mayo celebrates a victory that was soon followed by defeat, but the true victory for the Mexican people was that they didn't give up.

6: They kept fighting. Eventually, they won the greatest gift of all. Freedom.

7: So, happy Cinco de Mayo?

8: Happy Cinco de Mayo!

SECTION 3 NOTES:

Introduction to THEATRE ARTS 2

VOLUME TWO / SECOND EDITION

STUDENT WORKBOOK

WITH

ADDITIONAL NOTES FOR TEACHERS

CHAPTER 1
THEATRE FOR LIFE'S LESSONS

ADDITIONAL NOTES

INTRODUCTION

A young theatre teacher named Shayna had been doing her job for a couple of years when it dawned on her that she was not feeding the poor, healing the sick, or doing any of the things she had dreamt of doing in college. Sure, she was a teacher, and everyone knows that is an admirable job, but she was teaching theatre! While she loved her craft and her kids, she failed to see how she was changing the world or even making a difference. She was starting to wonder if she had made the right career choice.

She had one particularly unruly class of mostly boys. Arnie seemed to be the ring leader, and this was confirmed when he missed several days of school, and she was suddenly very capable of keeping order. The students joked about how peaceful it was with Arnie gone, but the teacher came to his defense. She said he was creative, imaginative, and full of extra energy. She added that one day he would make a great comedian and put their little town on the map.

The rest of the students were a little surprised at her response, and when Arnie returned, she welcomed him with concern, wondering if he had been sick. He explained that he had gone duck hunting with his father and had brought her back a souvenir. It was the curly tail feather of his duck. He said it was very prized by hunters, and he only had one. He was giving it to his favorite teacher because he heard what she had said about him, that he was funny and important and not just a class clown.

Arnie returned to his seat, opened his book, shot off a few quick one-liners, then gave the floor to his teacher. Her respect for him catapulted the two to a higher understanding. From that point forward, she allowed him to be "the comedian" briefly at the beginning of each class period. After his very short routine, he allowed her to be the teacher.

The young teacher grew with the experience, swiftly becoming the experienced teacher. She was making a difference in the world. Chances are Arnie would never become an actor or a comedian, but she was teaching him to respect his creative energy by harnessing it into something productive. He appreciated that she believed in him and didn't consider his absence something to celebrate.

Theatre is magical, and not just for the audience. Many young people, even those who were previously tagged as troubled, have found their niche in the theatre. Cary Grant had a horribly troubled childhood, as did Tom Cruise. Being onstage and escaping into a character allows these actors to leave reality momentarily; it is therapeutic.

Not all troubled teens who find refuge in the theatre become actors. Many find comfort in writing plays, directing, or being on a crew.

It doesn't matter where a young person is in the theatre; if they are involved in a play, they will hear the play's message over and over and over again. As their teacher and director, you are in a unique position. You have the power to guide them while allowing them to believe they are guiding themselves. By exposing them to character-building theatre, you are putting them in the position of the speaker in Robert Frost's poem "The Road Not Taken." He tells of standing at a fork in the road and remembers thinking that he "could not travel both and be one traveler." He decides to take the road that appears less traveled, remarking that he would save the other for another day. The poem ends:

> *...Yet knowing how way leads on to way*
>
> *I doubted if I should ever come back.*
>
> *I shall be telling this with a sigh*
>
> *Somewhere ages and ages hence:*
>
> *Two roads diverged in a wood, and I—*
>
> *I took the one less traveled by,*
>
> *And that has made all the difference.*

What the traveler does not say, or perhaps does not realize, is that he did not get to that fork in the road purely by accident. We come to those places in our lives because someone, perhaps a teacher or a parent, has shown us that there are more options than just the one. Frost's poem demonstrates how one person is faced with making a choice that he may or may not regret. Your plays have the potential to do the same for your students.

A teacher directed the play *Crying Out*, by Matthew Hunt (Concord Theatricals). The play deals with relationships, pregnancy, drugs, alcohol, succeeding in school, and many more topics that hit home with the students in the play and their classmates. Concerned that it was too mature for the inner-city high school student body, the principal asked to sit in on a rehearsal and brought all three members of the counseling staff. They were all in agreement that the play was something the students on their campus needed to see. Because many of their students were troubled, they tried to keep assemblies to a minimum, and when possible, they gathered in smaller groups. The theater, however, seated over 1,000 people, and there were just under that many students and teachers in the school. It was decided they would attempt one performance for the entire student body.

These particular students had never seen a play together at their school, and few had ever seen a drama. This director was fortunate to have a very gifted cast, and the two girls who played the mother and the daughter were especially talented. As the play progressed, their characters' troubled relationship erupted, and at one point, the actor playing the teen threw her schoolbooks.

The audience had become energized by the scene, and when the girl became enraged, they lost control of themselves and began yelling at the stage, laughing, and talking back and forth, yet the actors continued. Teachers began giving warning looks at those who were talking, the principal stood up and began circulating, and while a few hushed, some were just not familiar enough with live theatre to realize the negative impact of their unruly behavior.

Fed up with the outburst and concerned for her actors, the director stood up and yelled "Cut!" as loudly as possible. Surprisingly, the actors froze in place, and every member of the audience—shocked by the yelling—was instantly quiet. The director explained that the actors had worked hard, the play was their gift to the audience, and that the audience had only one choice—to be respectful. If they chose differently, the entire group would be released back to their classes and would never see how this play ended. Nor would they ever get to see another. Now, with a barely raised voice, the director asked, "May the actors continue?"

A single voice replied, "Yes, ma'am." Half a second later, a couple more repeated her reply, and before long, the audience, who had just been out of control and very disrespectful joined in applause to show the teacher they could do what had been asked.

A little disoriented by the entire string of events, the teacher waited for the applause to subside, then turned to the actors, who had remained frozen this entire time. The director thought, "I'm so glad I trained the actors to cut. I hope this next part goes well." The director then called "Action!" The frozen cast unfroze. The performer whose line had been interrupted picked up at the beginning of that line, and the emotionally moving play continued— uninterrupted—to the end.

The audience showed their appreciation and their respect with a huge round of applause, and a few students stood to show they really enjoyed the show. Afterward, the principal spoke, inviting any student

who needed to talk to a counselor to do so after the show.

Back in class, the actors were amazed that they had done so well and that they had all frozen on cue. They had been taught to stop and be quiet on "cut," but their spontaneous "freeze" was unrehearsed and unexpected. "The only thing I can say is that you are a team, and you were so used to working together that you sensed what the others would do," their director explained. It was difficult to get out of costume and back to class because they were continually interrupted by teachers and students congratulating them on a job well done.

Later the teacher learned that two students had visited the counselors because of the play. Only two. That's okay, the teacher thought. It's two more than might have gotten help had we not performed. Besides, there was success on multiple levels that day. There was no way to tell how many students were positively affected by the performance. The teacher knew the performance had reached at least two.

There are many types of literature that can be educational in nature without seeming preachy or which have lessons that are more subtle. For example, consider doing material based on a famous work of literature, especially those that are read in your district's language arts or other classes. Choosing the timing of these productions wisely will not only help your students to understand the literature, but it will also increase your attendance at performances. Say your school's eleventh grade language arts class is reading *Antigone* in March. Talk to the teachers who will be overseeing the assignment and discuss when they feel the production would be more beneficial. Some may want their students to see the play prior to reading it for a clearer understanding of what they will be reading. Some would probably prefer that their students see it after reading it—especially if they are being tested on what they read—to reinforce their understanding. By coordinating with the teachers ahead of time, you will gain their respect. They will know that you are aware of their curriculum and are making an effort to reinforce it. Your genuine interest in cross-curricular connections will be greatly appreciated. They will likely require students to attend the performance or offer credit to those who do.

You can do the same thing in history classes or with other lessons and events at school. Select a play from a time period or about an event in history that students will be studying at your school. Again, coordinate with the history teachers so that your play falls during or immediately before or after the unit. Your program, your actors, and your student body will all benefit from the thoughtful timing and selection of material.

How might these great pieces of literature or historical plays benefit in the area of character? That will depend largely on how the teachers approach the production in class. As with any event, teachers will want to discuss the impact and importance and relate it to students' lives. Discuss the moral of the story and how history tends to repeat itself. Make students feel involved and place them into the story by drawing parallels to life in their homes or on their streets.

There are many other types of educational plays, such as those dealing with parts of speech, math, science, technology, philosophy, religion, geography, culture, and so on. These will not only educate, they will also build character while entertaining. Anyone who has spent any time at all in a successful classroom realizes that making the lesson fun and taking the pressure out of a situation improves retention and enthusiasm.

How will you use character-building theatre in your classroom? You probably already are. Now it's time to introduce the idea to those in your charge—your students. It is they who will have the opportunity to bridge the gap between you and those in the school whom you do not reach on a daily basis.

THEATRE AS A TOOL FOR LEARNING AND TEACHING

As you review this chapter, consider the following extension activities for your students:

- **Investigate Your TV Lineup**: Have students look at one weekday's lineup for ABC, NBC, and CBS, and then present them with the following questions and assignment:

  ◇ Do you notice anything about the times that certain shows are aired?

  ◇ When are shows for your age group mostly shown?

  ◇ What are popular time slots for stay-at-home moms and dads?

  ◇ Who is being targeted for a show airing at 11:00 in the morning?

  ◇ What time do shows air that are mature or show adult themes?

  Select one thirty-minute time slot, and get your pen and pad ready. Record the name of the show, the age group you think it is intended to target, the types of colors, music, and language used, and every product for every commercial that comes on during that show. Most of the products will appeal to the same audience that the show does. Are there any that surprise you? If there are some products that do not seem to match the type of viewer for that show, why do you think the producers spent their advertising revenue on that time slot? Can you think of any connections or contradictions between the message or moral of the show and the products sold in the commercials? Write a one-page discovery of your findings including why commercial content is important to actors or those studying theatre.

- **Theme Chart**: Your students will learn a great deal in this chapter about theme and using their talents to reach others. First, to better make use of your in-class script library and to give them practice identifying the theme of different scripts, have your students help you get organized.

  With your entire library of scripts, have students divide them by publisher, then alphabetize the scripts within each publisher's group. Divide your class into groups and have each group work with one publisher's scripts. Each group will go to their assigned publisher's website, find the script, and record useful information into a table that you've created in Google Drive or something similar so all groups have access. Your table should look something like the chart on the next page.

TITLE	M	F	M/F	AUTHOR	PUBLISHER	GENRE	THEMES OR GENERAL DESCRIPTION	# COPIES
Charlotte's Web	5 to 7	7 to 9	+	White, E.B. adapted by Robinette, Joseph	Dramatic Publishing	Drama	Friendship; loneliness; sacrifice; love. Adapted from the classic novel.	1
The Great Gatsby	4	3	8+	Fitzgerald, F. Scott adapted by Peterson, Gary	Pioneer Drama Service	Drama	The American Dream; money; materialism; desire; love; jealousy. Stage adaptation of the classic novel.	15
Little Women	3	7 to 11		Alcott, Louisa May adapted by Davidson, Scott	Pioneer Drama Service	Drama	Family; duty; sacrifice; independence; work; selfless generosity; love. Adapted from the classic novel.	10
The Misanthrope	9	2		Moliére, translated by Harrison, Tony	Concord Theatricals	Comedy	Classic; social pretense; snobbery; hypocrisy. This is an updated version.	1
Phaedra	3	5		Racine, Jean, translated by Wilbur, Richard	Dramatists Play Service, Inc.	Drama	Betrayal; passion; jealousy; guilt; loyalty. This is the performance edition.	11

Now you can sort your table by any of the column headings, quickly finding scripts in your library by playwright, by number of males or females, etc. You can also add a column to the chart to help you keep track when students check out plays to read.

Most importantly, students learn how to recognize theme and use the different play publishers' websites. Students will also learn about their in-class resources for when they are ready to do student-directed productions. (Of course, even if you already have scripts, performance rights will have to be acquired by contacting the publisher.)

VOCABULARY WORD WALL

Employed by teachers in other subjects for years, the famous Word Wall is an innovation that can just as easily work in the theatre classroom. In short, it is a space visible by the entire class onto which the teacher or a student helper places new words. These may be words that pop up in any context, perhaps while reading a play, learning a new concept, in discussion, as dialogue in a scene, and so on. It is generally reserved for words repeated often or words students will see again.

This is how it works: say you are teaching about the parts of the stage. There are many difficult words that students will need to know, not only throughout the duration of the lesson, but also as they do scene work, are in plays, and as they study tech theatre. The teacher will write each word on a strip of paper large enough for the word to be read by the farthest student from the wall. The teacher will then discuss the word and place it on the wall with tape or sticky tack.

How is this different from other methods? First, the students see the words every day. There are constant visual reminders that the word is important on the walls of the classroom. They do not have to open their notes or their books' glossaries to find a word when needed for a quick reference, but students will also be given opportunity to add the words on the wall to their notes, so they will have them for more in-depth reference when needed.

There are many ways to create and maintain the useful teaching tools. The following are some suggestions, but you may find that you have a way that works better for you. Consider these ideas:

- Use a bulletin board as your Word Wall, but use it *only* for new words. Do not clutter the board with anything that will take your students' attention during Word Wall discussions. The backing on a bulletin board will also make it easier to put words up and take them down. You might want to cover the board with something a bit more durable than butcher paper, since it will experience more activity than a normal board.

- If you do not have a bulletin board large enough, frame a large piece of your classroom wall with bulletin board border.

- Title your space "Word Wall" so that students will know exactly where to look for new words. Word Walls are also impressive tools to use during your teacher evaluations and any other visits. However, they only make a good impression if your students have training on how to do their part. Teach students to reference the wall by encouraging and rewarding it. Try to avoid saying things like, "Don't look at the Word Wall; you should know this." Instead, because the wall is there for their benefit, perhaps say, "It's okay if you need to look at the Word Wall. That's why it's there." You may also hear other students call it cheating to reference the wall; it is your job to remind them that the wall is a tool, not a cheat. You will know the wall is working when students become comfortable referencing it regularly.

- You can either set aside time for students to put Word Wall definitions into their notes as they are placed onto the wall or you can make defining the words part of their bell work. "Bell work" is another name for the tasks students are regularly expected to complete after coming into the class and during attendance recording. Some teachers call them bell ringers, sponge activities, or even independent time.

- Consider making Word Wall quizzes a weekly occurrence, save them for tests, or quiz students orally as time allows.

- Use sturdy colored paper for the words on your Word Wall. If you go to a local print shop, they often have to cut paper for a job and will happily give teachers the leftover strips. A good size is about four inches tall by about ten or twelve inches wide, but a lot depends on how much space you have and how far away students sit.

- Write the word on one side of the paper and the definition on the other. Use a fat black marker that will not bleed through the paper for the word. You can write the definition on the back much less boldly, as you will not need students to see the definition from far away.

- Leave the words on the wall until you are confident that your students understand them.

- As you take old words down from your wall, put them in a "holding basket." When you are absent, your sub can play Trash Can Basketball with the students. Students will make two teams, and each team will line up side by side with the trash can about fifteen feet (you decide what works for your group) in front of them. The sub will then ask the first person on one team to either define a word or give the word to match the definition (using the old Word Wall cards). If that team member is correct, they take a shot at the trash can with a "ball" made of wadded up paper (wrap it in tape for a more solid ball). If they score, their team gets a point. Do the same thing with the next team, and take turns until one team reaches a certain score or the bell rings.

- File used cards in alphabetical order for future use.
- Consider adding play titles, playwrights, and other factual information to your Word Wall.
- Some teachers have their Word Walls divided into categories, perhaps even color-coded. For theatre use, you might have Terms, People, Plays, and Script Words (words from scenes).

- Assign one student from each class to help maintain your Word Wall. Perhaps you can give this helper bonus points on the quiz or even replace a low grade or some other appropriate incentive for helping you keep your wall current and accurate. This helper will find words in your file, put them on the wall, take them down as students become more familiar with the words, and then file them alphabetically after you feel they are no longer needed in the holding basket.

VOCABULARY

In this chapter, you will learn about:

Advertising Revenue: Money made by the network or station from the sale of commercial airtime.

Antagonist: The people, things, or ideas that prevent or try to prevent the protagonist from reaching a goal.

Brainstorm: To write without censoring as you go, jotting every thought that comes to mind on the subject at hand.

Climax: The turning point in a story in which the protagonist either reaches or fails to reach their goal.

Company: Team of actors working together on a show.

Dramatic Structure: The basic form of a story; includes exposition, rising action, climax, falling action, and ending.

Dramatization: To turn something into a script so that it can be performed.

Ending: The final wrap-up of the dramatic structure.

Exposition: The beginning of a story in which readers or viewers learn about the characters and setting.

Falling Action: Following the climax, it is the short time when loose ends are tightened and any remaining questions are answered.

Goal: What a character wants in a scene or story.

Historical Plays: Plays that teach about people, places, and events of our past.

Inciting Incident: The bit of action that starts the characters on their upward journey toward the climax.

Issue Plays: Plays about modern challenges relevant to today's actors and/or audiences.

Knowing Your Audience: Understanding as much as possible about the group you will be performing for (or who will read your material), including their maturity, interests, challenges, goals, and so on.

Message: The lesson the playwright intends for the audience/readers to learn.

Morality Plays: Dramas that seek to teach people to make moral choices.

Obstacles: Things that stand in the way (often figuratively) of one's goal.

Passion Plays: Dramatic presentations of the suffering, death, and resurrection of Jesus.

Plot: The storyline or events in a story.

Protagonist: The lead character.

Rising Action: The development of the plot after the exposition and before the climax.

Setting: When and where a story takes place.

Slapstick Humor: Exaggerated, very physical comedy in which the boundaries of common sense are often ignored to elicit a laugh.

Theme: The lesson the story is attempting to impart.

Venue: Performance space or event setting.

Work Ethic: A strong impulse to do a job well; a belief that work should be done well.

3

CHAPTER I VOCABULARY

A great deal of the vocabulary from this chapter will be used not just later in this book but also in your students' other classes. As always, review vocabulary with them in advance and seek clarification as you read to ensure your students understand the words as they are used in context. The following suggestions will assist your students in retaining the vocabulary in this and all chapters:

- Add words to your Word Wall as they are reached in the chapter; most words from the glossary are in bold the first time they appear in the chapter, and if the word is easily defined in the same sentence or within a reasonable distance, the definition will be italicized.

- Define one or two words on the board each day and train your students to add the definitions to a word journal or notebook silently while you take attendance.

- Quiz students on their vocabulary using the puzzle at the end of this chapter; by telling students ahead of time that you will be quizzing them, they will have incentive to record the words and definitions as you make them available.

- If you do not have students record the definitions, you may want to consider allowing them to refer to this chapter when completing the puzzle.

- Save puzzles from the various chapters for a day when you will have a substitute. Your students will benefit from the review of the vocabulary, your sub will appreciate the quiet activity, and you will be able to quickly check the puzzles and record the grades upon your return.

THEATRE FOR LIFE'S LESSONS

Sesame Street, *Thomas the Tank Engine*, and *Dora the Explorer* are just a few of the shows children watch for entertainment, but having fun and passing the time are not the shows' ultimate **goals**. Most of the shows that target young audiences use cute characters, songs, and bright colors to draw in young viewers, but they are obviously educational too, which appeals to parents. As the children's young eyes are transfixed by what's on the screen, their minds are absorbing math, communication skills, and the tools needed for making wise choices.

As viewers grow from childhood to pre-adolescence, television programming designed for them grows too. For the most part, shows aimed at preteens still hope to teach valuable life lessons. But the short skits prevalent in shows for a younger audience are now replaced by longer, more involved plots and more complex characters. The audience is now at an age where they know the difference between entertainment and education, and few will watch a "lesson" unless it is well-disguised as humor, action, or adventure.

Now that you are older, you are probably aware of how producers worked hard to hold your attention when you were younger, but are you aware that they are still doing it? Viewers your age, according to those who plan your TV programming, are looking for more grown-up themes in their shows. Producers keep in mind that your generation is struggling through a period when difficult choices pop up on a daily basis. They understand that having these same choices acted out on TV helps you on your journey to adulthood by presenting healthy (or unhealthy, depending on the programming) solutions to life's dilemmas. If these same programming gurus do their jobs well, your television heroes become your role models. If a young person relates to a fictitious TV character and that character demonstrates how to avoid drugs, it makes an impression on that young person, the viewer. When such young viewers are tempted with drugs in their own lives, they will have been exposed to at least one way to say no, all thanks to a one-hour TV drama.

During that one hour, you were entertained with a riveting, entertaining **plot**, the network earned **advertising revenue** (*money made from the sale of commercial airtime*), and your parents were pleased that you were watching something beneficial.

Think of a TV show you have watched recently. Was there a **theme** or lesson? Could you relate to what the actors were going through because it was similar to a situation in your life or the life of someone you know?

Of course, we all know that TV shows, no matter how compelling and educational, cannot replace a healthy relationship with the adults closest to you. The truth is that many kids your age spend more one-on-one time with

---

What was your favorite educational show when you were in kindergarten through about second grade?

What kinds of lessons did it attempt to teach?

Are there any shows you watched as a child that you would not want your children to watch because you think they could be harmful? Explain:

NOTES: ____

____

____

____

____

____

____

CHAPTER I — THEATRE FOR LIFE'S LESSONS

the TV than they do with their parents. It's refreshing to know that most programming seeks to help young people make the right choices.

So, what does all this talk of TV programming have to do with you, a theatre student? Think about this: the desire to use entertainment as a teaching tool isn't a new one, and before television, there was theatre.

In the Dark Ages, few common people knew how to read because farming or tending to the family business took precedence over education. The church recognized this, but there was still a strong need to spread the Gospel. Since commoners made up the majority of most communities, this was quite a big challenge. The educated few had to reach the uneducated masses. They decided the best way to do this was to gather willing, eager audiences and entertain them with religious stories produced as plays. True, people could hear the same stories at church, but a church service, or Mass, was held in Latin, which very few people understood.

The church also recognized that common people responded better to action and **slapstick humor** (*exaggerated, sometimes violent comedy in which the boundaries of common sense are often ignored to elicit a laugh*). Consequently, the religious plays were written with a great deal of comedy and even brutality, but the humorous message was always straight from the Gospel and had very serious undertones.

Both humor and action still draw large crowds to the box office today, as do movies and plays with compelling messages, strong morals, and, of course, heroes. Important lessons are everywhere in the entertainment industry. **Historical plays** *teach about people, places, and events of our past.* **Morality plays** *seek to teach people to make moral choices.* **Passion plays** *teach about the suffering, death, and resurrection of Jesus.* The latter two types of plays have their roots deep in history and religion, and they continue to be popular today, especially with older audiences. However, there are a number of wonderful plays that are more popular with your generation. These are **issue plays**, *stories that dramatize (sometimes with comedy) the modern challenges faced by young people today.* Young actors take the stage as drug addicts to teach others how harmful drugs can be, or they play out dysfunctional relationships hoping that we, the audience, will not repeat the mistakes portrayed onstage.

Theatre is an invaluable resource that can be used to gather crowds, to give young people self-esteem, and to guide those without a goal in a more positive direction. When you perform a scene for your classmates, you are not just reaching the audience; you and your partners are also gaining from the experience.

EXAMPLES OF HISTORICAL PLAYS

1. *Abe Lincoln in Illinois*, Robert E. Sherwood (Dramatists Play Service)

2. *Stand and Deliver*, Ramon Menendez, Tom Musca; adapted by Robert Bella (Dramatic Publishing)

3. *Anne of the Thousand Days*, Maxwell Anderson (Dramatists Play Service)

4. *Johnny Tremain*, Coleman A. Jennings, Lola H. Jennings adapted by Esther Forbes (Dramatic Publishing)

5. *Saint Joan*, George Bernard Shaw (Concord Theatricals)

6. *Julian*, James Janda (Pioneer Drama Service)

On a larger scale, your teachers/directors are mindful of how the plays they select can impact those in the cast, crew, audience, and beyond. Your district has probably given your instructors guidelines of what is and is not considered appropriate. This is based on several factors. For one, since it is a school play, they assume students will be in the audience. Your district has taken an oath to teach those students, and in the minds of many in education, that can mean protecting them from subject matter or language that they feel should be reserved for **venues** (*performance spaces*) outside of the school environment. It is also based on the school's and district's desire to be seen in a certain light. Allowing a performance that is too mature for its own students or that has a message not shared by the general public can harm the district's or school's reputation.

Likewise, as actors and producers of classroom scenes, you, too, have the ability to select material that sends a strong **message**, if that is your goal. You possess a great deal of power to reach a broad **audience**. Whether you mean to educate or not, you will be making a strong impression on someone, so select your material with that in mind.

NOTES: ____

____

____

____

____

____

____

____

What messages are important enough to you that you would want to share them with your classmates?

____

____

____

____

____

____

____

____

____

How do you go about selecting the right material for your audience? Look in your own community. What are some of the problems or challenges facing your friends or those at your school? What about challenges you see outside of school, such as stories on the news or family issues? Your teacher probably has plays or scenes that deal with a range of topics, or you can find non-copyrighted material on various sites on the internet.

Some topics to consider adding to the list you made above might include:

- Abuse
- Dishonesty
- Drugs
- Sexual issues
- Relationships
- Peer pressure

- Pregnancy
- Alcohol
- Bullying
- Recycling
- Respect
- Gangs

There are other types of literature that can be educational in nature without seeming preachy and/or which have lessons that are less obvious. For example, consider doing material based on a famous work of literature. Many of the stories you read in your classes have been made into plays. If your teacher is looking for a good play that will draw a large audience—perhaps as a fundraiser—suggest the play version of a literary work required at school. You'll be a hero among your friends and with your English and drama teachers.

Why reach across curricula? Many teachers will give extra credit for attending a play, especially when it can be directly tied to their curriculum. Furthermore, becoming an expert on a scene cements the knowledge in a way few other lessons will, so you learn more and you learn better as an actor. But your audience also benefits. Many students find dramatic performances more understandable than text from required reading. And often audience members become emotionally invested in material they see performed, which is rarely accomplished by a lesson from a textbook.

Any time you are studying a period in history, a region, a cause, or an idea at school, research

EXAMPLES OF FAMOUS LITERARY WORKS OFTEN ADAPTED INTO DRAMATIZATIONS

Classic literary works, since they are in public domain, are often adapted into dramatic works. Below is a list of a few of the titles that are often adapted.

1. *The Adventures of Huckleberry Finn* by Mark Twain
2. *Alice's Adventures in Wonderland* by Lewis Carroll
3. *Anne of Green Gables* by L.M. Montgomery
4. *Antigone* by Sophocles
5. *A Christmas Carol* by Charles Dickens
6. *The Grapes of Wrath* by John Steinbeck
7. *The Great Gatsby* by F. Scott Fitzgerald
8. *Jungle Book* by Rudyard Kipling
9. *Little Women* by Louisa May Alcott
10. *A Midsummer Night's Dream* by William Shakespeare
11. *Pride and Prejudice* by Jane Austen
12. *To Kill a Mockingbird* by Harper Lee

Check the website of different play publishers and see if you can find these or other famous adaptations.

NOTES: _______________________________________

____

____

____

____

____

____

____

plays associated with the topic you're studying. There are plays about pioneers, biblical times, wars, depressions and famine, slavery and racism, women's rights, elections, assassinations, and so much more. By studying the play and the characters, you will have a deeper, more personal understanding of the time period or the event. There are also many other types of educational plays that deal with parts of speech, math, science, technology, philosophy, religion, geography, culture, and more.

Remember, however, that dramatizations of real events might not be 100% accurate. **Dramatization** means *to take something that is not a script and put it into script form; it is a dramatic representation of something else.* Often, important characters may be cut, several characters may be combined into one, locations might be changed, or relationships that did not really exist may be added for spiciness because romance sells. When you are using a play to reinforce what you've learned about an actual event, person, time period, location, or piece of literature, find discrepancies or differences between the stories told by the play and the textbook and talk about them. Why did the playwright feel it was necessary to make that change? Did it make the story more interesting? Did it replace material, bridge a gap, help eliminate multiple characters, etc.? When you perform one of these plays, be sure that your audience knows (just as is done in the movies) that the dramatization is based on actual events, but some changes were made for theatrical purposes.

What are some lessons or moments in history that you think might be interesting in play form? Who are some historical characters whose stories may have been made into dramas? Research these on publishers' websites and submit the titles to your teacher.

____

____

____

____

____

____

____

Do any of the plays you discovered in your research sound like something you would like to see produced at your school? If not, perhaps you can write scenes or plays based on the topics on page 6.

NOTES: ____

____

____

____

____

____

____

WRITING YOUR OWN CHARACTER-BUILDING SCRIPTS

There are so many jobs in theatre, but one that many theatre teachers forget to foster in their students is that of playwright. Allow and encourage students to write their own material, keep files of the best ones, and use them to guide future students toward this creative outlet.

There are many very successful plays written by young people, some of them your students' ages. Dramatic Publishing Company proudly boasts at least four:

Choices, Glimpses, and *Rites,* all attributed to "Many Young Playwrights" as the authors, and *In Sight,* by "Louisville's Young Playwrights." Pioneer Drama Service recommends their bestselling *Big Bad*, which Alec Strum wrote when still a teen. High school senior Nikki Mondschein won a national playwriting award with her play, *Characters*.

Still need some ways to encourage your students to write? Try these tips:

Start small. Teach students to write monologues and perform them. Then teach them dialogue;

WRITING YOUR OWN CHARACTER-BUILDING SCRIPTS

Sometimes finding just the right script for the cause you are hoping to promote is impossible. Don't worry! That's actually really good news. Over-saturation means there are plenty of scripts available, but under-saturation means there is an opportunity for a young playwright to fill a need. That's right... often your best resource for scripts will be your own imagination and familiarity with a topic—or your ability to become an expert through research.

Several years ago, a Texas community began a campaign to promote recycling. Most people had a basic understanding of recycling, but the campaign's leaders knew that by arming the community with a little more knowledge, they could increase the overall effectiveness. The best way to do this, they agreed, was by starting in the schools. It had been their experience that school-aged children and teens teach their families a great deal. Students learn about something important at school, it becomes important to the students, and they take their infectious enthusiasm for the cause into their homes. Before long, the whole family has an incurable case of enthusiasm!

George King was the principal of Wilson Middle School, a large school in the Dallas suburbs. Unlike many of the other schools in the area, which had lost a great deal of the surrounding nature to expansion, Wilson had retained its beautiful, fully enclosed courtyard. Not only had the courtyard been retained, but Mr. King and some of the teachers were also continually making improvements to it. Long after the school day was over, students would see the principal, the art teacher, or the health teacher planting, cleaning, dredging the pond, or repairing the waterfall. With window-lined halls on all four sides of the courtyard, the students could enjoy the beauty of pools of water, rock gardens, statues, rose bushes, herbs, irises, squirrels, and butterflies as they passed from one class to the next. Many teachers would hold class or silent reading sessions on the courtyard benches.

With this little oasis at the center of Wilson's learning environment, it was no wonder that Mr.

King was interested in promoting recycling amongst his student body. He asked the drama teacher to produce a series of videos, starring her students, aimed at promoting recycling. He even came up with the main character: Can Man. "Focus on him; beyond that, you have full creative license," he told her.

Can Man was a superhero who was "out to save the world one can (or bottle) at a time!" Armed with this one character and the goal of recycling awareness, the teacher began a discussion with her most advanced theatre class. They were honored to have had their school's leader ask them to take on such an important task. Once they got past the initial excitement, the creativity began to flow. The teacher wrote down every idea, no matter how silly it seemed. From this **brainstorming** process, the class began to plan their season—a series of about ten episodes of *Can Man*, each dealing with a different environmental issue. Can Man was even slated to take a short break from his normal agenda to talk to students about Halloween safety and staying healthy over the holiday break.

The small drama class abandoned their normal curriculum to become the video class. To justify this, the teacher was easily able to connect their new objective to even more of the target objectives and skills in the state's curriculum. The class's goal was to produce an episode every week and a half. On day one, they would jot down ideas for scripts. On day two, they would work together at the teacher's computer as she finalized the script using their input and ideas. Day three would be a rehearsal day. On day four, they would make or gather whatever props and set pieces were needed and rehearse again. On day five (and sometimes six), they would try to film the entire episode in one solid take. This was many years ago, and with no access to editing equipment, this was their only option at that time. Thankfully, advancements in technology have since made it easier to film and edit on most standard computers, tablets, or smart phones.

After each episode was completed, they aired it on their school's video announcement system.

---

i.e., responding to each other. Shorter scenes are easier than longer ones, so build on successes by focusing on easily mastered shorter scenes.

- Consider hosting a playwriting competition among your students.

- Let them work in pairs or small groups.

- Start by giving them the entire plot and have them twist it around a little. For instance, have them modernize *Cinderella*, or put the story of *Sleeping Beauty* in a hospital—instead of being under a spell, she's in a coma or very ill. Allow students to perform their scenes in a night of student-written scenes. Since you will not be paying royalties, this is a wonderful idea for a fundraiser! Other twists could include any fairy tale as a Western, as a soap opera, in film noir, as a slapstick comedy, as a silent film, or even as a reality TV show.

- After they are comfortable with writing, allow them to work on some original plots.

- Many believe that the ending is the hardest part, so some find it useful to decide on the ending first, then work your way backward from there.

- If handling a large selection of student-written plays is not working for you, select just one or two plots and have your students develop them differently. You can discuss what is working and what isn't, and if the groups want to try to get back on the same track, they can. Otherwise,

If your whole school can watch any kind of pre-recorded video in separate rooms at the same time, you probably have the same capability. It didn't take long for *Can Man* to become a hit with the student body. Teachers reported that the students would chat during announcements but would hush each other when *Can Man* started and stay glued to the screen the entire time. They began making requests for the characters to mention their names on the air to discuss certain issues, or to repeat certain comedic gags that they thought were funny. A few even asked if they could write episodes (and, of course, the team gladly accepted all reasonable offers for help). Most importantly, the school saw a dramatic increase in recycling. Teachers made regular requests to upgrade from the small recycling can to the larger bin, and students were often heard saying things like, "Make Can Man proud," as they tossed a can into the blue container.

To what did *Can Man* owe its success? The characters were fun, and the costumes were hilarious. The actors bravely performed gags that were ridiculously funny (such as attempting to fly, then realizing they couldn't, and heroes galloping off on invisible horses). They incorporated all the typical superhero phrases like "trusty sidekick," "same Ram time, same Ram channel" (the school mascot was the Ram), and the famous villainous last line "… and I would have gotten away with it, too, if it hadn't been for you meddling tree huggers!"

Each episode attempted to introduce a new character—some heroes, some villains. Some examples of synopses include:

1. "The Birth of Paper Boy"—Can Man's archnemesis, The Lazy Loser, litters his newspaper, and out of the pollution is born Paper Boy, soon to become Can Man's trusty sidekick. The script for this episode is included on page 12.

2. "Plastic No More"—Polly Peppergrinder wants to help the environment in a big way, but she doesn't feel that one person (a non-superhero, especially) can make a difference, so she adopts the identity of "Princess Plastic," a faux superhero. Can Man and Paper Boy show her that one person can make a difference and that she has more power as herself than she does trying to be someone she isn't. The script for this episode is included on page 13.

3. "Think Outside the Box"—The Lazy Loser and his wife, Mrs. Loser, move. However, rather than using recycled boxes and recycling them again after the move, the Losers litter by abandoning their boxes. The boxes come alive in the character of The Boxer (*very* fun costume project), and with Can Man and Paper Boy's help, they "contain" the Losers and teach them the value of both using recycled materials and re-recycling them afterward. The script for this episode is included on page 15.

4. "The Dirty Adventures of Captain Compost"—Sentenced to community service for littering his boxes (in the previous episode), the Lazy Loser and Mrs. Loser discover the benefits of composting.

5. "It's a Good Thing"—In true Martha Stewart style, Can Man, Paper Boy, and all the previous heroes and guests participate as audience members at the filming of a home crafts show. The hostess, Mother Nature, teaches her audience how to reuse items around the house that many discard as trash.

6. "Assault and Battery"—Can Man and Paper Boy go on a fishing trip, but they find that the fish are dead on the banks of the lake. After investigating, they discover the villainous Battery Acid has poisoned the waters because of improper disposal of used batteries. The heroes educate the community in proper disposal and recycling of batteries, and the villain is reformed and becomes a superhero who vows to guide all old batteries to a new life.

7. "Dr. Toxin and the Quest for Proper Disposal"—Dr. Toxin has a lab full of unwanted chemicals found commonly in homes and schools. He spends his life seeking to uncover the mystery of how to properly dispose of them without harming the environment. However, the chemicals become impatient, coming to life (fun puppetry project) and taunting him. He almost gives in to impatience and dumps the chemicals improperly, but voices in his head (the Narrator, Mother Nature, Can Man, and that one voice he can't understand, Paperboy) convince him he's either going crazy or the solution is a phone call away—to the city (who will probably come pick up the chemicals for him free of charge).

The scripts for the first three episodes of *Can Man* are provided at the end of this section. Synopses for the other episodes are above, so you and your students may write your own scripts, if you like. What other lessons might Can Man or a different superhero teach on your campus? Add your own synopses if you wish.

Maybe recycling isn't even a problem on your campus; find a different cause. Perhaps your class can come up with a new, exciting **protagonist** or *lead character* who may more effectively guide your student body toward wise choices.

allow them to venture off on their own creative writing journey with you as their guide.

- Start by teaching your students how to write dialogue. It seems very simple, maybe too simple to teach, but to them, dialogue is a brand-new concept. Even though they may have read a dozen or more scripts, the task of writing one may be very intimidating. Show them how to organize dialogue by separating the speaker's name from the dialogue. There are many options including:

Bob: Someone ate all the pepperoni off the pizza! *(He picks up the pizza and throws it on the floor.)* I paid for this pepperoniless mess!

BOB

Someone ate all the pepperoni off the pizza! [He picks up the pizza and throws it on the floor.] I paid for this pepperoniless mess!

Bob. Someone ate all the pepperoni off the pizza! [He picks up the pizza and throws it on the floor.] I paid for this pepperoniless mess!

BOB: Someone ate all the pepperoni off the pizza! *(He picks up the pizza and throws it on the floor.)* I paid for this pepperoniless mess!

The character's name needs to obviously stand apart from his spoken line. Any actions the playwright wishes to suggest may be put in brackets or parentheses; dropped to another line, although this takes a great deal of additional space; italicized; or a combination of any of these. Regardless of the method, it must be used consistently throughout the script.

Perhaps the easiest of the script-writing activities for your students to undertake successfully will be those along the lines of the Can Man series. Students write for their peers and select messages that they feel are important. Because of this, they will enjoy writing a great deal more than when they don't feel that they have a personal stake in the assignment.

Before you invest much time in character-building projects, investigate your broadcasting abilities. Coming to class with a solid understanding of how their shows will air and who their audiences will be will make students more enthusiastic participants. You will be surprised at how quickly word will spread that the theatre teacher is using broadcasting to help students learn. There are numerous grants available to help get such projects off the ground. Your own district probably has access to technology grant money for innovative student-written or student-produced broadcasts.

There are so many other lessons that you can put into scripts for production. Before you spend too much time writing scripts, ask yourself a few questions:

What are some areas of concern in my school or community?

____

____

____

____

____

Who is my audience? What are their ages, their interests, their challenges, their goals, etc.?

____

____

____

____

How will the audience see the shows? Will the performances be live stage performances or videos? If they will be recorded, how will I get them to the audience?

____

____

____

____

What information do we need to get to the student body or particular groups of students that

might be achieved with video? For example, might new, incoming students benefit from a "virtual tour" of the school? Might outgoing or graduating students need information on the next level—local colleges, grants, scholarships, or graduation procedures?

____

____

____

____

Are there any pieces of equipment available to the theatre students to help with filming? If not, are there any funds available to help purchase equipment for this cause?

____

____

____

____

____

____

If you are interested in theatre for character development, there are numerous ways to get your message to your listeners. If your audience is young (local elementary schools, daycares, Head Start Programs, or even the developmentally delayed program at your school), consider putting the message into a puppet show or a mime act as an alternative to using a traditional script. Younger people have shorter attention spans, so use brightly colored costumes and set pieces and oversized props, and keep your script short. Stay away from abstract messages. With young audiences, it is better to be direct and to the point. Probably your best presentation method for this age group is a live act, up close and personal, in which the young audience

---

Use the various script-writing tools available that are specifically designed for this type of project. They make writing your scripts a breeze. You can even do several of them weeks in advance, file them, and use them as needed. This is especially true if you are doing an episodic show.

Be mindful of the events on your calendar, such as cultural holidays and school events, and have your students take a break occasionally from their normal routine to write commercials or public service announcements. If your choir is having a concert, get the full information from them and have your students create an advertisement. Film a PSA about Chinese New Year (January or February) or Teacher Appreciation Week (May). Other special occasions include:

JANUARY:

Crime Stoppers Month

Diet Month

Blood Donor Month

New Year's Day—January 1

World Religion Day— January 15

Martin Luther King Jr. Day—Third Monday in January

National Book Week—Third week in January

FEBRUARY:

Black History Month

Valentine's Day—February 14

Presidents Day

MARCH:

Women's History Month

Audition Month for Summer Theatre (see auditions in your area)

National Nutrition Month

is made to feel involved. Ask them questions like, "What should Can Man do, boys and girls?" Then let them respond and guide them toward the correct answer. Young children love to interact with the players onstage.

Intermediate and middle school audiences (around ages ten to fourteen) tend to be interested in what is popular in culture. Even though their attention spans are longer, they become easily impatient. Keep your script short and avoid being preachy. At this level, your message can become more abstract or symbolic, but it cannot be confusing. Consider mimicking the main structure of their favorite TV shows, replacing the plot with your own. They will appreciate humorous references to the original show and will be more likely to tune in for your developing message. This age group still enjoys live performances, but they are probably a little old for audience interaction (unless there are some rewards, such as prizes). Perhaps your best presentation method for reaching this age group

is to prerecord the skit and show it on your video announcements or ask teachers to show the video in their classes. You can also use the idea of an old-fashioned radio show and record audio for your school's public address system. You can learn more about radio shows in Chapter 3.

Older audiences—high school and up—are a little more inclined to find messages deeply embedded in the abstract. In fact, they tend to prefer it. They have longer attention spans and will often consider the **ending** of a story as a chance to probe the futures of the characters beyond the ending. If the playwrights leave some questions unanswered, older viewers will see this as a challenge to fill in the blanks and seek the answers themselves. Finally, this age group is less interested in fiction and more interested in reality. You might want to consider adopting a news format, a reality show, a game show, or a melodramatic soap opera with ridiculous plots (but important messages). You will likely be successful with a live performance if the script is long, but if it is short, your best avenue will possibly be a video or audio presentation. Thanks to video editing software and ample opportunities to post on social media, many teens are becoming excellent videographers and editors and are thoroughly enjoying the process. And due to the magnitude of the podcast trend, you will likely have great success and fun with this type of presentation as well!

Read the following original scripts from *The Environmental Adventures of Can Man*. Decide if you think his adventures are right for your student body.

What are some of the schools and programs in your area that cater to very young children or developmentally delayed students?

____

____

____

GETTING INVOLVED

Consider making videos of the best readers in your class reading books and showing the pictures; videos about schoolyard safety; how to be safe walking home from school; eating healthy; proper hand washing techniques; or an instructional video on the parts of speech or writing in cursive. Children love learning a new language. You could teach them Spanish (or English) with a series of videos!

     11

Touring Theatre Month
Cinco de Mayo—May 5
Poetry Week—last week
Memorial Day—last Monday

JUNE:

National Safety Month
National School Grounds Week

JULY:

National Ice Cream Month
Independence Day—July 4th

AUGUST:

American Artists Appreciation Month
National Night Out

SEPTEMBER:

National Hispanic Heritage Month (September 15 through October 15)
National Literacy Month
National School Success Month
Anniversary of 9/11
Labor Day—first Monday
International Car-Free Day— September 22

OCTOBER:

National Fire Prevention Month
National Youth Against Tobacco Month
Bullying Awareness Month
National School Lunch Week— second week
Toastmasters Week—fourth week

NOVEMBER:

Child Safety and Protection Month
International Creative Child and Adult Month
National Epilepsy Month
National Diabetes Month

National Grammar Day
St. Patrick's Day—March 17
Easter (possibly)
Passover (possibly)

APRIL:

William Shakespeare's Birthday—April 23
Keep America Beautiful Month
Mathematics Education Month
Multicultural Communications Month
National Humor Month
Prevention of Cruelty to Animals Month
Alcohol Awareness Month
Easter (if not in March)
Passover (if not in March)

MAY:

Teacher Appreciation Week
National Radio Month

National Youth Work Week—first week
American Education Week—second week
Thanksgiving—fourth Thursday

DECEMBER:

Theatre Day—December 1
Christmas—December 25
Kwanzaa—begins December 26
Hanukkah
Ramadan varies each year; consult the internet

There are many other important days, weeks, months, and dates for which your students could make PSAs or videos. Some are very serious; others are quite humorous, such as Static Electricity Day (January 9). Challenge your students to find occasions and make videos that give your program the image you seek.

INTRODUCTION TO THEATRE ARTS 2

THE ENVIRONMENTAL ADVENTURES OF CAN MAN

R E C Y C L I N G   S E R I E S

EPISODE I: THE BIRTH OF PAPER BOY

CAST OF CHARACTERS

NARRATOR .... the voice of reason and segue in the Can Man series, but would very much like to be more than a voice; the NARRATOR'S many attempts to reveal themself to viewers are unknowingly thwarted by Can Man's clumsiness.

CAN MAN .... the trusty hero of our story, out to save the environment one can (or bottle) at a time!

MOTHER NATURE .... the beautiful heroine, but she is often the target of nasty villains who, through carelessness and laziness, jeopardize her beauty.

THE LAZY LOSER .... does not appreciate the beauty of the world around him and does not see that one person can make a huge difference, whether it be for good or bad.

PAPER BOY .... Can Man's "soon-to-be" trusty sidekick, is born of The Lazy Loser's trashy ways but vows to save the beautiful Mother Nature.

VARIOUS TOWNSPEOPLE

NARRATOR: *(Voice-over.)* Ah, the beautiful town of *(Insert your town's name here followed by -ville, such as Dallasville or New Yorkville.).* A place where people young and old can enjoy natural beauty! *(A few townspeople pass through the scene, laughing and in good spirits.)* But wait! What's this? The Lazy Loser? Why, he's the dirtiest super villain this side of the *(Insert the name of a lake, river, or some other point of interest near you.).* Will *(your town)*-ville survive the filth? Let's tune in…

LAZY LOSER: *(Sits on a bench, The World Gazette blocking his face from view; a huge pile of papers discarded by his side.)* Says here that one ton of recycled paper can save seventeen trees, seven thousand gallons of water, three hundred eighty gallons of oil, four thousand kilowatts of energy, and three cubic yards of landfill space! Crazy tree-hugging journalists! Recycle, recycle, recycle. I don't see what the big deal is! *(Glances at his watch, then exclaims.)* Great heaps of stinky trash! I'm late for my TV show, The Lazy and the Careless! Today's the day Sophia and Rolando don't go on a honeymoon because they are too lazy. So romantic! *(EXITS, tossing his paper onto the pile.)*

MOTHER NATURE: *(ENTERS.)* Ah, nothing like taking a walk in the clean park to welcome a fresh new day. *(Sees the pile of papers.)* Holy heaps of stinking trash! Some villainous reader has carelessly littered great gobs of recyclable material! *(Calls OFF LEFT.)* Help! *(Calls OFF RIGHT.)* Help! *(To AUDIENCE.)* Won't anyone help me? *(CAN MAN and GIRLS 1-3 ENTER.)*

GIRL 1: Bye-bye, Can Man. Call me!

GIRL 2: We love you, Can Man!

GIRL 3: He's so dreamy. *(CAN MAN blows all a kiss, and GIRL 3 faints into the others' arms.)*

CAN MAN: *(As GIRLS EXIT.)* Good-bye, girls. And remember to reduce, reuse, recycle!

GIRLS 1 and 2: We will, Can Man. *(GIRLS EXIT.)*

CAN MAN: *(Turns to see the pile of papers.)* Great gobs of garbage! Someone has carelessly and lazily littered, and Mother Nature is in trouble! Must *(Steps closer.)* put *(Steps again.)* papers *(Steps again but starts weakening.)* in *(Falls to ground.)* recycling. *(Looks at camera.)* Superman has his Kryptonite, and Can Man has his newspaper.

MOTHER NATURE: Oh, please, Can Man. If you can't help me, who can? *(The pile of paper begins to come to life.)*

NARRATOR: What is this? Has Can Man finally met his match? Is Mother Nature doomed? Will the Lazy Loser's littering ways infest our beautiful planet? Stay tuned for the next ep—

PAPER BOY: *(Springs up from the pile of papers.)* Nasofassmisserwarrader! *(Meaning "Not so fast, Mister Narrator!")* Wesillhafawiwledime. *(Meaning "We still have a little time.")*

12   Photocopying this page violates federal copyright law.

ABOUT *THE ENVIRONMENTAL ADVENTURES OF CAN MAN*

These scripts are written to be ridiculous, but the message is a very serious one. Encourage your actors to "ham it up," overdo the acting, and use a great deal of their own brand of humor. Study and research superhero postures, phrases, clichés, and even some of the ways the films were edited—such as the fight scenes in the old *Batman* TV series in which silly words like "Pow," "Bam," and "Smack" would pop up on the screen.

If your students are going to become spokespeople for a cause, they need to realize that all your efforts in class will go nowhere if they can't continue to be spokespeople outside of class. You will have a hard time getting the young students at your school to take "Don't Smoke" seriously if your lead actor is enjoying a Marlboro at the local hangout after school. And the same

CHAPTER 1 — THEATRE FOR LIFE'S LESSONS

CAN MAN: *(As PAPER BOY throws papers in a recycling bin, CAN MAN slowly regains strength.)* He said to hold your horses, Narrator. There are still two minutes left in this episode!

NARRATOR: Oh. Sorry.

MOTHER NATURE: Can Man. You're saved, and so am I! Thanks Mr., um, Mr. —

PAPER BOY: Faferfoy. *(Meaning "Paper Boy.")*

MOTHER NATURE: Um, yeah. Do you see what's happening here, Can Man? You're a super recycling hero who's allergic to newspaper, and here's this boy born of the pile of papers…

CAN MAN: I think I see your point, Mother Nature. *(Gets down on one knee, proposal style.)* Paper Boy, will you be my trusty sidekick?

PAPER BOY: Wheoo, shr. Yeshe, Isbornfshepiwoofafwsjsoicdcomnhewpyo, CnMn.

MOTHER NATURE/NARRATOR: What'd he say?

CAN MAN: He said… *(CAN MAN pantomimes, explaining what PAPER BOY said as NARRATOR continues.)*

NARRATOR: Born of the pile of papers is a new hero, Paper Boy, *(PAPER BOY strikes a superhero pose.)* trusty sidekick to Can Man. *(CAN MAN strikes a superhero pose.)* Our new dynamically clean duo is out to save (your town)-ville one can, bottle, and paper at a time! Will they ever defeat The Lazy Loser? And will Paper Boy learn to articulate? *(PAPER BOY shakes his fist in the air at NARRATOR.)* Tune in next time to The Environmental Adventures of Can Man!

CAN MAN: Come, Paper Boy. *(Both mount invisible "horses." To camera.)* And remember, folks… reduce, reuse, and recycle! *(The last words fade out as both "gallop" off on their steeds and camera FADES to BLACK.)*

END EPISODE 1

EPISODE 2: PLASTIC NO MORE

CAST OF CHARACTERS

MOTHER NATURE

POLLY PEPPERGRINDER/
 PRINCESS PLASTIC ………… A faux superhero who is really just a misguided recycler.

NARRATOR

CAN MAN

PAPER BOY

TOWNSPEOPLE

NARRATOR: When last we left the good, clear people of (your town)-ville, Paper Boy and Can Man joined super forces to defeat the Lazy Loser's villainous laziness. The people realized that one man—or boy or girl for that matter—can make a difference. *(TOWNSPEOPLE are seen picking up trash and happily throwing it away as Mother Nature looks on approvingly.,* But not everyone was in agreement.

PRINCESS PLASTIC: *(Dressed awkwardly in a sloppy, makeshift superhero costume that is more glamour and glitz than super. Stops MOTHER NATURE from tossing a plastic soda bottle.)* Stop! You, step away from the recycling bin.

MOTHER NATURE: Um, who? Me?

PRINCESS PLASTIC: That's right! I recognize a villain when I see one!

MOTHER NATURE: I see. And who are you?

PRINCESS PLASTIC: I'm Princess Plastic, *(Strikes a superhero pose, knocking her tiara off her head.)* out to save the world one bottle at a time.

MOTHER NATURE: You can't say that. That's part of Can Man's tagline! And I'm not a villain. I'm Mother Nature!

PRINCESS PLASTIC: You? Mother Nature? I don't think so, sister. *(Shakes her finger at MOTHER NATURE.)* Will you look at that! I broke a nail. *(CAN MAN and PAPER BOY ENTER on their invisible steeds and dismount.)*

     13

principle applies to your *Can Man* participants. They need to be stewards of the environment outside of your classroom.

If you have several theatre classes and would like to try using video in all of them, let each group have their own agenda. For example, one could do a series on not smoking, another might focus on commercials for school and other events, and another might make videos for the local elementary school children.

You can also challenge the classes to raise their standards by occasionally having them compete for a slot. For example, have each group come up with a fire safety video, pick the best, and show all groups the qualities that made that video your top choice. The next time you challenge them, they will all have a better understanding of your expectations.

INTRODUCTION TO THEATRE ARTS 2

PAPER BOY: Whawo. *(Waves flirtatiously to MOTHER NATURE and tips his hat to PRINCESS PLASTIC.)*

CAN MAN: Mother Nature! How's the cleanup campaign coming along? *(Realizing her mistake, PRINCESS PLASTIC puts on thick glasses to get a better look. She tries to slink away in embarrassment.)*

MOTHER NATURE: Oh, hello, Can Man, *(Flirting in a very large way.)* and heeeellllloooo Paper Boy! The campaign is going just great. Princess Plastic and I were just tidying up this one little section, and look how clean!

PRINCESS PLASTIC: Oh! Yes, we were... Oh, Mother Nature, I'm not really a superhero. I'm just a big, plastic fake!

PAPER BOY: Wha, whatschnotdru. Wherrywunshashufferairorinshide, wherritcontshmosht. Rhataftcherayruzbhern, rhyriddennorudmakmeschpechul. *(Very seriously, tenderly, as though explaining something to a child.)* Rhuhaftuwhookinschide definooyherrearryar.

PRINCESS PLASTIC: *(Who has been listening as though she understood every word.)* Oh. *(Pause.)* I see. *(To CAN MAN and MOTHER NATURE.)* What on earth did he just say?

MOTHER NATURE: I don't know, but it was beautiful!

CAN MAN: He said that you have to look inside yourself to see what makes you special.

PRINCESS PLASTIC: But you make so much difference, and you are superheroes. I'm just one person. I thought maybe if I became a superhero, I could make a bigger difference. I mean, will you look at the size of this place? What difference can one person make?

MOTHER NATURE: What difference can one person make?

CAN MAN: What difference can one person make?

PAPER BOY: Whaffernskinunmershumayk?

CAN MAN: He said—

PRINCESS PLASTIC: Yeah, I actually understood that one!

CAN MAN: It's easy. One person can reduce the amount of trash he makes by reusing what he can and recycling or properly disposing of the rest.

PRINCESS PLASTIC: Okay, reduce, reuse, recycle. I get that. But what about the mess?

MOTHER NATURE: If everyone creates less trash and recycles, that's a good start, and it's also the easy part. Then, every day you can make the world a little cleaner by picking up the trash around you and disposing of it properly.

CAN MAN: If you do your part and try to convince your friends to do the same, and they convince their friends to help, and so on, and so on...

PAPER BOY: Rhawerldilbemuschcreaner!

PRINCESS PLASTIC: So, I really don't have to be a superhero to make a super difference. Can Man, Paper Boy, Mother Nature... *(She removes her thick glasses.)* Hi, I'm Polly Peppergrinder. I'm just an ordinary girl, but I can make a big difference, so if you'll excuse me, I'm off to save the day by reducing, reusing, recycling, and recruiting my friends to help clean our little corner of the world. *(EXITS.)* Goodbye!

CAN MAN, PAPER BOY, and MOTHER NATURE: Goodbye, Polly!

MOTHER NATURE: Oh, watch out for that— *(SOUND EFFECT: BOOM.)*—ouch! Tree! I think she needs to keep the glasses on!

CAN MAN: That's what I call a tree hugger! *(Calls OFF.)* You okay, Polly? Alrighty, then. Bye! Well, Paper Boy, our job here is done! *(Mounts his trusty steed.)*

MOTHER NATURE: Um, Can Man—

CAN MAN: No need to thank us, Mother Nature. It's all in a day's work!

MOTHER NATURE: No, Can Man, I wasn't—it's just that—*(Points to the ground.)*

PAPER BOY: Wharwersesmaydariddlrinky! *(Fans his nose as though something smells.)*

CAN MAN: What? My trusty steed made a what? Oh! Sorry, Mother Nature! *(Dismounts and begins frantically looking for a way to clean the mess.)*

ARE YOU READY TO RECORD?

Take inventory of your classroom equipment, including cameras, editing software and hardware, props, sets, and costumes. Now take inventory of your people resources: actors, technicians, camera operators, playwrights, directors, and so on. Lastly, take inventory of your needs. What would the common thread in every episode be? School spirit? News? Crime relief? Do you have what it takes to bring the world of video into your classroom?

Your students probably already know how to make videos and edit them on their phones. You may need to get permission to use students' personal equipment for school use. You may also be able to procure equipment for your classroom so that students' phones and cameras are not needed.

NARRATOR: Well, who would've thought something that invisible would have made something that—um—well, never mind. Once again, the day is saved thanks to our heroes. Will Polly Peppergrinder really make a difference? Will you make a difference? Will Can Man clean up his horse's mess? Find out next time on The Environmental Adventures of Can Man with his trusty sidekick, Paper Boy.

CAN MAN: Come, Paper Boy. *(Walks as though he stepped in something as PAPER BOY laughs.)* You think this is funny? You could have warned me... *(Their voices trail off as camera FADES to BLACK.)*

END EPISODE 2

EPISODE 3: THINK OUTSIDE THE BOX

CAST OF CHARACTERS

NARRATOR

LAZY LOSER

MRS. LOSER

THE BOXER

CAN MAN

PAPER BOY

NARRATOR: Ahh. Another day in (your town)-ville. A wonderful opportunity to do a little—um—spring cleaning? Ahem. Hello? Hello? *(Louder.)* Hello!!

LAZY LOSER: *(Newspapers over his face and pizza box in his lap, lounging and napping.)* What? Who's making all that racket? Why I oughta... Can't a guy get some shut eye around here?

NARRATOR: Sorry. It's just that it's afternoon, so I didn't think anyone would be asleep.

LAZY LOSER: I sleeps when I wants. You got a problem with that? Huh? I've been unpacking all day... all week for that matter. I'm beat.

NARRATOR: Oh. *(Not believing him.)* Been doing a lot of unpacking, eh? So, these are all empty, then?

LAZY LOSER: Yea. Sure. *(Tries to lift a box, but it's dead weight; tries another, and then another. All are still full except the smallest one, which he holds up proudly.)* Ya see! Haa! EMPTY! Super, duper empty.

MRS. LOSER: *(From OFF.)* Who are you talking to? Are you talking to your pizza again?

LAZY LOSER: Pizza! *(Grabs the box.)* That's right! Another one I polished off! Empty!

NARRATOR: Oh, brother!

MRS. LOSER: *(ENTERS, sees two empty boxes.)* Oh, goodie!! You emptied one. It took you long enough. I thought we was going to have to live with these boxes forever. Well, now what?

LAZY LOSER: Whaddya mean, now what? It's nap time! *(Tosses both boxes onto a pile. From the pile we hear gurgles and see smoke; the pile shakes and starts coming to life. Add any other special effects your team wishes to provide to dramatize The Boxer's birth.)*

NARRATOR: That was no ordinary pizza, my friends. It was a spicy meat lover's with extra cheese. And that pile of boxes was no ordinary pile of boxes. It was an angry pile of neglected boxes. And you know what happens when you throw a dirty pizza box in with clean—and angry—cardboard!

BOXER: *(Growls.)* No pizza. NO PIZZA!

TWO LOSERS: *(Together.)* It's alive!

BOXER: *(Growls.)* No pizza. NO dirty cardboard! Unpack me!!!

MRS. LOSER: Unpack me. He's s-s-saying unpack me! *(Picks up a newspaper, rolls it, and begins smacking her husband.)* Look what you did! You created a monster!

NARRATOR: Meanwhile, across the hall, Can Man and Paperboy are taking out their recycling, like good citizens.

CAN MAN: Paper Boy, who eats five jars of pickles in one week? Five! Nope. Make that six.

NOTES: ____

INTRODUCTION TO THEATRE ARTS 2

PAPER BOY: Picklshrgud. Yumumumumum. Bshides, smyogurtnmybag. *(Takes out a single yogurt container to show Can Man.)*

CAN MAN: True! You did eat a yogurt. Wait. Listen.

PAPER BOY: Whshatsound? Growlgrowlgrowlllllllll. *(Puts his ear to the door of the Losers' apartment.)*

CAN MAN: *(Carefully places a bag of recycling on floor.)* Stand back. *(Rams the door; PAPER BOYS follows.)* The Lazy Loser! And his slovenly wife. What kind of evil are the two of you up to—and since when are you our neighbors?

LAZY LOSER: It's not us! It's him *(Pointing at THE BOXER, who is beating his large boxy fists together and growling "no pizza.")*

PAPER BOY: Slookslikmovinday.

CAN MAN: Yes, Paper Boy. It does look like move-in day, but judging by the smell, I'd say this pile has been collecting dust—and who knows what else?—for a year!

MRS. LOSER: Stop exaggerating. It's only been eleven and three-quarter months! *(BOXER growls at her.)*

CAN MAN: Didn't you know that cardboard is a favorite food of roaches?

LAZY LOSER: Big deal. So, we get a few roaches.

CAN MAN: And silverfish, spiders, rats, mice, centipedes, scorpions…

PAPER BOY: *(Looks around uncomfortably, stomps on a "roach" and then stomps on another; finally, he jumps onto Can Man's back.)* Ifonlikbugggs. *(Begins batting at flying bugs and stomping on crawling ones.)*

BOXER: Pizza!

CAN MAN: Hold up. Wait. Let's get real here, Loser. Did you throw a pizza box into recyclable cardboard?

LAZY LOSER: *(Looking guilty.)* Wha? Come on. Really? Me?

MRS. LOSER: You betcha your sweet pepper he did!

CAN MAN: Pizza boxes are not recyclable. Any paper or cardboard stained with grease or food is not recyclable.

LAZY LOSER: Fine. Fine. I won't do it again. I don't even like recycling; it was kind of an accident. B-b-but what do I do about him?

BOXER: GROOOOOOOWL. Unpack me!

PAPER BOY: Awww. Hejesswanstobeunpackt.

CAN MAN: That's right, my trusty and intuitive sidekick. If you don't want roaches, silverfish, and spiders—and box monsters—unpack, collapse, and recycle clean cardboard before pests can feast on them. *(BOXER sits and the others begin "unpacking" him.)*

NARRATOR: And with that, the Boxer was unpacked—and not a minute too soon! The pizza box was discarded in the trash, and the clean cardboard was recycled. With nothing to feast on, the bugs moved away. And our super duo learned to live with his new, slightly less slovenly neighbors—at least until their lease was up! *(PAPER BOY removes can of roach spray from the box he was taking to recycling and sets it inside his door, winking at NARRATOR.)* Just another day in (your town) -ville. Have the Losers finally learned their lesson? Will they become proactive stewards of their environment? And will Paper Boy's pickle habit be Can Man's undoing? Find out next time on… The Environmental Adventures of Can Man!

END EPISODE 3

NOTES: ______________________

____

____

____

____

____

____

____

CHAPTER I — THEATRE FOR LIFE'S LESSONS

NAME ____ PERIOD _______ DATE _____________

SCRIPT PLANNING GUIDE

Use the following prompts to brainstorm your script. Attach additional paper if needed. Keep files of your ideas for future use.

What is your message (what do you want your audience to learn)?

____
____
____
____

Brainstorm key words associated with your message (list every word you can think of that has anything to do with your message):

____
____
____
____

Who is your audience? ____

What are their interests? ____
____

With your message and audience in mind, circle formats you think would be effective and mark through those you think would be ineffective

Short (_______ min.)	Long (_______ min.)	Video/Film
Live stage show	Drama	Comedy
Audio only	Game Show	Superhero Show
Soap Opera	Reality Show	Crime Show
Puppet Show	Musical	Radio Show
News Show		

How many episodes do you predict? ___________

Create your protagonist:

Name: ____ Age: _______ Gender: __________

What is your protagonist's goal and/or message? _____________________________________

Describe your protagonist's personality, background, appearance, etc.: __________________
____
____
____
____
____
____

                    17

NOTES: ____

____

____

____

____

____

____

Who or what stands between your protagonist and the goal? This will become your antagonist.

____
____
____
____

Keeping in mind your main character's description, how will the protagonist overcome the antagonist and the obstacles presented?

____
____
____
____

What is your script's setting (it is easiest to have just one), and what role does it play in the outcome of the plot?

____
____
____
____

Who are your supporting characters? _____________________________

____
____
____
____

Now it is time to begin writing your first episode. Start by deciding how you want it to end. What is the protagonist's goal in the first episode? Does your protagonist reach the goal?

____
____
____
____

What is the result? Was there a lesson to be learned? ____________

____
____
____
____

Use the activity on the next page to take your script to the next level.

NOTES: ____

____

____

____

____

____

____

CHAPTER I — THEATRE FOR LIFE'S LESSONS

NAME ______________________________________ PERIOD _______ DATE ____________

DRAMATIC STRUCTURE ACTIVITY

Write your ending in box (E), and either work your way backwards or fill in the gaps. By starting at the end, you have done what many people consider the hardest part of writing. If this method does not work for you, ask your teacher if you may use a different one. After you have finished, write or type your script in dialogue form.

(A) Exposition: *(Focus on characters and setting)*

(B) Rising Action: First...

Then...

Then...

(C) Climax: Finally,

(D) Falling Action: *(Focus on wrapping up the story)*

(E) Ending: *(A great place for a moral)*

     19

NOTES: ____

____

____

____

____

____

____

____

TEAMWORK FOR THE THEATRE CLASSROOM

One of the greatest challenges for both new and seasoned theatre teachers is managing group work. Much of what is done in the drama classroom is cooperative, meaning at least two people will work together on a project. There are a number of complications that can come of this, and while they may seem like huge hurdles, it may be best to think of them as life tests. Yes, working in groups has both benefits and detriments, but at the same time, life is full of "group work" where one isn't always fully in control of all phases of a project. Consequently, learning to work in cooperative groups early teaches everyone in the group the benefits, dangers, rewards, and consequences of all levels of teamwork.

Some teachers are very strict about grouping their students, insisting that friends should not work together. While this may be true in some cases, most recognize the benefits of good chemistry shared between hard-working, responsible team members. On the other hand, many teachers have adopted a "make your bed and lie in it" attitude about grouping. They allow students to get into groups with whomever they want and let them learn for themselves who is or is not a compatible group member. Neither is right nor wrong. Teachers must discover what works best in their environments with their students.

But why must it always be one way? Why is it that some teachers have one set of rules that they expect all students to follow? In an effort to be overly fair, many shy away from saying, "You two may work together, even though you are friends, but you two may not, because you will not get the work done." Does this "one-size-fits-all" method work for every student in every situation? Perhaps these educators are not comfortable putting different "sizes" of rules on individuals whose pasts have proven that they are unique. If this is the case in your classroom, it is a teaching method that should quickly be reconsidered. If students are different— different *learning styles*, different *backgrounds*, different *skill sets*, and different *behaviors*—they will all have *different needs*. As a teacher, it is your job to educate your students about more than just your curriculum; you must also educate them about life. This may mean being painfully honest—as long as you do so appropriately. Learn to say something like, "I've enjoyed observing you these past few weeks, and one thing I have learned about you is that you perform wonderfully with certain people. I'm trying to continue that pattern of excellence by putting you where I hope you and your group members will excel. I'm sorry if you do not think it's fair, but I have a great deal of documentation that supports my decision. If you would like to discuss it further, have your parents schedule a conference, and we can discuss it as a group." A shorter way to say the same thing is, "You are each receiving the privileges you have earned."

There are many creative ways to group students when allowing them to group themselves is not your preferred option. You can use a random method:

- One teacher cuts the fronts of greeting cards into the number of pieces needed for each group. For example, if there are twenty students divided into four groups of five students each, four cards are cut into five pieces. Students draw from the lot, then they find their group by putting their "puzzle" together. It is so much fun that they forget about getting into a group with their friends and focus on the puzzle. However, it may be wise to have them sign the back of their card piece as they draw it to avoid quick switches once groups have been completed.

- Another favorite is drawing numbers, drawing colors, etc.

If some form of random assignment does not work for you, try one of the following teacher-guided matching systems:

- Try introducing your students to information about their classmates that they didn't know using a "profile" system of matching students. For example, if you are doing a readers theater and need large groups, create a short questionnaire of silly questions such as "If you were going to be stranded on a deserted island and could only take one of the following, what would you take: A) supplies to make a message in a bottle, B) supplies to plant a small garden, or C) your smart phone. Limit questions to about three, match students with similar responses, allow the class to discuss their responses (you will learn a great deal about how your students think!), then put them into groups. This method leaves the final decision up to the teacher.

- Put students in groups according to how you think they will learn the most and perform to their best abilities. This usually means mixing ability levels, avoiding placing students together who distract each other, and pre-planning a safe, suitable amount of peer pressure. In other words, put students together who will encourage each other rather than harass and berate their peers into participating. This is probably the best and thus the most common means of matching students. The only downfall is that if you use the same system repeatedly, students will end up in the same—or perhaps similar—groups over and over again.

- Pass out a list of students in your class and assign "making groups" to every student, and have them provide an explanation as to why students should go into certain groups. You will find a great deal of honesty in their responses. Students who consistently fall below their ability levels tend to put themselves into high-performing groups. Overachievers tend to group themselves with students they can easily control. You can either select one student's grouping of the class, and perhaps give them bonus points, or use student responses as a guide to create well thought-out groupings.

- If your assignment is group scenes, allow students to select the scenes they like best and that fit your criteria first: time, number of participants, content, appropriateness. Then have table readings, where the class listens as the scene is read aloud. After all scenes are presented, discuss which ones interest the class for further exploration. Use the discussion participation to gauge interest and to gauge leadership. At this point, you may either cast the scenes or select student directors to cast them, either by holding auditions or by using previous performance experiences. Students with smaller roles may be cast in multiple groups or given additional responsibilities. Oftentimes, student directors take on small roles or sometimes multiple small roles within their scenes, as well.

As the teacher, consider acting in your students' scenes, if needed. Many times, teachers have students who experience a great deal of absences. A teacher once had a rising star as a student. The young woman would miss several days a week to travel to country and western music performances. While at school, she wanted to participate in drama, and she was good! The others wanted her in their groups, but all too often, her absences negatively affected the performances. Eventually the teacher took on the role of understudy to this young performer. The student, singer LeAnn Rimes, soon reached her stardom and continued to act as well as to sing.

Regardless of what you decide works best for you in your classroom, stay flexible. Each student is different, and every class will have different personalities depending on the dynamics, the chemistry, the time of day, your mood, and so on. As you work with your class on various projects,

remind them—not only with words but also with your actions—that you, too, are on their team. In the end, you want each of them to be the best they can be, and in order to achieve that goal, you make the best decisions you can based on their ability to accept responsibility.

In this chapter, you will find a number of helpful forms and activities designed to make group work within your classroom more successful, and you will even come across some activities intended to exercise your students' abilities to function as teammates.

You may want to enlarge the table in the Student Workbook, *Addressing Teamwork Issues Within the Theatre Classroom*, to poster size and place it in your room. This simple "troubleshooting guide" addresses four of the more common theatre teamwork issues. While it cannot be expected to address everything your students may encounter, many of the steps are common sense and can be applied in a broader sense than that which is implied.

Suzanne Petryshyn, a mediation specialist, says that the first thing to do in a conflict situation is to name the issue. This should be the topic of the conversation rather than anyone's position on the topic. For example, instead of "One student wants to do this scene, but everyone else wants to do a different one," the issue would be "selecting the scene." By naming the issue without emotion, students are forced to get to the root of the problem. Sometimes a group will think there is a conflict, but when each member is asked to name it, they realize they really wanted the same thing—they either find arguing more stimulating than agreeing, or they are experiencing a personality conflict. Perhaps there really is trouble, but when the group puts the problem into an emotionless phrase or word, they are reminded that they have a job to do. This tactic gives them a focal point so that they can move to the next step in conflict resolution.

Once the problem is named, if the conflict remains, each student should state their position or what they want or need. Again, this may be a point where everyone agrees, and they realize there was no reason to argue. If there is still disagreement, however, they will begin working together to mutually reach an agreement by brainstorming options, evaluating each one quickly, and coming to an agreeable resolution. Petryshyn recommends having the students write down their resolution.

Once they have an agreement, check on them often. Even though you may have trained them to work problems out on their own, be prepared to intervene again if disagreement interferes with progress.

How do you give grades when students perform in groups? Most of the time, grading is objective and fair. Occasionally you will have a group that is so mixed that the lines are not so easy to discern. Take, for example, one six-member group. Two of the six were top students, and all the others were very capable. The four capable students had all done well on their other assignments, but the teacher had to remind them often to stop talking about other things and focus on their scripts. The two who were at the top of their class chose to be in the group but later asked the teacher to put them elsewhere. By that time, it was too late in the project for such a major change, so the teacher continued to monitor the group's progress.

When they performed, it was chaos. The four talkers broke character, blamed each other, and looked lost and frustrated. The other two stayed in character, led their group back on track when they strayed from the script, and were not blameful afterward. As a matter of fact, when the teacher asked what went wrong, the latter two were humble, saying that their group (themselves included) just didn't work hard enough.

TEAMWORK FOR THE THEATRE CLASSROOM
WORKING IN GROUPS

In most of your classes, you are reminded to do your own work, keep your eyes on your own paper, be original, don't copy, and don't work together. However, in many creativity-based classes, especially those that exercise students' gifts and talents, working individually is rare. Instead, students are told to help each other, share ideas, try what another student is doing, and work in pairs and groups.

There are many benefits to working in groups.

For one, students share more in common with their peers than they do with their teachers, so there is positive chemistry.

Regardless of the ability levels within the group, as long as there is drive, there are advantages. For example, if a group member is very skilled and hardworking, they may combine their talents to achieve success. A mixed group has the potential to work together to capitalize on everyone's skills, and a group of all beginners may all develop skills on an even keel, allowing each group member to contribute and shine, leaving no one in the shadows.

Working in groups keeps an assignment interesting, allows students to see a goal from several perspectives, and breaks up the monotony of always having to be quiet and work at one's desk. Think of how a team is made up in business. Each member has an area of expertise, but they all have the same goal and can work together to accomplish it quickly and with a higher level of success than any one person alone. Theatre is very similar, and that is one reason the word **company**, *a team of actors working together on a show*, is so appropriate.

Of course, we are all aware that there are the inevitable **obstacles**. If it was a perfect scenario every time, there would be no need to include a lesson on teamwork in this book. No, more often than not, a group—regardless of its chemistry—will encounter problems. Because so much of the work in theatre is done in groups, each member of the company must possess conflict management skills and learn to implement them in daily practice.

TOP FIVE GROUP WORK CONCERNS

5. **PERSONAL PROPERTY:** Each student will be asked to bring items from home such as props, music, and costumes, and they'll be expected to keep up with them in the theatre classroom. When items are forgotten or misplaced, work lags behind.

4. **SKILL AND TALENT COMPATIBILITY:** Some groups have a wide range of ability levels within the group. It is easy for those who feel like they don't fit in—either because they are ahead of their group or not as advanced—to feel frustrated.

3. **BEHAVIOR:** With the entire class divided into groups and with each group working aloud on different projects, spreading out becomes a necessity. You must be able to work independently with your partners while your teacher works with other groups. As a part of this topic, there will be "down time" for certain group members, so staying engaged takes discipline.

2. **CUES:** Most theatre is based on dialogue or other types of cues. If you fail to give your partner or group the required cue, they have to cover for you and, in doing so, they are in danger of skipping others' cues.

1. **CLIQUES:** Because of numbers 5, 4, 3, and 2, it is easy to see why cliques might form. Students migrate to others like themselves—to teammates they know will have similar goals. Consequently, there are those who want to break free of their low-performing group who cannot do so because cliques have formed bonds that keep outsiders out.

The students in the group were given individual grades for teamwork and progress rather than on their performance. This was based on several things. First, even though they selected their group, all had worked hard in the past with direction from the teacher, so it seemed safe to assume the group would make a good team. Second, the two did attempt to break away from the group when it started going badly, but time was not on their side. Lastly, they followed some, but not all, of the steps in the *Addressing Teamwork Issues* table. In the end, it was agreed that the two students who gave it the greatest effort tried as hard as they could. They were given grades that reflected their efforts rather than their results—not a reward, but not a punishment. The others also received grades based on their efforts which were, incidentally, similar to what their performance grades would have been.

The only scenario in which it may be fair to penalize a group for one member's failure to contribute might be when all of the following factors were present from the beginning:

- The non-contributing member had a history of similar teamwork prior to this assignment.

- The group knew of the student's lack of effort and still made the choice to bring the student into the group.

- The students in the group did not follow the steps in the *Addressing Teamwork Issues* table.

Regardless of how you choose to handle grading group work, try to look at the situation from your

CHAPTER I — THEATRE FOR LIFE'S LESSONS

What happens when everyone in a group lacks drive and does not wish to attempt to achieve success? Believe it or not, this is *not* the worst-case scenario because if everyone lacks drive, they will all get the grade on their project they have earned: a failing one. So, what is the worst-case scenario? Perhaps it is one where those with a desire to make good grades and complete a successful project are grouped with those who do not care and cannot be persuaded to try.

The following table will help your group, teacher, and you work together to become better at resolving teamwork issues.

ADDRESSING TEAMWORK ISSUES WITHIN THE THEATRE CLASSROOM

PROBLEM	FIRST	THEN TRY ...	IF THAT DOESN'T WORK, TRY ...	IF YOUR GROUP IS STILL HAVING TROUBLE, TRY ...
Our group cannot agree on a project.	DETERMINE EXACTLY WHAT THE PROBLEM IS, WHY IT IS HAPPENING, AND THE CONSEQUENCES FOR THE GROUP OR INDIVIDUAL.	... reading the rubric again. What are some of the things it says that might help you narrow your choices? Now have each member write their choice anonymously on a piece of paper and see if you have a majority that meets the requirements of the rubric.	... eliminating half the choices. Put your very best and most popular (within your group) ideas on paper, and list the advantages and disadvantages of each. Allow every group member to have input. Hold another anonymous vote.	... asking your teacher for input. Your teacher may have more information about why one idea is better than the other, and that may sway your group. If your teacher does not have an opinion, continue the process of elimination until only one choice remains.
Our group argues too much.		... determining if your group is arguing because they cannot agree or if there are underlying issues that are getting in the way.	... assigning a leader and possibly a secretary, timekeeper, and other jobs that will establish a role for each person within the group.	... setting short-term goals and time limits for meeting those goals. If students continue to argue to the point of not being able to reach these short-term goals, you may have to ask your teacher to intervene, possibly reassigning certain students to other groups.
Our group is easily distracted or gets off task.		... avoiding distractions. Position yourselves in such a way that group members are focused on each other and on the task at hand. Remove distracting objects.	... assigning specific short-term goals to each member and time limits for meeting those goals. If two group members distract each other, separate them.	If students continue to get off task to the point of not being able to reach these short-term goals, you may have to ask your teacher to intervene and possibly reassign the distractible students to another group.
One or more members of our group does not do their part.		... assigning specific jobs to each member and time limits for completing those jobs. Determine if each person is capable of and willing to do the job assigned to them.	... get email addresses and phone numbers of members in your group. Don't pester or nag them; instead, remind them of deadlines and duties.	... letting the teacher know there is a problem, having the more responsible members assist in picking up the slack, and documenting your attempts to assist or encourage.

Special thanks to Suzanne Petryshyn, Teen Peer Mediation Expert

 21

MAKING THE MOST OF GROUP WORK

Read this section with your students and talk to them at length about how businesspeople would lose money if they never put anyone but friends in their groups. Your students may say things like, "That's why we want to do it now because we'll have to be more serious when we're older." It's not an altogether silly statement. Middle and high school students are young, and they should be enjoying these years. At the same time, it is still school, and they are here to learn as much as they can. One of the lessons you must impart is that their decisions will have consequences.

When they have finished reading, decide whether you think they are ready to use the short *Theatre Work Ethic Survey* on page 84 of this Teacher's Guide to receive feedback on how their peers perceive them as team members. It is important that the survey not be completed until after students have had the opportunity to learn about one another's work habits. If your class is very small or if it is combative, you will probably want to skip the survey. Have students put their name at the top of all three columns, cut them along the dotted lines, and fold them in half. Put them in a hat and allow each student to draw three, returning their own if they happen to draw it. Check to ensure that no one has their own survey and that all are using pencil (adds to the anonymity). Take up completed surveys and return them to their owners. Do not allow students to say who had another's survey, as this may cause undue conflict. But do discuss the results.

As your discussion continues, remind them that what they are practicing now will be habit-forming. Perhaps the habits are already deeply ingrained in their personalities. One bad habit is taking the position that they're "just kids, so it doesn't matter." College admission boards look at transcripts all the way back to ninth grade. Some students will argue

students' perspectives. Give grades individually based on each participant's contributions and efforts, taking into consideration the obstacles they faced and the application of what they learned prior to the performance. When it comes to conflict, encourage them to resolve issues on their own, make yourself present should they need you, and involve yourself with their group regularly. If all this is done, there should be no doubt that your grading is justifiable and fair.

that theatre is just an elective, so it doesn't really count. That is completely untrue. As a matter of fact, a low grade in an elective can look much more alarming than a low grade in a core class.

Another bad habit is being uncomfortable saying "no." If a solid group of high performers is approached by a person who has fallen short of the team's standards but is seeking group admission, what do they do? Maybe the high performers believe they are strong enough to be able to focus a little more time on this individual in hopes that they can help the admission seeker. It is possible. Perhaps they believe this person has potential but has always been in bad groups—also possible. Maybe they really want to say "no" but are afraid of hurting the person's feelings.

What would you have your students do? You could compromise with them, allowing the student into the group but giving the original group members permission to change their minds at the first sign of trouble (limit this permission to early in the rehearsal process). If they are successful, you have found a win/win solution to their problem. If not, the group still has time to pull it together and

---

> INTRODUCTION TO THEATRE ARTS 2
>
> # MAKING THE MOST OF GROUP WORK
>
> **OBJECTIVE** You will understand your role as a team member and will explore the importance of forming project groups wisely.
>
> In educational theatre, many activities are done in groups. Most of the time, your teacher will allow you to select your partners, but many teachers—fearing the obvious magnetic draw of friendship—assign students to groups ahead of time. Both methods have their benefits and their drawbacks.
>
> Your teacher's goal is that everyone be placed into groups where each can perform at the highest level and no one will be left out. By spreading levels of achievers around in different groups, perhaps there will be fewer instances of groups being off task—the workers will keep the non-workers in line. The problem is that these teams may lack chemistry or have little in common, and because theatre is an art, the final performance may lack the energy and passion that can result from collaboration among friends.
>
> You have probably discovered that groups of friends can become easily distracted, and instead of working on their project, they will talk about the things they have in common. Teachers will hear, "We're going to work on it at home," but the truth is there are even more distractions and reasons not to work at home. It may be a comfort to say that "it's just a grade," but that is little more than a weak excuse. At some point, your grade starts affecting your future in a serious way; perhaps it already has.
>
> The first advantage of forming your own groups is that high achievers will tend to drift to other high achievers, and those who do not care as much will also attract one another. This allows those who want a solid performance to focus all their energy on that goal. It also requires each person to be accountable for their own success (or failure).
>
> Secondly, if a team is made up of friends—and some do have a good performance as their goal, while others do not—it forces the goal-minded to think like managers. Participating in group work is a part of life. Workers must either learn to form their teams more carefully or learn to manage team members whose goals are not set to the same standards as
>
> > Think of your grade as income. If you were an advertising executive and your team was working on a high-dollar project where each grade point equaled $1,000, would you be willing to give up $30,000 so that your friends could be on your team? Habits you form in school will follow you throughout life. If you must have your lower-performing friends in your group, what tricks can you use to tap into their most valued skills and talents? What motivates them? Or what distracts them, and can you avoid it? Or, if you know that including them will hurt your grade, how can you assert your independence while remaining a loyal friend?
>
> their own. Needless to say, it is easier to reach a goal when everyone is in agreement as to what it is and everyone works hard to reach it.
>
> It can be painful to say, "Sorry, I want to make a good grade, but I don't think that's as important to you." As a young person, this may feel like the meanest comment; it is not. It may be the most important thing your friend will hear, putting them on the right track—or at least offering the opportunity to change paths. Likewise, if someone must say this to you, it can hurt. But listen with your mind, not your heart. If grades are less important to you, you will: (a) mature enough to know that you must raise your personal standards; (b) risk failing the class and jeopardizing your friends' grades in the process; or (c) watch as your friends enjoy success with new groups—and new friends.
>
> As you begin forming performance teams, ask yourself this question: *If I were in charge of hiring someone to successfully manage an office, and if I could be fired for making a bad choice, would I hire this person?* Along with the privilege of selecting your teammates comes the responsibility for that team's success. If a member does not produce (does not bring supplies or fails to contribute), another member must take up the slack. Passing blame will not improve your grade, so be prepared to work extra hard if you bring a low performer onto your team.
>
> 22

---

you can give the individual an alternative assignment. See ideas for alternative assignments below.

A simple solution to the problem is to teach your students to become more comfortable saying "no." If they cannot refuse a student who wants into their group, will they be able to say no to other negative offers in the future? Try the activity starting on the bottom of page 83 with them. They will soon learn the value of saying no and meaning it.

ALTERNATIVE ASSIGNMENTS

In some classes, there will be one or two students whom others do not select for group projects. This could be for a number of reasons: the student doesn't complete assignments in other classes or has a history of doing poorly, the student does not work well with others or is perceived as negative, or maybe the student has a learning disability and has difficulty in group culture. Some students prefer solo work; and while this is commendable to a degree, all students should be encouraged to explore working in pairs and groups.

And in those same classes, certain students will stand out and be favorites. Every group will want them, and they may, as overachievers, try to please everyone. These students may need to be pushed to explore solo work.

Working in groups is an important skill. Working alone is also a skill. Both will be required in life and in business, and both must be encouraged. Balance is important, and despite student successes in one form or the other, every student should develop both sets of skills.

As a theatre teacher, you must get creative with group work so that every student—even the difficult ones—have the opportunity to work in groups or alone. One way to do this is to allow students to pick from a few options each performance—provided that, at the end of the six weeks or nine weeks, each student completes one individual performance, one duet performance, and one group performance. Furthermore, each student should complete at least one memorized performance and one with script in hand.

As you make assignments, consider your classroom dynamics and what is being studied. If you are studying duets but have some students who will not be ideal partners, get creative.

TWO-PERSON TEAM ASSIGNMENTS:

- A memorized seven-minute duet for a high grade of 100.

- A seven-minute two-person newscast using a teleprompter (or alternative) for a high grade

of 90 (or high grade of 100 if the students have reading difficulties).

SOLO ASSIGNMENTS:

- A memorized monologue. If this is a student's first monologue, it must be at least three minutes for a high grade of 100; if this is their second, a minimum of five minutes is required.

- A memorized seven-minute demonstration of how to complete a task, complete with visual aids, for a high grade of 100.

- A five-minute solo newscast using a teleprompter (or alternative) for a high grade of 90 (or high grade of 100 if at least seven minutes and all news is from the current week).

- An engaging solo reading of a children's book, at least five minutes for a high grade of 90; a high grade of 100 can be achieved if the student can provide signed documentation that the book was read to a group of four or more children.

NO!

Have your classes horizontally cut notebook paper into five two-inch-wide strips. Before you begin, have them sign their names on one side of the strips, and then flip them over so that the blank side is facing up. This is an important step in ensuring appropriateness.

Next, give them some ideas as to the types of questions or comments you want them to write. The answer to all should be "no." They can be as creative as they want, so long as they are clean (how clean depends on your standards in your classroom and your students' ages). Samples include:

- Can I borrow your homework?
- Will you help me get even with someone?
- Can I get your locker combination?
- Can we skip school tomorrow?
- Can I borrow your car?
- Can I be your partner on the English project?
- Will you send me some pictures?

Have the students fold the piece of paper a couple of times, then put them into a hat or bucket. Divide your class into two groups. Line the groups up like two trains coming face to face on the same track with the folded papers between them.

The first two students will each take a question. This should be fun for your students, so allow and encourage them to act. Without breaking eye contact, one will ask the question first. The other

must say "no" but cannot smile or break eye contact. This needs to be believable, so if the responder sounds hesitant or weak, the questioner can repeat the request or comment until the response is believable. Then switch roles. When they have both been successful, they may go to the back of their lines. Each group member will take turns saying "no" and learning to mean it.

Make this activity a game by giving points. In order to score points for their team, the player must not smile or break eye contact. Another option is to play it like the game Red Rover. Line your groups up facing each other and allow them to make "challenges." If the person they challenge smiles or breaks eye contact, they add that person to their team. If the person does not smile or break eye contact, they take the next turn trying to gain a member for their team.

Talk to your students about the importance of learning to say "no" without feeling guilty and without feeling compelled to make excuses. You can even incorporate this into your activity by allowing the person who asked the question to probe and beg. You may want to put a limit on this too.

NAME ____ PERIOD _________ DATE _______________

THEATRE WORK ETHIC SURVEY

What kind of worker are you? Do you see yourself as others see you? Are you happy with where you have "placed the bar," or would you like to change that? Are you on the road to success, or did you get lost on a detour? Can you handle the truth?

Put your name at the top of each survey and give them to your teacher. They will be returned once they are completed anonymously.

THEATRE WORK ETHIC SURVEY FOR: _________________

1. The subject of this survey is...
   A. Always hard working.
   B. Mostly hard working.
   C. Hardly working.

2. As for bringing required items from home, this student is...
   A. Very dependable.
   B. Mostly dependable.
   C. Rarely dependable.

3. When faced with obstacles, this student...
   A. Hurdles them eagerly.
   B. Ponders, calculates, then hurdles carefully.
   C. Worries, then seeks help.
   D. Quits.

4. This student's bar is placed...
   A. Very high.
   B. High enough to get by.
   C. Not high enough.
   D. What bar?

5. As for group work...
   A. This person would be a great partner.
   B. This person takes work way too seriously for me.
   C. This person's bar is set too low for my standards.

Please do not identify yourself. Feel free to make comments on the back.

THEATRE WORK ETHIC SURVEY FOR: _________________

1. The subject of this survey is...
   A. Always hard working.
   B. Mostly hard working.
   C. Hardly working.

2. As for bringing required items from home, this student is...
   A. Very dependable.
   B. Mostly dependable.
   C. Rarely dependable.

3. When faced with obstacles, this student...
   A. Hurdles them eagerly.
   B. Ponders, calculates, then hurdles carefully.
   C. Worries, then seeks help.
   D. Quits.

4. This student's bar is placed...
   A. Very high.
   B. High enough to get by.
   C. Not high enough.
   D. What bar?

5. As for group work...
   A. This person would be a great partner.
   B. This person takes work way too seriously for me.
   C. This person's bar is set too low for my standards.

Please do not identify yourself. Feel free to make comments on the back.

THEATRE WORK ETHIC SURVEY FOR: _________________

1. The subject of this survey is...
   A. Always hard working.
   B. Mostly hard working.
   C. Hardly working.

2. As for bringing required items from home, this student is...
   A. Very dependable.
   B. Mostly dependable.
   C. Rarely dependable.

3. When faced with obstacles, this student...
   A. Hurdles them eagerly.
   B. Ponders, calculates, then hurdles carefully.
   C. Worries, then seeks help.
   D. Quits.

4. This student's bar is placed...
   A. Very high.
   B. High enough to get by.
   C. Not high enough.
   D. What bar?

5. As for group work...
   A. This person would be a great partner.
   B. This person takes work way too seriously for me.
   C. This person's bar is set too low for my standards.

Please do not identify yourself. Feel free to make comments on the back.

NAME _______________________________________ PERIOD _______ DATE _____________

REHEARSAL PEER EVALUATION

Once you feel your scene is polished, have two groups (or individuals if scenes are solo performances) watch an uninterrupted rehearsal and critique your performance. Discuss what your evaluators think you are doing well and what they think could use some more work. Remember, this is their opinion. Even if you do not agree with what they say, you should listen, consider their point, and be grateful for their input. Likewise, you should evaluate two individuals or groups. Remember to be helpful, not hurtful, with your feedback.

Rehearsal Evaluation #1

Performer or Performers: ____

Evaluated by (list all): ____

Evaluators: Rate the above performer(s) on each of the following items on a scale of 1 (low or not present) to 5 (high), then return the form to the performer(s). Discuss your findings with them.

____ Intro (if required)	____ Articulation/diction	____ Memorization or familiarity
____ Confidence	____ Flow	____ Energy/enthusiasm
____ Blocking/movement	____ Timing/pacing	____ Ending
____ Facial expressions	____ Characterization	____ Overall acting
____ Gestures	____ Staying in character	____ Overall entertainment value
____ Eye contact	____ Preparation	
____ Volume	____ Focus	

Notes: ____

____

Rehearsal Evaluation #2

Performer or Performers: ____

Evaluated by (list all): ____

Evaluators: Rate the above performer(s) on each of the following items on a scale of 1 (low or not present) to 5 (high), then return the form to the performer(s). Discuss your findings with them.

____ Intro (if required)	____ Articulation/diction	____ Memorization or familiarity
____ Confidence	____ Flow	____ Energy/enthusiasm
____ Blocking/movement	____ Timing/pacing	____ Ending
____ Facial expressions	____ Characterization	____ Overall acting
____ Gestures	____ Staying in character	____ Overall entertainment value
____ Eye contact	____ Preparation	
____ Volume	____ Focus	

Notes: ____

____

　　　　23

REHEARSAL PEER EVALUATION

The *Rehearsal Peer Evaluation* page will assist your students in becoming better at something they are probably already doing: critiquing one another. Have students use the forms later in the rehearsal process, when scenes are mostly prepared. It is meant to be a shared experience. If students are working in groups, pair groups up or put them into clusters of three performance groups. In these clusters of groups, two groups will watch as the other performs. The groups who watched will make suggestions, write notes, and then they will rotate. If you end up with an odd group out, either make a set of four groups or two sets of two and then allow them to switch out.

Performers' names will go on the top line and their evaluators will put their names on the line below. Each critiquing group will work together to rate the performers on a scale of 1 (low) to 5 (high) on the various elements. If you prefer for each group member to complete a form individually, you will need to provide them with additional copies.

After the activity, gather to discuss the groups' findings and what changes they plan to make based on what their evaluators had to say. Discuss the importance of the activity.

VOCABULARY REVIEW CROSSWORD KEY

ACROSS

3. PASSION
5. ISSUE
9. FALLING
10. AUDIENCE
16. DRAMATIC
20. RISING
22. ANTAGONIST
23. SETTING
24. EXPOSITION

DOWN

1. MESSAGE
2. INCITING
3. PROTAGONIST
4. VENUE
6. SLAPSTICK
7. THEME
8. PLOT
11. CLIMAX
12. DRAMATIZATION
13. BRAINSTORM
14. ENDING
15. HISTORICAL
17. MORALITY
18. OBSTACLES
19. REVENUE
21. GOAL

VOCABULARY REVIEW CROSSWORD

ACROSS

3. Plays that teach about Jesus's death and resurrection.
5. Plays that teach about the modern challenges faced by young people today.
9. After the climax, the _________ action begins, wrapping up loose ends and answering any unanswered questions.
10. When you are writing for this group of people, it is important to know as much about them as possible, including challenges, their attention spans, and what will appeal to them.
16. The basic formation of a play is called the _________ structure.
20. The _________ action begins with the inciting incident and carries the action toward the climax.
22. The person, thing, or idea that prevents or tries to prevent the protagonist from reaching their goal.
23. When and where a story takes place.
24. The beginning of a story in which readers or viewers learn about the characters and setting.

DOWN

1. The lesson the playwright intends for the audience to learn.
2. The bit of action that starts the characters on their upward journey toward the climax is called this type of incident.
3. Lead character.
4. Performance space or event setting.
6. Exaggerated, sometimes violent comedy in which the boundaries of common sense are often ignored to elicit a laugh.
7. The lesson the story is attempting to impart.
8. The storyline or events in a story.
11. The turning point in a story in which the protagonist either reaches or fails to reach their goal.
12. Something that has been turned into script form so that it may be performed.
13. To write without censoring as you go, jotting down every thought that comes to mind on the subject at hand.
14. To some playwrights, this is the hardest part of a story to write; for the purpose of this section, it will contain your moral or lesson.
15. Plays that teach about people, places, and events of our past.
17. Plays that seek to teach people to make Godly choices.
18. Things that stand in the way (often figuratively) of one's goal.
19. Money made by the network or station from the sale of advertising air time.
21. What a character wants in a scene or story.

VOCABULARY REVIEW CROSSWORD SOLUTION

CHAPTER 2
THEATRE FOR THE EYES

VOCABULARY

MOVEMENT—THEATRE FOR THE EYES

LIP-SYNC

> *Lip-sync Project*
> *Lip-sync Performance Peer Evaluation*

PANTOMIME

> *Pantomime Elements Chart*
> ***Activity #1—Pantomime Warm-up***
> ***Activity #2—Solo Scene***
> ***Activity #3—Solo Scene Set to Music***
> ***Activity #4—Duet Scene Set to Music***
> ***Activity #5—Large Group Scene Set to Music***
> ***Activity #6—Silent Film***
> ***Activity #7—Pantorhythms***
> ***Activity #8—Slow-motion Pantomime***
> ***Activity #9—Backward Pantomime***
> ***Activity #10—Pantodance***
> *Pantomime Planner*
> *Pantomime Performance Peer Evaluation*

ADDITIONAL NOTES

INTRODUCTION
> ***Photo Activity***

LIP-SYNC
> ***Additional Grading Options***
> > Lip-sync Performance Rubric
> > Self-Improvement Plan

PANTOMIME
> Matching Answer Key
> ***Pantomime Activity Notes***
> > Pantomime Performance Rubric

VOCABULARY

In this chapter, you will learn about:

Action: Movement.

Body Language: The messages sent with one's body position, posture, facial expressions, and gestures.

Cheat Out: To turn out more toward the audience; similar to "opening up to the audience," only may be more involved, such as moving a chair or shifting one's whole body.

Choreography: Planned dance movements.

Creativity: Use of artistry and originality in a performance.

Dance: To interpret music or feelings with rhythmic and/or patterned movements of the body.

Facial Expressions: The messages sent with one's face.

First Impression: The way the performer comes across the moment the audience sees him; can include appearances, confidence, timely set up, preparation, professionalism, and so on.

Force Focus: To position actors, props, lighting, and scenery in such a direction as to "command" that the audience look a certain way.

Gender Bending: To place an actor into a role that was intended for an actor of the opposite sex; to put a boy in a female part or a girl in a male part without changing the gender of the character.

Gestures: Hand movements that are expressive.

Gimmicks: Devices used to win the approval of the audience.

Hook: A figurative term for getting the audience's attention and holding it.

Lip-sync: A type of performance in which an actor or actors act as though they are the ones singing a song by synchronizing their lip movements to the words of the song; also includes acting out the story of the song and/or dancing.

Lyricist: A person who writes song lyrics.

Lyrics: The words in a song.

Movement: In theatre, the way an actor uses their body for interpretation.

Narrative: A story.

Open Up to the Audience: To turn one's body out slightly toward the audience, usually by a simple shift of the foot.

Opposing Synchronization: Forces actors to work together to create movement that appears to be "cause and effect."

Pantomime: To act out a specific movement without the use of a prop (example: to act like one is holding a phone to the ear to tell a friend to get the phone).

Perfect Synchronization: Two or more actors are doing the exact same thing for a sustained period of time.

Plane: A flat surface that is not always readily visible; may include stage left to stage right, downstage to upstage, and floor to ceiling.

Props: The things used by actors onstage.

Set: Anything that indicates a place or setting or that turns a nontraditional performance space into a suitable performance area.

Stage Picture: A term used to describe each moment onstage as though it were a photograph; the desirable stage picture is one in which actors are focused, a story is being told, and there is a focal point.

Synchronize: To match or align two or more things exactly.

Tableau: Meaning "picture" and also meaning "scene," refers to creating meaningful pictures onstage.

Take Center: To make one's self the center of focus.

Teamwork: The result of more than one person using their assets and working together to reach a common goal; cooperation.

Upstage Hand (or Foot): The Upstage body part is the one farthest away from the audience at that moment; it will change as actors move around on the stage.

Upstage One's Self: To poorly position one's self so that the audience's view will be obstructed.

27

INTRODUCTION

Movement may be one of the hardest concepts to teach using a textbook. The very idea of movement requires that someone be present to guide, demonstrate, and motivate students. It also helps to have a theatre teacher who is willing to get on the floor, jump over chairs, and take risks with the students.

Contrary to what we may have done in college or what is stereotyped in the movies, movement doesn't have to be all black tights and intensity. Learning movement through pantomime and other creative methods can be a joyful and pleasurable self-guided tour.

This book focuses on lip-sync and pantomime for movement study.

MOVEMENT—THEATRE FOR THE EYES

"I like your silence, it the more shows off / Your wonder."
William Shakespeare, *The Winter's Tale*, Act V, Scene 3

Here's a challenge for you and your classmates: try to go one class period without speaking or making any other sounds. No, you cannot sleep. You must still participate in class as usual, but you will rely on your abilities as a master **pantomime** artist to do so. Is it possible? Okay, in theatre, this might be a little like cheating, but imagine holding class silently in science or math! Is it possible to make do without sound? Have we become such a society of speakers and listeners that we have forgotten that we can communicate without words? You may have difficulty meeting the challenge outside of this class, but in theatre, you are taught to communicate silently with the audience when necessary. As Shakespeare said in the quote above, silence "shows off your wonder."

About a third of what happens on the stage is for the eyes, a third for the ears, and a third to be consumed by the brain and heart. The three parts work together to create theatre. Theatre is everywhere, and with today's passion for entertainment, it's no longer reserved for the stage. It is what takes a football game from a mere outing to a spectacular event. Theatre is why thousands watch the fireworks after a home run instead of watching the batter round the bases. It is why home decorating shows, shopping shows, and reality TV are more popular than ever. If a producer can make everyday life dramatic, they will draw an audience and make money!

None of the pageantry will ever do any good if the director and actors cannot get the audience's attention, right? There are several ways to grab attention onstage. One is to touch the audience's imagination with a captivating story. But it takes time to build interest, so there must be a better way to **hook** the audience early in the production. There is! Engage them with sound and pictures. Your audience craves theatre for the ears and eyes.

We'll start with *theatre for the eyes*. What makes appreciators of the arts want to look at something, study it, and become lost in it? Color, action, drama, light, darkness, mystery, connectivity, pain, suffering, and growth. People want and need to feel,

but as a director, it's not enough to just feed emotions to your audience. Your job is to stir something deep inside them.

Take, for example, the cover of a magazine that shows a mother holding a thin baby, his dark legs discolored with ash-colored dust, his weak head resting heavily on his mother's bare shoulder. The child looks off in the distance, not seeing much but feeling the weight of hunger and illness in every cell of his tiny body. The mother silently pleads with the camera to take a picture of her poverty and share it with the world. Perhaps they will send help, maybe medicine for her baby.

It's a snapshot of one one-hundredth of a second of this small family's life, but it tells a long story, and in a very real way, it is theatre. The photographer submitted hundreds of pictures, but this one caught the editor's eye because of the drama. It was perfectly framed and lighted to include the silhouette of an old man with his head hung low, passing by an armed guard who looked like he should be in school. The mother's once-red wrap is dirty and tattered, but it speaks of a life that was not always this hard. She appears too old to be the child's mother, but her sad eyes are younger than her skin. This photo won out over many others because it could do what they could not: hook the audience.

But how is a photograph like theatre? A director sits in front of the actors while blocking the show. The director looks at the stage a lot like you look at the cover of a magazine and judges the composition of the **stage picture**. Does it tell the story the director seeks to share? Is it balanced? Can everyone be seen? Is there focus? How will the lighting director approach this scene? Finally, the director takes into consideration the costumes, the **set**, **props**, makeup, and even how sound will play a part in the effect. If the director cannot get the audience to look at the stage, it will all be for nothing.

It is not uncommon to hear directors tell actors that they have two primary jobs: to be seen and to be heard. After they have accomplished that, then

NOTES: ____

____

____

____

____

____

____

____

they can act. This means that they have to learn to stage themselves well within the context of a scene. Because they also are almost always dealing with "being heard" or delivering their lines, they are really trying to do two jobs at once. For younger actors especially, staging one's self is challenging. That is why directors will often be heard using phrases like **"cheat out," "open up to the audience," "use your upstage hand," "don't upstage yourself," "force focus," "take center,"** and so on. These are all theatre phrases that deal with making good stage pictures.

A **stage picture** is *a view of what the audience will see at a given moment in the show.* It's a particular moment frozen in time like a photograph—something you would spend money to print and put in a frame. Because the audience has many things to see in a theatre besides what they came to see—your show—you must give them thousands of reasons not to become distracted. Your show must be full of interesting stage pictures. If you were to line all of your stage pictures up in a photo album, a person viewing the album should be able to follow the story from start to finish.

There is more to creating a captivating stage picture than spacing the actors. There are several "planes" on which to work. A **plane** is *any flat surface,* even—and often—an invisible one. Theatrical planes include stage left to stage right, downstage to upstage, and floor to ceiling. The director must consider all of these. How the director chooses to

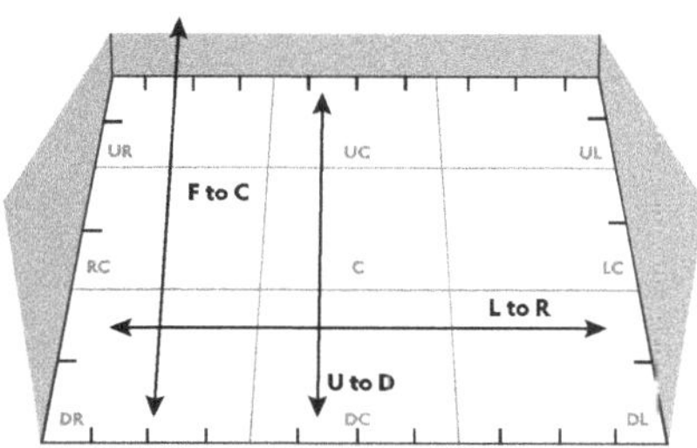

arrange actors depends a great deal on the way the director wants the audience to feel about the message of the show. The director may choose a concept that is bold and "in your face," where the audience feels as if it is a character in the show. In that case, the director may position actors facing full front with the stage extended out into the audience

and down center being the focal point. This would take advantage of the downstage to upstage plane (U to D in the diagram). The director might choose to use minimalism with only five cubed set pieces spaced evenly in five spotlights across the entire downstage area (L to R in diagram). The director may want to build complex scaffolding that extends high into the rafters, allowing actors to hang off the set by the backs of their knees or do tricky entrances like sliding down fire poles or entering trapeze-style. In that case, the director is taking advantage of "air space," or the area between the floor and ceiling (F to C in diagram).

But placing actors along a plane isn't the only consideration a director must make. The director must position actors so that focus is drawn to the right place, the actors' bodies must be telling the right story, everyone must be seen, and it must all be visually appealing. All of these things can depend on many different factors.

Take a look at the three groups of people below. Each group is set up to draw attention to one of the figures. Can you tell which figure is meant to take the focus and explain why?

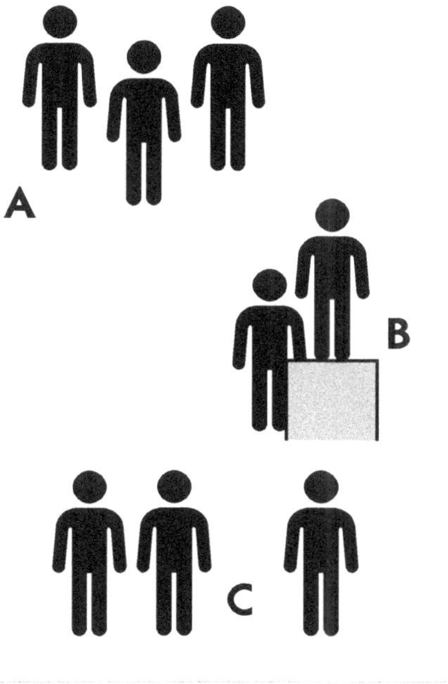

PHOTO ACTIVITY

From the audience's perspective, movement is visual, as is a stage picture, which is like a snapshot of what the audience sees at any time in the show. Before diving into stage movement activities, it is helpful to heighten students' awareness of the stage picture their movement choices create at any given moment.

You can easily teach about stage pictures or stage composition with just newspapers, a few phone cameras, and this two-day activity. To prep for this activity, sort through the newspapers and cut out interesting headlines. Mount each on a brightly colored piece of paper so that they will be difficult to miss when you hang them around your classroom at about eye level.

Announce the activity a few days in advance to ensure you have enough students willing to use the cameras on their phones who are responsible enough to make sure their phones are fully charged for class on the given day. When you divide your class into groups of five to seven, each group will need at least one photographer.

On the day of the activity, divide your class into groups consisting of at least one photographer plus four to six other students, who will be the actors. If you have more than one photographer in a group, they can rotate roles.

Point out the headlines you have hung around the room and tell students they have the entire class period to take ONE picture to go with each headline, using as many or as few actors as they feel necessary. They must interpret the headline appropriately and should consider space, body language, eye contact, and action. Explain that this would be the picture that appears with the headline in the newspaper, so while having fun, they also need to take the activity seriously (unless, of course, the headline is humorous).

You may also want to allow props. You could provide a box of generic props such as various pieces of scrap lumber that could "stand in" as various items.

You don't want excess clutter in the photographs, so if you do not have a lot of blank wall space for students to use as backdrops in their photos, it may be better to do this activity on your stage or even outside against the building walls. Emphasize that you really want your actors and photographers to have a clean area so they can focus their viewers' attention on a captivating stage picture. Another option is to provide each group with a piece of muslin or a large sheet to use as a backdrop.

At the end of the class period, have each photographer send you a single photo for each headline. Before the next class session, print these photos or create a slide show with them so you can lead a discussion with your students about their choices. For each photo, you might ask:

- Where is the focus in this picture?

- What is the action?

- What does each character want in the picture?

- Does each actor in the photo have a character?

- Is each actor in the picture making an important contribution?

- How might lighting or costuming change things?

- Are actors using a variety of planes (left to right, front to back, floor to ceiling)?

You may want to keep some pictures from year to year to use as examples. You can even add some photos from your own shows to help students make the link between this activity and stage pictures.

Here's another idea: during your productions, take pictures of the students when they are not creating good stage pictures, then stop them and have them build a better one. Create a slide show of before and after pictures so that they can understand how much thought must go into each and every moment in the show—stage pictures do not make themselves!

INTRODUCTION TO THEATRE ARTS 2

In Group A, the center figure is closest to the audience and in the middle. With all other things being equal, that figure will be the focal point. In group B, the figure on the cube is higher and appears to be closer to the audience, so that figure will take focus. In group C, all are on the same plane, but one is apart from the others, so that figure will take focus. This assumes that all other factors are equal. However, in any of these groups, the lighting director could change focus easily by spotlighting one of the other figures. The costumer could change the focus by introducing a new color to the stage or a large costume, such as wings. Even the use of a prop could affect focus. Take another look at group B. Imagine the figure behind the cube with a large sword and a bright red hood while the figure on the cube is in white. The various new elements of color and prop as well as lighting, action, and acting will change the audience's attention immediately.

Perhaps the best way to focus attention is with **action**. The audience's attention will drift to the most dynamic part of the stage. If ten actors are down center standing still and one actor is moving up left, the audience will focus on the up left actor, even though the up left actor is in a weaker stage area. Is it a bad choice to bring in the focal point from a weak stage position? Not necessarily. Theatre is an art, and as long as the director can achieve the desired goal, there is no "right" or "wrong" way to stage a scene—but there may be a more artistically appealing way. Even directors are still students, so as a continuing student of the theatre, continue to try different things. Take pictures and study them, and don't be afraid to say, "I don't like it. Let's start over."

You will learn more about the technical aspect of theatre later in this book. For now, let's focus on action. At the beginning of this section, you were challenged to go an entire class period without speaking. Could you do it? How would you communicate? No sign language or writing allowed! You are an actor, so you would act! That's right—**pantomime**, **gesturing**, **facial expressions**, **body language**—all of these would surface naturally if you could not speak. However, because you can speak, these instincts are repressed.

Have you ever seen one of your parents tell you to do something with just the lift of an eyebrow? Or has a parent ever gotten you to move simply by taking a small step backward, perhaps gesturing with a hand? What if you were told you had to act out an entire scene with just your feet? Could you do it? These are all challenges you will face and defeat—or de-feet—with the fun, energetic, and expressive activities in this chapter.

So, are you ready to move?

LIP-SYNC

Long before MTV or VH1 began airing music videos in the 1980s, would-be entertainers were singing along with their favorite songs. When they thought no one was watching, they may have even danced, acted like rock stars, or held their heads at dramatic angles while holding out passionate, long notes. If the faux musicians could not sing but their hearts still ached to be musical stars, they probably faked it by *lip singing*, or *moving their mouths along with the words without making any sound*. If they were good, their faces and mouths would be **synchronized** with the original recording.

GROUP SIZE & TEAMMATES

Can you think of some classmates who would be fearless partners for this project?

What would be some benefits or drawbacks to working alone?

Over time, this type of performance came to be known as **lip-sync** (or lip-synch, according to some). While it may not hold the status of a well-performed Shakespearean soliloquy, it does have its place in the theatre curriculum. Some of the benefits of learning lip-sync include:

- Learning to move to the music without having to learn to dance.
- Experiencing musical theatre without having to be a singer.
- Learning to make appropriate facial expressions fearlessly.
- Discovering the fine art of synchronization.
- Learning to find a theme and decipher a storyline.
- Pulling various elements together for a full-scale performance, including character development, costuming, special effects, and possibly dance.
- Focusing on teamwork and energy to elevate a performance.

LIP-SYNC GROUPS

Lip-sync can be done by as few as one person or by groups of up to six performers. Your group's size and makeup must fit the song, at least from the audience's perspective. If the song has one singer and you have five people in your group, only one person will logically be able to lip-sync. The others will have to act or dance. At the same time, if your group has two people and the audience can easily detect many more voices, it will be difficult to convince them that two people are enough to perform the song.

If the song is sung by a male, the character singing should be male, but that doesn't mean the actor must be male. **Gender bending**, or *taking on a character of a different sex*, is a fun way to make all songs accessible to everyone. Imagine a girl dressed like Ken and a boy dressed like Barbie performing the "Barbie Girl" song by Aqua. While gender bending is an acceptable form of entertainment, having a girl character sing a male song without any attempt to create a male character—or vice versa—will send confusing messages to the audience.

to be as successful as your more advanced students. At the same time, every learner can excel on their own level. If you have extremely creative actors, they will probably produce unique, memorable lip-syncs. If you have studious, hard-working actors, they will likely produce well-organized and thorough lip-syncs.

Dancers, actors, singers, and those who cannot sing will all find something enjoyable about the project. For those who love musical theatre but cannot sing, lip-sync affords them the opportunity to feel like a star and a musical performer.

And there are very few projects that combine costuming, makeup (optional), small-scale scenery, directing, acting, props, movement and/or dance, and even some writing, all in the same performance.

You may want to invest some of your departmental money in musical soundtracks and other appropriate songs for the classroom. You do not have to use songs from musicals for lip-sync. Almost any type of song will work. Your students will actually be more challenged if a published musical number is not available for copy (although this, too, has its benefits).

LIP-SYNC

Some teachers do not see the value in doing lip-sync. While it is very unlikely any of your students will make their fortunes by lip-syncing, there are a number of worthwhile skills taught through lip-sync projects.

First, there are many different challenging and appealing elements—something for every type of student. Second, lip-sync is a great tool to get even your most reluctant learners interested in performing.

Next, it is not as challenging as some acting projects, so your beginners will have the opportunity

Read the lip-sync lesson with your class. It has a lot of useful information on selecting groups, choosing a song, and creating a storyline from the lyrics.

Give your students the necessary information to fill in the additional information portion of the lip-sync section, including your performers' deadlines for choosing their music (unless you will provide music for them).

They will need the means to play their music. If your school does not allow phones in class, figure out in advance how you can provide technology to each group, whether a CD and CD player or an MP3 player. Or seek permission for an exemption from the rule for this project.

Also, each group will need a copy of the lyrics. It may be beneficial to consider the appropriateness of the lyrics if students are allowed to choose any song.

Discourage the use of Wi-Fi for musical selections, as this is less reliable than an actual downloaded or physical copy. And each student should bring a copy of the music daily so that it is always in class even if key group members are not.

Depending on their skill level and maturity, your students will probably need about three to five hours to rehearse and at least two hours to make a simple set. If you will require anything more complex, you will want to give extra time. For most classes, and depending on how much out-of-class time you require, a week and a half to two weeks is plenty of time to put together a well-rehearsed lip-sync project.

Next, on the students' pages, there is space for each group member to volunteer to bring items and a place for their phone numbers so that reminder calls can be made.

On performance day, make sure each student has their *Lip-sync Performance Peer Evaluation* form. Students should be critiquing one another either orally or in writing for every performance. The form provided is designed to make the task of peer evaluating easy but effective.

As each group takes the stage, give them group numbers. This will help students stay organized and make it easier to know if they missed a group. Have each performer in the group give their initials (it goes faster than names and is easier to write) for those in the audience to write on their forms. If students do not know a performer's name, you may want to have them write some identifying feature in the margin, like "braids" or "black pants."

After the group performs, have each audience member rate the group members individually on a scale of your choosing (1 to 5 or 1 to 10) and tell at least one thing that the performer did well and one thing to focus on improving. You can grade peer evaluations on thoroughness or completeness, but try not to criticize your students' judgment. Reward very specific comments and discourage vague ones. For example, the comment "dance" means nothing to the performer, but "great choreography" is a clear, helpful comment.

On page 99, there is a rubric for you to grade the performance. Each group will turn in one rubric. The first page of the rubric is for grading the group's joint efforts. The second page is for grading the individuals' contributions. Under "Name," have them write the name of their song. On the second page of the rubric, each actor will write their name in one of the dark rectangles marked "Actor." Record the group score from the first page (from a possible 45) and the individual's score (from a possible 55) in the first two shaded boxes below each actor's name. Then record any applicable bonus points. Add the three together to get the actor's final grade. Together both pages of the rubric equal 100 points.

ADDITIONAL GRADING OPTIONS

On pages 99-100, you will see a *Lip-sync Performance Rubric* for evaluating each performance. The front is for evaluating the group as a whole, the back is for each individual in the group. You will need one two-sided rubric per group, with the performers' names listed on the front as well as written on the back. Directions are provided on the rubric itself for compiling a grade for each student based on a 100 point scale, 45 points based on the Group Score and 55 points from the Individual Score.

You might consider giving a blank rubric to each group in advance so they can see what their grade will be based on and how their final grade will include both group and individual metrics. It will be the group's responsibility to write in their own names front and back along with their song title, then hand you back this rubric before their performance. If you choose not to do this, you'll need to be prepared in advance on the day of performances.

Besides evaluating their final performance, there are other aspects of this unit you could grade either on a group or an individual level. Alternatively, these might be the basis for Bonus Points on the rubric.

Here are some ideas:

- Rehearsal Grade: having all materials, staying on task, and being respectful of others who are trying to work.

- Lyrics and Music Grade: having lyrics approved by teacher by deadline, having music in class for all rehearsals, and properly storing the music and music player after rehearsals.

- Set Grade: fulfilling commitments to bring material from home and assisting with the completion of the set.

- Peer Evaluation Grade: properly completing and turning in the *Lip-sync Performance Peer Evaluation* page and making comments specific and helpful.

- Audience Grade: being a respectful, quiet, supportive member of the audience during all performances.

- Self-improvement Plan Grade: thoughtfully completing a copy of the *Self-improvement Plan* (page 101 of the teacher's guide) after receiving feedback on their lip-sync performance.

NAME ____ PERIOD _________ DATE _______________

LIP-SYNC PROJECT

OBJECTIVE You will interpret the story or theme of a song in an energetic musical routine in which singing is mimicked and movement may be dance and/or theatrical in nature.

SONG SELECTION

Not only must your song have an appropriate number of voices for your group (or your group an appropriate number of people for the song), but you must also pick a song that will not be offensive to your audience and that will be in line with your school's code of conduct. Avoid songs with any graphic language, even if the words have been bleeped over or removed. Your audience is intelligent enough to know the offensive language was once there, and even if the song doesn't say the words, their minds will fill in the blanks. Stay away, too, from songs that use slang to mean something inappropriate. Your teacher can veto anything for any reason if it gives cause for concern.

What are some songs you think would make good lip-syncs? ______________________________________

____

____

____

SONG LYRICS

For this project, the song's lyrics are your script. Make sure you have enough copies of the song lyrics for each person in your group. Each performer will highlight their lines, and all will write in their movements.

Your lip-sync lines must be memorized. It is important that you are fully in sync with the singer on the recording; your mouth and face must move the same way the singer's did when they made the recording. Simply moving one's mouth will not be convincing; if a performer's lyrics are not memorized, it will be obvious to the audience and not believable.

STORY AND DANCE

What is the song about? Is there a story? If so, your song is **narrative**, meaning *like a story*. Other songs may not have an obvious plot. That's because many songs are written very poetically, and some focus on ideas and themes instead of plot. While it may be a little harder to connect these to figure out what the **lyricist** is trying to say, most of the time it is possible.

Write the story of your song below. If you cannot detect a story, write one key word from each line of the song and see if a story begins to form. If you still cannot see a plot, ask your teacher for help or research the meaning of the lyrics online.

Story or key words: ____

____

____

____

____

NOTES: ____

____

____

____

____

____

____

CHAPTER 2 — THEATRE FOR THE EYES

The story is the most important part of the performance because it will be what connects the audience to the song. Your group will work together to portray the characters and act out the story in a musically entertaining way. If your group is capable of it, **dance** can also be important by both commanding and holding the audience's attention. Combined with the story, it can be even more effective than acting alone because it adds energy and becomes a magnet for your audience's eyes. Have you ever noticed that it is difficult to look away when someone is dancing, especially when a group is doing a good job dancing together? Dance can also be a useful tool for making a good grade, because when done well, there is no doubt in the teacher's or the audience's mind that the group worked hard and was well-prepared. In other words, it's more difficult to fake being prepared with a dance than it is with acting or lip-syncing.

Don't worry, if you aren't a dancer, you still have some options. Start small. Act out your lip-sync but move in time with the music. Each time you rehearse the song, add a little more to the difficulty level by making your acting movements a bit more dance-like. If you shake your finger at a character, do it to the beat of the music. Then do it with attitude to the beat of the music. Then add a little head fling and strut off. You may not be dancing, but you'll soon be moving like a dancer.

OTHER IMPORTANT THINGS TO REMEMBER
- Create interesting stage pictures.
- Ensure that everyone can be seen at all times.
- Be **creative**; try some fun **gimmicks** such as throwing candy to the audience or using puppets. Or if you have a special skill like hula hoop tricks, performing gymnastics, or magic, use your skill to improve your performance and intrigue the audience.
- Create energetic, unique, and interesting characters.
- Incorporate as many elements as may be justified by the story without stealing focus or crowding the stage (smoke or bubble machine, special lighting, props, set, costumes).
- Make the audience feel involved and special, almost as though your performance was intended especially for each audience member.
- What is *not* a lip-sync? It is not a band pretending to play instruments!

ADDITIONAL INFORMATION
- ☐ Students will provide their own music by ________ /________ .
- ☐ Teacher will provide music.
- ☐ Students must provide CD or MP3 player or other device to play their music by ________ /________ .
- ☐ Teacher will provide CD or MP3 player or other device to play music.
- ☐ Teacher must see lyrics by________ /________. (Teacher approval:_____________________________)

GROUP MEMBER	WILL BRING	CONTACT INFO

　　　33

NOTES: ____

____

____

____

____

____

____

____

NAME _______________________________________ PERIOD _______ DATE _____________

LIP-SYNC PERFORMANCE PEER EVALUATION

Evaluate each aspect of the performer's lip-sync
on a scale of 1 (worst or not present) to 5 (best).

Group #	Performer's initials	1st impression	Lip-syncing	Creativity	Facial expressions	Movement/Dance	Character	Props	Costume	Set	Preparation	This performer was best at...	This performer could use a little more work on...

After all performances are completed and grades are recorded, cut the evaluators' names off the top of the peer evaluations. Place your class in a large circle and have them read the comments made about them on each evaluation. After they have read each one, they will pass it to the right. This is also a great time to return the evaluation you completed. Then use a *Self-Improvement Plan*, like the one on page 101, to encourage students to think of ways to apply what their peer evaluators had to say to future performances.

NOTES: ____

____

____

____

____

____

____

LIP-SYNC PERFORMANCE RUBRIC

PERFORMERS:

____

____

____

____

____

SONG TITLE:

____

1. The group made a good **first impression**, setting up in a timely manner and clearly understanding who would do what job and where each item would be placed.

   1 2 3 4 5

2. The group was **creative** and original in their performance.

   1 2 3 4 5

3. The lip-sync performance had well-planned, creative, synchronized, and organized **movement** and/or **dance** that assisted in telling the story or supporting the theme.

   1 2 3 4 5

4. The **set** was appropriate to the performance, added to the audience's entertainment or understanding, and when needed, offered the performers a "backstage."

   1 2 3 4 5 6 7 8 9 10

5. The group had appropriate **props** or was able to justify using pantomime throughout, and did so effectively.

   1 2 3 4 5 6 7 8 9 10

6. **Teamwork** was evident in the way performers interacted in rehearsals, during their performance, and after the performance. Voices and movements were synchronized when appropriate, and the group appeared well-rehearsed.

   1 2 3 4 5 6 7 8 9 10

GROUP SCORE

Record the total group score from this page (out of a possible 45) in the box to the left. Transfer this to each performer's group score on the next page. Finish rating each individual's performance (out of a possible 55 points). Add any applicable bonus points. The total of the group, individual, and bonus points will give you a grade for that performer.

LIP-SYNC PERFORMANCE RUBRIC, CONT.

Performer:

First impression

1 2 3 4 5

Lip-syncing

1 2 3 4 5 6 7 8 9 10

Creativity

1 2 3 4 5

Facial expressions

1 2 3 4 5 6 7 8 9 10

Movement/Dance

1 2 3 4 5

Character

1 2 3 4 5 6 7 8 9 10

Costume

1 2 3 4 5 6 7 8 9 10

Group Score	Individual Score	Bonus Points	TOTAL

Performer:

First impression

1 2 3 4 5

Lip-syncing

1 2 3 4 5 6 7 8 9 10

Creativity

1 2 3 4 5

Facial expressions

1 2 3 4 5 6 7 8 9 10

Movement/Dance

1 2 3 4 5

Character

1 2 3 4 5 6 7 8 9 10

Costume

1 2 3 4 5 6 7 8 9 10

Group Score	Individual Score	Bonus Points	TOTAL

Performer:

First impression

1 2 3 4 5

Lip-syncing

1 2 3 4 5 6 7 8 9 10

Creativity

1 2 3 4 5

Facial expressions

1 2 3 4 5 6 7 8 9 10

Movement/Dance

1 2 3 4 5

Character

1 2 3 4 5 6 7 8 9 10

Costume

1 2 3 4 5 6 7 8 9 10

Group Score	Individual Score	Bonus Points	TOTAL

Performer:

First impression

1 2 3 4 5

Lip-syncing

1 2 3 4 5 6 7 8 9 10

Creativity

1 2 3 4 5

Facial expressions

1 2 3 4 5 6 7 8 9 10

Movement/Dance

1 2 3 4 5

Character

1 2 3 4 5 6 7 8 9 10

Costume

1 2 3 4 5 6 7 8 9 10

Group Score	Individual Score	Bonus Points	TOTAL

Performer:

First impression

1 2 3 4 5

Lip-syncing

1 2 3 4 5 6 7 8 9 10

Creativity

1 2 3 4 5

Facial expressions

1 2 3 4 5 6 7 8 9 10

Movement/Dance

1 2 3 4 5

Character

1 2 3 4 5 6 7 8 9 10

Costume

1 2 3 4 5 6 7 8 9 10

Group Score	Individual Score	Bonus Points	TOTAL

Performer:

First impression

1 2 3 4 5

Lip-syncing

1 2 3 4 5 6 7 8 9 10

Creativity

1 2 3 4 5

Facial expressions

1 2 3 4 5 6 7 8 9 10

Movement/Dance

1 2 3 4 5

Character

1 2 3 4 5 6 7 8 9 10

Costume

1 2 3 4 5 6 7 8 9 10

Group Score	Individual Score	Bonus Points	TOTAL

NAME ____ PERIOD _________ DATE ________________

SELF-IMPROVEMENT PLAN

Answer each question honestly. Any honest answer will be given credit. This worksheet is intended to help you and your teacher analyze the success of your class performance and to create a strategy for the next performance.

1. *How* and *where* did you practice (both in class and outside of class)?

2. Did anyone in particular help you? Who was it and how did they help?

3. How much time did you practice outside of class?

4. Did you use all of the class time the teacher gave you? If not, what were you doing instead of practicing?

5. In what areas did you score highest from the teacher and what were some of the comments?

6. In what areas did you score lowest from the teacher and what were some of the comments?

7. According to your peers, what were some of your strengths?

8. According to your peers, where do you need to focus your efforts to improve?

9. In your opinion, what areas of your performance need the most attention?

10. What exercises or activities will you use to sharpen the skills that need improvement?

11. What can your teacher do to help you achieve success for the next performance? Is there anything you would like to have explained or taught again?

PANTOMIME

Pantomime is the ability to communicate without speaking. It also refers to a play or story in which the entire performance is done without speaking.

Helen Keller, one of the subjects of William Gibson's play *The Miracle Worker*, spent much of her life in the public eye. It's ironic, considering that Keller, deaf and blind from an early age, spent most of her childhood unable to communicate with others. It took a very special woman, Anne Sullivan, to teach her how to articulate words with her mouth and then how to make her voice pass through those articulators. But that was still only part of the battle. Keller had to learn to read what others were saying to her by feeling sign language in her hands. Once she learned to communicate with others and they learned to communicate with her, her career as one of the world's most famous public speakers soared.

The need to communicate is instinctive, but as babies, humans cannot speak. Instead, they observe the world around them and then find simple ways to tell parents or caregivers what they need by using non-verbal communication (any message sent without words). A hand to the mouth means "I'm hungry," pointing to an object means "I want that," and clapping means "I like that." These are all forms of non-verbal communication, the foundation for pantomime.

However, as babies learn to speak, they replace pantomime with vocabulary. Before long, pantomime has become a language reserved for worship services (a parent holds a finger to their mouth in a "shushing" gesture), secrets (your friend frantically gestures to you to not say something because of mixed company), and the classroom (teachers may point to their eyes and then to your paper meaning "keep your eyes on your own test"). Interestingly, the language of gesturing and pantomime transcends language barriers. Most of the movements are recognizable in any country. Therefore, pointing to one's eye for the word "I" is not acceptable pantomime; instead it is a type of wordplay.

Think of ten simple messages you use on a daily basis that can be said with pantomime. Record these in the following blanks. Stand (for greater movement) and perform the various messages for the class, and see if your classmates can guess each one. Create a pantomime "dictionary" on the board of the various daily tasks that could be communicated without speaking.

> **FOR FURTHER CLARIFICATION AND PRACTICE...**
>
> Study "Dramatic Structure" and "Character Development" in Chapter 5.
>
> **THESE PROJECTS WILL...**
>
> - Improve understanding of non-verbal communication.
> - Encourage higher levels of physical creativity.
> - Encourage **teamwork**.
> - Promote attention to detail.
> - Require actors to strongly consider the audience's point of view.
> - Reinforce understanding of dramatic structure and character development.
> - Both teach and entertain!

1. ____

2. ____

3. ____

4. ____

   35

PANTOMIME

There are ten pantomime exercises in this chapter. Do one or any combination of the ten to assist your students in learning to use their bodies onstage. A *Pantomime Planner* is provided for each student on page 44 of their workbook.

You may want to declare one day in class to be "Silent Day." Just as some Spanish teachers do not allow their students to speak English, a silent day as a study of pantomime would require that your students find other ways of communicating besides speaking. To write messages is only acceptable after all other efforts to communicate have been exhausted. Speaking of exhausting—wear comfortable clothing and shoes on your class's silent day. You will be doing a lot of movement, as will your students.

Because pantomime is about creating a story, use it before introducing script writing as a way of easing your students into the idea of becoming playwrights.

INTRODUCTION TO THEATRE ARTS 2

5. ____

6. ____

7. ____

8. ____

9. ____

10. ____

The point is, when you need to communicate but are not allowed to speak, you find a way to get your message across. What gestures did you and your classmates use to send your messages? It is very likely you used one or more of the methods below. Can you match the strategies on the left with the proper definitions on the right?

1. Gestures ________   A. To precisely copy an observed activity

2. Postures ________   B. Hand movements

3. Facial expressions ________   C. The way in which a person walks or runs

4. Gait ________   D. The ways in which a body may be positioned

5. Mimicry ________   E. The ways in which a person shows emotions from the neck up

6. Movement ________   F. Any physical expression in which the body is manipulated

ANSWER KEY:

1: B
2: D
3: E
4: C
5: A
6: F

What does all this have to do with acting? When film was first introduced in the 1890s, movies were silent simply because the technology did not exist to add voices. The experience was a visual one until music was eventually added. Before long it advanced again, and a short bit of text would pop up onto the screen to explain what was happening. But the greatest burden (or joy) of communicating the message was left to the actors. Movements were large, exaggerated, and even somewhat ridiculous—that is, compared to today's standards. But because the entire story had to be told without voices, this melodramatic acting style was necessary.

As the technology evolved and voices, sounds, and music became commonplace in films, the acting style changed too. Early "talking pictures," the term used for movies in which the characters' voices were heard, showcased acting very similar to that of silent films. It did not take long, though, for it to be replaced by the more subtle, realistic acting we see in films today.

Silent acting is still common. A more exaggerated yet still highly popular form of silent acting is the art of mime. Mime artists entertain with short situations. Rarely are these intended to take the form of an entire plot-driven story. A less exaggerated form is the pantomime used in a play. A script may call for actors to pretend to use props, or this may be a style the director chooses to use for artistic reason. Then there are scenes that are completely pantomimed. Some of these are set to music, some to a rhythm, and some are simply silent.

Actors who study theatre—movement in particular—will often say pantomime is the gateway to really understanding the body and how to communicate effectively with it. Some young actors are intimidated by the style because it eliminates the first tool they rely on to communicate: the voice. Once they master the style, these same actors will say pantomime became their most valued acting gateway.

Another thing that makes pantomime unique is the fact that most gestures are created by the actors rather than being pre-scripted. Although there are a few pantomime "scripts," most of the time the actor or actors performing the piece create the entire story.

And that brings up one of the most important things. The scenes you will be performing will be stories, meaning they will follow dramatic structure (see Chapter 5). Even though you will not be writing the scenes—although you may, if you wish—you will be creating them from start to finish. The concept is the same. It is important that your pantomime have the following elements:

NOTES: ____

____

____

____

____

____

____

____

PANTOMIME ELEMENTS CHART

PLOT ELEMENT	EXAMPLE
A clear beginning (the exposition) in which interesting **characters**, their relationships to one another, and the **setting** are defined; one of the characters (or all) must make their goal apparent.	A greedy landlord demands rent from his tenant, a beautiful lady. She makes it known that she can't pay the rent because she is poor, cold, and hungry. She wants extra time (her goal). He says she won't have to pay if she'll marry him (his goal).
There must be an **inciting incident** or initial problem that occurs after the exposition that gets the story's momentum moving toward the climax and also manages to **hook** the audience.	He makes a pass at her, but she declines and pushes him out the door. He struggles, but she manages to close the door in his face. This fuels his rage and he begins to scheme. The audience sees the ideas forming in his evil head.
There must be **rising action** that builds in intensity, keeping the audience interested.	He tries sneaking into her apartment by crawling in a window. She is cooking and without realizing he is there, discards her tasteless (but hot) broth out the window and into his face. He tries other tactics, but all are thwarted by her clumsiness.
There must be a **climax** in which the characters either achieve their goals or are denied them.	He finally gets into the apartment and is slowly sneaking up behind the unsuspecting lady, who stands at the window. He gets a running start, hands outstretched in "choking" formation, but she remembers something and steps aside (still not seeing him). He flies out the open window.
There must be a short—very short—bit of **falling action** leading toward the ending.	She fumbles in her pocket, pulling out several items and tossing them over her shoulder; they plunk the fallen landlord on the head as he is about to rise. Finally she finds what she is seeking.
There must be a satisfying **ending**.	She hears a sound and moves to the window, where she sees her landlord below. She tosses him the rent, closes the window, and exits. Still on the ground, he starts to rise, but instead gives up and is out cold.

NOTES: ____

____

____

____

____

____

____

____

ACTIVITY #1—PANTOMIME WARM-UP

(No props, costumes, or set pieces will be used in this activity.)

Write an item on each of five index cards—for a total of five items—from the category of the month of your birth. This will ensure a variety of items. Think creatively so that your prompts will not be too easy, but also think realistically; some things will be very difficult for even the most seasoned actor to pantomime.

Categories:

January—Things in the kitchen	July—Things in nature
February—Things in the garage	August—Things on vacation
March—Things in a child's room	September—Things people like
April—Things on a farm	October—Things people dislike
May—Things in an office	November—Things around the house
June—Things in a hospital	December—Things around work

Your teacher will collect all of the cards, mix them up, and then pass them out again randomly. It is not a problem for you to get some of your own cards back. The point is to be secretive yet challenging. Arrange the cards in order of what you think will be easiest to pantomime to what you think will be the hardest.

For the first round, the class will sit in a circle, you and your classmates will stand and pantomime your easiest card one at a time. You may sit when someone guesses your object. You might want to time the individuals in this round and reward the actor and guesser with the shortest times.

For round two, the class will be divided into two equal teams, Team 1 and Team 2. Each team will then divide into two parts, Group A and Group B. The groups on each team *do not* compete against each other. They are still all on the same team.

Each of the four groups will now combine their individual players' remaining cards by turning them face down in a single pile. Each group will have its own pile of cards. Group 1-A will start by randomly selecting (without peeking) one card from its pile. The team will have one minute to pantomime the word for Group 1-B. Every member of the pantomiming group should pantomime the word, either as a team or separately. If group 1-B correctly guesses the card, Group 1-A gets to pick one player from either group on Team 2 to join their team (similar to the game Red Rover). There is no penalty for not guessing correctly. Group 2-A will go next, then 1-B, then 2-B, then you will start over. If a team is down to one group, that group may continue to divide until there is just one player. When a team has only one player, the other team wins, or the team with the most players at the end of class wins.

ACTIVITY #2—SOLO SCENE

(No props, costumes, or set pieces will be used in this activity.)

You will have one class period to plan a two- to three-minute solo pantomime scene with solid dramatic structure. Use one of the prompts below or, if your teacher allows, create one of your own.

• Trying on pants	• Feeding a pet
• Eating a meal	• Using an appliance
• Getting ready for school	• Taking a test
• Brushing your teeth	• Studying
• Making a bowl of cereal	• Watching TV

Can you think of some (you will need at least three) funny things that might happen to get your scene moving toward a climax? For example, have you ever found two different shoes, but you couldn't find the mate

For ***ACTIVITY #1***, you may wish to time the individuals in the first round and reward the actor and guesser with the shortest times. In the second round, consider an even shorter time limit if you have more advanced students.

NOTES: _______________________________________

____

____

____

____

____

____

____

to either? Of course, this always happens when you are running late! Just when you think you have found a match, you realize you have actually found a third different shoe. Finally you settle on wearing two different shoes, and as you leave the room and pick up your backpack, you discover a match (under the backpack, of course). You put it on only to feel something crunchy inside. You take it off, turn it over, and out falls a dead spider (probably alive when your foot went in). Deathly afraid of spiders, you do the "freak out" dance on your bed, scream (pantomime, of course) for a parent who removes the carcass, you bang the shoe like crazy to make sure there are no spider relatives inside, check it out, put it on, and leave the room. You suddenly remember your backpack, return cautiously to get it, wipe it furiously, and exit, scratching with paranoia on the way out.

Complete the *Pantomime Planner* later in this chapter and present it to your teacher for a grade. Use the remaining time to rehearse.

ACTIVITY #3—SOLO SCENE SET TO MUSIC

(No props, costumes, or set pieces will be used in this activity.)

Either instead of—or in addition to—the previous activity (whatever your teacher allows), set the solo pantomime scene to instrumental music. It is important that the music not have any words so that the actors and audience may focus on the message rather than the **lyrics**. The entire class may practice their solo pantomimes to the same song, or individual actors may use headphones and work to their own music.

Guidelines:

- Begin and end with the music.
- Make use of the various musical elements in the scene.
- Loud cymbal strikes can be an alarm sounding.
- Flutes can be birds outside a classroom window.
- Use quiet moments in the music for sneakiness or suspicion.
- Use the beat and rhythm of the music to pace your scene and to motivate movement.

Complete the *Pantomime Planner* later in this chapter and present it to your teacher for a grade. Use the remaining time to rehearse.

ACTIVITY #4—DUET SCENE SET TO MUSIC

(No props, costumes, or set pieces will be used in this activity.)

Like the solo music scene, this is a pantomimed scene in which the story is performed to the beat and rhythm of instrumental music. The biggest difference in this activity is the presence of a second actor.

In life it is not unusual to experience an event like the ones in Activity #3 without speaking. Most people do not speak aloud if they are the only ones in a room, so a solo pantomime may not be the greatest test of your non-verbal communication skills. By adding a second person to the scene, you are taking it to the next level and can introduce comedic devices like misunderstandings and secrecy.

Again, the entire class may practice to the same song or groups may work to their own music. This will be loud in a large room, so be sure to keep your music at a personal level. By focusing, each group will be able to ignore other groups' music and hear only their own.

Guidelines:

- Begin and end with the music.
- Make use of the various musical elements in the scene.
- Experiment with **synchronization** now that there are two players.
  - ◊ Find opportunities to mimic each other's movements exactly, as in a mirror.

NOTES: ____

- ◇ Challenge yourselves to mimic each other's movements without being in a position to see each other.
- ◇ React to the other player's actions by timing movements with the music rather than visually: A has their back to B; B throws a tomato, hitting A in the back of the head; A reacts as though hit, even though A could not see the partner "throwing" the tomato.
- React facially, physically, and in character to your partner's actions.

Complete the *Pantomime Planner* later in this chapter, present it to your teacher for a grade, and then use the remaining time to rehearse.

ACTIVITY #5—LARGE GROUP SCENE SET TO MUSIC

Form a group of between six and twelve participants. Discuss and agree upon a single theme or event. Some suggestions include celebrating Independence Day, remembering 9/11, any number of religious holidays, Memorial Day, or an event in history. Find music—instrumental or not—to fit your pantomime's message. With a large group, you will probably want to stick with a serious scene. Comedy tends to work best with smaller pantomime groups.

While the preceding pantomime activities have limited the use of props, costumes, and set pieces, this one will not. On the contrary, this is an exceptional opportunity to prepare a simple presentation for an assembly or other special event, so make the most of your resources.

The earlier music activities also required only instrumental music. For this activity, you may select music with singing, but be certain that the message in your song is the message you want to portray in your pantomime. Avoid music that is religious or political in nature so that your entire audience feels entertained.

Because of the size of your group and the seriousness of your message, you may want to work with a tableau-style presentation. **Tableau**, meaning "picture" and also meaning "scene," refers to *creating meaningful pictures onstage*. To create a tableau, think of a headline in a newspaper that would be appropriate for your theme. The tableau would be the full-color picture that would accompany that headline, tugging at the hearts of readers and driving even non-readers to stop and stare.

Use the following activity to form your tableaus:

- Actors are not to speak. The activity should be done from instinct rather than direction.
- While the music plays, take the stage (one student at a time) and get into a frozen position; it is important that this not be rushed; it is also okay to start over again if you or your classmates get "stuck" or lose motivation.
- After the first student takes the stage, the second will play off the first's position; in other words, the first player up becomes the foundation for the rest of the picture.
- The tableau is finished when either the students or director feel that the message is clear; it may have as few as one actor or the entire class—as many as it takes to create the message.
- Once the tableau is formed, it is still a work in progress; this means the director or students can tweak it as needed to correct focus or ensure that all players can be seen.
- You may have up to three different tableaus, depending on the size of your pantomime group, frozen onstage at the start of your scene; repeat the activity as needed until all players in the group are staged.

Now that you have your tableau, you will use it to create the opening to your pantomime.

If your group has more than one tableau:

- Consider using levels of height and depth onstage so that each has its own distinct area; platforms and cubes that do not distract from the scene are great ways to ensure all actors and groups can be seen.

NOTES: ___________________________________

____

____

____

____

____

____

____

____

- Consider having all the tableaus frozen at the beginning and having only one tableau come to life at a time during the music so that the audience may focus.
- Consider having the individual tableaus come together at some point in the scene to become whole.
- Use slow motion for effect; do not let it become a distraction.

If your group has just one tableau:

- Consider using the opposite effect as your scene progresses by breaking off individual members or small groups and having them freeze in meaningful but smaller frozen pictures to end your scene.

Out of these perfectly still tableaus, your individual scenes will develop in the pantomime.

- Each tableau will take turns pantomiming a different scene or part of a scene until the music ends.
- Enjoy experimenting with blending the tableaus, freezing in tableaus at the end of your music, using actors to create backgrounds, focus, slow motion, lighting, levels in your staging, and more.
- Avoid over-costuming these scenes.
  - ◊ Focus on simplifying and coordinating.
  - ◊ Consider wearing all jeans and all solid-colored T-shirts, but not matching exactly (in a scene like this, matching too closely will make it difficult for the audience to distinguish between players).
  - ◊ Perhaps each tableau can have its own wardrobe plan.

Complete the *Pantomime Planner* later in this chapter, present it to your teacher for a grade, and then use the remaining time to rehearse.

ACTIVITY #6—SILENT FILM

Spend a day or two watching silent movies, which are available from your local library or online. Pay special attention to the ways the actors used and positioned their mouths, eyes, hands, and postures. Take note of the makeup, costumes, setting, and any text displayed on screen.

Select a scene from one of the films you watched. Your job is to mimic what you observed so that you may better understand the melodramatic style. Props, costumes and set pieces are allowed and encouraged. Mimic the acting style of the film and the makeup. You may have another participant display the text. You may use the music from the film or replace it with music of your own.

For a fun twist on the activity, set up your laptop near the performance area and perform simultaneously with the actors in the film.

ACTIVITY #7—PANTORHYTHMS

Every person, situation, family, environment, etc., has a rhythm. It is a part of the environment. The rhythm can be an actual sound, or it may be the slow, steady creep of a band of sunlight working its way across the floor. Think of the sounds on a playground: The chains on the swing set create a very definite, rhythmic squeak that slows as the swing comes to a stop. Children's laughter can add energy to the rhythm, and jumping rope can create a steady beat. The climax is when the bell signals the end of recess, the falling action is the slowing and decreasing volume and speed of the rhythms, and the scene ends when the school door slams shut and all sound suddenly ceases.

What role do rhythms play in pantomime? Imagine that the people in an environment are unable to speak. Instead, they use beats, sounds, and pantomime to communicate. These become their voices, words, and sentences. A story still evolves, but instead of being accompanied by an instrumental piece of music, the characters provide the sounds themselves.

Create a pantomimed scene in which you create rhythms with your hands, feet, mouths, props, and even select words—but no dialogue—to express yourselves. You can also pantomime. Think of this as a cross between the show *Stomp* and any of the previous pantomimed scenes.

  41

ACTIVITY #7 is recommended for advanced students as it is a very challenging project. It can also be extremely rewarding. How can using an activity such as this help students in a play performance? Plays have rhythms, as do the individual characters within the plays. Use this activity the next time you rehearse your play (after lines are memorized). Instead of the actors saying their lines, spend a rehearsal running the play using only the strategies from this activity. As students are disallowed the ability to say each line, they will instead discover new ways to express the lines' internal messages non-verbally.

ACTIVITY #8—SLOW-MOTION PANTOMIME

Select a song that is short and slow, building to a climax, and then dropping off with an appropriate amount of "falling action" time. There are many musical pieces that will work very well. Below is a list of musical selections that will work for this activity.

"Quiet Village," Martin Denny, Exotica; 3:40

"Jungalero," Les Baxter, The Exotic Moods of Les Baxter; 3:27

"12 Bagatelle a 3: No. 5," Andantino; 2:09

"Soul Bossa Nova," Hollywood Classics; 2:41

"Flute Song," Mamer, Eagle; 2:40

"Electric Counterpoint: II, Slow," Steven Reich, Reich: Different Trains; 3:22

"Lyrical Dance," Terem Quartet, Terem; 2:34

"Khomus Solo," Shu-De, Voices from the Distant Steppe; 2:19

"River Flows in You," Yiruma, First Love (Yiruma Piano Collection); 3:05

"Box Car Racer," Box Car Racer; 1:57

"Here's That Rainy Day," Pat Coil, Cocktail Party Jazz; 3:18

In groups of one or two, create scenes around a mundane task in which the task is made overly dramatic. One example might be a scene in which you wake to discover a horrible taste in your mouth. You rush—in slow motion—to brush your teeth, but you can't get the top off of the toothpaste. You struggle to loosen it, try to bite it off, then bang it on the counter (note the three bits of action leading to the climax). Finally, you get a great idea: you'll cut the end off the tube of toothpaste. Victorious, but messy, you brush your teeth and freshen your breath (falling action and satisfying ending).

What are some other daily tasks that might make fun pantomimes if performed overly dramatically?

____

____

____

____

____

____

SUGGESTED SCENES

For one person:

◇   Making a large sandwich

◇   Getting up the nerve to call a boy/girl

◇   Taking a test

◇   Putting on a tight pair of pants

◇   Replacing a light bulb

◇   Walking a dog

For two people:

◇   Two siblings fighting for the bathroom

◇   Racing to be first in the lunch line

◇   Reeling in the "big" fish

◇   Changing a flat tire

◇   Inventing the wheel

◇   Building a house of cards

◇   A first date

ACTIVITY #8 is a superior introductory tool and a highly effective activity for advanced actors. Try the activity with one or two actors per team. To form teams, have students draw a name from a hat, plan for one minute, then perform.

ACTIVITY #9—BACKWARD PANTOMIME

Perform scenes in "rewind" mode either with or without music. Starting fresh or using a previous scene, perform the scene backward, including facial expressions. You will do everything in their scene backward, including walking, stepping on and off of objects, expressing emotions facially before the event that inspires the facial expression, and working your way to the beginning of the scene. The order of events will be: ending, falling action (only in this case it is rising), climax, rising action (but because you are in rewind, it is falling), inciting incident, and exposition or beginning.

ACTIVITY #10—PANTODANCE

Start by studying Pantomime Activities 3, 4, or 5. The Pantodance will follow the same basic story structure, but unlike those activities in which the acting is more natural, a Pantodance is so **choreographed**—that is, each movement planned to happen on a certain beat of the music—that naturalness is replaced with precision and synchronization. At the same time, it is *not* a dance. At no point should you be using dance steps; all movement is exaggerated, rhythmic, synchronized pantomime.

A Pantodance with more than one actor should include some synchronized movement. One type of synchronization is "**perfect synchronization**," in which *two or more actors are doing the exact same thing for a sustained period of time*. Another type of synchronization, however, can be "**opposing synchronization**," such as "tug-of-war." This type of synchronized movement *forces actors to work together to create movement that appears to be "cause and effect."* One actor pulls the rope toward themself, and the other actor acts as though they are being pulled forward. Consequently, the second actor pulls harder, which forces the partner forward. Both types of movement are synchronized, but their actions are slightly different.

Again, the music used should be instrumental only. You want *your movement* to tell the story, not the lyrics. Each actor should give as many hints as to their character as early as possible, and all actors should assist in making the setting obvious—again, as early in the scene as possible.

ACTIVITY #10 is a cross between a pantomime and a dance in which each movement is performed so precisely to the beat of the music that it becomes fully choreographed while still managing to tell a story.

NOTES: ____

NAME ____ PERIOD _______ DATE _____________

PANTOMIME PLANNER

Time limit: __________   Due date:___________

Check all that apply:

| _______ No music | _______ Music with singing | _______ Instrumental music |
| _______ Set | _______ Costumes | _______ Props |

Which are you performing?

_______ Activity #2   –   Solo Scene
_______ Activity #3   –   Solo Scene Set to Music
_______ Activity #4   –   Duet Scene Set to Music
_______ Activity #5   –   Large Group Scene Set to Music
_______ Activity #6   –   Silent Film
_______ Activity #7   –   Pantorhythms
_______ Activity #8   –   Slow Motion Pantomime
_______ Activity #9   –   Backwards Pantomime
_______ Activity #10   –   Pantodance
_______ Other – ___________________________________

1. Music title (if applicable):
    ____

2. What is the scene about? _____________________________________
    ____
    ____

3. Where does the scene take place? _____________________________

4. List each character, starting with your own, and describe each character's goal.

Character	Goal

5. Describe each character in detail, starting with your own.

NOTES: ____

____

____

____

____

____

____

6. What are some things you can do as a silent actor to introduce your characterizations early in the scene?

7. What are some things you can do as a silent actor to let your audience know your setting early in your scene?

8. What is your inciting incident?

9. What is the first obstacle your character will face in pursuit of the chosen goal?

10. What strategy will your character use to overcome this obstacle? (The strategy should in some way relate to your character's personality.)

11. What is the second obstacle your character will face in pursuit of the chosen goal? (This obstacle should be different and slightly more intense than the first.)

     45

NOTES: ____

____

____

____

____

____

____

12. How will your character attempt to deal with this obstacle?

13. What is the final obstacle your character will face in pursuit of the chosen goal? (Again, this obstacle should be different than the first and second obstacles and should be of the greatest intensity. At this point the character either will or will not achieve the goal.)

14. What final strategy will your character use to try to overcome this last obstacle?

15. Now that the goal has or has not been reached, what must your character do to resolve the scene?

16. End your scene with a short, satisfying ending.* Describe it here.

*If you have a difficult time ending your scene the way you have written it, try starting with the ending and working your way back toward the beginning. It may mean changing some of your events, but it will probably result in a more solid scene and a more satisfying ending.

NOTES: ____

____

____

____

____

____

____

____

NAME _______________________________________ PERIOD _______ DATE _____________

PANTOMIME PERFORMANCE PEER EVALUATION

Evaluate each aspect of the actor's performance
on a scale of 1 (worst or not present) to 5 (best).

Group #	Actor's initials	1st impression	Setting introduced	Creativity	Facial expressions	Pantomime	Character	Creativity	Story/Plot	Timing/Music use	Movement	This actor was best at...	This actor could use a little more work on...

NOTES: ____

____

____

____

____

____

____

____

____

PANTOMIME PERFORMANCE RUBRIC

ACTORS:

____

____

____

____

____

1. The group made a good **first impression**, setting up in a timely manner and clearly understanding who would do what job and where each item was to be placed.

   1 2 3 4 5

2. The group used pantomime to clearly introduce a **setting**.

   1 2 3 4 5 6 7 8 9 10

3. The pantomime had well-planned, creative, synchronized, and organized **movement** that assisted in the telling of the story.

   1 2 3 4 5 6 7 8 9 10

4. The group was **creative** and original in their **story**, and the story was easy to follow.

   1 2 3 4 5 6 7 8 9 10

5. **Teamwork** was evident throughout the performance.

   1 2 3 4 5 6 7 8 9 10

6. The **plot** was constructed with an exposition, rising action, climax, falling action, and a satisfying ending.

   1 2 3 4 5 6 7 8 9 10

GROUP SCORE

Record the total group score from this page (out of a possible 55) in the box to the left. Transfer this to each actor's group score on the next page. Finish rating each individual's performance (out of a possible 45 points). Add any applicable bonus points. The total of the group, individual, and bonus points will give you a grade for that actor.

PANTOMIME PERFORMANCE RUBRIC, CONT.

Actor:

First Impression

1 2 3 4 5

Pantomime

1 2 3 4 5 6 7 8 9 10

Creativity

1 2 3 4 5

Timing/Use of music (if applicable)

1 2 3 4 5

Movement

1 2 3 4 5

Character

1 2 3 4 5 6 7 8 9 10

Facial expressions

1 2 3 4 5

Group Score	Individual Score	Bonus Points	TOTAL

Actor:

First Impression

1 2 3 4 5

Pantomime

1 2 3 4 5 6 7 8 9 10

Creativity

1 2 3 4 5

Timing/Use of music (if applicable)

1 2 3 4 5

Movement

1 2 3 4 5

Character

1 2 3 4 5 6 7 8 9 10

Facial expressions

1 2 3 4 5

Group Score	Individual Score	Bonus Points	TOTAL

Actor:

First Impression

1 2 3 4 5

Pantomime

1 2 3 4 5 6 7 8 9 10

Creativity

1 2 3 4 5

Timing/Use of music (if applicable)

1 2 3 4 5

Movement

1 2 3 4 5

Character

1 2 3 4 5 6 7 8 9 10

Facial expressions

1 2 3 4 5

Group Score	Individual Score	Bonus Points	TOTAL

Actor:

First Impression

1 2 3 4 5

Pantomime

1 2 3 4 5 6 7 8 9 10

Creativity

1 2 3 4 5

Timing/Use of music (if applicable)

1 2 3 4 5

Movement

1 2 3 4 5

Character

1 2 3 4 5 6 7 8 9 10

Facial expressions

1 2 3 4 5

Group Score	Individual Score	Bonus Points	TOTAL

Actor:

First Impression

1 2 3 4 5

Pantomime

1 2 3 4 5 6 7 8 9 10

Creativity

1 2 3 4 5

Timing/Use of music (if applicable)

1 2 3 4 5

Movement

1 2 3 4 5

Character

1 2 3 4 5 6 7 8 9 10

Facial expressions

1 2 3 4 5

Group Score	Individual Score	Bonus Points	TOTAL

Actor:

First Impression

1 2 3 4 5

Pantomime

1 2 3 4 5 6 7 8 9 10

Creativity

1 2 3 4 5

Timing/Use of music (if applicable)

1 2 3 4 5

Movement

1 2 3 4 5

Character

1 2 3 4 5 6 7 8 9 10

Facial expressions

1 2 3 4 5

Group Score	Individual Score	Bonus Points	TOTAL

CHAPTER 3
THEATRE FOR THE EARS

VOCABULARY

THE ARTISTIC VOICE

- ***Earth Day Public Service Announcement***
- ***Radio Commercial***
- ***Newscast***
- ***Cartoon Practice***
    - *Voice Self-Evaluation*
- ***Can You Karaoke?***
    - *Karaoke Performance Peer Evaluation*

RADIO AS THEATRE

- ***The History of Radio***
- ***Radio as Theatre***
- ***Sound Effects in Radio Theatre***
    - *Sound Effects Match-up*
- ***Produce Your Own "Old Time Radio" Show***
    - *Zombie High School*
    - *Radio Theatre Puzzle*
    - *Radio Theatre Extension Activities*

PODCASTS

- ***Opportunity for the Masses***
    - *Podcast Practice*
    - *Podcast Project*
    - *Podcast Practice Peer Evaluation*

ADDITIONAL NOTES

INTRODUCTION

THE ARTISTIC VOICE
- *Voice Self-Evaluation*

KARAOKE
- ***Additional Grading Options***
    - *Karaoke Performance Rubric*

ABOUT RADIO THEATRE
- *Sound Effects Match-up Key*
- *Radio Theatre Puzzle Key*
- *Podcast Production Rubric*

VOCABULARY

In this chapter, you will learn about:

Audibility: The ability to be heard.

Clarity: The quality of being easy to understand.

Confidence: Belief in one's self; in performance, confidence is "fearlessness."

Dialect: A regional accent.

Federal Communications Commission (or FCC): Government agency in charge of overseeing licensing and enforcing legislation regarding radio broadcasting in the U.S. and its possessions.

Habits: Distracting tendencies, such as shifting weight nervously or saying "um," that can be corrected with practice.

Inflection: A change in the pitch of one's voice.

Karaoke: A form of entertainment in which people sing popular songs into a microphone over prerecorded backing tracks.

Manual Sound Cues: Sound cues made using various contraptions and devices and that were made "live" during broadcast.

Networks: Groups of radio stations owned and run by the same company.

Old Time Radio: The term used to describe radio from its beginnings to the age of television, when radio was replaced by TV as the center of family entertainment.

Pitch: How high or low one's voice is.

Podcast: A digital file that can be downloaded and enjoyed at the convenience of the listener.

Pre-recorded Sound Cues: Sound cues played from CDs, tapes, or digital files.

Rate: How fast or slow one speaks.

Selling the Performance: The ability to fully engage the audience in the performance.

Sound Effects: Audio created to enhance a performance or used to indicate a bit of action, such as the sound of footsteps to indicate a person walking.

Tone: The sound of your voice.

51

INTRODUCTION

For this chapter, you will need as many recording devices as possible. Solicit help from your students, fellow teachers, parents, and neighbors. If your school allows, encourage students to use their smart phones, as most have voice recording applications. Laptops and tablets will also record voices if they have the right applications and/or software. Reasonably priced digital voice recorders are also available.

You may want to encourage students to bring earphones or earbuds. A splitter or Y cable will allow two earbuds to connect to the same device, which will be beneficial for duos. Your more technically advanced students may have microphones, mixers, amplifiers, and more. While you can certainly complete the activities low-tech, consider expanding the lesson to allow some student-led discussion and instruction, if it is within your lesson's boundaries.

THE ARTISTIC VOICE

There are many careers in theatre for actors with unique and flexible voices. You've been enjoying their talents for years on the radio and in cartoons, and they bring you valuable information daily in commercials and as the invisible personalities in public service announcements. While a great many of these actors make their living doing camera work, many are strictly voice artists whose faces are never seen. This is such easygoing, enjoyable work that famous actors also see the benefits. Today, cartoon movies are voiced by some of the most famous names in the business.

How flexible and unique is your voice? This lesson is not meant for you to decide if you have what it takes to do the job. Rather, it is meant to help you exercise your voice, to become familiar with its finer characteristics, and to become an expert at manipulating and changing it.

YOUR VOICE HAS CHARACTER

- **Audibility**: Can you be heard? Can you control how loud or soft your voice is for added effect?
- **Tone**: How pleasant is the sound of your voice?
- **Pitch**: How high or low is your voice, and how much control do you have over it?
- **Inflection**: Does your voice naturally change pitch in a pleasant and natural way when you speak? The opposite of nice, natural inflection would be a monotone or boring voice.
- **Dialect**: Does your voice have a strong dialect? If so, can you control it? Are you capable of pulling off other dialects? Are you able to speak with no dialect at all?
- **Clarity**: Are you easy to understand?
- **Rate**: Do you speak at a rate that is easy on listeners' ears? Can you manipulate that rate to draw interest?
- **Habits**: Are you free of bad vocal habits like dropping sounds—saying "se'en" instead of "seven" or "go'n" instead of "going"; adding sounds, such as saying "year-uh" instead of "year" or "cow-uh" instead of "cow"; or adding trash words like "um" and "uh"?

Is there anything about your voice that you don't like? The great thing about voices is they are fixable with practice.

Very few people like the way they sound when they first start hearing themself on recordings. They think they don't sound like themselves or they start noticing their bad habits or vocal issues. This is not a reason to stop performing! Instead, this is exactly why you should practice making your voice one you like to listen to.

Use the following activities to listen to and study your voice. Take notes about things you would like to change and practice making those adjustments. Never erase or delete your old recordings. Even after you have made improvements, save them to remind yourself how far you have come in your quest for an artistic voice.

THE ARTISTIC VOICE

There are three scripts provided for practice in *The Artistic Voice*. The Earth Day public service announcement is written for your students to be able to use on their school's public address system if desired. For optimum impact, you may want to plan this activity about two weeks before Earth Day, which is April 22. The radio commercial may also be used as a public service announcement by deleting references to Mike's Bikes. The last practice activity is a news report. Your students may also practice writing and saying their own news reports. Use events around your school and create a school news show.

Have students record themselves performing each script, listen to the recording, rate themselves on the *Voice Self-Evaluation*, and practice for improvement. There are seven opportunities to record, evaluate, and rate. They may also evaluate each other; when this is done, the evaluating student

EARTH DAY PUBLIC SERVICE ANNOUNCEMENT

April 22 is Earth Day, one day out of 365 each year when we celebrate the natural beauty of the world around us. What is it, and how did it come to be?

What ultimately came to be Earth Day started as a small seed in 1962 when Senator Gaylord Nelson, disappointed in the lack of political concern over the environment, convinced President John Kennedy to help bring the environment into the spotlight. In response, the president began a five-day, eleven-state conservation tour in September of 1963. While the tour was not the success both had hoped, it planted the seed that would one day grow into Earth Day.

Despite the popular president's efforts, evidence of environmental degradation was appearing everywhere, and everyone seemed aware of it except for the politicians. Senator Nelson realized what his idea needed was a grassroots campaign, similar to what he was witnessing in the Vietnam War protests on campuses across the US. He decided to tap into the students' anti-war energy and utilize it for his environmental cause. The politicians were noticing the anti-war protests; maybe they would finally notice the weakening state of the environment!

In 1969, Senator Nelson invited everyone to join him in a nationwide grassroots demonstration on behalf of the environment that would launch the following spring. Finally, American environmentalists had a voice! They were able to talk about what was happening to the land, rivers, lakes, and air, and the politicians were starting to listen. Earth Day was about to blossom!

And blossom it did! As the first official Earth Day neared in 1970, the entire campaign was forced to relocate when it became apparent it had outgrown its founder's original vision. The environment was now at the forefront of the political agenda. Senator Nelson had achieved his dream.

This year we celebrate the ___________* Earth Day on April 22. Join us in pledging to do more than our part to make the Earth—our Earth—a better place to live.

(To fill in the blank, the first Earth Day was in 1970.)

RADIO COMMERCIAL

CHRIS: Mom! *(Or Dad, if actor is male)* I'm going outside to ride bikes.

PARENT: Wear your helmet.

CHRIS: I always do. *(Door slams, and children can be heard playing outside.)*

NEIGHBOR: I wish I could get Rendon to wear his helmet, but he won't. He says it looks dorky.

PARENT: It's not a fashion statement. It's there for protection.

NEIGHBOR: I know. You know how boys are.

PARENT: You're my best friend, so please don't take this the wrong way— you're the parent here! Chris doesn't get a choice. If he doesn't wear his helmet, we give the bike away. That's all there is to it.

NEIGHBOR: But he says the helmet is uncomfortable.

PARENT: Yeah. You're right. A little brain damage would feel so much better!

NEIGHBOR: Wow. That's a little harsh.

PARENT: You want to hear harsh? About five hundred people die each year from bike crashes, forty percent of them kids Rendon's age and younger! About eighty-five percent of those deaths could have been prevented with a good helmet.

NEIGHBOR: You're right. I'll make him start wearing one.

PARENT: Not just Rendon. I've seen you riding bikes with him. If you don't show him you're willing to do it, he'll never take you seriously.

NEIGHBOR: I don't even go that fast!

53

---

should record their initials next to the number at the top of the column. Each card should be used for only one type and piece of copy. If students will be practicing with all three pieces, they will need extra copies of the *Voice Self-Evaluation*.

Your students will also have fun playing the dubbing game for practicing cartoon voices. Rarely is a teacher able to work cartoons into the curriculum, but this is a lucrative theatre-related business that could be a career option for your vocally gifted students.

With the popularity and ease of new voice recording technology, all of these voice-related careers are available to actors whether they live near a major acting hub or not. Many are finding that they can cash in on the voice-over industry from their homes, regardless of their location.

PARENT: Even a low-speed fall can result in serious brain damage or even death.

RENDON: Can I go outside and ride bikes with Chris?

NEIGHBOR: Only if you wear your helmet.

RENDON: But—

NEIGHBOR: No helmet, no bike.

RENDON: No problem. *(Door slams.)*

NEIGHBOR: That was easy.

PARENT: Now for the hard part.

NEIGHBOR: What's that?

PARENT: Where's your helmet? *(Both laugh.)*

ANNOUNCER: May is Bicycle Safety Month. No helmet, no bike! No problem. Brought to you by Mike's Bikes, Lennay County's busiest bike shop with the largest selection of safe—and fashionable—bicycle helmets. 1010 West Blue Ridge Trail. Like bikes? See Mike!

NEWSCAST

Good evening. I'm _______________________, and this is your six o'clock update. If you were at Town Hall today, you were probably seeing spots! That's right, spots. Don't worry. There's probably nothing wrong with your eyes. The spots were the efforts of one college student to raise money for a local dog shelter. Twenty-two-year-old law student Lindsie Clowe discovered a shivering, hungry puppy on her doorstep last week. Her campus apartment would not allow her to keep the starving dog, so she took it to the See Spot Run Dog Shelter in neighboring Jenny County. See Spot Run is the only no-kill shelter in the region, and it relies entirely on donations to stay afloat. Over the years, contributions have been sluggish, and complaints about safety prompted a city inspection. The city found numerous code violations and gave the organization one week to fix the problems or close shop. The shelter had to turn the tiny pup away. Afraid of what would happen to Baby Stephanie at any of the other shelters, Clowe and her fellow law students stepped in. They sold paper spots around town for a dollar apiece, placing donor's names on each. Today, Clowe and her entourage of helpers decorated Town Hall with over twenty-five-hundred spots and presented the See Spot Run Dog Shelter with a check *(Pause.)* and a brighter future. If you are interested in adopting Stephanie or any of the other dogs at See Spot Run, you will find a link to the shelter on our webpage. Now for the weather...

CARTOON PRACTICE

A fun way to practice cartoon and other character voices is by experimentation with a game called "Dubbing." Gather several videos or DVDs of cartoons. Play the cartoons without any sound, and with some fellow actors, add in your own dialogue using cartoon voices. You can practice mimicking the characters' original voices or make your own. Enjoy the humor of the spontaneous dialogue that usually has nothing to do with the cartoon's actual plot, and hear your voice begin to take on a new flexibility.

NOTES: ____

Also appears as page 55 of the Student Workbook

NAME ____ PERIOD _________ DATE _____________

VOICE SELF-EVALUATION

Practice reading the script assigned to you. Then record yourself, listen to the recording, and rate yourself by circling 1 (worst or not present) through 5 (best) in the first column, noting anything needing special attention. Continue practicing, recording, and evaluation yourself until you achieve the desired effect.

Script: ____

	1 Date: _____	2 Date: _____	3 Date: _____	4 Date: _____	5 Date: _____	6 Date: _____	7 Date: _____
Audibility: My voice can be heard at all times, and I manipulate my volume for added effect.	1 2 3 4 5	1 2 3 4 5	1 2 3 4 5	1 2 3 4 5	1 2 3 4 5	1 2 3 4 5	1 2 3 4 5
Tone: My voice is pleasant sounding.	1 2 3 4 5	1 2 3 4 5	1 2 3 4 5	1 2 3 4 5	1 2 3 4 5	1 2 3 4 5	1 2 3 4 5
Pitch: My voice overall is neither too high nor too low in pitch.	1 2 3 4 5	1 2 3 4 5	1 2 3 4 5	1 2 3 4 5	1 2 3 4 5	1 2 3 4 5	1 2 3 4 5
Inflection: Changes in pitch are present but unnoticeable because they sound natural.	1 2 3 4 5	1 2 3 4 5	1 2 3 4 5	1 2 3 4 5	1 2 3 4 5	1 2 3 4 5	1 2 3 4 5
Absence of Noticeable Dialect: I can speak "neutrally" without my normal accent.	1 2 3 4 5	1 2 3 4 5	1 2 3 4 5	1 2 3 4 5	1 2 3 4 5	1 2 3 4 5	1 2 3 4 5
Dialect Mastery: I can convincingly sound as if I'm from a particular place.	1 2 3 4 5	1 2 3 4 5	1 2 3 4 5	1 2 3 4 5	1 2 3 4 5	1 2 3 4 5	1 2 3 4 5
Clarity: My speech is clear and easily understood.	1 2 3 4 5	1 2 3 4 5	1 2 3 4 5	1 2 3 4 5	1 2 3 4 5	1 2 3 4 5	1 2 3 4 5
Rate: I can control and manipulate my speaking pace and use pauses effectively.	1 2 3 4 5	1 2 3 4 5	1 2 3 4 5	1 2 3 4 5	1 2 3 4 5	1 2 3 4 5	1 2 3 4 5
Habits: These are tendencies I need to control or manipulate so they don't distract.							

KARAOKE

Karaoke has become extremely popular, and it's no wonder. There's a little rock star in all of us, but for actors, the stage and spotlight are a natural. Add a microphone to the mix, and you have an instant show off!

Can You Karaoke? is just a fancy way of getting your kids to perform using their voices. And while you may use a basic karaoke machine, there are websites and applications that turn any computer or cell phone into a portable party machine. The instrumental tracks from your previous musical might also do the trick and shouldn't involve royalties as long as this is limited to a class project and not a public performance.

This project is very similar to the lip-sync project, except that students will focus on actual voiced singing and not on the sets, props, costumes, etc. For a bigger project, consider combining the two and encouraging students to add those visual theatrical elements to their karaoke performance. Other options include permitting students to sing backup if they would feel more comfortable with their voices blended among others or allowing students to be dancers rather than singers.

Other important things to remember:

- Create interesting stage pictures. Because it is musical theatre, you can be "larger than life."
- Stage your performance so that no one is upstaged.
- Be creative and original. If you are going to use gimmicks, they should be appropriate to the song, the musical or selection, and the characters.
- Be original in your characterizations, too!
- Make the audience feel involved and special, almost as though your performance was intended especially for each audience member.

Additional information:

- ☐ Students will provide their own music by (date) _______________.
- ☐ Teacher will provide music.
- ☐ Students must provide the CD player, karaoke machine, MP3 player, or other device to play their music by (date) _______________.
- ☐ Teacher will provide players or other devices to play music.
- ☐ Teacher must see lyrics by (date) _______________. (Teacher approval:_______________)

GROUP MEMBER	WILL BRING	CONTACT INFO

ADDITIONAL GRADING OPTIONS

- Rehearsal Grade: having all materials, staying on task, and being respectful of others who are trying to work.

- Lyrics and Music Grade: having lyrics approved by teacher by deadline; treating music responsibly including upkeep and accessibility at each rehearsal and properly storing music device after rehearsal.

- Set Grade: bringing what they committed to bring and assisting with the completion of the set.

- Worksheet Grade: completing this sheet and returning it after all groups have performed.

- Audience Grade: being a respectful, quiet, supportive member of the audience during all performances.

INTRODUCTION TO THEATRE ARTS 2

NAME ____ PERIOD _______ DATE _____________

KARAOKE PERFORMANCE PEER EVALUATION

Evaluate each aspect of the "singer's" performance
on a scale of 1 (worst or not present) to 5 (best).

Group #	Performer's initials	1st impression	Confidence/ Selling the song	Creativity	Facial expressions	Movement/Dance	Character	Props/Pantomime	Costume/ Appearance	Set	Teamwork/ Preparation	This performer was best at...	This performer could use a little more work on...

As with all projects in this book, a rubric is provided for you, and a peer performance evaluation is provided for your students. After all performances are completed and grades are recorded, cut the evaluators' names off the top of the peer evaluations. Place your class in a large circle and have them read the comments made about them on each evaluation. After they have read each one, they will pass it to the right. This is also a great time to return the evaluation you completed. Then use a *Self-Improvement Plan*, like the one on page 101, to encourage students to think of ways to apply what their peer evaluators had to say to future performances.

KARAOKE PERFORMANCE RUBRIC

PERFORMERS:

____

____

____

____

____

SONG TITLE:

____

1. The group made a good **first impression**, setting up in a timely manner and clearly understanding who would do what job and where each item would be placed.

   1 2 3 4 5

2. The group was **creative** and original in their performance.

   1 2 3 4 5

3. The group moved in a way that helped sell the song and fit the selection. **Movement** and **choreography** appropriately fit the selection.

   1 2 3 4 5

4. The **set** was appropriate to the performance, added to the audience's entertainment or understanding, and when needed offered the performers a "backstage."

   1 2 3 4 5 6 7 8 9 10

5. The team had appropriate **props** throughout or was able to justify using pantomime throughout, and did so effectively.

   1 2 3 4 5 6 7 8 9 10

6. **Teamwork** was evident in the way actors interacted in rehearsals, during their performance, and after the performance. Voices and movements were synchronized when appropriate, and actors appeared well-rehearsed.

   1 2 3 4 5 6 7 8 9 10

GROUP SCORE

Record the total group score from this page (out of a possible 45) in the box to the left. Transfer this to each performer's group score on the next page. Finish rating each individual's performance (out of a possible 55 points). Add any applicable bonus points. The total of the group, individual, and bonus points will give you a grade for that performer.

KARAOKE PERFORMANCE RUBRIC, CONT.

Performer:

First impression

1 2 3 4 5

Confidence

1 2 3 4 5 6 7 8 9 10

Creativity

1 2 3 4 5

Facial expressions

1 2 3 4 5 6 7 8 9 10

Movement/Dance

1 2 3 4 5

Character

1 2 3 4 5 6 7 8 9 10

Costume

1 2 3 4 5 6 7 8 9 10

Group Score	Individual Score	Bonus Points	TOTAL

Performer:

First impression

1 2 3 4 5

Confidence

1 2 3 4 5 6 7 8 9 10

Creativity

1 2 3 4 5

Facial expressions

1 2 3 4 5 6 7 8 9 10

Movement/Dance

1 2 3 4 5

Character

1 2 3 4 5 6 7 8 9 10

Costume

1 2 3 4 5 6 7 8 9 10

Group Score	Individual Score	Bonus Points	TOTAL

Performer:

First impression

1 2 3 4 5

Confidence

1 2 3 4 5 6 7 8 9 10

Creativity

1 2 3 4 5

Facial expressions

1 2 3 4 5 6 7 8 9 10

Movement/Dance

1 2 3 4 5

Character

1 2 3 4 5 6 7 8 9 10

Costume

1 2 3 4 5 6 7 8 9 10

Group Score	Individual Score	Bonus Points	TOTAL

Performer:

First impression

1 2 3 4 5

Confidence

1 2 3 4 5 6 7 8 9 10

Creativity

1 2 3 4 5

Facial expressions

1 2 3 4 5 6 7 8 9 10

Movement/Dance

1 2 3 4 5

Character

1 2 3 4 5 6 7 8 9 10

Costume

1 2 3 4 5 6 7 8 9 10

Group Score	Individual Score	Bonus Points	TOTAL

Performer:

First impression

1 2 3 4 5

Confidence

1 2 3 4 5 6 7 8 9 10

Creativity

1 2 3 4 5

Facial expressions

1 2 3 4 5 6 7 8 9 10

Movement/Dance

1 2 3 4 5

Character

1 2 3 4 5 6 7 8 9 10

Costume

1 2 3 4 5 6 7 8 9 10

Group Score	Individual Score	Bonus Points	TOTAL

Performer:

First impression

1 2 3 4 5

Confidence

1 2 3 4 5 6 7 8 9 10

Creativity

1 2 3 4 5

Facial expressions

1 2 3 4 5 6 7 8 9 10

Movement/Dance

1 2 3 4 5

Character

1 2 3 4 5 6 7 8 9 10

Costume

1 2 3 4 5 6 7 8 9 10

Group Score	Individual Score	Bonus Points	TOTAL

RADIO AS THEATRE

THE HISTORY OF RADIO

Today, entertainment almost always means watching something. Perhaps you and your friends like watching movies or music videos, watching sports, or just watching television. Sure, you listen to these things, too, but for the most part, unless our eyes are busy doing something else, like driving, we are a society of watchers when it comes to being entertained.

THIS UNIT WILL...

- Introduce a form of family entertainment common in your great-grandparents' time but rare today.

- Help you understand the origin of radio theatre and how it has changed throughout the years.

- Promote an appreciation for acting and writing for audiences who can hear but cannot see the action.

- Guide you in understanding the fundamentals of radio as a business, radio commercials, and Old Time Radio vocabulary.

- Introduce the fundamentals of the art of **sound effects**.

- Encourage teamwork.

- Allow you to experience a rare form of theatre firsthand.

Before television, movies, and certainly before music videos, people entertained themselves in different ways than they do today. Families attended sporting events together, and if they didn't have time or money to go see a professional team, they would watch local or traveling teams. They attended the theatre, eagerly lapped up the drama, music, and gospel in the Sunday sermon, and enjoyed stories. While some preferred reading, others liked to sit back and listen. Grandparents would recount tales of their younger years. Parents instilled moral values with entertaining stories about staying out of trouble. And young people made campfires and scared one another with tales of ghosts, escaped convicts, or haunted mansions.

When radio emerged in the early 1920s, entertainment changed. Suddenly families could enjoy the big game from the comfort of their own homes. Days were planned around radio schedules. The radio's importance in the home was sealed.

It did not take long for the little box to grow into a huge phenomenon. There was a little something for everyone. In 1920, Warren G. Harding was announced as the winner of the presidential election on Pittsburgh's KDKA. Months later, the same listening audience also enjoyed the first religious broadcast: KDKA aired the Calvary Episcopal Church's Sunday service. In 1921, the famous Dempsey-Carpentier fight was broadcast "wirelessly" by radio phone, making it the first sporting event to make it to the airwaves. Record dealers and sheet music companies began "sampling" their music on the air followed by purchasing information.

Before long, listeners were enjoying radio shows, musical events, and news bulletins, but they also had to pay the price by listening to commercials. As a matter of fact, most radio stations were owned by companies seeking to promote their products. There is some debate about the first radio commercial, but most agree it was a five-day broadcast for a real estate company at a cost of about fifty dollars. Others claim ownership of the "first" radio commercial, but their claims cannot be verified.

By 1922, five hundred stations were licensed to broadcast to over two million radios in American homes. In 1926, NBC (the National Broadcast Company) was formed alongside a second network, RCA (Radio Corporation of America). **Networks** allowed stations to work together to broadcast shows simultaneously in various parts of the country. Within two years, CBS (Columbia Broadcasting System) started a radio network as well, and the golden age of radio began.

59

ABOUT RADIO THEATRE

Some students might be familiar with the old-time radio shows, but even they might not realize the impact radio had on families before television. Because it was such an important part of the entertainment industry in America and abroad, and because of a renewed popularity, this chapter will end with an in-depth view of "Radio as Theatre."

A sample script, *Zombie High School,* is included that will allow your students to experience radio theatre and sound effects. Consider allowing your most advanced class to prepare the show as a live radio theatre program and present it to your school or to select classes as a Halloween project or an opening act to your fall show.

As the business of radio grew, it was only natural that the government would have to become involved. In 1934, the **Federal Communications Commission**, or **FCC**, was formed to *oversee licensing and enforce legislation regarding radio broadcasting*. The commission is still busy today regulating interstate and international communications by radio, television, wire, satellite, and cable. Its jurisdiction covers all fifty states, the District of Columbia, and all U.S. territories.

By 1945 and the end of World War II, most homes in America (about ninety-five percent) had at least one radio. However, as television became more popular in the early 1950s, radio began to lose its appeal as the center of family entertainment, although it did remain an important part of American family entertainment. The era of **Old Time Radio**, or OTR, ended in 1962 as *Suspense* and *Yours Truly, Johnny Dollar* aired their final radio broadcasts. CBS attempted to revive OTR with *Radio Mystery Theater* from 1974 to 1982, but it could not compete with the lure of television.

WHY DO RADIO STATIONS HAVE COMMERCIALS?

Over-the-air radio is free for listeners, but it costs a great deal of money to run a station. Stations sell commercial time slots so that radio stations' listeners can hear about various products and services. In turn, those listeners get to listen to free music, news, or talk shows. Those same listeners purchase the products from the advertisements, and then the company buys more airtime from the radio station. It's a cycle.

A great deal of thought is put into when and where to air certain products. Is 11:30 a.m. on a Tuesday in October a good day to advertise a product that appeals mainly to young teens? Think about your radio listening schedule and the products you hear advertised. Is there any connection?

program director of WGY, and in September of 1922, *The Wolf*, an adaptation of Eugene Walter's stage play, was aired. It was cut down to forty minutes so as not to test the attention limitations of listeners, and it featured Smith's fellow actors and actresses from his theatre company. It was so successful that the theatre company received fan mail from over five hundred miles away! Smith's company of actors continued to perform radio show adaptations of famous plays and was very successful throughout the rest of the decade.

Perhaps the most famous radio series was *Amos 'n' Andy*. Having been previously known as *Sam 'n' Henry*, it became *Amos 'n' Andy* in 1928 when it was picked up by NBC. The program's success kept it on the air until 1960, making it the longest-running radio show in history.

The single most famous radio drama, however, is probably the 1938 airing of Orson Welles' *The War of the Worlds*. Written to simulate a dance program, actors playing newscasters would break in with information about a Martian attack. Some listeners reported that it sounded so real they believed it, despite a number of reminders to the audience that the story was fiction. There were reports of police stations, hospitals, churches, and phone lines seeing the effect of frightened audience members who were overcome by the realistic-sounding drama.

Today, fans of Old Time Radio can go online to listen to shows our great-grandparents enjoyed. Perhaps the most famous is *A Prairie Home Companion*. Originally broadcast in 1969 to a live audience of just twelve people, the program quickly grew in popularity and only ended well into the 21st century. Its variety-show format with unique musical guests and commercials for fictitious products captivated audiences. The commercials were a large part of the entertainment, but the show was actually sponsored by real companies.

RADIO AS THEATRE

Radio has many connections to theatre. Many disc jockeys and other radio personalities started as actors or have a history in theatre. For those who discover that their talent lies in their voices, radio is a natural career move. Additionally, the airwaves are thick with commercials, which are another type of theatre. Actors take on characters who sell the products or ideas to listeners. Most young people, however, have little experience with actual radio theatre.

In the early 1920s, as America was getting its first taste of radio, an actor by the name of Edward H. Smith of The Masque, a theatre company in New York, had the idea of adapting some popular plays into radio dramas. He pitched his idea to Kolin Hager,

NOTES: ____

____

____

____

____

____

____

____

CHAPTER 3 — THEATRE FOR THE EARS

SOUND EFFECTS IN RADIO THEATRE

Today, there is a growing trend toward performing non-broadcast radio theatre plays in front of live audiences. These shows look, sound, and are even produced just like Old Time Radio, but they are not for the radio. One of the appeals of being in the live audience at these "radio" shows is watching the sound effects person perform their cues. While real Old Time Radio eventually used a combination of **pre-recorded sound cues** and **manual sound cues** *performed live using a variety of props and machines*, the allure of the non-broadcast shows lies in watching the sound person "perform." After all, seeing the sound person push a button on an electronic device wouldn't be nearly as interesting.

Besides captivating storylines, one of the things that allowed early radio listeners to become "caught up" in radio drama was the subtle layering of sound effects. In its infancy, before competition increased the need for realism, crudely created sounds were acceptable. At that point in radio history, few entertainers received pay for their time on the air, and most sound people (mostly men) worked for free hoping to work their way into paying positions. However, as more and more radio shows emerged, each one bringing with it higher standards, the demand for captivating sound also grew. Unfortunately, it would be many years before the industry began fully integrating trained and specialized sound personnel into their network broadcasting.

Sound effects historian Jack French of Fairfax, Virginia, says sounds in a radio drama or comedy fall basically into one of two layers. The top layer consists of those sounds that keep the storyline moving along. Behind those primarily important sounds is the second layer—background and mood setting sounds. All of the sounds in both layers are either produced manually or pre-recorded. The recorded sounds have become more and more popular due to the ever-growing amount of props needed to make manual sounds. It is easier to play a storm from a pre-recorded track than to store the giant wind and rain machines needed to make the sound live in the studio.

SOUND EFFECTS MATCH-UP

Match the effects on the right with the action that makes them on the left.

1. Twisting cellophane or plastic grocery bags
2. Squeezing a box of cornstarch
3. Blowing air through a straw into a tub of water
4. Rubbing ice skate blades against each other
5. Quickly snapping open an umbrella
6. Pulling wet cork from bottle then popping a balloon
7. Squeezing folded, unused sandpaper
8. Squirting water into a pail from distance
9. Shaking BBs in a stapled paper cup
10. Twisting a new leather wallet near the microphone
11. Shaking a chain against a piece of leather
12. Hitting a piece of plywood with two coconut halves alternately

______ Rattlesnake
______ Footsteps in the snow
______ Sudden ignition of a fire
______ Crackling fire
______ Water boiling
______ Sword fight
______ Milking a cow
______ Opening a bottle of champagne
______ Running horse
______ Breaking eggs
______ Getting out of a saddle
______ Horse harness

SOUND EFFECTS MATCH-UP KEY

1.	Crackling fire	7.	Breaking eggs
2.	Footsteps in the snow	8.	Milking a cow
3.	Water boiling	9.	Rattlesnake
4.	Sword fight	10.	Getting out of a saddle
5.	Sudden ignition of a fire	11.	Horse harness
6.	Opening a bottle of champagne	12.	Running horse

PRODUCE YOUR OWN "OLD TIME RADIO" SHOW

Read the following script, inserting as many sound effects as you can. Some have been suggested for you.

ZOMBIE HIGH SCHOOL

Radio Theatre Script by Suzi Zimmerman

CAST OF CHARACTERS

LAUREN	COACH
KRISTEN	BOY 1
MARC	BOY 2
MRS. ANDERSON	BOY 3
CODY	GIRL
LEILA	MS. TUCKER

LAUREN: *(School sounds; the GIRLS are at their lockers; a thunderstorm rages in the background.)* Kristen, I'm so excited about the social tonight. You are going, right?

KRISTEN: I don't know. I have so much work left on the science fair. I really need to finish. Besides, this storm has me a little spooked. *(The bell rings.)* Oh, great! *(A locker closes.)* I can't believe I'm late again. Mrs. Anderson is going to kill me! *(Running footsteps.)*

LAUREN: Think about it! Hey, watch—*(An "oof" sound is heard as KRISTEN runs into MARC; books fall to the floor.)* Oh, Marc, I'm so sorry. I wasn't watch—

MARC: Hey, no problem, Kristen. You okay?

KRISTEN: *(Rustling papers.)* Yeah, I just—

MARC: Kristen, you're bleeding.

KRISTEN: It's nothing. I just bit my lip. *(Laughs.)* Flesh wound!

MRS. ANDERSON: *(A door opens.)* Kristen, you're late again. Hello, Marc.

MARC: Hi, Mrs. Anderson. I wasn't watching where I was going and I ran into her. She's hurt.

LAUREN: *(Approaching footsteps.)* Kristen, you okay? He's captain of the debate team, not the football team. You'll break him trying to tackle him like that! *(ALL laugh.)*

MRS. ANDERSON: Marc, you go on to class. Tell Mrs. Craig not to use the lab today. We still have a little cleanup to do from our star tackle's science experiment yesterday.

MARC: Yes, Ma'am. See you, Kristen. Hope you're okay.

KRISTEN: Bye, Marc. *(Fading footsteps as MARC leaves.)* Mrs. Anderson, about yesterday… I'm so sorry. I haven't been getting much sleep lately with the science fair and the speech tournament coming up. I guess I kind of dozed off.

MRS. ANDERSON: I'm just glad you and the others are okay. I may never get rid of the smell, though! It was like something crawled in the vents and died! *(Loud clap of thunder.)* Whew! I guess I'm a little on edge, still. Lauren, take Kristen to get some ice for that lip. Here are some passes. *(Paper sound.)* See you both tonight, right?

KRISTEN: *(Mumbles, half-dazed.)* Yeah.

LAUREN: *(Two pairs of slow footsteps as GIRLS walk down the hall.)* So you're going to go? I'm so glad. What made you change your mind?

KRISTEN: What? I, uh—I don't know. Maybe I've been focusing on school too much lately.

LAUREN: I think that little bump knocked some sense into you! Speaking of Marc…

KRISTEN: Oh, don't start!

LAUREN: Wear that new sun dress. And don't be late. Here we are. You get some ice, and I'll see you at the social.

NOTES: __________________________

____

____

____

____

____

____

____

KRISTEN: See you. (*Music to indicate scene change: the social.*)

CODY: (*"Oof" sound.*) Hey! Watch it, loser! You almost spilled my drink. (*Slurps.*)

BOY 1: There's no need to be rude. It was an accident. No harm done, right?

CODY: Not yet, loser. (*Fist to palm noise.*)

MARC: Lay off him, Cody.

CODY: I was just trying to teach him a lesson. Whoa! Who's that?

MARC: Wow! Hey, Kristen!

KRISTEN: (*Her voice is slightly sultry and she is obviously distracted.*) 'Lo, Cody. Beat up any sixth graders today?

CODY: No. You look pretty.

KRISTEN: Marc… You look very nice. Very.

MARC: Thanks. You look… amazing! You're different somehow!

LEILA: Hi, Cody. Want to dance?

CODY: I, uh—sure. See you, Kristen. Maybe you can save me a dance later.

KRISTEN: (*Ignores CODY.*) I'm glad you like my new look, Marc. It's like I've got a whole new attitude. I don't know. I think school had taken over my life. When we bumped into each other in the hall today, it was like you dislodged something that had gotten stuck in my brain.

LAUREN: Hey, you two! Kristen, I just talked to Ms. Tucker, and she—

KRISTEN: Not that. Not now. It's not up for discussion.

LAUREN: But you've always—

KRISTEN: I'm going to grab a bite to eat.

MARC: I'll come with you.

KRISTEN: No! Stay with Lauren. I have something I want to do.

LAUREN: Did you know she dropped out of the tournament?

MARC: What? You're joking.

LAUREN: No. I just ran into Ms. Tucker. She said Kristen came to her after going to the nurse and dropped out. She said she dropped out of science fair too. Just like that. (*Snaps her fingers.*)

MARC: That's not like Kristen. (*LEILA screams.*)

LAUREN: What in the world?

MARC: Freshmen! They always have to spoil—

LEILA: He's dead! Cody's dead! (*Music stops; the crowd noise begins to grow.*)

MRS. ANDERSON: (*Quick footsteps.*) Ladies. Gentlemen. Everyone just calm down. Leila, what's going on?

LEILA: We were out in the hall. He went around the corner to the water fountain, but I heard a noise. I saw someone running—or stumbling—and there was Cody. There was so much blood! (*Crowd noise in response to "blood"—gasps, exclamations.*)

COACH: Everyone stay put. I'll check it out.

BOY 2: I'll go with you, Coach.

BOY 3: Me too. (*Three sets of footsteps leaving.*)

MRS. ANDERSON: Leila, are you sure?

LEILA: I wouldn't lie about something like this. She killed him! She—

LAUREN: She? It was a girl?

KRISTEN: (*Calm.*) Hey, what's all the excitement?

LAUREN: Something happened to Cody.

LEILA: He's dead!

  63

NOTES: ______________________________

KRISTEN: *(Unemotional.)* Gee, that's too bad. Maybe someone got tired of his bullying… his constant, annoying, irritating bullying.

MRS. ANDERSON: Kristen! Listen, everyone. I don't know what's going on or what kind of prank this is, but it needs to stop. Now!

KRISTEN: Ms. Anderson. It isn't a prank.

LAUREN: What are you talking about, Kristen?

BOY 1: She's right. You had all better take this very seriously. *(Some monstrous moans from the crowd, they start low and build as the scene progresses.)*

GIRL: There's blood on her hands!

MARC: And on his!

LAUREN: What's happening? Why does everyone have blood all over them? *(Slow, rhythmic footsteps approaching.)* Mrs. Anderson, Ms. Tucker, help!

MS. TUCKER: No one can help you now.

BOY 1: Don't worry. It won't hurt.

KRISTEN: We just need one little drop of your blood, then you can be one of us!

MARC: Get away fr— Lauren, get behind me! *(Rustling sounds.)*

LAUREN: Kristen, don't. Oh, Cody! Thank God, you're okay!

MARC: Cody! *(Sound of heavy footsteps approaching.)*

KRISTEN: Hello, Cody, dear. You're looking very dead.

LEILA: Cody, what happened back there?

KRISTEN: Yes, Cody. Tell Leila all about it. She's scared.

CODY: Just be still. If you run like me, it'll hurt. *(LEILA screams, but it is cut short.)*

KRISTEN: *(There is a struggle, and MARC is overcome; he screams, but it is cut short.)* There, Marc. That wasn't so bad, was it?

LAUREN: No, Marc! Please, Kristen, don't! No… no… no…

KRISTEN: Lauren! Wake up. Lauren! You're having a nightmare.

LAUREN: *(Catches breath.)* Oh, my gosh. It was horrible. We were at the dance, and you and all the others were zombies, and you were trying to kill us. Thank goodness, it was just a dream!

KRISTEN: Or was it? *(Sounds of zombies and LAUREN screaming; scary music.)*

NOTES: ____

____

____

____

____

____

____

____

NAME _______________________________________ PERIOD _______ DATE _____________

RADIO THEATRE PUZZLE

Answer each question, then place the letters and spaces that appear in parentheses following the correct answer into the puzzle grid under the question's corresponding number. If you have correctly answered each question, you should see *New York Times* headline that followed a very famous radio broadcast.

2.	4.	9.	1.	5.
3.	6.	10.	14.	12.

16.	13.	8.	15.	11.	7.

October 31, 1938 Late City Edition, *The New York Times*

RADIO THEATRE PUZZLE KEY

Radio Listeners in Panic, Taking War Drama as Fact

Many Flee Homes to Escape 'Raid from Mars'

Phone Calls Swamp Police at Broadcast of Welles Fantasy

Name the famous broadcast to which the article refers:_________________________________

1. Even though the radio was invented many years earlier, its popularity soared in the _________.

   a. 1920s (king War D)
   b. 1930s (as Raid Fr)
   c. 1940s (rama as Fact)

2. In 1920, _________________ was announced as the new president, the first major use of the radio as a means of bringing newsworthy political information to the public.

   a. Franklin D. Roosevelt (f Welles Fantasy)
   b. Warren G. Harding (Radio List)
   c. Calvin Coolidge (o Escape 'G)

3. For which of the following was radio not used in the early 1920s?

   a. church services (e 'G)
   b. to announce traffic problems (Many Fl)
   c. to sell sheet music and records (pe Gas R)
   d. to broadcast sporting events (Is S)

4. Even though most radio shows were owned by large companies as a means of promoting their own products, it did not take long to discover that there was a profitable market for _________________. These allowed companies (perhaps those who could not afford an entire radio show) to sell their products, introduced consumers to goods and services, and allowed shows to bring music, theatre. and other forms of entertainment and news to their listening audiences.

   a. commercials (eners in P)
   b. networks (Phone Calls)
   c. the FCC (road)

1. a	9. b
2. b	10. c
3. b	11. b
4. a	12. a
5. a	13. a
6. c	14. b
7. a	15. c
8. b	16. a

     65

5. By 1922, __________ stations were licensed to broadcast to the over two million radios in American homes.

   a. 500 (rama as Fact)
   b. 622 (king War D)
   c. 917 (o Escape 'G)

6. By the end of World War II, about __________ of American homes had at least one radio.
   a. 50% (eners in P)
   b. 75% (Many Fle)
   c. 95% (ee Homes)

7. __________________ allowed stations to work together to broadcast shows in various parts of the country simultaneously.

   a. Networks (Welles Fantasy)
   b. Trusts (f Wel)
   c. Teamwork (ls Fa)

8. The Federal Communications Commission was formed in 1934 to __________________.

   a. investigate panic created by *The War of the Worlds* broadcast (Many Fle)
   b. oversee licensing and enforce legislation regarding radio broadcasting (Police at B)
   c. explore the possibilities of broadcasting across the nation's borders (as Raid Fr)

9. Radio lost its position as the center of family entertainment due to the popularity of __________________ in the early 1950s.

   a. film (Radio List)
   b. television (anic, Ta)
   c. rock 'n' roll (e Homes t)

10. The era known as __________________ ended in 1962.

    a. The Golden Age (road)
    b. Radio Across America (o Es)
    c. Old Time Radio (to Es)

11. Radio theatre probably owes its birth to an actor by the name of __________________ of The Masque, a theatre company in New York. In September 1922, he and his colleagues produced *The Wolf*, an adaptation of Eugene Walter's stage play, and they remained successful throughout the remainder of the 1920s.

    a. Jack French (pe 'Gas R)
    b. Edward H. Smith (cast of)
    c. Orson Welles (om Mars')

12. The longest-running and one of the most famous radio series was __________________, which ran from 1928 to 1960.

    a. *Amos 'n' Andy* (aid from Mars')
    b. *The War of the Worlds* (o Escape 'Gas R)
    c. *The Lone Ranger* (Phone Calls)

NOTES: ____

____

____

____

____

____

____

____

13. The 1938 airing of Orson Welles' _______________ may be the most famous radio show despite the fact that the broadcast itself was not a series. It earned its position in history because its news-style format and alien attack storyline frightened some listeners who thought it was real.

    a. *The War of the Worlds* (Swamp)
    b. *Amos 'n' Andy* (Phone Calls)
    c. *World War II* (Radio List)

14. A more recent alternative to Old Time Radio was Garrison Keillor's _______________ , a variety show with musical guests and humorous commercials for products that don't actually exist.

    a. *The Family Hour* (o Es)
    b. *A Prairie Home Companion* (cape 'R)
    c. *Hour of Nostalgia* (f Wel)

15. Pre-recorded sound cues are easier and less expensive to use, but _______________ sound effects are more entertaining, especially when performed in front of a live audience.

    a. layered (o Es)
    b. actor-performed (cap)
    c. manual (road)

16. In radio theatre, _______________ fall into one of two layers: one helps establish the mood and setting, and the other aids in keeping the action moving along.

    a. sound effects (Phone Calls)
    b. cues (king War D)
    c. commercials (p P)

NOTES: ____

____

____

____

____

____

____

____

____

NAME ____ PERIOD _______ DATE _______________

RADIO THEATRE EXTENSION ACTIVITIES

1. Record the sound effects below one at a time using three different intensities for each. Do not make any character (voiced) sounds when recording. Mark how to find each one on your recording by indicating below the time at which each appears.

	CALM	URGENT	PANICKY
a. Knock on door			
b. Footsteps walking indoors			
c. Footsteps running indoors			
d. Footsteps walking in snow or gravel			
e. Footsteps running outdoors			
f. Sword fight			
g. Splashing in pool			
h.			
i.			
j.			

2. Create twenty sound effects of your own that might be useful in an Old Time Radio show. Record your effects.

3. Write a five-minute Old Time Radio show, including at least twenty sound cues. Five of your cues may be music cues, but the rest must be either action sounds or background sounds to establish the mood or setting. You do not have to create the sounds. As the playwright, your job is to create the script.

4. Create an interesting time line of Old Time Radio theatre, highlighting the most impacting events. Include a few important non-radio events, too, so that those using your time line will see how world history and radio history affect one another. Include a lot of color, pictures, diagrams, etc.

5. Research and write a five-page, typed, double-spaced essay on one of the following:

   a. A famous radio comedy or drama.

   b. A famous radio actor or actress.

   c. A current radio theatre program.

   d. The original *The War of the Worlds* broadcast and its impact on listeners.

6. Create an entertaining recording of Dr. Seuss's *Mr. Brown Can Moo, Can You?* book including all of the sound effects mentioned in the story. Find five teachers of young children to email your recording to. With each one you send, include an engaging, artistically designed letter that explains how many of the sounds were made. Your letter should also encourage young readers to experiment with creating their own sound effects.

NOTES: ____

____

____

____

____

____

____

____

PODCASTS
OPPORTUNITY FOR THE MASSES

There are very few performance opportunities as accessible to the masses as podcasts. And for young performers, this means the future very well could be in your pocket. On your smart phone, that is.

A podcast is a digital file that can be downloaded and enjoyed at the convenience of the listener. The word **podcast** is a combination of the words iPod and broadcast, because the iPod was originally the preferred method for collecting and storing the broadcasts. However, iPods have already been replaced by smart phones, laptops, and tablets. But basically, a podcast can be downloaded onto any digital media device. That makes them portable, and a favorite source of entertainment and information for people on the go.

Podcasts were developed when Dave Winer and Adam Curry wrote a program to download radio broadcasts in 2004. Since then, the idea has been significantly improved upon and is now used for a variety of platforms: interviews, solo opinion or commentary, group panel discussion, storytelling, a hybrid mixture of platforms, and repurposed content. Among these could be dozens of additional sub-platforms; the possibilities are endless. Rather than producers attempting to read the minds of their audience members and produce shows they will like, episodes can be produced and published, and those that are desirable survive and thrive. Those that lack a following sink to the bottom. Because there is little cost involved (or can be little cost involved), this is a safe method for testing content.

Some very popular podcasts include *Serial, This American Life, Planet Money, Teen Life, Stuff You Should Know, The Moth*, and far too many more to list. To find podcasts you'll enjoy, search on the internet, or ask your friends what they enjoy. Because it is a fluid and rapidly growing industry, the broadcasts available at the date of this book's publication may quickly become outdated or even unavailable.

Anyone can create a podcast. Even you! What are your areas of expertise? What excites you? Maybe your area of expertise is advice. Maybe you are the one person your friends come to for a good heart-to-heart talk, and you are good at it. Could you come up with a single episode about advice? Could you plan ahead and ask for various questions from your friends and then create an interesting outline for your show based on those questions and your impending answers? Don't think of it as a script, because it's not. It's a casual discussion. Your listener should feel like they are a part of a lighthearted conversation. And while you will likely have a basic outline in mind, be flexible in what you will say.

Because podcasts aren't always scripted, it's important to be careful about what you say. It should not be mean-spirited or judgmental; try to keep it fun for your entire audience.

What are some topics you feel you could discuss with some level of expertise? The list has been started for you. Add to it!

Books_______________________________________

____

Sports _______________________________________

____

Movies _______________________________________

____

TV Commercials _______________________________________

____

Music _______________________________________

____

Comics_______________________________________

____

     69

NOTES: _______________________________________

____

____

____

____

____

____

What are some topics you would like to hear others discuss? Are there already podcasts about any of these subjects? "Supply and demand" is the idea that if consumers need or want something, there should be a product—in your case, a podcast—to supply that demand. If you have a broadly appealing interest but there are no podcasts for your listening pleasure, there is a demand but no supply. What does that tell you? Fill the need! Create a podcast to supply the demand.

____

____

____

Many podcasts have guests or multiple speakers. This helps to move the subject along. On Car Talk, for example, each episode discusses a topic related to cars. There are two speakers, Tom and Ray, and they work off each other to expand on the topic. Sometimes they have guests, and they take calls from listeners who are having car trouble; the panel helps diagnose problems and advise callers.

Who are some friends, either in class or outside of class, you feel would make good podcast participants? Explain.

____

____

____

Listening to your podcast should be fun. You, the host, and your guests should always keep in mind that there are others present: your audience. While you might be having fun, ask yourself if they are. Find ways to bring them in, to involve them, to make them feel like they are part of the show. What are some tricks you can use to keep the audience intrigued and to help them feel a part of the broadcast? Could you read their letters during the podcast? Issue

challenges? Take their advice on show content, or maybe even give them advice?

____

____

____

Not only do you need a catchy beginning to keep your listeners' interest, you also need to keep your podcast concise and wrap it up neatly.

Here are some ideas to help you create a natural, conversational ending:

- It seems everyone has a different idea about what makes the ideal school lunch. Some people like salad bars, and others prefer pizza. I love pizza myself, but it's track season, so salad it is! Whew. After all this talk about food, I'm hungry! And that's *What's for Lunch*, Dallas's best resource for hungry teens. I'm Kiara Kennedy, and she's Brianna Bagly. Until next time!

- So you're telling me that you'd rather wear beat-up kicks than a new pair of Nikes? Dude! I guess that's your choice. And you know, that's the great thing about shoes. There are so many to choose from! And there are seven days in the week to experiment. So until we meet again, I'm Basil.

  And I'm Kai.

  And we're *Two Guys Talking About Shoes!*

- So, after 25 years of firefighting, you finally get to retire. Congratulations, man! That's exciting! Thank you so much for joining us today and telling our listeners about another career option. I think you've given them something to think about. Speaking of retirement, it's time to say "so long," till next time, that is. My name is Henry Miner, and this has been *The Art of Growing Up*.

For a 5-minute podcast, relate whatever you're discussing at the 4- to 4½-minute mark back to your title so that you've come full circle. Maybe even throw in a quippy expression. Then reintroduce yourself, play your music, and fade out.

NOTES: ____

____

____

____

____

____

____

NAME _________________________________ PERIOD _______ DATE _____________

PODCAST PRACTICE

Create a five-minute podcast with a partner. Your partner may be a co-host, like you, or they may be a guest.

Your teacher will tell you if your podcast will be live or recorded.

______ Live   ______ Recorded

For the purpose of this practice, your subject is *shoes*, or you may adapt it to some sort of clothing.

OPENING MUSIC

What music will you play? _____________________________________

What section of the song will you play? _____________________________

How will you play it? ____

Will you play the same section at the end? _____Yes _____No

If no, what music will you play at the end? ______________________________

INTRODUCTION

Write an introduction for yourself and your co-host, if you have one. If you have a guest, you will need to introduce them as they are about to speak. At this time, you will also introduce the title of your podcast, and if you have one, the title and number of your episode.

How will you introduce your subject?

____

How will you introduce your guest, if you have one? What will you say about them?

____

BODY

In your five-minute podcast, what will you say about your subject? Why is this subject important? Why will the audience want to listen?

____

____

List at least three different topics that will be discussed during the podcast. Below each one, give yourself hints of things you can discuss about each of the three topics. For example, if your subject is shoes, maybe first on your list could be athletic shoes; letter "a" could be trendy athletic shoes and "b" could be high-performance shoes.

Here's a partial outline as an example:

1.   Types of shoes
         a. comfortable shoes
         b. fashionable shoes

          71

NOTES: ____

____

____

____

____

____

____

2. Memories of shoes from my childhood
   a. ____
   b. ____

3. If I was designing the perfect shoes
   a. ____
   b. ____

Now, create your own sample outline about shoes:

1. ____

   a. ____

   b. ____

2. ____

   a. ____

   b. ____

3. ____

   a. ____

   b. ____

If you can't think of something important or interesting to say about your topic fairly quickly, it may not be a good topic for you.

Remember, you have five minutes. You might not get to each subject on your list. That's okay. If your podcast is entertaining, it doesn't matter. Save unused material for future episodes! The key is to keep your listeners engaged; if they aren't itching to comment, think of ways you can be more engaging.

CONCLUSION

At about four minutes, you'll want to work your way to a close, but it's important to cap off the dialogue so it has a finished feel. Closing any unscripted piece can be difficult! Keep it natural. Don't try too hard, or you'll find yourself stuck in new dialogue. If you have a guest, use this time to thank them. If you don't have a guest, simply restate your topic in a new way and add a final thought or two. Always repeat your name and the title of your podcast. If you have a sponsor (or would like to pretend you have one), this is a great time to thank them as well.

Then reintroduce yourself, play your music, and fade out.

NOTES: ____

____

____

____

____

____

____

____

NAME ____ PERIOD _______ DATE ______________

PODCAST PROJECT

OBJECTIVE: Now that you've practiced with the subject of shoes, create a five-minute podcast on a topic of your choice with a partner. Your partner may be a co-host, like you, or they may be a guest.

Your teacher will tell you if your podcast will be live or recorded.

_____Live   _____Recorded

OPENING MUSIC

Select music appropriate to your subject. How much will you play? How loudly will you play it? It is up to you to practice playing your music so that it runs smoothly during your performance, whether live or recorded.

What music will you play? ____

What section of the song will you play? ______________________________________

How will you play it? ____

INTRODUCTION

Write an introduction for yourself and your co-host, if you have one. If you have a guest, you will need to introduce them as they are about to speak. At this time, you will also introduce the title of your podcast, and if you have one, the title and number of your episode.

How will you introduce your subject?

____

How will you introduce your guest, if you have one? What will you say about them?

____

BODY

In your five-minute podcast, what will you say about your subject? Why is this subject important? Why will the audience want to listen?

List at least three different topics that will be discussed during the podcast. And below each one, give yourself hints of things you can discuss about each of the three topics. If you can't think of something important or interesting to say about your topic fairly quickly, it may not be a good topic for you.

1. ____

   a. ____

   b. ____

                    73

NOTES: ____

____

____

____

____

____

____

____

2. ____

   a. ____

   b. ____

3. ____

   a. ____

   b. ____

CONCLUSION

At about four minutes, you'll want to work your way to a close, but it's important to cap off the dialogue so it has a finished feel. Closing any unscripted piece can be difficult! Keep it natural. Don't try too hard, or you'll find yourself stuck in new dialogue. If you have a guest, use this time to thank them. If you don't have a guest, simply restate your topic in a new way and add a final thought or two. Always repeat your name and the title of your podcast. If you have a sponsor, or would like to pretend you have one, it's a great time to thank them as well.

Then reintroduce yourself, play your music, and fade out.

FOR DISCUSSION

1. Why do you think podcasts have become so popular?

____

____

2. Which of the podcasts from your class do you feel could be successful topics? Is there anything you would change?

____

____

3. Which podcasters seemed to have a knack for this type of performance? What traits do you feel work well in this type of performance?

____

____

4. Now that you've heard a few practice podcasts, can you think of some additional topics that would make interesting discussions?

____

____

5. Listen to an actual podcast. What sets it apart from other genres? What is the draw? And lastly, who makes an ideal listener?

____

____

NOTES: ____

____

____

____

____

____

____

CHAPTER 3 — THEATRE FOR THE EARS

NAME ____ PERIOD _________ DATE _______________

PODCAST PRODUCTION PEER EVALUATION

Evaluate each aspect of the podcaster's performance
on a scale of 1 (worst or not present) to 5 (best).

Group #	Performer's initials	1st impression	Selection	Introduction	Topic structure	Voice	Focus	Timing	Familiarization	This performer was best at...	This performer could use a little more work on...

　　75

NOTES: ____

____

____

____

____

____

____

____

PODCAST PRODUCTION RUBRIC

PODCASTER: ____

1. The podcaster took the stage or started the recording with confidence, making a good **first impression**.
   1 2 3 4 5 6 7 8 9 10

2. The content **selection** was engaging, interesting, and appropriate for the audience.
   1 2 3 4 5 6 7 8 9 10

3. The **introduction** was well-written and effectively prepared the audience for the topic.
   1 2 3 4 5 6 7 8 9 10

4. The **music selection** was appropriate and fit the topic well.
   1 2 3 4 5 6 7 8 9 10

5. The actor's **voice** was loud and clear.
   1 2 3 4 5 6 7 8 9 10

6. The co-host or guest was effectively integrated into the production.
   1 2 3 4 5 6 7 8 9 10

7. The podcast was wrapped-up well, with an effective conclusion.
   1 2 3 4 5 6 7 8 9 10

8. The podcaster was **focused** from beginning to end and stayed on topic.
   1 2 3 4 5 6 7 8 9 10

9. The **timing** was within the limitations; the podcaster was not rushed, progressed at an acceptable rate, avoided hesitant pauses, and used dramatic pauses to their advantage.
   1 2 3 4 5 6 7 8 9 10

10. The podcaster was **familiar** with the piece and delivered it without hesitation.
    1 2 3 4 5 6 7 8 9 10

TOTAL SCORE

CHAPTER 4
SKILL BUILDING ACTIVITIES
THEATRE PROJECTS, MINI-UNITS AND SELF-GUIDED LESSONS

VOCABULARY

In this chapter, you will learn about:

Ad-lib: To add lines to a scene "spur of the moment."

Assignment: A short or simple task.

Characters: The fictitious personalities in a scene.

Choral Reading: Another way to say "readers theatre."

Delivery: The act of saying the lines; often the term used to describe the quality of how the lines are said.

Dropping Off: Allowing final sounds or words to become inaudible.

Echo Effects: To repeat lines, words, phrases, and sounds creatively onstage.

Engage: Actively listening, understanding, and reacting.

Ensemble Reading: Another way to say "readers theatre."

Event: An important bit of action in a play.

Familiarize: To learn a piece well enough that the performer must look at the script only occasionally.

Focus: The actor's ability to concentrate on the moment and not be distracted by memorization issues, distractions, and nervousness.

Fourth Wall: The imaginary wall between the performers and the audience.

Freeze: To be absolutely still onstage, either for effect or to simulate being "off" or "offstage."

In the Scene: Being an active, listening character; also "in the moment."

Introduction: A small section written by the speaker at the beginning of some scenes that helps connect the piece to the audience and often gives the author and title of the piece.

Jingle: The song used to advertise a product.

Levels: Taking advantage of various visual planes including height, width, and depth; changes in pace, pitch, or volume to add interest and draw audience's attention.

Logo: The symbol used to identify a product for advertising.

Losing the Audience: Becoming so creative that it becomes a distraction or becoming so creative that the audience doesn't get it.

Memorize: To learn a piece so that it can be performed without prompting or looking at a script.

Motto: The short phrase that summarizes the product and/or what the advertiser wants the buyer to think of it.

Onomatopoeia: The term used to describe words that sound like what they mean, like "pop" and "drip."

Project: A series of tasks that work together like a system.

Readers Theatre: A piece for which actors use scripts onstage; other than that, it is very similar to other performances.

Segue: (SEG-way) To make a connection from the current topic to the next topic for the purpose of flowing smoothly.

Set-up: The moments after the performer is called to the stage and before their performance begins; often the act of preparing the stage for the performance.

Sing-song Cadence: The effect of sounding like the lines have a musical quality; this is usually a negative effect caused when actors become too used to each other, and becoming "sing-songy" replaces true interpretation.

Slate: To give one's name and other vital information prior to a performance, particularly an audition.

Slogan: The short phrase that summarizes the product and/or what the advertiser wants the buyer to think of it.

Stealing Focus: To take the focus away from the performer who should be the center of the audience's attention at that moment.

Teaser: A small section of the scene delivered in character prior to the introduction; after the intro, the scene continues where the teaser left off.

Timing: The effective use of pausing, pace and rate, silence, and building of suspense in scene work and performances; may also include movement.

Unison: Together.

Voice-over: A type of acting in which only the actor's voice is used; cartoons use voice-over, as does radio, and even many TV commercials are voice-over on top of action; narration is often voice-over.

          79

INTRODUCTION

This book focuses a great deal on both group and independent projects, since being successful in theatre requires skills in each area. Projects require thinking on several levels. Whether working as part of a group or independently, students must complete research, use artistry, and pull from various directions to complete a finished product that is worthy of the time and effort put into it. Theatre students must learn to become reliable, independent workers as well as good team players. During the course of the semester or year, one of your students' goals should be to earn your trust to work independently, whether alone or with a group.

SKILL BUILDING

Think about the various places you see professional actors doing their craft. They perform in commercials, movies, and TV shows, do **voice-over** for cartoons and radio, perform onstage, and are all over the internet as virtual guides on websites. They are everywhere doing different types of work. Yet theatre classrooms everywhere are full of actors honing their skills with only duets and monologues. These are two wonderful ways to learn to act, but they are not the only ways.

Most students who study theatre in school will not become actors. At the same time, they will *always* act. What you learn in theatre classes will be useful in a variety of jobs. This chapter will bring all of the elements of theatre and full-scale projects together to help you sharpen the skills you will use both on the stage and off.

The difference between a **project** and an **assignment** is simple: an assignment has a basic objective, and a project is more like a system. Each project you do will incorporate a number of smaller elements to create a larger, more involved performance. In completing a project, you will learn a great deal about leadership, taking and following direction, time management, teamwork, quality, presentation, confidence, controlling stage fright, lights, sound, props, special effects, and successfully selling a final product that makes the audience want to see more.

Because theatre is so diverse, you will find a variety of projects throughout this book. The lip-sync project, for example, involves creating a set, costumes, and props, and it requires a great deal of time, energy, creativity, and teamwork. Similarly, any time you write a script it becomes a project because of the amount of rewriting, peer reviewing, and the sheer amount of effort needed to complete the task. Basically, anything that requires multiple resources (including people, books, the internet, and so on), takes more than one or two class periods to complete, and is worthy of some sort of presentation would be considered a project.

So what does that mean to you? As you get older and your life becomes richer and more complex, it becomes a little more difficult to earn your place in the world. In business, for example, the stakes are higher because people's income is on the line. Consequently, when it comes time to compete—yes, compete—for a promotion, a new title, a new division, a raise, or to keep one's job, all of your skills must be sharp. Rarely is a task on a high-stakes job simple, like an assignment. It is almost always going to be a project, such as managing a large account, overseeing the completion of a campaign, or successfully upgrading to a new kind of software. Business is all about being able to successfully reach goals (your company's goals, that is), hitting a number of different targets along the way, and avoiding problems. Successful businesspeople make it look easy, no matter how hard the task. They are organized, creative, and fearless. Why? They learned early how to take a project, find a goal, plan, implement, overcome obstacles, and charge forward. They are prepared, and preparation is invaluable.

Each of the projects in this book will exercise the skills you need to become a better project manager and participant, but they are all also designed to be fun. What skills can you build for future success?

NOTES: ______________________________________

CHILDREN'S BOOK READING

The art of reading a children's book aloud is not that different from telling a story. In both, you relate directly to the audience or listeners. When reading a children's book, you must **engage** with the audience more than the book. You should make eye contact with the audience 75 to 90 percent of the time but should refer to the book and its illustrations often. You should use character voices, talk to the children, redirect distracting behavior, and use character and drama to keep them interested and focused. In storytelling, you have no script or text, but you can still use character voices, engage the audience, redirect hecklers, and use keen speaking skills to draw them in or grab their attention.

And while reading a children's book and telling a story are similar, each one deserves its own place in performance. If you know how to read, you have probably read aloud to a child. Children are fascinated by books and stories long before they are capable of sounding out the words themselves. They rely on those who are able to read to help them decipher the mystery. It is a practice as old as books themselves.

Reading is a bridge. It connects young, eager listeners to more mature, educated performers—even if those performers are simply siblings or cousins or grandparents. In schools and libraries, reading aloud is used to focus children, to teach reading and listening skills, and to introduce concepts. It is often the activity used just before nap time because it channels energy toward the imagination rather than action.

And for both the reader and the listener, it is educational. Reading aloud is one of the best ways to practice language, to improve fluency, to become a better speaker and articulator, and it is actually a wonderful way to calm nerves. Many actors credit storybook reading with instilling in them a love of acting. Perhaps this is why so many actors are also playwrights! And for children, having stories read to them introduces new concepts and new vocabulary. Most importantly, it teaches a love of words, books, stories, creativity, performance, and listening.

What is your favorite children's book or bedtime story? Why is it your favorite? Some children love the nonsensical whimsy of Dr. Seuss, while others have memories of Shel Silverstein's creative rhymes and silly situations. Still others relate more to fairy tales or books in which the illustrations are as important as the written word.

For the purpose of this activity, choose books that are not dependent on illustrations. Books may be illustrated, but the pictures should be supportive of the story rather than part of the structure of the story. Imagine your audience is visually impaired. You should not have to explain the pictures in order for the story to make sense.

You should also select books appropriate to the audience. For example, if your school is a religious school, religious books would be appropriate; if your school is a public school, your religious views might not be shared by your entire audience. For this assignment, selecting a book that fits your audience is part of your grade; therefore, religious or controversial books should be avoided.

CHILDREN'S BOOK READING

For the purpose of this activity, students should choose books that are not dependent on illustrations to complete the story. Books may be illustrated, but the pictures themselves should be supportive of the story rather than part of the structure of the story. Imagine your audience is visually impaired. You should not have to explain the pictures so that the story makes sense.

Advise students to select books appropriate to the audience. For example, if your school is a religious school, religious books will be appropriate. But if your school is a public school, your religious views may not be shared by your entire audience. For this assignment, selecting a book that fits the audience should be part of the grade, so religious books should be avoided.

You can provide students with a list of recommended books to choose from such as:

- *17 Things I'm Not Allowed to Do Anymore*, Jenny Offill
- *Wordy Birdy*, Tammi Sauer
- *The Book with No Pictures*, B.J. Novak
- *Alexander and the Terrible, Horrible, No Good, Very Bad Day*, Judith Viorst
- *Interrupting Chicken*, David Ezra Stein
- *We Found a Hat*, Jon Klassen
- *Lady Pancake and Sir French Toast*, Josh Funk and Brendan Kearney
- *President Taft is Stuck in the Bath*, Mac Barnett

(Search "Fun Read Aloud Children's Books" for current suggestions)

CHILDREN'S BOOK READING RUBRIC

READER: ____

1. The reader took the stage with **confidence**, making a good **first impression**.
1 2 3 4 5 6 7 8 9 10

2. The **selection** was engaging, interesting, and appropriate for the audience.
1 2 3 4 5 6 7 8 9 10

3. The **introduction** was well-written and effectively prepared the audience for the story.
1 2 3 4 5 6 7 8 9 10

4. The reader's **voice** was loud and clear, and characters' voices were distinct and interesting.
1 2 3 4 5 6 7 8 9 10

5. The reader maintained good **eye contact**, looking at the audience 75-90% of the time.
1 2 3 4 5 6 7 8 9 10

6. **Movement** and gestures were well-planned, interesting, and supported what the reader was saying without being distracting.
1 2 3 4 5 6 7 8 9 10

7. The reader thoroughly **developed characters**, including giving each a unique voice and physical characteristics as well as using supportive facial expressions.
1 2 3 4 5 6 7 8 9 10

8. The reader was **focused** from beginning to end and stayed in character.
1 2 3 4 5 6 7 8 9 10

9. The **timing** was within the limitations; the reader was not rushed, progressed at an acceptable rate, avoided hesitant pauses, and used dramatic pauses to their advantage.
1 2 3 4 5 6 7 8 9 10

10. The reader was **well-familiar** with the piece or had it memorized, delivering it without hesitation.
1 2 3 4 5 6 7 8 9 10

TOTAL SCORE

STORYTELLING PERFORMANCE RUBRIC

STORYTELLER: ____

1. The storyteller took the stage with **confidence**, making a good **first impression**.
   1 2 3 4 5 6 7 8 9 10

2. The **selection** was engaging, interesting, and appropriate for the audience.
   1 2 3 4 5 6 7 8 9 10

3. The **introduction** was well-written and effectively prepared the audience for the story.
   1 2 3 4 5 6 7 8 9 10

4. All parts of the story's **dramatic structure** were evident.
   1 2 3 4 5 6 7 8 9 10

   ______ Exposition (setting)   ______ Event 1   ______ Climax
   ______ Exposition (characters)   ______ Event 2   ______ Falling Action
   ______ Inciting Incident   ______ Event 3   ______ Ending

5. The storyteller's **voice** was loud and clear, and character voices were distinct and interesting.
   1 2 3 4 5 6 7 8 9 10

6. **Movement** was well-planned, interesting, and supported what the storyteller was saying without being distracting.
   1 2 3 4 5 6 7 8 9 10

7. The storyteller thoroughly **developed characters**, including giving each a unique voice and physical characteristics, as well as using supportive facial expressions.
   1 2 3 4 5 6 7 8 9 10

8. The storyteller was **focused** from beginning to end and stayed in character.
   1 2 3 4 5 6 7 8 9 10

9. The **timing** was within the limitations; the storyteller was not rushed, progressed at an acceptable rate, avoided hesitant pauses, and used dramatic pauses to their advantage.
   1 2 3 4 5 6 7 8 9 10

10. The storyteller was **well-familiar** with the piece or had it memorized, delivering it without hesitation.
    1 2 3 4 5 6 7 8 9 10

TOTAL SCORE

STORYTELLING

Small children aren't the only ones who love a good story. Storytelling is an ancient art form, older than book reading, because books are relatively new for the common person. Where illustrations were not available, the storyteller would spark the listeners' imaginations with detailed accounts of the costumes and castles and the witch's green teeth and hairy mole.

The practice of storytelling is just as beneficial to the speaker as to those listening. Telling stories is an art form; you may recall that it was also a precursor to theatre. For those with reading difficulties, telling stories builds vocabulary and reinforces reading skills. Perhaps most importantly, it pairs the written word with the word's meaning, its inflection, its use in a sentence, its mood, its context, and its pronunciation, all of which lead to better reading comprehension.

The art of storytelling almost always relies on a basic format: The storyteller takes a complex idea—a lesson—and puts it into a dramatic format, thus helping the listener to grasp the complex idea. For example, a little girl might complain that her grandmother walks too slowly, so rather than talk about age, Grandma might tell her the story of the tortoise and the hare. Soon the child is no longer focused on her grandmother's speed but rather on her grandmother's wisdom.

And that brings us to the second point of storytelling: It is a connection. A story is a thread that binds the listener to the speaker. Throughout history, those who tell stories skillfully have been revered. Audiences are drawn to these people, and as a result, there is power in the ability to tell a story.

And this leads to another point. If storytelling is powerful, then a smart society uses storytelling to motivate its people, thus enriching their shared culture. Perhaps the most famous collection of motivational or inspirational stories is the Bible. Each story guides readers toward a goal: the enhancement of faith and adherence to rules. Actually, all religions have stories that help connect believers to their faith. In Hawaii, where the ancient culture embraced many gods, stories were used to encourage a respect for natural beauty.

Storytelling introduces your audience to reading, to listening skills or audience skills, to story structure, spelling, and the art of weaving a tale. And for more mature audiences, storytelling is a break from reality, an opportunity to learn a little about you, the storyteller, and an **introduction** to your piece of prose. This is your chance to move them or make them laugh or cry.

Could you retell a famous story that you heard as a child without having a book to read? Select one of the familiar storylines below. If needed, perform a little bit of research to **familiarize** yourself with the basic plot. And then, in groups of two or three, tell your stories in about three to five minutes. Do not start with "Once upon a time." Instead, come up with an alternate opening. Feel free to use **characters** and voices, but don't focus on that. Instead, use your time to mesmerize your partner(s) with the twists and turns and the adventure while exploring your own abilities as a teller of tall tales.

Beauty and the Beast	*Puss in Boots*
Cinderella	*Rapunzel*
The Emperor's New Clothes	*Rumpelstiltskin*
	Sleeping Beauty
The Gingerbread Man	*Snow White and the Seven Dwarfs*
Jack and the Beanstalk	
King Midas	*The Ugly Duckling*

Was it easy or difficult to tell the story?

What was easy about it?

ABOUT STORYTELLING

You probably already teach some form of storytelling. Prose, for example, is like storytelling, only scripted, and speakers use binders. In a way, monologues are a type of storytelling, and if you have students present children's books, you're getting even warmer.

Storytelling is one of the oldest art forms in the world. Simply put, it's communicating—only in great detail. Prior to radio, it was a staple in most homes. Radio dethroned grandparents from their perch as the center of the family's attention, and then TV did the same to radio. Because watching TV is still the reigning favorite American pastime, storytelling is an art form that has almost been forgotten.

Encourage students to act out as much of the action in their stories as they can, even if it feels a bit ridiculous. All movement should be larger than life, and characterizations should be very exaggerated. Most importantly, students should have fun with their delivery. If it isn't fun for them, imagine what it must be like for the audience!

What were some obstacles you faced?

GROUP DISCUSSION

In groups of four or five, discuss stories that revolve around the following central themes. Do any of the stories from the list on the previous page fit into the following categories?

Honesty	Courage
Hard work	Creativity
Trustworthiness	Helpfulness
Family bonds	Laziness
Self-confidence	Foolishness
Strength	Greed

Did you learn any performance skills from your partner? _________ If so, explain:

____

____

____

Now that you've told the story once, switch partners and tell your story again. Was it easier or harder this time? Explain.

____

You can tell a story using a famous tale, or you can tell your own story, like the time you broke your leg at recess and had to leave school in an ambulance. Part of the problem with telling a personal story is that it is often too short to use as an assignment. But if you practice, you can usually come up with enough interesting details to make it a three to five minute fully developed plot. You will want to include a beginning, a few bits of detail to build up the middle, and a well thought out ending.

It is also important to tell your story, not someone else's—even if you were there. When you tell others' stories, it can seem like gossip or as though you are sharing secrets. Let others tell their stories, and for the purpose of this lesson, stick to telling your own.

What role does practice play in a telling a story even if you aren't reciting it from memory?

What are some stories from your own experiences you would be willing to share with a partner? In pairs, practice telling the stories. After each person has told their story, take turns asking questions, and then tell your stories again—including anything that might have been missing or confusing the first time.

What skills do you think a good storyteller needs?

How was it? What were some beneficial parts of practicing telling your own story? What were some obstacles? Is your story interesting enough that you'd want to tell it to a larger audience? What would you change to make it more successful?

NOTES: _______________________________

____

____

____

____

____

____

____

____

NAME ____ PERIOD _______ DATE ____________

STORYTELLING PROJECT

OBJECTIVE: Learn to create settings, develop characters, build excitement, and successfully tell stories.

Children have limitless imaginations. As their bodies grow, their minds are growing too. They crave images, information, and stories the same way a plant craves water. The more stories they get, the stronger their imaginations become. Do you remember a favorite story you heard in your childhood? Was it from a book, or was it something a relative passed on to you?

Before radio and television, storytelling was how many families passed the time. Grandparents would tell of their adventures, and young, eager ears would cling to each and every word. However, when radio became popular in the 1920s and actors began telling or enacting stories for massive audiences, an unfortunate thing happened. The eager ears that used to listen to and pass on family histories began hushing their elders until their show was over. Slowly but steadily, family story time faded away. Sadly, the art of storytelling has suffered as well.

This is one of the few projects in this book that is intended to be completed alone. There are no props, costumes, set pieces, or other items used. This is purely the actor and their craft. In the next few days, you will explore the art of telling a story from beginning to end, creating a setting, developing all the characters by yourself, engaging the audience with growing excitement, using timing, and enacting a satisfying ending.

You can use any children's story, or you can perform a true story so long as it can be worked into the "Learning the Story" pages following this one.

SELECTING YOUR STORY

As always, remember that your goal is to entertain the audience, so select a story appropriate for them. If you are performing for your classmates, you can still select a children's story, but you can update it to include more mature characters or maybe take advantage of fun stereotypes. Or you can take a story from popular culture, such as attempting to summarize the entire Harry Potter series in seven minutes! If you are performing for young children, any classic tale will do, and the larger the characters, the better!

Quickly brainstorm a few story ideas that you might enjoy retelling:

____

____

____

____

LEARNING THE STORY

Familiarize yourself with the basic sequence of events and the characters' names in your story. You may want to memorize a few key lines, such as the traditional "I'll huff and I'll puff, and I'll blow your house in" from the story of The Three Little Pigs. If you got your story from a book, you will also need to memorize the author's name so you can credit the original storyteller in your introduction.

You have already learned a great deal about writing stories using dramatic structure, and now it is time to tell stories using the same basic format. You may think that this is additional work added onto storytelling, but it will actually save you a great deal of extra work. By dissecting your story into parts (the structure), you will be able to remember the details to retell it much more easily.

NOTES: ____

____

____

____

____

____

____

____

CHAPTER 4 — SKILL BUILDING ACTIVITIES

USE THE FOLLOWING BLANKS TO DISSECT YOUR STORY'S DRAMATIC STRUCTURE.

1. The exposition is where the storyteller introduces key characters and the setting. Where is your story set?

   ____

2. What words describe your setting? Fill in every blank, and remember to appeal to all the senses when possible.

   _____________________________   _____________________________
   _____________________________   _____________________________
   _____________________________   _____________________________

3. When does your story take place? ____

4. How will the setting—the place and time—be reflected in the way you play the characters?

   ____
   ____
   ____
   ____

5. Complete the following character grid for all of the characters in your story; use additional paper, if needed.

CHARACTER	GOAL	POTENTIAL OBSTACLES	PHYSICAL TRAITS/ VOICE	PERSONALITY TRAITS, QUIRKS

6. What is the inciting incident in the story?

   ____
   ____
   ____

     85

NOTES: ____

____

____

____

____

____

____

____

7. Who is the protagonist and what is their goal?

8. Who or what is the antagonist? Explain the reason this person or thing is an obstacle to the protagonist's goal.

9. What is the first event that happens after the inciting incident? Remember: walking, thinking, and sitting are not events; an event is action-oriented.

10. Then what happens?

11. What is the most exciting part, or climax, of your story?

12. What is your story's falling action?

13. How does your story end? Seek a more solid ending than "They lived happily ever after." Stick to the story, but find an original way to say it.

14. Finally, what lesson does your story seek to teach? How can you reinforce that lesson with the way you tell your story?

NOTES:

REHEARSING YOUR STORY

The first few times you rehearse your story, you might want to consider having your script in hand. Your script could be your book, notes, or your answers from pages 85 and 86. Or you might want to retype your story into note form just for the purpose of being able to retell the main parts. Remember, the same copyright laws apply with storytelling books as with play scripts. Check the individual publisher's page in the book you are using—if you are using a book—or any other resource you are using to ensure you are not in violation of copyright law.

Find a private place, or if one is not available. find a place where you can move freely. If several students are rehearsing in the same area, concentrate on yourself, but be aware of the other students so that everyone stays safe. Storytelling can involve many large movements, and you do not want to end up giving or receiving a black eye.

Your story should be told in your own words. Start by setting the audience up for something exciting. You will eventually add an introduction, so keep this in mind as you format the beginning; save room for a bit more.

Start by making the audience see the setting, smell the odors, feel the temperatures, relate to the characters' feelings. You can do this with volume, word choice, postures, and even the ways in which you approach the audience. Occasionally change your pace, lower your volume, make penetrating eye contact, and fill each of your characters with a great deal of personality. Make it fun for you, and your audience will have fun watching.

Try to make your audience forget they are hearing a story. Don't say things like, "In the story I'm about to tell..." You want it to feel more personal than that. Try to create an atmosphere where the audience forgets they are hearing a story and instead feels like they have been absorbed into one. You might even experiment with making the story "nonfiction." What if you, the storyteller, were the little girl in the red hood or one of the three little pigs? Even if you are not one of the characters, what if the story itself was a true story?

Focus on action. Avoid telling what people are thinking; instead, work it into dialogue or an **event**. Instead of saying, "Jack thought to himself that he'd been climbing a long time," say, "Jack climbed for what seemed an eternity, looked down, and nearly lost his grip at what he saw! His house was a tiny speck and almost unnoticeable through the dense clouds."

As the story approaches the climax, you should increase the intensity. Build the audience's interest and curiosity with changes to your voice, picking up the pace, and making your listeners want more. Create anticipation; draw it out just enough to intrigue—but not enough to make it old—then hit the climax hard. Your climax should be full of action words and lots of physical reinforcement on your part.

Physically act out as much of your story as you can. For humorous stories, this can be exaggerated almost to the point of it being ridiculous, especially considering that you will be playing several characters. If you are not tired at the end of your story, you may not be working hard enough! If your story is serious, focus more on the story's action, the message, and the relationships between the characters and less on your own physical action.

You will portray all the different characters in your story, including the narrator, and each character should be unique and well-defined. When you are playing more than one personality, you are asking the audience to try to keep them all straight and separate in their minds. This is easily done if the storyteller does their job.

First, imagine that you have two people in your audience: one in a blindfold and one in soundproof earplugs. Both of these audience members must be able to keep your various characters straight. That means you must make your characters' voices and dialects very different for the person in the blindfold, and their postures, body language, and gestures must look different for the person in the earphones. At the same time, when their blindfolds and earplugs are removed, the vocalizations and physical characteristics you have assigned to the personalities must work harmoniously with the plot. Avoid combinations that seem funny at the time but will just confuse the audience, such as making Cinderella cynical, unless that is the version of the story you are telling.

Because you will be working alone, you will want to rehearse at least a few times with a couple of other people and get their advice before you perform for your grade. Use the *Rehearsal Peer Evaluation* form in Chapter 1 to record their suggestions.

NOTES: ____

INTRODUCTIONS

Rarely would someone start telling a story out of the blue without first introducing it. They would find a reason to tell the story at that moment in time. Somehow they would **segue** or *find a connection between what was happening at that moment and the story.*

In theatre, this is referred to as an introduction or a **slate**. A slate is a *formal introduction, similar to what is done before an audition.* It consists of factual, vital information, and it might vary from one audition to the next. Very often it is just the actor's name, their agent (or their school), and sometimes it will include their audition number and the title of the piece they are performing. An introduction, on the other hand, may still provide that same information, but it generally revolves around the piece to be performed.

You will find an entire lesson on preparing creative introductions in the next chapter. For now, you should remember:

- Intros are usually performed out of character.

- Intros are usually performed through the **fourth wall** (with audience eye contact).

- Serious pieces should have serious intros and comic pieces should start with something equally lighthearted.

- Intros are memorized.

Your introduction may be inserted after a short **teaser**. This is when *the speaker begins their piece, then a few lines into it, they stop, step out of character, deliver the intro, then step back into character and finish the piece.* There is no formula for correctly inserting an intro after a teaser, but it needs to happen within the first two minutes and no more than about one-fifth of the way into the piece. The break into which the intro is inserted should be natural so that the piece flows again when resumed. Usually, the break offers a natural segue into the intro. Look for a place early in the piece in which the theme is mentioned or is presented as an obstacle.

It is time to prepare for your performance. You will be graded using the rubric that your teacher will hand out. Familiarize yourself with its finer points so that you will be prepared for a great performance.

NOTES: ____

____

____

____

____

____

____

____

CHAPTER 4 — SKILL BUILDING ACTIVITIES

NAME _______________________________________ PERIOD _______ DATE ______________

STORYTELLING PERFORMANCE PEER EVALUATION

Evaluate each aspect of the storyteller's performance
on a scale of 1 (worst or not present) to 5 (best).

Storyteller's name	1st impression	Selection	Introduction	Story structure	Voice	Movement	Characterizations	Focus	Timing	Familiarization/ Memorization	This storyteller was best at...	This storyteller could use a little more work on...

NOTES: ____

____

____

____

____

____

____

____

READERS THEATRE

OBJECTIVE Your group will use teamwork and creativity to turn one or more related pieces of literature into a non-memorized performance with scripts in hand.

One of the wonderful things about **Readers Theatre**, also known as **ensemble reading** or **choral reading**, is that everyone seems to have a different way of doing it. It is a very flexible form of performing art, and the opportunities for creativity are limitless. About the only rule that everyone agrees on is that the actors must remain true to the name, so rather than memorizing their lines, they read from binders.

Readers Theatre can be done with just about any piece of literature. Plays work well, as do short stories, children's books, humorous pieces, poems, and even comic books. Today, there is an abundance of material young people can sink their teeth into. There are scripts for video games, short web-based movies, and, of course, all of those emails affectionately known as "forwards." These have been floating around in cyberspace, sent from one reader to friends and all of their friends. Dan Morrow of Wilson Middle School in Plano, Texas, jokes that the lists of ingredients in some of the foods we eat would make a good readers theatre piece, and he even challenged his students to make scripts using only the dictionary. They did it, and it worked great!

Readers Theatre does not have to be humorous. Serious pieces can be very moving. This is a wonderful chance to combine music (humming or singing), poetry, and other literature to create a chilling effect. For example, a group may commemorate Independence Day by writing a readers theatre script that is a combination of hummed Revolutionary War-era battle music, the poem "Paul Revere's Ride" by Henry Wadsworth Longfellow, and facts about the fight for America's independence.

What makes this art form so interesting? First, the actors will get a break from having to memorize. It reduces the anxiety, especially for beginners. Secondly, most pieces are fairly short, averaging about ten minutes. There are very few rules, you get to turn your chairs and binders into just about any prop you want them to be, there is room for limitless creativity, and it's just plain fun! Lastly, nowhere will teamwork be more important than in this type of performance. You work together to create an illusion using very little other than your voices, your bodies, your books, and your chairs. In the end, the actors are producing their entire performance without a crew. They will even make all of their own sound effects!

Look at the comic piece about stupid laws later in this chapter. It isn't like the dialogue in most plays. You may notice that the characters will often address the audience directly, they often speak in unison, they sing, dance, and even fish off the back of a giraffe. They can use their binders to drum their fingers or to "whack" their neighbor on the back of the head. They identify the fifty different settings by singing songs that relate to certain parts of the country, using unique eye contact, and using their chairs creatively. Each actor will have to play many different characters, often switching from one to the next instantaneously.

Each actor needs a half-size (5½ x 8½-inch) black binder. This is so that they can all be uniform, and the attention is on the actors, not their books. Small binders are less cumbersome than the full-size binders, and they can easily be held in one hand. Most office supply stores sell these smaller binders with one-inch rings. If you do not want to buy binders, make them. A regular sheet of black construction paper folded in half will conceal half sheets of copy paper stapled inside. The actual vinyl-covered binder is recommended to avoid the temptation to fold the homemade ones back, exposing the papers inside. The construction paper will also deteriorate, which can become a distraction during performances.

Lastly, using props might be common in readers theatre in some parts of the world, but most will probably agree that props are hard to handle with notebooks in tow, so for the purposes of this lesson, we will assume that actors are not allowed to use props.

ABOUT READERS THEATRE

Maybe you haven't tried readers theater because you consider it boring. After all, students are using their scripts. How challenging can it be? The truth is that it is very challenging and extremely creative. It's one of the few types of performance where students can become scenery or props, play multiple characters, gender bend, make their own sound effects, enjoy the freedom of ad-lib, and even sing and dance.

Remember to have students write introductions to their readers theater pieces. Intros may be placed at the beginning of the pieces or inserted after a short teaser. Because so many students participate in the performance, there are plenty of people for a fun, energetic, and creative introduction. For more information on writing introductions, see Chapter 5.

Put Your Master on a Leash, the script in this book, is about twenty minutes long uncut. If that is too long, give the first half to one group and the second half to another. There is also the *Cinco de Mayo* readers theater script in Section 3, but your students do not have this in their books, so you will need to make copies.

READERS THEATRE TIPS

- Five or six actors make the ideal group size; remember, actors can be more than one character, and even narration can be shared amongst the group.

- Characters should be unique, especially when it comes to comic pieces; use clues within the script to give each character you play a different personality including voice, posture, style, dialect, mannerisms, and personality.

- All readers theatre pieces should start with a creative introduction; one has been provided for the script in this chapter, or you may write you own.

- The script in this book, *Put Your Master on a Leash*, is about twenty minutes, uncut.

- Each actor may have a chair, if desired; chairs may be used for just about any purpose.

  ◇ Actors may crawl under them, sit in them, lie down in them, stand in them, move them into various positions, or tip them over; creatively using chairs and the floor adds **levels** and depth to the stage.

  ◇ Chairs could be shopping carts, lawn mowers, baby carriages, etc., but using them as props other than chairs may limit actors' creativity, whereas using pantomime may work better.

- Binders could also be used as props for movements like tossing pizza dough, fanning yourself, or, as mentioned earlier, "smacking" another character. It may be necessary to use tabs to mark your place so that you can quickly get back to your place if the binder is closed. Or practice holding your place with a finger.

- In a humorous readers theatre, people who are not characters in a given scene may become other objects, like benches, pets, or even doors; be certain that this works for you and not against you; in other words, avoid **stealing focus**.

- Introduce as many vocal and sound effects as possible.

  ◇ A slamming binder might be a door closing.

  ◇ Drumming fingers on binders could be rain.

  ◇ Tapping the metal part of a chair could be someone tapping on a window.

  ◇ Humming or singing TV theme songs can add humor.

  ◇ Making sound effects with the actors' mouths, feet, hands, and so on, can add personality (as in an old radio show) to the performance.

- Experiment with **ad-lib** (but don't allow it to become overbearing or change the playwright's intent).

- Experiment with **echo effects**, where *one actor says a line, and the others echo the last word*; **onomatopoeia**, or *emphasizing how a word sounds like its meaning*, as in the buzzing in the sample readers theatre provided in this chapter; using **freezes**, when some of the *actors freeze in position while the others continue acting*; saying lines in **unison**, where *two or more actors say a word, phrase, or line together*; or even splitting sentences into individual words or phrases, where several actors take turns saying part of a line, such as "and they lived" "happily" "ever" "after" said by four actors instead of one.

- Be careful not to become rhythmic, a common side effect of ensemble reading; also avoid getting into a **sing-song cadence** or **dropping off** the ends of lines.

- Even though this is not memorized, it should be very familiarized; by the performance, actors should be looking up ninety-five percent of the time.

- Actors who are "offstage" should always be visible but in a position that takes them out of the scene, such as heads dropped, frozen, as set pieces, backs turned, etc.

- Actors who are onstage should be **in the scene 100%**; because it is readers theatre, some will be inclined to read as the others act, but with practice, they will learn to memorize page turns and look down only as a line is needed.

- It is very important that all actors listen and respond when in the scene, unless it has been staged otherwise (for example, the director might stage a poem with all eyes forward and expressionless faces, except when the actor himself is speaking).

- Remember to be as creative as you can without **losing the audience**, i.e., *being so creative that it becomes a distraction or that your audience doesn't get it*.

- Look up videos of readers theatre performances—especially if the idea is completely foreign to you. Make note of what you like and don't like about performances you've studied.

Many schools take their readers theatre pieces to competitions. Because the art form itself is so flexible, it is very likely that the rules and judging styles will change from one contest to the next. If you take your performance to a contest, familiarize yourself with the event's rules, as the suggestions in this book may differ.

NOTES: ____

____

____

____

____

____

____

____

INTRODUCTION TO THEATRE ARTS 2

NAME _______________________________________ PERIOD _______ DATE _____________

READERS THEATRE PERFORMANCE PEER EVALUATION

Using a scale of 1 (worst or not present) to 5 (best), rate each performer's (not each group's) final reader's theatre performance and write two useful, detailed, politely constructed comments. Remember to critique yourself too. Write a comment for the group as well. Do not leave any blanks; if a group had less than 6 performers, mark through the remaining spaces.

Group #	Performer's initials	Voice	Movement	Facial expressions	Character	Familiarization	Final Impression	This performer was best at...	This performer could use a little more work on...
1									

Comment for group:

2									

Comment for group:

NOTES: ____

____

____

____

____

____

____

____

CHAPTER 4 — SKILL BUILDING ACTIVITIES

READERS THEATRE PERFORMANCE PEER EVALUATION, CONT.

Group #	Performer's initials	Voice	Movement	Facial expressions	Character	Familiarization	Final impression	This performer was best at...	This performer could use a little more work on...
3									

Comment for group:

Group #	Performer's initials	Voice	Movement	Facial expressions	Character	Familiarization	Final impression	This performer was best at...	This performer could use a little more work on...
4									

Comment for group:

Group #	Performer's initials	Voice	Movement	Facial expressions	Character	Familiarization	Final impression	This performer was best at...	This performer could use a little more work on...
5									

Comment for group:

NOTES: ____

____

____

____

____

____

____

____

READERS THEATRE PERFORMANCE RUBRIC

ACTORS:

1. The group **set up** in a timely manner, knew who was responsible for which items, and appeared to know exactly where everything would go.

   1 2 3 4 5

2. The chairs were used to create varying and interesting **levels** such as depth (front to back), width (left to right), and height (floor to ceiling). Changes were well-choreographed and added to the scene rather than interrupting flow or becoming a distraction.

   1 2 3 4 5 6 7 8 9 10

3. The **introduction** effectively prepared the audience for the scene, was well-memorized, and was balanced among team members.

   1 2 3 4 5 6 7 8 9 10

4. Group **pantomime** and **movement** were used effectively to create interesting stage pictures. The movement added to the overall performance.

   1 2 3 4 5 6 7 8 9 10

5. **Teamwork** was evident in the way actors interacted in rehearsals, during their performance, and after the performance. Voices and movements were synchronized when appropriate, and actors appeared well-rehearsed.

   1 2 3 4 5 6 7 8 9 10

6. Actors were **focused** and **engaged** from beginning to end and created a solid and confident ending for their scene.

   1 2 3 4 5 6 7 8 9 10

GROUP SCORE

Record the total group score from this page (out of a possible 55) in the box to the left. Transfer this to each actor's group score on the next page. Finish rating each individual's performance (out of a possible 45 points). Add any applicable bonus points. The total of the group, individual, and bonus points will give you a grade for that actor.

READERS THEATRE PERFORMANCE RUBRIC, CONT.

Actor:

Voice

1 2 3 4 5

Movement/Blocking

1 2 3 4 5

Facial expressions

1 2 3 4 5

Characterization

1 2 3 4 5 6 7 8 9 10

Energy

1 2 3 4 5 6 7 8 9 10

Familiarization

1 2 3 4 5 6 7 8 9 10

Group Score	Individual Score	Bonus Points	TOTAL

Actor:

Voice

1 2 3 4 5

Movement/Blocking

1 2 3 4 5

Facial expressions

1 2 3 4 5

Characterization

1 2 3 4 5 6 7 8 9 10

Energy

1 2 3 4 5 6 7 8 9 10

Familiarization

1 2 3 4 5 6 7 8 9 10

Group Score	Individual Score	Bonus Points	TOTAL

Actor:

Voice

1 2 3 4 5

Movement/Blocking

1 2 3 4 5

Facial expressions

1 2 3 4 5

Characterization

1 2 3 4 5 6 7 8 9 10

Energy

1 2 3 4 5 6 7 8 9 10

Familiarization

1 2 3 4 5 6 7 8 9 10

Group Score	Individual Score	Bonus Points	TOTAL

Actor:

Voice

1 2 3 4 5

Movement/Blocking

1 2 3 4 5

Facial expressions

1 2 3 4 5

Characterization

1 2 3 4 5 6 7 8 9 10

Energy

1 2 3 4 5 6 7 8 9 10

Familiarization

1 2 3 4 5 6 7 8 9 10

Group Score	Individual Score	Bonus Points	TOTAL

Actor:

Voice

1 2 3 4 5

Movement/Blocking

1 2 3 4 5

Facial expressions

1 2 3 4 5

Characterization

1 2 3 4 5 6 7 8 9 10

Energy

1 2 3 4 5 6 7 8 9 10

Familiarization

1 2 3 4 5 6 7 8 9 10

Group Score	Individual Score	Bonus Points	TOTAL

Actor:

Voice

1 2 3 4 5

Movement/Blocking

1 2 3 4 5

Facial expressions

1 2 3 4 5

Characterization

1 2 3 4 5 6 7 8 9 10

Energy

1 2 3 4 5 6 7 8 9 10

Familiarization

1 2 3 4 5 6 7 8 9 10

Group Score	Individual Score	Bonus Points	TOTAL

PUT YOUR MASTER ON A LEASH & OTHER STUPID LAWS

Readers Theatre by Suzi Zimmerman

CAST OF CHARACTERS

1: Animal lover, any gender

2: Any gender

3: Any gender, but preferably male

4: Female

5: Any gender, but preferably male

6: Any gender

Suggested Introduction (or you may write your own):

1: Did you know that in Alabama, it's illegal to flick boogers into the wind?

2: And in Alaska, it's illegal to push a live moose from a moving airplane?

3: And in San Francisco, you are a criminal if you use unwashed underwear to dry cars in a car wash.

4: Now, that's just gross, but still. You can't tell me these are actual laws.

1, 2, & 3: Yep.

5: You mean, some state paid their legislators to come up with those?

1: You got it!

6: So what? You act like three outdated laws is a big deal! It's not like every state has them.

1: Every one.

2: From Alabama...

3: To Wyoming.

4: Don't tell me. And all the states in between?

1, 2, & 3: Yep.

5: Put Your Master on a Leash and Other Stupid Laws.

6: By Suzi Zimmerman. The Wonderful United States of America, *(1 through 5 begin humming "The Star-Spangled Banner" quietly under 6's narration; this continues even as discussion does. Actors will take turns humming.)* Founded by those seeking freedom from religious persecution, our country has always prided itself on an outstanding legal system, designed to ensure that all citizens—

1 through 5: ...and their pets...

6: Pets?

1: Sure. Giraffes...

6: Giraffes.

1: Yeah. Georgia had to pass a law against tying your giraffe to a telephone pole or streetlamp.

2: Must have been a problem there, or they wouldn't have written the law. Same thing with the alligators...

6: Alligators?

2: Oh, sure. In Alabama, you can't chain your alligator to a fire hydrant.

6: Makes sense, I guess.

3: Belvedere City, Arkansas, has a Council order that dictates that a dog can't be in a public place without its master on a leash.

6: Its master has to be on a leash? Now I know you're pulling my leg. There's no law that—

4: *(Dramatic.)* And, oh! The poor, poor chickens.

6: Wait. What about chickens?

4: In Quitman, Georgia, it is illegal for a chicken to cross the road.

2: Why does a chicken cross a road?

1, 3, 4, 5, & 6: To get to the other side!

ALL: *(In vaudeville style.)* Da da da da da da!

6: It sounds like every state—

OTHERS: Every one.

6: —has its share of outdated laws!

5: That's right, and nowhere do they get any dumber than in the proud South!

1, 2, 3: *(Sing.)* Oh Susanna, don't you cry for me. I come from Alabama—

4: Alabama!

1, 2, 3: *(Continue song.)* —with a banjo on my knee.

4: Did you know that in Alabama, it is illegal to drive blindfolded?

OTHERS: No!

4: Yes!

6: Okay, I have heard that in Alaska it is illegal to whisper in someone's ear while they are moose hunting.

NOTes: ____________________

____

____

____

____

____

____

____

CHAPTER 4 — SKILL BUILDING ACTIVITIES

1: In Arizona *(Someone whistles "The Good, the Bad and the Ugly" theme music.)* criminals must be very color-conscious. A misdemeanor committed while wearing a red mask—

4: Hmmmm. Should I wear the red *(Pantomimes a mask in the left hand.)* or the blue? *(Pantomimes a mask in the right hand.)*

1: —used to be considered a felony.

4: Blue it is!

1: Hey, what state is next?

5: Arkansas. *(Pronounces it wrong with "Kansas" at the end; OTHERS turn in horror.)* What?

1, 2, 3: (To tune of the Dragnet theme song.) Dun, dun, dun, dun…

4: In that state, Arkansas must be pronounced 'Ar-kan-saw."

1, 2, 3: *(Finish.)* Dun, dun, dun, dun, dun.

6: You know, not all stupid laws are really stupid.

5: What do you mean?

6: In California…

1, 2, 3: Let's go surfin' now, everybody's learning how. *(Stop abruptly and act like nothing happened.)*

6: …a city ordinance states that a five hundred-dollar fine will be given to anyone who detonates a nuclear device within city limits.

4: Where would they go to pay the fine?

5: Good question.

1: Okay, here's one that will set everyone's minds at ease. In Colorado it's now perfectly legal to remove the furniture tags that say "Do Not Remove Under Penalty of Law."

2 through 6: Whew!

2: So, Colorado doesn't have any stupid laws?

1: I didn't say that. In Sterling, cats may not run loose without a taillight.

3, 4, 5, 6: *(Cat-like.)* Reow!

3: *(Bounces objects from a pantomimed jar onto the ground. Some bounce, in which case the character's eyes follow them on their course. Some do not, in which case the character looks disappointedly at the object on the ground. This goes on for several seconds and is well-choreographed with the others.)*

4: What on earth are you doing?

3: I'm testing pickles.

4: Why?

3: You see, in Connecticut, a pickle is not officially a pickle…

OTHERS: Go on…

3: … unless it bounces.

4: *(Licks her lips as one pickle bounces especially high.)* Um, you gonna eat that?

3: Are you kidding? It touched the floor!

4: But they all—

5: Ladies and gentlemen, I've got the best stiffs in all of Delaware. You want corpses? I've got 'em. Need a skeleton? Then I'm your guy.

6: Um, sir, in Delaware you can't sell dead people without a license.

5: Spoil sport!

1, 2, 3: M-I-C-K-E-Y.

4: In Miami, it is forbidden to imitate an animal.

1, 2, 3: M-O-U-S-E.

4: Well then, it's a good thing Disney World is in Orlando!

6: Ah, Georgia! Any crazy laws there?

5: Crazy laws? Did you say Georgia had crazy laws?

6: No, sir, I—

5: Them's fightin' words! *(Turns to AUDIENCE, very matter-of-factly.)* In Georgia, you have the right to commit simple battery if provoked by "fighting" words. *(5 and 6 pantomime a fight. 1, 2, and 3 hum a Hawaiian song and hula while 5 and 6 huddle from their fight.)* In Hawaii, coins are not allowed to be placed in one's ears.

6: *(Yells, as if hard of hearing.)* What?

5: Never mind. Hey, what's going on there? *(1, 2, 3, and 4 are all in a row as though straddling a bench, fishing.)*

1: Yeeeehaw, this is fun.

2: Caught one. *(Reels a fish in.)*

3: Yep, me too. *(Reels a fish in.)*

4: I don't know why we didn't think of this sooner! Whoa, got one!

6: *(Pulls quarters out of ears.)* Hey, if we can't stick coins in our ears, then I don't think it's fair that you get to break the law!

1, 2, 3, 4: Break the law? *(Stunned.)*

6: That's right. In Boise, Idaho, you can't fish from a giraffe's back. *(1, 2, 3, and 4 climb "down" from a "giraffe," but continue fishing.)*

4: That's fine.

3: Yeah, not a problem.

1: We'll just climb down and then we'll just go fish in Chicago.

2: Yeah.

95

NOTES: ____

169

6: Um, guys, in Chicago, Illinois, it's illegal to fish in pajamas.

2: Told you we should have put pants on!

5: What's that smell?

6: What? I don't smell anything.

OTHERS: It's you. *(Point to 6.)*

6: Sorry. In Indiana, you can't take a bath in the winter.

1: No, it's not him. I smell smoke.

2: Me too. Fire, fire! (OTHERS start scrambling.)

3: Patience, everyone. You know the rules.

5: But there's a—

6: I know, there's a fire and the whole city is in peril, but in Fort Madison, Iowa, you know we firefighters have to practice for fifteen minutes before attending a fire.

2: But the—

6: You know what they say…

OTHERS: Practice makes perfect.

1, 2, 3: In Kansas, if two trains meet on the same track … *(Lined up like a train going toward 4, 5, & 6.)*

4, 5, 6: Neither shall proceed until the other has passed. *(Lined up like a train going right, toward 1, 2, & 3.)*

1: After you.

4: Oh, no, no. After you.

1: But I can't go until you do.

4: And I can't go until you do.

ALL: Then we'll just fly! *(ALL split and begin buzzing like bees.)*

4: So, bzzzz, where you headed?

3: Kentucky. Bzzzz.

1: Kentucky, eh? Bzzzz. You sure you want to go there?

3: Sure. Bzzzz. Why?

2: By law, all bees entering Kentucky shall be accompanied by certificates of health. Bzzzz. You got yours?

3: Not on me. Bzzzz. Well, that bites!

5: Speaking of biting, *(Slowly they morph out of bee characters.)* did you know that in Louisiana, biting someone with your natural teeth is "simple assault," but biting someone with your false teeth is "aggravated assault"?

6: You don't want to bite under false pretenses, do you?

OTHERS: Bite under false pretenses?

6: Let's move on. Okay, remember how I said some stupid laws just aren't that stupid? *(OTHERS ad-lib agreement.)* This next law is just good sense. In Maine, it is illegal to step out of a plane in flight.

4: Geronimoooo! *(OTHERS watch 4 fall.)*

1: And there's another one I'm glad they wrote. It's long past due! In Baltimore, Maryland, it is illegal to mistreat oysters.

3: How is that long overdue?

1: Oysters have feelings too!

2: You know, I think Massachusens, Massachutens… people from Massachusetts deserve your sympathy more than the oysters!

5: What do you mean?

2: Well, on the one hand, it is illegal to go to bed without first having a full bath. But at the same time, it is illegal to take more than two baths a month in Boston.

3: Do you think that means they only get to go to bed twice a month?

1: Poor Massachutens. And I thought oysters were mistreated!

4: Oh, shoot! I'm late for my haircut! See you guys later.

OTHERS: Hold it!

6: Did you get permission?

4: Permission. To get my hair cut?

5: In Michigan, by law a wife's hair legally belongs to her husband.

4: Oh, really? Why, I've got half a mind to—

5: He owns that too.

4: What?

5: Your mind. He owns the whole head!

2: Speaking of heads, in Minnesota, a person may not cross state lines with a duck on their head.

6: And in Tylertown, Mississippi, you'd better not shave in the center of Main Street.

3: Okay, this one is just plain irresponsible. On Sundays in Kansas City, Missouri, children can buy real shotguns… but not toy cap guns.

5: Have you noticed that a lot of the stupid laws are about women?

4: And fishing.

5: In Montana, it is illegal for married women to go fishing alone…

4: While in Nebraska, it is illegal to go whale fishing.

1: And it's a good thing too. Whales have rights!

NOTES: ___________________

OTHERS: There are no whales in Nebraska!

1: Change the subject. This one really does make good sense.

6: More animal rights?

1: No. In Nevada, smarty pants, don't try to pawn your dentures to pay gambling debts, and keep your camel off the highway!

2: Yeah, yeah, we know. "Camels have rights too!"

3: *(To 1.)* Okay, here's the grandfather of all stupid laws. In New Hampshire, if a person is caught cleaning up the countryside, he can be fined one hundred and fifty dollars for "maintaining the national forest without a permit." *(1, 2, 3, 4, 6 pantomime picking up trash.)*

5: Excuse me, folks. You got a permit to pick up that trash?

OTHERS: Permit? *(They frown.)*

5: You hooligans better wipe those frowns off your tree-hugging faces.

6: Why? It's not like we're in New Jersey.

1: What does he mean, New Jersey?

2: In New Jersey, it is illegal to frown at a police officer.

5: What beep through yonder beep beeps. It is the beep and Juliet is the beep.

4: And in New Mexico, Shakespeare caused such a stir that state officials ordered four hundred words of "sexually explicit material" to be cut from Romeo and Juliet. *(ALL look way up.)*

1, 2, 3: *(Sing softly.)* Start spreading the news.

6: Don't do it! *(As if calling to a jumper.)*

1, 2, 3: *(Sing softly.)* I'm leaving today.

5: Don't jump!

1, 2, 3: *(Sing softly.)* I got to be a part of it...

4: You have your whole life ahead of you.

1, 2, 3: *(Sing softly.)* New York, New York.

4, 5, 6: *(Eyes slowly start watching "jumper" fall.)*

1: In New York...

2: It is illegal to jump off the Empire State Building.

3: The penalty for jumping off a building is...

1, 2: *(Jumper "lands" right in front of them.)* Splat!

4, 5, 6: Death.

4: You know, you three *(Speaking to 1, 2, 3.)* have pretty good voices.

1, 2, 3: Thanks.

4: *(5 begins humming.)* Did you know that in Nags Head, North Carolina, you can be fined for singing out of tune for more than ninety seconds? *(5 stops humming abruptly.)*

3: And in North Dakota...

1: *(Points.)* What's that?

2: My elk.

1: Your elk, eh? Well, what's he doing?

2: Sitting in a sandbox.

1: An elk... in a sandbox... and in North Dakota, of all places. You criminal!

5: *(Sneaks up on something and whispers.)* Hot dawg! That's a big one!

4: Where?

5: There. *(Pause.)* In the cheese. *(Pause.)*

4: *(To AUDIENCE.)* Cleveland, Ohio.

5: I've almost got 'em.

4: *(To 5.)* Um, excuse me, sir. In our fair state, it's illegal to catch mice without a hunting license!

1, 2, 3: *(Sing.)* O, K, L, A, H, O, M, A, Ooooklahoma, where—

6: *(Spoken.)* You'd better tie your car up when leaving it outside a public building.

2: *(1 whistles.)* What are you up to?

1: Getting ready to go swimming in Oregon.

2: What? *(Shocked.)* Man, are you out of your mind? Don't you know that in Oregon, people may not whistle under water?

1: Um, I hate to tell you this, but it's physically impossible to whistle under water.

2: Yes, and I'm sure that's why it's the law!

3: Oh, this is a really good one. By law, "watch stuffers" are unwelcome in McKeesport, Pennsylvania.

5: What's a watch stuffer?

3: What's a watch stuffer? What's a watch stuffer? To tell you the truth, I don't have a clue, but whatever it is, he'd better do it somewhere else.

5: You're a lunatic!

3: Oh, yeah? Well, you're an idiot!

5: Lunatic!

3: Idiot!

4: In Rhode Island, any marriage where either of the parties is an idiot or lunatic is null and void.

1: On Hilton Head Island, South Carolina, it is illegal to shine a flashlight on a sea turtle.

2: *(As a sea turtle.)* Ugh! My eyes! You've blinded me! Quick, someone write a law!

6: Um, excuse me. Do you sell horse pants?

NOTES: ____

INTRODUCTION TO THEATRE ARTS 2

5: Horse pants. Why, no, sir. We have horseshoes and saddles, but no pants.

6: Darn. I'm a horse, and I have no pants. In South Dakota, horses aren't allowed into Fountain Inn unless they are wearing pants.

5: Well then, it's a good thing you're in Tennessee!

6: Oh! Tennessee? Well, in that case, got any hollow logs?

5: Shhhh! You want to get us both thrown in jail? It's illegal to sell those things here! Listen, I've got a nice lasso, though, but there's just one hitch.

6: What's that?

5: You'd better not be caught using it to catch fish in these here parts!

1: Everything's big in Texas…

2: Even the stupid laws!

3: A recently passed anti-crime law requires criminals to give their victims twenty-four hours' notice, either orally or in writing, to explain the nature of the crime to be committed.

4: In Salt Lake City, Utah, no one may walk down the street carrying a paper bag containing a violin.

1: We're almost there!

2: And in Vermont, women must obtain written permission from their husbands to wear false teeth.

5: In Virginia, you need a permit to run a barbershop in the town of Christiansburg.

6: That's not stupid.

5: You got to be careful. The law says your permit will be taken away if you're caught operating without a permit!

6: Oh, I get it!

4: In Seattle, Washington, it is illegal to carry a concealed weapon that is over six feet in length.

3: How would you conceal it if it was over six feet in length?

OTHERS: Exactly!

2: And in Wisconsin, there's a cheesy law that requires a license to make cheese, and making Limburger cheese requires a master cheesemaker's license.

1: In Wyoming, you may not take a picture of a rabbit during the month of June. May is fine, and July's good too. But in June…

OTHERS: We know! Rabbits have rights!

1: No, in June they are notorious for having bad "hare" days. *(Pause.)* Get it? Bad "hare"? H-A-R-E? *(Pantomimes a microphone.)* Hello? Is this thing on?

6: Okay, guys. I kept count, and that's only forty-nine states with stupid laws.

4: No, there are stupid, outdated laws in all fifty states. We saved the best for last.

6: Good, I'm getting hungry.

5: Great, then you'll love this one!

1, 2, 3, 4, 5: In West Virginia…

2: The law states that…

4: It is entirely legal…

3: To take roadkill home for dinner!

ALL: MMMMmmmm, mmmm.

NOTES:

NEWSCAST

Newscasts are how many of us receive updates on daily world events. Those events range from the very important to the trivial but inspiring. There is no formula for creating a newscast. What matters is that **delivery** is clear and that the listener feels important.

You may deliver your newscast from paper notes, from a digital source, from a teleprompter, from a large placard, or from memory. For the purposes of this lesson, you are encouraged to use a teleprompter such as a tablet or a laptop, hand-held notes, or a placard.

Hand-held notes should be neat, printed clearly, pages numbered, and rehearsed.

Teleprompter notes should be in large print with proper punctuation and delivery notes, and they should be set at a comfortable reading speed. They should also be rehearsed. There are numerous ways to turn TVs, tablets, computers, laptops, and even video monitors into teleprompters. Because there are so many options, and because technology changes rapidly, it will be up to you to research recent innovations. Do not spend money on this lesson. If you cannot create a teleprompter using resources already at your disposal, move to a different method. You will get more points for innovation than you will for spending unnecessarily.

Placards should be written in dark print, large enough to be seen clearly from the news desk, numbered if there is more than one, and in order. The person holding the placards should practice handling them quietly and with proper fluidity. The person reading them should be well-rehearsed.

What do all four of the previous paragraphs have in common? Rehearsal. While professional newscasters do not rehearse each night's news over and over again, they do get rehearsal time. They are bringing news into homes. They need listeners to trust them, and blowing lines over and over again erodes trust.

The basic structure of a newscast involves an introduction of one's self and the name of the news show. Sometimes, if it is not a busy news night, journalists might talk amongst themselves a bit, giving their show a human touch. This is generally kept to a minimum, because it is ultimately about the news. Each news segment answers five or six questions: who, what, when, where, why, and how.

And as they go from one story to the next, they tend to **segue,** *a verbal bridge that leads gracefully from one story to the next.*

At the end of the broadcast, there is a wrap-up of the episode and then the signoff.

Producers try to make their newscasts more interesting by providing a number of visually interesting elements, including diagrams, statistics, interviews, field reports, photos, sound bites, and anything else that will be more attractive than the newscasters themselves.

Speaking of attractive, newscasters do tend to look good. And while there is a new trend toward individuality, it is important that those delivering the news feel "welcomed" in our living rooms. We want them to be clean, polite, and carefully put together. When delivering the news, avoid graphic T-shirts unless they fit your particular show or support your newscast, and try to look like your general listening or viewing population.

On the next two pages are three newscasts you can use for practice.

NOTES: _______________________________________

NEWSCAST PRACTICE 1—SINGLE NEWSCASTER

BARNEY: Good afternoon. I'm Barney Specklefrashter, and this is your Four O'Clock Countdown. This morning, Mayor Goodall Gootenberry announced, after much speculation, that he would not be running for reelection. As suspected, the Mayor has accepted an offer to take over the Rinky Dink, Fort Myers' very own roller derby roller rink! That's great news for the Rinky Dink, but sad news for the town of Fort Myers. Under Mayor Gootenberry's tenure, the town has seen crime decrease by 22 percent, and we are enjoying record-low unemployment. He will be missed. But don't be sad! Rumor has it he will be rolling with the Fort Myers Maelstrom every Friday at 7 p.m.!

Speaking of maelstrom, last night's storms brought in a little over an inch of rain, much needed precipitation. So far in September, we've only seen 1.7 inches, far below average for the second-rainiest month of the year.

But I'll tell you what's not below average: The Corn Queen! That's right, Fort Myers. Saturday marks the crowning of the 77th annual Corn Queen, and this year's contestants are all stunners! Each year, our town nominates ten farm animals to compete in the beauty pageant. Last year, Daisy the milk cow won by a landslide. And she has served well, visiting schoolchildren at each of our K through 5 campuses, But alas… MOOOOOve over, Daisy. Hey, if you want to see Daisy crown her successor, join us at the clock tower Saturday at 10 a.m. And if you haven't voted, see Ray Ray at Heath Automotive.

Last week, Alice Quegmire noticed a man walking down 4th street. He seemed confused, but he was an adult, so she went on about her business. A few minutes later, she noticed the same man wandering near Lake Conchitrail. As you may know, that Lake has steep drop-offs, and Alice became worried. She tried to speak to the man, but he kept walking away from her, so she called Sandy at the town office. Sandy sprang into action. He fit the description of a man who had wandered away from a nursing home seven miles away. His family had been searching for him. Thanks to Sandy and Alice's quick thinking, he was reunited with his family, safe and sound. So this week's Citizenship Award goes to Alice Quegmire and Sandy Sterling for being caring neighbors! Good job, ladies!

And that wraps up today's update. I'm Barney Specklefrashter. Until next time!

NEWSCAST PRACTICE 2—TWO NEWSCASTERS

KAY: Good morning, Houston! I'm Kay Novak.

TIBERIUS: And I'm Tiberius Spear. And this is Gulf Coast Sunrise. Harris County woke up to a shocker this morning. Nope. It wasn't a spectacular show of thunder and lightning. It was a countywide power outage. No word yet on what caused the four-minute blackout, but school kids' sighs were heard as far north as Waco when power returned just before 6 a.m.

KAY: That's right, Ti. Officials are in the dark about the origins of the outage.

TIBERIUS: In the dark! Good one, Kay!

KAY: Thanks, Ti. Did you hear we're getting a new ice cream parlor at City Hall?

TIBERIUS: Ice cream? Really?

KAY: That's right. Now when you go to City Hall, you can order up a single, a double, or even a triple scoop of your favorite sweet treat! The old pass-through window where citizens once paid parking tickets was no longer in use, so the city has contracted with Saul's Sweets, a local hand-churned ice creamery, to use the nine-foot by eight-foot space. Saul says there's just enough room to launch his first retail venture. And city workers say they welcome the smell of waffle cones in the morning! Good for them! I wish we had an ice cream parlor here at the studio.

TIBERIUS: We'd never get any work done! Say, Kay, you know Gus, the security guard?

KAY: I love Gus! Of course!

TIBERIUS: Did you know Gus is 91 years old today?

KAY: 91! Well, happy birthday, Gus!

TIBERIUS: For those of you watching at home, Gus is our beloved front door greeter. I started here at WFGN eleven years ago, and on my first day, Gus welcomed me and told me to always pack snacks because you never know when you're going home. And he was right! He has always had a smile and a firm pat on the back for each of us. He's the glue that holds our little news station together, so happy birthday, Gus! May you have many more!

KAY: Sweet guy. He's been here 34 years.

TIBERIUS: 34! Wow!

KAY: That's right. He was a basketball coach for 35 years before that. Which leads us straight into

NOTES: _______________________________

____

____

____

____

____

____

____

our next story. Houston ISD is holding a job fair, but not for teachers. Nope. This fair is different. It's a job fair for parents of ISD students. If you are a parent in need of full- or part-time work, log on to our website for more information.

TIBERIUS: Kay, do you know what time it is? It's time to announce the Whiz Kid of the Week! Gerardo Ortiz was just 14 when his family immigrated to the United States. He spoke no English, but right away he began volunteering at his local library. He taught himself English by studying children's books and then increasing the difficulty of the reading material. He became a volunteer story hour reader in both English and Spanish, and by the time he was 15, he was a confident bilingual speaker. But still, there was a lot of catching up to do, so Gerardo began attending after-school tutorials. There, he won the attention of Dr. Ian Caskill, who saw something special in Ortiz. Soon, Dr. Caskill recommended emergency placement at the STEM magnet school, where Ortiz's interest in

robotics earned him a spot on the team. Because of his language hurdles, he repeated 11th grade, voluntarily! Ortiz will graduate this May with a 4.0 GPA and ranked 9th in his class of over 300. He's been offered scholarships at a dozen colleges but will be attending Texas A&M University on full scholarship, where he will double major in engineering and English. Congratulations to our Whiz Kid of the Week, Gerardo Ortiz, for being an inspiration to us all.

KAY: Wow. Great story, Ti. What is he hoping to do after college?

TIBERIUS: Rumor has it he's got his eyes on the stars... as in NASA!

KAY: Future astronaut. Good for him. Well, that's all the time we have this morning. Join Elliot and Franky at noon right here on Channel 7. Have a great day!

TIBERIUS: Take care!

NEWSCAST PRACTICE 3—FIELD REPORTER, INTERVIEW

MICHAEL: Good evening. This is Michael Bennet with the Six O'clock News on 8. We have a breaking story. Let's get right to it. We were just informed that the pink bunny in the claw machine at Eric's Pizza Palace is closer to being set free. That's right. The plush pink bunny that had been infamously wedged between the blue otter and the yellow sponge creature has been loosened. He's not yet free. Let's get straight to our field reporter, Chesney Botox. Chesney, what can you tell us?

CHESNEY: Well, Michael, it's true. Tots and their parents have for years dropped quarter after quarter into the claw machine at Eric's Pizza Palace. In that time, they've won a lot of prizes, but pink bunny had remained elusive—that is until Mia Thomas got her claws on him. Ms. Thomas. Congratulations! No one has ever moved the bunny. Not once. What strategy did you use?

MIA: Well, Chesney, I used my eyes. I lined him up this way, and then I scooted around to the side of the machine and lined him up that way, and $24.50 later, he was wiggling. So I kept at it

CHESNEY: $24!

MIA: And fifty cents. That's an important fifty cents, because that's when his little paw popped up.

CHESNEY: His left paw or his right paw?

MIA: It was his left one. Then it looked like he was patting the sponge guy on the back. It was kind of cute, but short-lived.

CHESNEY: Short-lived? How so?

MIA: Well, I blew another ten bucks or so and got his other arm free. Then it looked like he was riding a roller coaster. Wheeeeee! And then he popped out, like a primed pimple! Ploop! (Toward the machine.) Hey, kid! Step away from the claw machine! That baby's mine! (To Chesney.) Gotta run. Some little jerk's gonna get my pink bunny!

CHESNEY: Say, Mia, where's your kid?

MIA: My kid? What? Naw, man. No kids for me. I'm too busy! Whoo!

CHESNEY: Well, Michael, looks like the infamous pink bunny is about to meet his match. Ooh. And the Pac-Man machine is available. Yes! Back to you at the studio!

MICHAEL: Nothing like a good arcade to bring out the kid in all of us! And now for the weather...

NOTES: ____

NAME _______________________________ PERIOD _______ DATE _______

NEWSCAST PERFORMANCE PEER EVALUATION

Evaluate each aspect of the newscaster's performance
on a scale of 1 (worst or not present) to 5 (best).

Newscaster's name	1st impression	Introduction	Delivery	Newscast structure	Voice	Additional elements	Confidence	Timing	Familiarization/ Memorization	This newscaster was best at...	This newscaster could use a little more work on...

NOTES: ____

____

____

____

____

____

____

____

TELEVISION COMMERCIAL

Dan Morrow, theatre and speech teacher in Plano, Texas, submitted the information for this project. The following are the guidelines for the tournaments in which they compete, but your teacher may change the specifications. Always consult your teacher before making guideline changes.

In the "real world," most TV commercials are only thirty seconds long. There are some exceptions, but because advertising can be very expensive, it's important to say as much as possible in a short amount of time.

For this project, however, your commercial will be three minutes long. Contrary to the heading, these commercials are not intended for broadcast unless your teacher takes it to that level. Instead, you and your partners will perform live for your classmates. The performances may be filmed for future enjoyment, self-improvement, or for broadcast, should you have that option.

GUIDELINES

- Two to three people per group.
- All participants will act and share equally in all phases of the project.
- Teams will create their own unique product and write the commercial's script.
- Each group will create an actual sample of its product.
- Props must be used and will not be pantomimed.
- A set is required.
- Costumes are required for each group member.
- You may have special effects, music, sound effects, or lighting, but these are all optional.
- Unless your teacher says otherwise, each script will be three minutes, give or take fifteen seconds; in other words, the final performances must be no less than 2:45 and no more than 3:15.

Additional Guidelines: ____

____

____

BEFORE DOING THIS ACTIVITY...

- Review "Making the Most of Group Work" on page 22.
- Study "Character Development" on page 140-142.
- Study "Dramatic Structure" on pages 135-136.

THIS PROJECT WILL...

- Exercise time management skills.
- Improve broad-scale project management.
- Allow for higher levels of creativity.
- Encourage teamwork.
- Require self-accountability.
- Improve organization.
- Require attention to detail.
- Improve presentation technique.
- Be extremely fun!

103

ABOUT COMMERCIALS

In Plano, Texas, where this lesson originated, middle school speech and drama students attend tournaments and compete against one another in twelve different events. Most of the twelve events are commonly found at similar tournaments across the country. In an effort to diversify and attract interest, the directors introduced a new competition where students would create imaginary products and write and perform commercials about them.

Commercials are not uncommon in theatre; teachers have been using them to train actors for years. But this type of commercial is unique. Your students will love the idea of creating one-of-kind products, and you will find yourself saying, "Now that would be a great TVC product!" TVC is short for TV commercial.

One of the shortcomings of this type of activity is that students sometimes migrate toward the unsavory. Do not allow them to use bathroom humor or to make fun of other students or teachers. Teach them that there are other ways to be funny and that they do not have to be gross or insulting to get laughs.

Change the rules to suit your needs or your group of students. If you are working with younger actors, you might want to shorten the commercials

---

GRADING

Your teacher will discuss the various parts of the project with you and explain which steps will receive an individual grade, which will not, and the dates by which each must be completed. Mark the steps accordingly so that you and your group members will be prepared.

GRADE	NO GRADE	DUE DATE	ASSIGNMENT
			Choose one product and begin writing scripts.
			Create slogan, logo, and jingle.
			Complete and time script (typed/un-typed).
			Rehearse.
			Design and make set.
			Make or gather costumes.
			Make or gather props, including product sample.
			Complete two *Television Commercial Rehearsal Peer Evaluations*.
			Other:
			Other:
			Perform.
			Complete and turn in *Television Commercial Performance Peer Evaluations*.

PRODUCT

The first thing you must do is decide on a product. Your commercial will be humorous, so you do not want to select a product that is too common or predictable. Instead, look for something that is ridiculously funny without being negative. Look at the following list of products and their purposes. Can you add to the list? Can you mix things up to create new products? Can you change one word and make something even better?

- **Edible School Supplies**—Eraser Gum, Pencil Pops, and Gulpable Glue for those in-class cravings.
- **Moose Mousse**—To tame the mane on your pet moose.
- **Bodyguard Mime**—An annoying personal protector who will use mime to irritate those who would do you harm.
- **Test Taker 3000**—A double who will take all your tests for you.
- **Deodorizer Suit**—A large, conspicuous suit that emits perfume every few seconds or at the press of a button.

If you have a hard time thinking of a product, use the table on the left. How about "Drive-Thru Haircuts" or "Dial-a-Dingbat"? Even if you don't use the ideas in that list, they may get your imagination moving in the right direction.

The best way to discover your product is to brainstorm. Brainstorming is a process that encourages spontaneity and creativity. Start by grabbing a timer and pencils and paper for each member of your group. Then start the timer.

- For the first minute, each group member should write everything—literally *every* word—that comes to their head without talking. Get inspiration from the room around you.
- At one minute, stop the timer and take turns reading everything you wrote aloud. As ideas come to you and your partners, write them down—no matter how seemingly unimportant. Circle everything you and your partners seem to like.

---

to a minute and a half. Three seems to be the ideal group size, but you may find that, especially in larger classes, you have better luck with groups of four.

Put a new twist on TVC and have your students use it as a means of exploring problems at school. Create a public service announcement commercial in which there is no product; instead, students are promoting random acts of kindness or some other worthy cause. It can still be humorous, but it meets a campus-wide need.

Invest in several timers for this project, or have students use the timers on their phones.

Perhaps the most beneficial aspect of TVC is the simple way in which sets are designed and built. You can use this same concept for several different projects. It works especially well with lip-sync and anything where an inexpensive, lightweight set is required.

As with all performances in this book, a rubric is provided for you and a *Television Commercial Performance Peer Evaluation* form for your students. Encourage students to become master critics, both orally and in writing.

A sample script is also provided.

- Start the timer again, writing everything that comes to mind. This time, take more time with detail and feel free to discuss with your group members. You should brainstorm for two full minutes this time.

- Stop the timer and discuss the results. By this time, you and your group members will probably be focusing on two or three ideas you like.

PRODUCT IDEAS
~ fill in the blanks ~

______________________ in a Can
______________________ in a Box
______________________ Spray
______________________ Shoes
______________________ Glasses
______________________ Remote
______________________ Cream
______________________ -inator
______________________ Repellent
______________________ -on-a-Stick
______________________ -ilizer
______________________ Are Us
______________________ Olympics
Invisible ______________________
Dial-a- ______________________
Bottled ______________________
Disposable ______________________
Book of ______________________
Insta- ______________________
Drive-Thru ______________________
Magic ______________________
Edible ______________________
Techno- ______________________
One Hour ______________________

- Write all the ideas you do not plan to use on the board in your classroom. All the groups will be doing this. This is a form of idea *recycling*. Look at the ideas your classmates are throwing away. Can you use any of them? Hopefully, your discarded ideas will be of use to some of them too.

Write your five favorite product ideas and their purposes here:

1. ______________________

____

2. ______________________

____

3. ______________________

____

4. ______________________

____

5. ______________________

____

Take a few minutes to discuss your top five ideas. Cross off anything that is not funny enough or that does not inspire a great deal of discussion. These discarded ideas may now be recycled for the rest of the class so other teams can see them and become inspired. Keep discussing your remaining ideas until you and your team can agree upon one product. Be certain you choose wisely; after the product decision deadline you will not be allowed to change your product.

NOTES: ______________________

____

____

____

____

____

____

____

INTRODUCTION TO THEATRE ARTS 2

NAME ____ PERIOD ________ DATE ____________

TELEVISION COMMERCIAL PRODUCT BASICS

Now it is time to learn as much about your product as you can. The more you know about it ahead of time, the easier it will be to write your script when the time comes, so write as much as you can in the spaces below. You can always mark things off that you choose not to use, but failure to write something can mean a good idea will be forgotten later in the process.

1. What is the name of your product? ____

2. Can you think of other names that might be even funnier?

3. What does your product do? List all the benefits.

4. Can you think of some humorous side effects? These should have something to do with the nature of the product.

5. What kinds of consumers will want to buy your product? Men or women, adults or children, human or non-human, tall or short, etc.?

6. If your product is used by someone famous, who would use it and how might it have changed their lives? For example, might Einstein have benefited from the Test Taker 2000, or how about someone less brilliant?

7. What sizes, flavors, colors, or other important descriptors might make your product more appealing to the public?

8. Sometimes having an interesting history or complex science to back it up makes a product more appealing. This can also add to the humor. How was your product developed? Is there some amazing science behind it?

106

NOTES: ____

____

____

____

____

____

____

____

9. Does your product have competition? What are their names and what makes yours better?

10. Where can consumers purchase your product? How much will it cost? Are there any special deals you are offering?

PRODUCT RECOGNITION: JINGLES, LOGOS, AND SLOGANS

Have you ever had a jingle stuck in your head? A **jingle** is a product's theme song, and the advertisers purposefully seek out catchy tunes that will get consumers' feet tapping or get stuck in their heads. Either is effective, because once the jingle gets them, the name of the product—or at least the idea of the product—runs through the mind of the buyer for longer than the thirty-second commercial. While the company pays good money for the half-minute commercial, they don't pay a thing for what your mind does with the information afterward. Each time you hum the jingle or even think about it, that's free advertising for them.

Another important element of advertising is the **logo**. That is *the little design the company uses to symbolize its product; it might or might not include the company's name or initials.* There are the Golden Arches, the yellow bouncing smiley face, the Swoosh, and the mouse ears. You probably don't need to be told that those stand for McDonald's, Walmart, Nike, and Disney—in that order. A logo is usually the first thing a reader recognizes, especially the very young, because it is more visible than words from a distance and usually involves more color or flair than the written part of an ad.

Look around you or use recall to draw three or four famous logos:

Why do you remember these logos? Were you exposed to them more than others? Is something about them more appealing than others? Use this knowledge to fix your own logo in the minds of your commercial's viewers.

Begin brainstorming a logo for your product.

NOTES: ____

____

____

____

____

____

____

____

SLOGAN/MOTTO KEY

1. Verizon

2. Nike

3. Pork

4. M&M's

5. Bounty

6. McDonald's

7. De Beers Group

8. Lay's potato chips

Finally, you will need a **slogan** or **motto**. This is the short phrase that summarizes the product and/or what the advertiser wants the buyer to think of it. How many of the following slogans can you complete or identify?

1. Can you hear me now? ____

2. Just Do It ____

3. The Other White Meat® ____

4. Melts in your mouth, not in your hands ________________________________

5. The Quicker Picker Upper ____

6. I'm lovin' it ____

7. A diamond is forever ____

8. Betcha can't eat just one ____

If you were able to recognize even half of these products, you can understand why a slogan is so important. Like the jingle and the logo, it carries the point of the advertising message beyond the ad itself. It stretches the advertising dollar and encourages more sales.

For the purpose of your project, these three items will add to the humor and the impact of the final performance. Your commercial will be more polished, and your product, while only imaginary, will remain with the audience longer. If your project is for competition, this means your judges will be more likely to remember your product. If it is for class, this will translate to a better grade.

Product Name: ____

1. The Slogan: Look at your product name. Think about what it does. Brainstorm as many slogans as you can. Give yourself two minutes. Begin.

Reword your favorite slogan until your group agrees on it. Keep it simple, avoid wordiness, focus on your product's message, and use creative devices (like rhyming, alliteration, and originality) to make it stick in the consumers' heads. This is a great place to work in a little humor too. Write your final slogan here for safekeeping.

Our product's slogan is…

2. The Jingle: Now that you have your slogan, you can start thinking about your jingle. This does not have to be finished right away. As you write your commercial, your ideas about your jingle may change. However, it is important to write down all ideas while they are fresh in your head. You may think you will remember a fleeting thought later, but it wouldn't be called a fleeting thought if it was going to stick around!

NOTES: ____

____

____

____

____

____

____

____

TOP TEN TIPS FOR WRITING COMEDY

10. Never be cruel; remember that being hurtful will likely backfire on you.

9. Inside jokes may be funny to you, but they are not funny to your audience.

8. Keep it clean.

7. Shock—and add energy—by introducing the unexpected.

6. Develop unique characters that not only contrast with one another, but clash.

5. If you use a running gag (a joke that repeats), it needs to build, and each repetition needs a twist; comedy works best in groups of three (three falls, three misunderstandings, etc.).

4. Use what works; if a pie in the face makes you laugh, use it in your scene.

3. Use (and misuse) a lot of props (think of Carrot Top).

2. Keep it simple; if a joke or gag requires explanation, it doesn't work.

1. Timing is everything; synchronize when possible, use unique timing gags (like performing tasks in sequence and rhythm), and maintain an energetic pace.

You can create your own tune, or (only because this is not real advertising) you can use a famous song that the audience will immediately recognize. A jingle can be from any genre of music. If your group can't sing, consider rapping your song, or use your lack of musical ability to add humor to your commercial. It is important to keep it short. If your jingle is longer than about thirty seconds, you are probably neglecting something else within the body of your commercial.

Use this space to brainstorm famous songs that have anything to do with your product in any way (such as "Let it Snow" for a dandruff product):

Now write down other songs to which you think your audience will relate:

When the time comes, write your jingle here. You will probably want to do your planning on scratch paper and save this space for your rough draft.

Our product's jingle, to the tune of ____, is...

3. The Logo: In real advertising, a logo is quite important, but for your project, it is only slightly important. Do not spend more than a few minutes on this, or save it for your spare time. When you do decide to work on it, keep it simple. It can be a straightforward picture, initials arranged in a creative manner, a combination of the two, or it can even be a symbol. When it comes to logos, most will agree that less is more.

Sketch your final logo here:

NOTES: ____

____

____

____

____

____

____

____

____

____

CHARACTER DEVELOPMENT

Before you can begin writing, you need to spend a little time talking about your various characters. A scene without well-built characters will lack a strong foundation. Remember the "Deodorizer Suit"? Give yourself a moment to think about ideas for a commercial for the product. Can you come up with something? Maybe you can, but with a little more information, your team will find writing much more fun and rewarding.

Here is what we got when we took the classical idea of nerds versus bullies:

A nerdy boy has exhausted all the store-bought deodorizers in search of the one that will make him smell "popular." He has his eyes on a freckled, similarly nerdy girl in his science class with the cutest row of titanium braces—seeking to correct the loveliest tooth gap—in history. The only thing standing between him and his love is the school bully, who is dating the nerdy girl so that his grades will be good enough to keep him on the hockey team. The bully exits, but the same actor returns as a new character, half-angel and half-devil. This new split personality switches between selling the Deodorizer Suit and trying to get the nerd to pull pranks on the bully. Our nerd decides on the suit but keeps the prank idea as a "Plan B," and the suit is delivered immediately by the actress who plays the freckled girl and who is now playing a clumsy bicycle delivery person. As promised, the Deodorizer Suit emits the smell of popularity, which attracts the girl, but now even the bully wants to be his friend. The commercial ends when the suit emits the smell of "responsibility," the only bully repellent known to mankind.

Keep in mind the skills you and your team already possess. Do you do a great British accent? Consider working it into your character. Can you do gymnastics? Maybe your character could be an excitable cheerleader who flips when happy.

(For much more on Character Development, see Chapter 5, page 140.)

TIME TO WRITE YOUR COMMERCIAL

You are finally ready to get started. As you write your commercial, stay flexible. Sometimes it works out differently than planned, and being able to work outside your original plans will often allow you to create a funnier, more workable script. When you think you are done, refer to the ten items on the *Television Commercial Product Basics* on page 106. Have you included all of the necessary parts of the script? Is it funny? Did you use dramatic structure, and did you complete your jingle? The tips below will help you if you get stuck or feel you are not progressing quickly enough.

COMMERCIAL TIPS

- Start at the end and work backward.
- Stay in one setting, two at the most; jumping from setting to setting confuses the audience and interrupts the smooth flow of the scene.
- Use your characters to create gags or jokes; comedy is funniest when it springs from a clash between a character's personality and the setting or situation: "dumb" cheerleader badly sells Chinese language lessons.
- Stay focused on your product—sell, sell, sell!
- Think of all the things you hear in commercials when you watch TV and use them.

- ◇ "Sunday, Sunday, Sunday!"
- ◇ "A limited-time offer"
- ◇ "But wait, that's not all! Buy today and you'll receive this second…"
- ◇ "Side effects may include…"
- ◇ "Some assembly may be required; batteries not included!"
- Avoid "child's play" like chasing, pointless arguing, wrestling, or fighting.
- Time your scene often during rehearsal!
- After you have written your scene, it should follow simple dramatic structure so that you can fit it into the following sentence with ease: "Our commercial starts when ___________. It gets even funnier when ___________. But it gets even funnier when ___________. Finally, ___________ (this would be the climax), and then we top it off with ___________."

In other words, it should have a clear start in which a problem is introduced, at least two additional points of rising action, a climax, and a satisfying ending.

When you are happy with the script, time it. It should be between 2:45 and 3:15. Record the time at

NOTES: ________________________

____

____

____

____

____

____

CHAPTER 4 — SKILL BUILDING ACTIVITIES

each rehearsal until you fall between the minimum and maximum with every attempt for five rehearsals in a row. This will ensure you do not exceed the time limit for your final performance.

Do not time just the dialogue without movement. Your blocking will add to the length of the scene, as will costume changes, using the product, dealing with props, going "backstage" behind your set, if you have one, and so on. Always time your scene with all of the elements, even if it means writing the names of props on scratch paper and rehearsing with mock props, set, and costumes. As the performance date approaches, however, you must begin working with the actual items to ensure that everything comes together as you planned.

Use rehearsal time wisely. Knowing that your scene is prepared will give you and your group members confidence, and nothing improves acting skills more than feeling sure of one's team and one's self.

TIMING AND REHEARSAL

REH. 1	REH. 2	REH. 3	REH. 4	REH. 5	REH. 6	REH. 7	REH. 8	REH. 9	REH. 10

REH. 11	REH. 12	REH. 13	REH. 14	REH. 15	REH. 16	REH. 17	REH. 18	REH. 19	REH. 20

Rehearsal Times: Time every rehearsal until you fall between the minimum and maximum time requirements for five rehearsals in a row. After that, you may only have to time a rehearsal when changes are made or props and costumes are added.

PROPS, PRODUCT SAMPLE, COSTUMES, AND SET

Now that you have your performance in good shape, it's doubtful you will make any major changes. It is time to finalize any unfinished props, the product, costumes, and your set. Use the following chart to decide who will bring which items. Find out ahead of time how your teacher would like these items stored while awaiting your performance.

Because this is comedy, the visuals—the props, product, set, and costumes—should be "outrageous." This could mean a number of things:

- Larger than life (or ridiculously small).
- Like something from a bad science fiction movie.
- Shockingly colorful.
- Cartoonish.
- Glittery, shiny, fuzzy, or with springy pipe cleaners and pompoms sticking out in every direction.

Look at the examples in the chart on the next page from the products suggested on page 104.

111

NOTES: ____

____

____

____

____

____

____

____

INTRODUCTION TO THEATRE ARTS 2

PRODUCT	SUGGESTED PRODUCT SAMPLES & PROPS*	SUGGESTED COSTUMES	SUGGESTED SET
Edible School Supplies	• Giant pencils and erasers from novelty shops or homemade out of edible materials (like cookie dough)	Very exaggerated school uniforms with a Japanese anime-inspired boldness	Anything to suggest a classroom with a number of things that remind the characters they are hungry (a clock that seems to stand still, a large apple on the teacher's desk)
Moose Mousse	• Chocolate-flavored whipped cream in a can with a label covering the original one • Giant foam moose antlers attached to a can	• Moose: actor with frizzy hair and antlers • Spokesperson: lumberjack or ranger	Mountains or woods with a stream that doubles as a mirror
Bodyguard Mime	• Newspaper for character needing bodtguard • Autograph pad, pen, and camera for pesky character	Mime: black pants with a bar code, striped shirt	A giant box decorated like a doll's box from which mime would emerge (to do the "mime in a box" stunt)
Test Taker 3000	• Thick test • Cardboard cutout shaped roughly like a student • Remote control to operate Test Taker 3000	Teacher dressed like an older person; thick glasses and hearing aid	Student desks and chairs; teacher desk and chair
Deodorizer Suit	• Science beakers and test tubes filled with colored water and a tiny piece of dry ice • Blue ribbon	• Students: nerdy outfits • Bully: large jersey, cap	• Typical science classroom with pictures of famous scientists on walls

*Unlike many of your other scenes, you cannot pantomime props in this project. As you rehearse, write down any props your team needs for the scene.

Perhaps the most challenging part of a TV commercial project is the set. If your team will actually be competing, you will probably want to spend a little more time and perhaps invest a little money into this part of the project. If it is strictly for class, your teacher can give you an idea about what they expect for the completed set. If you exercise your creativity, you won't need to spend a dime. The following are some suggestions for putting together an inexpensive or even free set for your commercial project.

When planning your set...

• Think small and simple; the larger the set, the more time and money you may have to spend.

• Use materials you already have around the house like spare doors in your garage, room dividers, shower curtains or sheets that can be painted and hung from a frame, lumber, or cardboard.

• Stack two project display boards on top of each other and duct tape them together (see sample); with enough tape, your boards will fold for storage or open and stand freely for your performance; decorate them with paper, paint, or fabric.

• If your set has two sides (most will), use one side to create a setting and the other to post information about your product.

• Create "storage" on your set by attaching boxes that can become cupboards or sturdy

NOTES: ____

sheets of cardboard that can serve as shelves or countertops (see sample). But keep it as lightweight and simple as possible. The heavier your set becomes, the more quickly it will deteriorate because of all the movement.

- Make your set "pop" out at the audience by adding some three-dimensional elements. In the example, the cupboard (a box attached to the back with a cut-out) made it difficult to use the back side of the set, so a large poster of the group's logo was attached to the protruding box. It made the logo seem larger while allowing the group to still use both the front and back of their set.

- Be creative; holiday lights, hidden doors or windows, and other simple additions to your set can give it something special.

- Learn from what others do.

- Ask for help; if you are not comfortable with your ability to do this, get an older student or adult to help you and learn from them.

BACK VIEW

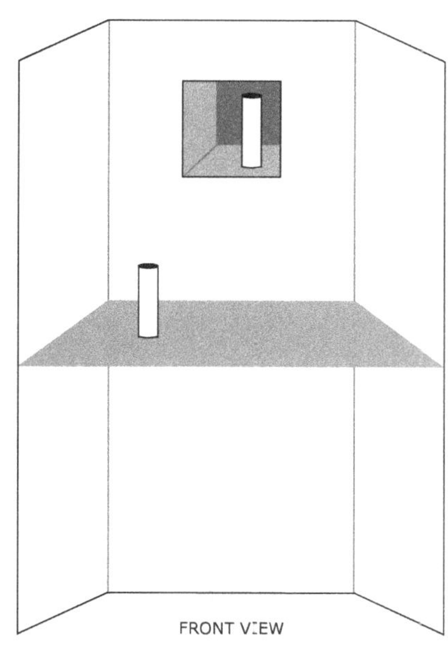

FRONT VIEW

113

NOTES: ____

____

____

____

____

____

____

____

____

____

INTRODUCTION TO THEATRE ARTS 2

NAME ____ PERIOD _________ DATE _______________

Plan the rest of your project here, including who will provide certain items.

ACTION (What needs to be done or brought?)	MEMBER	MEMBER	MEMBER	DUE DATE	COMPLETE? (If no, explain alternate plan)

You may also want to get phone numbers or email addresses from each member so that reminders and other communication will be possible.

NOTES:

NOTES: ____

____

____

____

____

____

____

____

____

SAMPLE TV COMMERCIAL SCRIPT

PRODUCT: Moose Mousse

LOGO: (at left)

SLOGAN: Tame your wild beast's wild hair!

CAST OF CHARACTERS

BUBBA .... The pet moose who has bad hair.

ARNOLD .... The boy with equally bad hair.

MOM .... A believer in the Moose Mousse product; she has perfectly styled, huge hair.

SETTING: The family breakfast room before school.

MOM: *(Calls off.)* Arnie, baby! You're going to be late for school. *(To AUDIENCE.)* That boy! He'd sleep all day if I let him.

ARNOLD: *(ENTERS with really bad hair.)* Morning, Mom.

MOM: *(Sees ARNOLD.)* Aaaagghhhh! Oh, Arnie, you scared me!

ARNOLD: Sorry, Mom. I'm having a really bad hair day.

MOM: I can see that. I mean, it's not that bad. It's just a little wild, that's all. Call Bubba. If he's late one more time, he'll have to graze by himself for a full week.

ARNOLD: Bubba, time for breakfast!

BUBBA: *(From OFFSTAGE.)* Just—one—second. I'm—having—a little prob—lem. Ugh. There. *(ENTERS.)*

ARNOLD: Aaaagghhhh!

BUBBA: Aaaagghhhh!

MOM: Oh, my! You're both a sight for sore eyes.

BUBBA: Here's your comb, Mom. *(Hands her a comb with huge clumps of moose hair tangled in it.)* Sorry about the fur. It got stuck in this wild, mangled, mess of a hairdo.

BUBBA and ARNOLD: And today's picture day!

MOM: Picture day? Noooo!

BUBBA and ARNOLD: Yeeeessss! What are we going to do?

MOM: *(Takes out a fake butcher knife.)* I guess we could cut it all off! *(Gives AUDIENCE an evil look.)*

BUBBA: Not that!

ARNOLD: Anything but that!

MOM: Then perhaps I could try to comb it out. *(She grabs Arnold's hair and tugs, then takes a fork from his hair.)* I thought I was missing a fork. How did this get in there?

ARNOLD: I broke every comb in the house. I had to use something!

BUBBA: *(Removes some random object from his hair.)* Oh, speaking of that. Here. I've had this a while. *(MOM stares, confused. With ARNOLD.)* Don't ask!

MOM: Wait a minute! Wait a minute! I just remembered. I think I have just the thing for your beastly hair! *(Produces two cans of hair mousse.)* Moose Mousse—when you need to tame your wild beast's wild hair!

BUBBA and ARNOLD: Moose Mousse?

MOM: That's right. From the makers of Hoof Gloss, Moose Mousse is a specially formulated hair product that softens coarse hair, removes grass, fleas, knots, tangles, and forks, and instantaneously forms hair into an impressive, impermeable coiffure that will last an amazing seven to ten days!

BUBBA: *(Teases.)* Mom, you've been holding out on us!

MOM: Well, boys, a woman's got to protect her beauty secrets! Now go tame those beastly heads! The Super Strong Formula for you, *(Tosses a can to BUBBA.)* and the Mild Formula for you. *(Tosses a can to ARNOLD. Both EXIT.)* Moose Mousse is perfect for growing boys and mooses. It comes in three formulas—Mild, Regular, and Super Strong, plus it comes in a variety of scents. I like Peat Moss and Silt. They are so natural. But perhaps Sweaty Hide or Pasture Breath will suit your loved ones better. *(ARNOLD and BUBBA ENTER with large, perfect hair.)* Well, will you look at that! Perfect!

ARNOLD: Mom, you're the best. Where can we get more of this amazing Moose Mousse?

MOM: You can buy it at your local feed store, the veterinarian's office, and from participating park rangers. Or you can call or order online.

NOTES: ____

____

____

____

____

____

____

____

The next ten people to purchase Moose Mousse will receive a four-ounce sample of Hoof Gloss absolutely free!

BUBBA: Oh, my! Look at the time. I don't want to be late. With this hair, I think I'll be grazing with that cute little 800-pound moose today!

MOM: Do you think you can spare a few seconds for the Moose Mousse jingle, Bubba?

BUBBA: You betcha, Mom!

ALL: *(To the tune of "Baby Got Back.")*
We like big hair and we cannot lie
Those other guys look so wild
But my mane's tame
Moose Mousse is to blame
And now I'm one handsome guy!
(Spoken.) Moose Mousse, tame your wild beast's wild hair today!

NOTES: ____

____

____

____

____

____

____

____

NAME _______________________________________ PERIOD _______ DATE _______________

TELEVISION COMMERCIAL PERFORMANCE
PEER EVALUATION

Evaluate each aspect of the performance on a scale of 1 (worst or not present) to 5 (best).

Group #	Actor's Initials	Voice	Movement	Facial expressions	Character	Memorization	Final impression	This actor was best at...	This actor could use a little more work on...
1									

Comment for group:

Group #	Actor's Initials	Voice	Movement	Facial expressions	Character	Memorization	Final impression	This actor was best at...	This actor could use a little more work on...
2									

Comment for group:

Group #	Actor's Initials	Voice	Movement	Facial expressions	Character	Memorization	Final impression	This actor was best at...	This actor could use a little more work on...
3									

Comment for group:

Group #	Actor's Initials	Voice	Movement	Facial expressions	Character	Memorization	Final impression	This actor was best at...	This actor could use a little more work on...
4									

Comment for group:

Group #	Actor's Initials	Voice	Movement	Facial expressions	Character	Memorization	Final impression	This actor was best at...	This actor could use a little more work on...
5									

Comment for group:

 117

NOTES: _______________________________________

____

____

____

____

____

____

____

192

INTRODUCTION TO THEATRE ARTS 2

TELEVISION COMMERCIAL PERFORMANCE PEER EVALUATION, CONT.

Group #	Actor's initials	Voice	Movement	Facial expressions	Character	Memorization	Final impression	This actor was best at...	This actor could use a little more work on...
6									

Comment for group:

7									

Comment for group:

8									

Comment for group:

9									

Comment for group:

10									

Comment for group:

NOTES: ____

____

____

____

____

____

____

____

TELEVISION COMMERCIAL PERFORMANCE RUBRIC

ACTORS:

____

____

____

1. The group **set up** in a timely manner, knew who was responsible for which items, and appeared to know exactly where everything would go.

   1 2 3 4 5

   NOTES:

2. The **set** met the teacher's requested standards for size, sturdiness, neatness, content, and overall appeal. The set added to the scene and was not a distraction.

   1 2 3 4 5 6 7 8 9 10

   NOTES:

3. **Props** were used rather than pantomimed. Props were appropriately exaggerated, humorous, and added to the performance's message.

   1 2 3 4 5

   NOTES:

4. **Product sample** or samples were exaggerated, customized, fit the description in the script, and added to the performance's message.

   1 2 3 4 5 6 7 8 9 10

   NOTES:

5. **Teamwork** was evident in the way the actors interacted in rehearsals, during their performance, and after the performance.

   1 2 3 4 5 6 7 8 9 10

   NOTES:

6. The actors were confident in their overall **memorization** and **delivery**, and the scene flowed without confusion or hesitation.

   1 2 3 4 5 6 7 8 9 10

   NOTES:

GROUP SCORE

Record the total group score from this page (out of a possible 50) in the box to the left. Transfer this to each actor's group score on the next page. Finish rating each individual's performance (out of a possible 50 points). Add any applicable bonus points. The total of the group, individual, and bonus points will give you a grade for that actor.

TELEVISION COMMERCIAL PERFORMANCE RUBRIC, CONT.

Actor:

Voice

1 2 3 4 5

Movement/Blocking

1 2 3 4 5

Facial expressions

1 2 3 4 5

Characterizations

1 2 3 4 5 6 7 8 9 10

Costume

1 2 3 4 5

Energy

1 2 3 4 5 6 7 8 9 10

Memorization

1 2 3 4 5 6 7 8 9 10

Group Score	Individual Score	Bonus Points	TOTAL

Actor:

Voice

1 2 3 4 5

Movement/Blocking

1 2 3 4 5

Facial expressions

1 2 3 4 5

Characterizations

1 2 3 4 5 6 7 8 9 10

Costume

1 2 3 4 5

Energy

1 2 3 4 5 6 7 8 9 10

Memorization

1 2 3 4 5 6 7 8 9 10

Group Score	Individual Score	Bonus Points	TOTAL

Actor:

Voice

1 2 3 4 5

Movement/Blocking

1 2 3 4 5

Facial expressions

1 2 3 4 5

Characterizations

1 2 3 4 5 6 7 8 9 10

Costume

1 2 3 4 5

Energy

1 2 3 4 5 6 7 8 9 10

Memorization

1 2 3 4 5 6 7 8 9 10

Group Score	Individual Score	Bonus Points	TOTAL

Actor:

Voice

1 2 3 4 5

Movement/Blocking

1 2 3 4 5

Facial expressions

1 2 3 4 5

Characterizations

1 2 3 4 5 6 7 8 9 10

Costume

1 2 3 4 5

Energy

1 2 3 4 5 6 7 8 9 10

Memorization

1 2 3 4 5 6 7 8 9 10

Group Score	Individual Score	Bonus Points	TOTAL

THEATRE HISTORY TIME LINE
WITH INFLUENTIAL POLITICAL AND SOCIAL WORLD EVENTS

BC

c. 2560 BC: The Great Pyramid of Giza completed in Egypt.

2000 BC: Stone tablet depicting first known performance in Egypt.

c. 1800 BC: World's oldest surviving narrative, Epic of Gilgamesh, carved into The Old Babylonian tablets.

1000 BC: Greeks rebuilt their civilization after its collapse in the Late Bronze Age.

776 BC: First documented Olympic Games.

750 BC: Greeks learned the alphabet from Phoenicians; Homer composed The Iliac and The Odyssey about the Trojan War and the Fall of Troy.

c. 563-400 BC: Buddha born in India.

551-479 BC: Life of Chinese philosopher and politician Confucius.

534 BC: Thespis became the first "actor," stepping from the traditional chorus to act as an individual.

c. 529 BC: Greek thinker Pythagoras developed theories about music, physics, and mathematics, including what became recognized as the Pythagorean Theorem, a fundamental of geometry.

525-456 BC: The life of Aeschylus, Greek playwright, "Father of Tragedy."

509 BC: Roman Republic established.

508 BC: Cleisthenes introduced democratic governance in Greece, ushering in the Classical Period, a high point in culture and the arts that lasted until the death of Alexander the Great in 323 BC.

496-406 BC: The life of Sophocles, Greek playwright, author of Antigone, Oedipus Rex, and Electra.

490 BC: Greeks repelled Persian invaders at the Battle of Marathon.

480-406 BC: The life of Euripides, Greek playwright, author of Medea, Hippolytus, and The Trojan Women.

445-385 BC: The life of Aristophanes, Greek playwright, "Father of Comedy."

438 BC: Construction of the Parthenon completed.

431-404 BC: Greek city-states Sparta and Athens fought the Peloponnesian War.

c. 400 BC: Women first allowed to attend the theatre.

342-290 BC: The life of Menander, prolific Greek playwright of comedies. Only Dyskolos survives today.

336-323 BC: Macedonian King Phillip II conquered Athens to control Greece. Upon Phillip's assassination, his son Alexander the Great led armies to conquer Persia, Syria, Egypt, and parts of India before dying suddenly in Babylon.

335 BC: Greek philosopher Aristotle penned Poetics, the earliest surviving work of dramatic theory. A year later he opened the Lyceum.

254-184 BC: The life of Plautus, Roman playwright, who adapted most of his works from earlier Greek plays.

221-206 BC: China, unified under Emperor Qin Shi Huang. Construction began on The Great Wall.

190-158 BC: The life of Terence, Roman playwright.

146-60 BC: Roman conquest of Greek regions introduced Greek philosophy and theatre to Rome.

146 BC: Rome destroyed Carthage bringing an end to the Third (and final) Punic War, and to the Carthaginians.

44 BC: Assassination of Julius Caesar signaled the end of the Roman Republic and the beginning of the Roman Empire.

3 BC-65 AD: The life of Seneca, Roman philosopher, statesman and playwright, author of Medea, Thyestes, and Phaedra.

First through Tenth Century AD

33 AD: Crucifixion of Jesus of Nazareth.

43 AD: Romans conquered Britain.

79 AD: Pompeii is buried in twelve feet of volcanic lava and ash.

80 AD: Built amid a nearly 200-year stretch of prosperity and relative peace known as Pax Romana, the Roman Colosseum was completed, allowing for seating of up to 80,000 spectators.

300-645 AD: During the Yamoto period, Japan organized a unified state and established ties to mainland Asia.

c. 350 AD: Indian poet Kālidās composed Shakuntala, which would become one of the first Sanskrit works translated into English.

390 AD: Theodosius the Great declared Christianity the official religion of Rome.

410 AD: Visigoths shocked the world by conquering Rome, the "Eternal City."

476 AD: Flavius Odoacer revolted against and replaced Emperor Romulus Augustulus, effectively ending the Western Roman Empire.

500-800: The lotus of Roman power shifted to Constantinople in the East, in what's now known as the Byzantine Empire, and Western Europe fell into disrepair. Since Christians generally opposed theatre, it became virtually non-existent in Western Europe.

574-622: Emulating China, Shōtoku Taishi began to transform Japan, centralizing the government, emphasizing a bureaucracy of merit, and reverence for Buddhism and Confucianism.

630: Mohammed entered Mecca in triumph; two years later the Qu-ran was completed.

119

NOTES: ____

____

____

____

____

____

____

____

INTRODUCTION TO THEATRE ARTS 2

710-794: Japanese court built a new capital in Nara modeled upon Chang-an in China; emperors are Shinto chiefs. They adopted Buddhism hoping that its teachings will bring peace and protection.

711: The Umayyands conquered the Iberian Peninsula spreading Islam to Europe. The Islamic state, or caliphate, would by 750, rule from the Atlantic Ocean in Northern Africa in the west into modern day Afghanistan in the east.

794-1185: In Japan, the Imperial Court moved to Heian-kyō (now Kyoto) to escape domination of Nara's Buddhist establishment.

800: Frankish king Charlemagne crowned the first Holy Roman Emperor.

800-1000: Height of Byzantine Empire, hub of world commerce and industry.

c. 800: Chinese accidentally created gunpowder.

900: The Roman Church resurrected theatre by introducing religious performances to Easter services.

c. 950: Hrosvitha, a member of German nobility, wrote six plays based on Terence's comedies but featuring religious figures. Her work became the first known example of Western dramatic theatre since the Classical Era.

Eleventh Century

1002: Japanese court women produced the best literature of the era; Murasaki Shikibu's *Tale of Genji* is the world's first novel.

1046: Pope Gregory VII took steps to unify the Roman Church and strengthen its rule in Rome.

1066: William I, Duke of Normandy, conquered England.

1095-1271: The Crusades: first of many attempts by the Roman Church to reclaim the Holy Lands from Islamic rule.

Twelfth Century

1100-1220: Troubadour poetry spread throughout France, Spain, and later Italy. Themes mainly concerned chivalry and courtly love.

1100-1300: Origin of universities in Western Europe.

1140-1260: Aristotle's works translated into Latin.

1150-1500: Gothic style in architecture and art.

1192: Shogun Minamoto no Yoritomo overthrew the Taira Emperor, establishing what would become 675 years of military rule in Japan.

Thirteenth Century

1206-1260: Genghis Khan unified tribes of Mongolia and conquered territory throughout China, the Middle East, and as far northwest as Poland. His empire expanded after his death and then contracted after Islamic Mamluks defeated Mongols at the Battle of Ain Jalut.

1212: Spanish victory over Muslims at Las Navas de Tolosac.

1215: King John of England signed the Magna Carta, which would inspire those seeking liberty for hundreds of years hence.

1271-1295: Life of Italian merchant and explorer Marco Polo, whose stories in The Travels of Marco Polo inspired Europeans to build trade routes eastward.

1290: Mechanical clock invented.

Fourteenth Century

1314: Italian statesman and poet Albertino Mussato wrote *Ecerinis*, the first tragedy written since Roman Times.

1315-1317: Famine choked Northern Europe.

1337-1453: England and France fought the Hundred Years' War, which helped establish their respective national identities.

1347-1350: The Black Death, a pandemic of the bubonic plague, killed between 75-200 million people in Europe, Asia, and North Africa.

1387-1400: Geoffrey Chaucer penned *The Canterbury Tales*.

Fifteenth Century

1415: Italian inventor Giovanni Fontana wrote *Bellicorum instrumentorum liber* (Book of Instruments of War), an illustrated book about military technology, including a discussion of rockets and torpedoes.

1429: Joan of Arc led French to free Orléans from the English. She was burned at the stake two years later.

1440: Johann Gutenberg invented the printing press. This technological breakthrough allowed the spread of information faster than ever before.

1450-1600: The Renaissance Period: the rediscovery of classical Greek philosophy led to a new, expanded way of thinking, that reverberated through all facets of life.

1453: Ottomans captured Constantinople, leading to the end of the Byzantine Empire. The Ottomans would control Constantinople (later named Istanbul) until the end of the First World War in 1917.

1455-1487: Civil wars, called the Wars of the Roses, were fought between the House of Plantagenet and the House of Lancaster over the English throne.

1467-1477: The ten-year-long Ōnin no Ran (Onin War) brought disintegration of the central government in Japan and led to the beginning of the Sengoku period.

1475-1564: The life of Italian sculptor, painter, and poet Michelangelo di Lodovico Buonarroti Simoni.

1476: Ulrich Han first printed a book containing music, in Rome.

1478: Catholic leaders Ferdinand II of Aragon and Isabella I of Castile implemented the Spanish Inquisition, which would persecute Jews, Muslims, and (so-called) heretics for the next 300 years.

1483-1520: Life of Italian painter and architect Raphael Sanzio de Urbino; his best known work is *The School of Athens* in the Vatican.

1492: Italian explorer Christopher Columbus crossed the Atlantic Ocean and landed in the Bahamas, opening the door for the European colonization of the Americas.

c. 1495: Writing of *Everyman*, a morality play whereupon one's good and evil deeds are tallied by God in a ledger. It has seen many adaptations since.

Sixteenth Century

c. 1500: Transatlantic Slave Trade: Sailing from Europe, merchants kidnapped and enslaved men, women, and children from Western Africa.

1503: Italian painter, scientist, and engineer Leonardo da Vinci began painting the *Mona Lisa*.

1504: Michelangelo completed *David*, a masterpiece in marble.

NOTES: _______________________________

____

____

____

____

____

____

____

____

CHAPTER 4 — SKILL BUILDING ACTIVITIES

1508-1512: Michelangelo painted the ceiling of the Sistine Chapel in Rome.

1516: In the Venetian Republic, a law limited Jews to San Girolamo Parish, establishing "Ghetto Nuova" as the first ghetto in Europe.

1517: Martin Luther nailed his *Ninety-five Theses* to All Saints' Church in Wittenberg, beginning the Protestant Reformation—and eventually splitting Western Christianity into Catholics and Protestants.

1519: Spanish conquistador Hernán Cortés met Aztec leader Montezuma in one of the world's largest cities Tenochtitlan (modern Mexico). Within two years, the Aztec Empire was destroyed

1520-1566: Under Suleiman the Magnificent's reign, the Ottoman Empire entered its "Golden Age," expanding to include over 25 million people.

1521: Voyage of Magellan completed with his crew, having circumnavigated the globe.

1524: Italian diplomat and writer, Niccolò Machiavelli published *La Mandragola*, a five-act satire.

1533-1603: Life of Queen Elizabeth, long-reigning ruler of England, patron of the arts.

1542: Pope Paul III established the Roman Inquisition to combat Protestantism.

1543: Firearms introduced in Japan by shipwrecked Portuguese.

1549: Christianity introduced in Japan by Frances Xavier.

1551: Commedia dell'arte gained popularity in Italy and Western Europe.

1562-1589: Catholics and Huguenots Protestants fought the French Wars of Religion.

1564-1593: Life of Christopher Marlowe, English playwright best known for tragedies, wrote *Hero and Leander*, *Tamburlaine the Great*, and *The Tragical History of Doctor Faustus*.

1564-1616: Life of William Shakespeare, English playwright, wrote *Hamlet*, *Romeo and Juliet*, *Macbeth*, *Othello*, *A Midsummer Night's Dream*, and many more.

1568-1600: Oda Nobunaga started the process of reunifying Japan after a century of civil war, laying the foundation for modern Japan.

1570: The Elizabethan masque, an elaborate combination of dance, music, and costumes performed for aristocrats, debuted.

1572-1637: Life of English poet and playwright Ben Jonson, author of *Every Man in His Humour*, *The Alchemist*, and *Bartholomew Fair*.

1576: The first Elizabethan playhouse, The Theatre, opened in London.

1581: First ballet performance, "The Comic Ballet of the Queen," staged in Paris.

1582: Pope Gregory XIII instituted the Gregorian Calendar.

1588: English defeated the Spanish Armada.

1590-1681: The Golden Age of Spanish Theatre: Spain produced four times more plays than the English during their theatrical renaissance. Playwrights included the prolific Lope de Vega, soldier and priest-turned-playwright Calderón de la Barca, and former nun Juana Inés de la Cruz.

1594: The foremost Elizabethan theatrical company, Lord Chamberlain's Men, formed with William Shakespeare as its chief playwright and Richard Burbage as its most famous actor.

1598: Edict of Nantes allowed Protestants in France to practice their religion in peace.

Seventeenth Century

1600: The Globe Theatre staged its first production, *Julius Caesar*.

1600-1750: Baroque Period: encouraged by the Catholic Church to counter the simplicity of Protestant art, Baroque art used color, detail, and movement to create works that would create a sense of awe in the viewer. Later baroque works, known as rococo, became even more extreme and ornamental.

1605: Spanish writer Miguel de Cervantes published *Don Quixote, Part I*, considered among the most important novels ever written.

1607: Englishman John Smith founded the first colony of Virginia at Jamestown.

1609: Italian inventor and scientist Galileo Galilei published *The Starry Messenger*, a compilation of his astronomical discoveries.

1611: The King James Bible was published.

1613: Fire destroyed the Globe Theatre.

1620: Pilgrims sailed to America on the Mayflower.

1622-1673: Life of French writer and actor Molière (born Jean-Baptiste Poquelin), author of *Tartuffe*, *The Misanthrope*, and *The Learned Women*.

1631-1700: Life of critic, poet, and playwright John Dryden, England's first Poet Laureate.

1631: Mt. Vesuvius erupted, destroying everything around the volcano and killing between 3000 and 6000 people.

1636: Harvard College founded in Cambridge, Massachusetts.

1637: The first public opera house, the Teatro San Cassiano, opened in Venice.

1639-1699: Life of French playwright Jean Racine, a tragedian, who wrote *Andromaque*, *Phèdre*, and *Athalie*.

1640-1689: Life of Aphra Behn, one of the first English women to make her living as a writer.

1641-1716: Life of English dramatist William Wycherley, writer of *The Country Wife* and *The Plain Dealer*.

1642-1660: English Civil War: Tensions between King Charles I and Parliament erupted in armed hostilities. Throughout the war, the Puritan majority ruled, and Parliament closed all theatres in England.

1643: Molière founded Illustre Theatre in Paris.

1651: First public comedy house opened in Vienna, Austria.

1653-1725: Life of Japanese dramatist Chikamatsu Monzaemon, innovator in bunraku and kabuki, writer of *The Courier for Hell*, and *The Love Suicides at Amijima*.

1660-1710: The Restoration Period: The reopening of English theatres led to a theatre boom that welcomed women to the stage, diversity to the audiences, and popularized comedy.

1661: Lincoln's Inn Fields, London's largest public square, opened.

NOTES: ____

____

____

____

____

____

____

____

INTRODUCTION TO THEATRE ARTS 2

1662: The English Royal Patent mandated that women perform female theatrical roles.

1663: The Theatre Royal, Drury Lane, London, opened.

1665: *Ye Bare and Ye Cubb*, on record as the first English-language play presented in the colonies in the colony of Virginia.

1665-1666: Bubonic plague killed an estimated 100,000 people, nearly a quarter of all Londoners.

1673-1841: Golden age of kabuki theatre: Japan starts to flourish with kabuki and bunraku theatre and broader access to education and books.

1681: Professional female dancers appeared in Paris for the first time.

1687: English physicist, theologian, and astronomer Isaac Newton published *Mathematical Principles of Natural Philosophy.*

Eighteenth Century

c. 1700: Italian Bartolomeo Cristofori invented the first modern piano.

1705: The Queen's Theatre opened in London.

1707-1793: Life of Italian playwright Carlo Goldoni, founder of modern Italian comedy, author of *Servant of Two Masters* and *The Mistress of the Inn.*

1711-1785: Life of Kitty Clive, English actress.

1714: Italian composer Antonio Vivaldi (1678-1741) became the impresario of the Teatro Sant' Angelo, helping popularize opera throughout Europe.

1720-1860: Life of Italian playwright Carlo Gozzi, revitalized commedia dell'arte by bringing an intense satirical edge to it.

1728-1774: Life of Irish writer Oliver Goldsmith, author of the plays *The Good-Natur'd Man* and *She Stoops to Conquer.*

1730: *Romeo and Juliet,* performed in New York, is the first play by Shakespeare to be presented in America.

1737: One of the largest theatres in Europe, Teatro di San Carlo, connected to the Royal Palace, opened in Naples.

1737: English Parliament passed the Stage Licensing Act, which required all public performances to be examined and, if necessary, censored by the government. It would exist in some form until 1968.

1748: The excavation of Pompeii, buried by a volcano eruption 1700 years earlier, inspired what will become known as the Neoclassical Period (1750-1815), an embrace of Greeco-Roman ideals, of simplicity and grace. In theatre that meant decorous plays, acted very broadly, with meticulous costumes and sets.

1749-1803: Life of Italian dramatist and poet Vittorio Alfieri, the founder of Italian tragedy.

1750: First resident theatre company established in New York City.

1751-1816: Life of English playwright, poet and politician Richard Brinsley Sheridan, author of *The Rivals, The School for Scandal, The Duenna,* and *A Trip to Scarborough.*

1751: The Virginia Company of Comedians, the colonies' first professional theatre company, opened a temporary playhouse in Williamsburg, Virginia.

1766: The first permanent American theatre building, Philadelphia's Southwark Theatre, was built.

1766-1839: Life of American playwright, actor and historian William Dunlap, author of over 60 plays and the encyclopedia *History of the Rise and Progress of the Arts of Design in the United States.*

1768: Italian naturalist Lazzaro Spallanzani proved that boiling and sealing food products will keep them free of microorganisms, thus creating modern-day canning.

1775-1783: The American Revolution, prompted by Americans drafting the Declaration of Independence, declaring their intent to secede from Great Britain.

1784: Pierre Beaumarchais' comic play, *Marriage of Figaro,* premiered. It was later developed into an opera composed by Mozart and a libretto written by Lorenzo Da Ponte.

1788: United States ratified The Constitution. The next year, George Washington became the first US president.

1789-1815: The French Revolution and Napoleonic Wars: Inspired by the ideals of liberty, equality, and fraternity, civilian insurgents stormed the Bastille, a symbol of monarchy rule in Paris. Political struggle, wars with other European nations, the beheading of King Louis XVI, and the abolishment and reestablishment of the Catholic Church culminated in dictatorial rule by a council known as the Directorate—which was subsequently commandeered by Napoleon Bonaparte. Napoleon and the *Grande Armée* engaged nearly every other European power in battle until his ultimate defeat at the Battle of Waterloo. The peace, negotiated at the Congress of Vienna, re-drew the borders of Europe, and established the British Empire as the world's foremost power.

1791-1861: Life of French playwright Eugène Scribe, who developed the "well-made play," a popular, though criticized genre that emphasized rigid plot structure and entertainment over didactic-ism.

Nineteenth Century

1800s: Using simple characterization and exaggerated emotions, melodrama—as written by August von Kotzebue and René Charles Guilbert de Pixérécourt—dominated French theatre.

1800-1890: Born from Germany's sturm und drang movement, Romanticism offered artists and thinkers an opportunity to focus on emotion and individualism instead of the encroaching modernity and industrialization.

1808: German writer Johann Wolfgang von Goethe published *Faust, Part I.*

1816: Philadelphia's Chestnut Street Theatre became the earliest gas-lit playhouse in the world.

1821-1881: Life of Russian writer Aleksey Pisemky, who introduced psychological realism to playwriting, authored *A Bitter Fate* about serfdom.

1828-1910: Life of Russian author Leo Tolstoy, author of the novels *War and Peace, Anna Karenina,* and the play *The Power of Darkness.*

1837: A London theatre first used Thomas Drummond's limelight, similar to today's spotlight.

1848: Germans Karl Marx and Friedrich Engels published *The Communist Manifesto,* a political document describing society through the lens of class struggle.

NOTES: __________________________

1854-1900: Life of Irish poet and playwright Oscar Wilde, author of *The Importance of Being Earnest*.

1856-1950: Life of British/Irish playwright George Bernard Shaw, writer of *Man and Superman, Pygmalion,* and *Saint Joan.*

1859: English naturalist Charles Darwin published *On the Origin of Species*, founding the science of evolutionary biology.

1861-1865: American Civil War: After the election of President Abraham Lincoln and fearing the abolition of slavery, seven southern states seceded from the United States and formed the Confederate States of America. During the war, Lincoln issued The Emancipation Proclamation, freeing slaves in rebel territory. Shortly before the war's end, John Wilkes Booth assassinated Lincoln.

1861: The transcontinental telegraph linked the east and west coasts of the United States.

1868-1912: Emperor Meiji transformed Japan from a feudal island nation into an industrialized world power.

1869: The Transcontinental Railroad was completed at Promontory Point, Utah.

c. 1870s: Realism: Following the trend of French painters, dramatists sought to represent life as it appeared. In realistic plays, characters spoke without verse or meter, sets were dressed as if they were actual locations, and psychological considerations motivated characters' decisions.

1871: To create *Thespis*, English producer John Hollingshead introduced librettist W.S. Gilbert to the composer Arthur Sullivan. Gilbert and Sullivan would write 14 comedic operas, including *H.M.S. Pinafore, The Pirates of Penzance,* and *The Mikado.*

1879: Eadweard Muybridge invented the zoöpraxiscope, forerunner to the motion picture projector.

1879: *A Doll's House*, Henrik Ibsen's drama about the repression of women, premiered at the Royal Theatre in Copenhagen.

1881: The first building lit entirely by electric light, The Savoy Theatre, opened in London's West End. The West End and New York City's Broadway would become the pinnacles of professional theatre in the English-speaking world.

1884: European leaders divided Africa into imperial colories at the Berlin Conference.

1884: First elevator stage constructed at the Budapest Opera House.

1888-1953: Life of American playwright Eugene O'Neill, whose *Long Day's Journey into Night* is considered one of the best American plays of the 20th century.

1891: First public demonstration of a working motion picture at Thomas Edison's lab.

1896: First US movie theaters opened in Buffalo, NY and New Orleans, LA.

1897-1975: Life of American playwright Thornton Wilder, who authored *Our Town* and *Skin of Our Teeth*.

1898: Spanish-American War: The United States conquered Cuba, destroyed the Spanish navy in the Pacific and decisively ended the Spanish Empire.

Twentieth Century

1900: At Broadway's Casino Theatre, *Floradora* opened, introducing the Floradora sextet, a forerunner to the modern day chorus line.

1902: Los Angeles built its first movie theatre.

1904: Anton Chekhov's play of modern realism, *The Cherry Orchard*, premiered at the Moscow Art Theatre.

1904-1905: The Russo-Japanese War pitted Japan and Russia against one another for competing colonial claims in Korea. Japan surprised the world with their resounding victory.

1905-1984: Life of American dramatist Lillian Hellman, who wrote *Foxes* and *Toys in the Attic*.

1907: Broadway producer Florenz Ziegfeld Jr. introduced his legendary theatrical revue Ziegfeld Follies.

1908-1981: Life of novelist and playwright William Saroyan, who authored *The Time of Your Life, My Name Is Aram,* and *My Heart's in the Highlands*.

1909: Russian theatre actor and director, Konstantin Stanislavsky, introduced "method acting," whereupon a character's internal decisions influence their external action.

1911-1983: Life of American playwright Tennessee Williams, writer of *The Glass Menagerie, A Streetcar Named Desire, Cat on a Hot Tin Roof, Sweet Bird of Youth,* and *The Night of the Iguana*.

1913: Featuring an all-black cast, the large scale musical *Darktown Follies* helped launch Harlem as an African-American cultural center.

1914-1918: World War I: Ultimately, the war resulted in nearly thirty million casualties, the end of all empires in Europe (Germany, Russia, Austria-Hungary, Ottoman), and ongoing political upheaval.

1915-2005: Life of American playwright Arthur Miller, writer of *All My Sons, Death of a Salesman, The Crucible,* and *A View from the Bridge*.

1917: Russian Revolution: The March and October Revolutions in Russia deposed Emperor Nicholas II and instigated the Russian Civil War that would end in 1922 with the founding of the USSR, led by Vladimir Lenin.

1920: *Beyond the Horizon*, Eugene O'Neill's first full-length play, won the Pulitzer Prize, marking the beginning of modern American drama.

1920: The African-American migration to northern cities ignited the Harlem Renaissance.

1921: America's first resident professional theatre, The Cleveland Playhouse, opened.

1927-2018: Life of American play- and screenwriter Neil Simon, author of *Biloxi Blues, Come Blow Your Horn,* and *The Odd Couple*.

1927: Jerome Kern and Oscar Hammerstein's musical *Show Boat* debuts on Broadway. Despite heavy themes involving race and tragic love, *Show Boat* is chock-full of song, dance, and spectacle, marking Broadway and musical theatre as a distinctly American art form.

1927-1949: Chinese Civil War: The Chinese Nationalist Party (CNP) and Communist Party (CPC) of China vied for control of the largest country on Earth, suspending hostilities during Japan's invasion from 1937-1945. Ultimately CPC, led by Mao Zedong gained control of mainland China, while CNP took residence in Taiwan.

          123

NOTES: ____

1929: The New York Stock Market crashed and the Great Depression followed.

1930: American Jean Rosenthal pioneered stage lighting and the idea of it as a career.

1930-1965: Life of Lorraine Hansberry, whose *A Raisin in the Sun* tells of an African American family's experience in Chicago.

1932: Radio City Music Hall opened in New York City. The "Showplace of the Nation" is home to the leggy dance company, The Rockettes.

1935: Opening in Boston, George Gershwin's *Porgy and Bess* featured a cast of classically trained African-American actors.

1937-1945: World War II: The war and its consequences ultimately killed up to 85 million people, including 6 million Jews and 5 million others killed in the Holocaust. It also led to the formation of the United Nations, established the United States and the Soviet Union as the world's only superpowers, and kicked off a nuclear standoff between them, called the Cold War, that would last until 1991.

1950: Frank Loesser, Joe Swerling, and Abe Burrows's *Guys and Dolls* debuted on Broadway.

1952 - : Life of American playwright Beth Henley, winner of the Pulitzer Prize for her play *Crimes of the Heart*.

1954: In Brown v. Board of Education, the US Supreme Court declared that segregated schools were unconstitutional per the 14th Amendment.

1955-1975: Vietnam War: In one of the Cold War's proxy wars, the US and the USSR took opposing sides in a civil war in Vietnam. In the US, where the government conscripted young men to fight, the war became a cultural flashpoint.

1957: Leonard Bernstein, Stephen Sondheim, and Arthur Laurents brought *West Side Story* to Broadway. Its complex and enduring music, societal themes, and extended dance numbers still influence Broadway theatre.

1957: Both the Tony Award and the Pulitzer Prize are awarded to Eugene O'Neill's *A Long Day's Journey into Night*.

1957: The Soviet Union launched Sputnik 1 into Earth's orbit.

1963: Civil rights leader Martin Luther King Jr. delivered the "I Have a Dream" speech in Washington DC, a call for racial equality. Five years later he was assassinated.

1968: The controversial rock musical, *Hair*, opened on Broadway. *Hair* dealt frankly with profanity, drug use, and sexuality and notoriously included a nude scene.

1969: The United States landed astronauts Neil Armstrong and Buzz Aldrin on the moon with pilot Michael Collins delivering them back to Earth.

1982: Andrew Lloyd Webber's *Cats* opened. It became Broadway's longest running play until it was surpassed by Webber's own *Phantom of the Opera*.

1989: The Fall of the Berlin Wall led to the reunification of Germany (which had been split since 1945) and symbolized the end of the Cold War. The USSR dissolved two years later.

1989: English engineer Tim Berners-Lee wrote the code for the World Wide Web, the first web browser, allowing what had started as an U.S. Department of Defense project, ARPANET, to develop into a global network serving 3.2 billion people and counting.

1991: In the Gulf War, America forced Iraqi dictator Saddam Hussein's armies out of Kuwait.

1998: Osama Bin Laden and his Al-Qaeda terrorist network destroyed two American embassies in eastern Africa.

Twenty-First Century

2001: Al-Qaeda terrorists hijacked four planes and used three of them to bring down the World Trade Center Buildings in New York City and to attack the Pentagon; the fourth plane, which is thought to have been heading for the White House, crashed in an empty field.

2003: US invaded Iraq a second time to eject tyrannical leader, Saddam Hussein, and to install a democratic system of government.

2008: Barack Obama became the first African-American President of the United States.

2012: Simon Stephens' play, *The Curious Incident of the Dog in the Night-Time,* premiered on Broadway, showcasing an autistic main character.

2013: Scientists successfully cloned human stem cells.

2015: Lin Manuel Miranda's musical *Hamilton* debuted on Broadway featuring an ethnically diverse cast portraying America's founding fathers and music drawn from hip hop and R&B.

2020 - : A worldwide pandemic shut down countries around the globe. In the US, state-at-home orders forced businesses, schools, and theatres to close. Broadway shows and national tours were cancelled, as schools and amateur theatres scramble to create Virtual Theatre.

NOTES: _______________________________________

____

____

____

____

____

____

NAME ____ PERIOD _______ DATE _____________

THEATRE CURRENT EVENT

Theatre, like all forms of art, is very dynamic A play written and produced today will have very few elemental similarities to one written and produced fifty years ago. That is because there are so many pieces that work together to become a play—numerous areas in which various artists will contribute, changes in technology, trends, experimentation, and countless other facets in which "differences" can occur. On top of that, the demands of the locale, the audience, the culture, world events, politics, commerce, music, and even fashion all can have huge impacts on the evolution of theatre.

As a student of the theatre, whether you are onstage, behind the scenes, or sitting in the director's chair, it is important that you know what is happening in the world around you. Just as a doctor subscribes to medical journals, you should consider subscribing to theatre journals. There are many, and some directly target students. Your newspaper is also very likely to have an "Arts" section; if you are not in an urban area, you can access many metropolitan newspapers online. Another option for staying current is to subscribe to theatre newsletters. Some larger theatres and theatre companies have them, as do many theatre organizations.

What is "current" and what is an "event"? *Current* means up-to-date or recent, and is up to interpretation. In most cases, if you complete a **Theatre Current Event** assignment often enough, *current* simply means that the article was written since the last assignment was completed. Your theatre teacher will tell you how recent your current event needs to be. An *event* is an occurrence. In your case, a current event can be any article relating to theatre today. In other words, an article about Tennessee Williams' impact on theatre in 1940 would not be current, even if it was published today, but an article about his continued impact on theatre today would be current. Lastly, your teacher may allow you to venture into an article about film or TV, but unless this is specifically noted, limit your findings to live theatre. If you are not sure about an article, clear it with your teacher ahead of time.

ASSIGNMENT

A. Find a recent article about theatre and print it out or attach it to a full sheet of paper.

B. Read the article thoroughly, highlighting important facts, names, and main ideas.

C. Complete this assignment, staple the article to it, and turn it in by ____________________________.

D. Be prepared to present your current event to the class or to answer the teacher's questions about the article.

1. Article Title: ____

2. Author: ____

3. What does the article tell you about the author? _____________________________

____

____

4. Article Source: ____

5. Check one from each column in reference to your article:

   ☐ Very useful   ☐ Very interesting   ☐ Very easy to read

   ☐ Somewhat useful   ☐ Somewhat interesting   ☐ Somewhat easy to read

    125

CURRENT EVENTS

One way to get your students thinking about theatre outside of school is to require a regular current event submission. Students find a recent article about theatre, read it, and present it in summarized form for a grade.

Some teachers have students present these to the class, finishing their presentation with the three questions at the end of the worksheet. This gives you additional applicable and pertinent information for quizzing or testing your students on what they have read and heard about theatre in class.

---

6. What is the article mostly about?: (circle one)

   Acting   *Writing/Playwrights*

   Directing   *Producing/Finance*

   Technical Theatre (specify): ________________________________

   Other (specify): ________________________________

7. Summarize the current event: ________________________________

   ____

   ____

   ____

8. Why is this important to you, your organization, or to theatre today? ____________

   ____

   ____

   ____

9. Write three significant questions about theatre today and answer them using quotes from the article.

   Question 1: ____

   ____

   Answer: ____

   ____

   ____

   ____

   Question 2: ____

   ____

   Answer: ____

   ____

   ____

   ____

   Question 3: ____

   ____

   Answer: ____

   ____

   ____

   ____

NOTES: ____

____

____

____

____

____

____

NAME _______________________________________ PERIOD _______ DATE _____________

TIME LINE PROJECT

Make a visual aid of the time line on pages 119-124. Divide into groups of two to four. Each group will complete a section of the theatre history time line by neatly matching each event to its appropriate place on the time line. Groups will need a blank time line page for each century they have been assigned to record. After completing each century, cut pages along the dotted gray lines and tape them together in chronological order.

SUPPLIES

Sharpened pencils, fine-point markers
Rulers
Computer, research materials

HELPFUL HINTS

- Assign jobs to group members so that everyone contributes and no one duplicates another's work.

- Start with pencil.

- Write small, but not so small that reading your completed time line is difficult. Try to write your entries straight across on one line; paraphrase if needed.

- Use the top of the time line for theatre and other art dates, and the bottom for non-theatre and non-art related events.

- One rectangle represents 10 years; the entire page is 100 years. The small mark in the middle of each small rectangle is the 5-year mark—not the mark for the beginning of the decade

EXAMPLE

<table>
<tr><td>1905-1984 Life of Lillian Hellman   1907 Ziegfeld Follies introduced</td><td>1913 Darktown Follies Harlem now Black cultural center</td><td></td></tr>
<tr><td>1900</td><td>1910</td><td>1920</td></tr>
<tr><td></td><td>1915 Germans sink Lusitania   1917 U.S. enters WWI</td><td></td></tr>
</table>

ENRICHMENT

- Further your understanding by adding events from your other classes like history, English, science, music, and foreign languages. How do the major events of the world influence art, theatre, and literature? How do the arts impact one another?

- Color code the events, making theatre one color and non-theatre events another. You may even want to find various colors to represent music, dance, visual art, religion, inventions, and so on.

- Share your completed time line with the other classes within the school and invite them to also record significant dates.

- Find pictures online to accompany your events.

- Add the dates of all significant plays and playwrights' lives not already included.

    127

TIME LINE PROJECT

The *Time Line Project* can be a quiet, educational activity for the whole class to work on together. Teach a concise history of theatre by having students plot hundreds of dates and events on a time line that will stretch across your classroom. Give each pair of students a different century to prepare and present. Or, have students fill out a century each time you have a substitute teacher in your classroom.

Cut the time lines from the Student Workbooks (page 128) on the dotted lines and tape them together for a great visual effect. You can use this time line to discuss current events and trends in theatre too. Have students draw connections between the past and present.

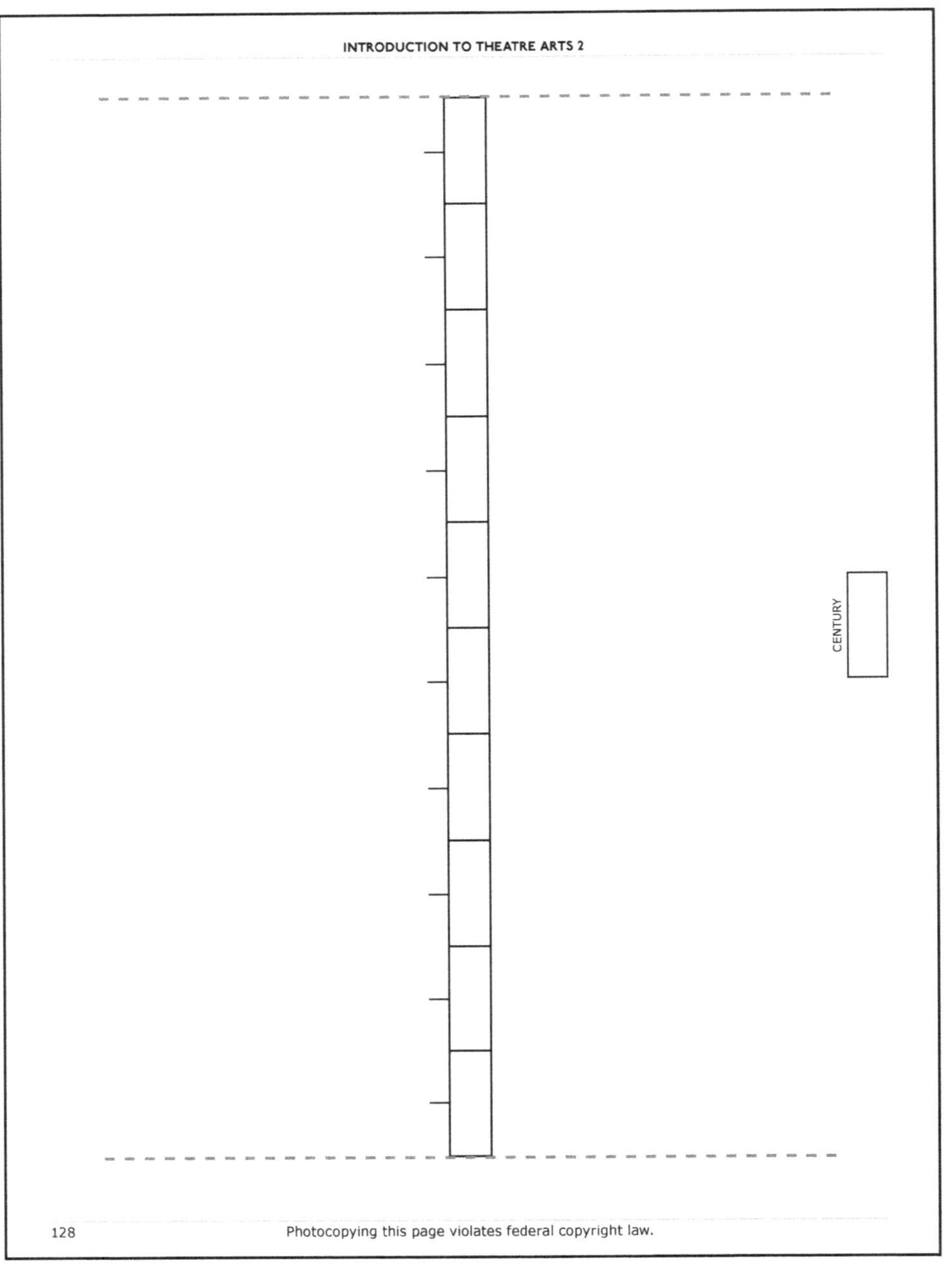

NOTES: ____

____

____

____

____

____

____

____

____

FAMOUS CLASSICAL PLAYWRIGHTS PROJECT

Complete the classical playwright project by selecting three assignments, one from row A, one from row B, and one from row C. The squares do not need to form a straight line. Remember to pay attention to the rules below, but also pay attention to the requirements in the squares you select.

GUIDELINES

- Type all essays (double spaced, size 10 or 12 standard legible font, fully developed paragraphs).
- Use cover sheets for any written work.
- Your visual aids should be appropriate for your grade level and should reflect the general expectations of this class.

A	Read a play written before 1450 and write a play evaluation.	Read a play written between 1450 and 1750 and write a play evaluation.	Read a play written between 1750 and 1879 and write a play evaluation.
B	Research the playwright of the play you read and the time and place in which it was written. Write a two-page essay.	Research the playwright of the play you read and the time and place in which it was written. Create a fictitious three- to four-page scene in which a journalist interviews your playwright, revealing important clues about their life, period in history, works, and more. This should be written in the classical style of the play you read.	Research the playwright of the play you read and the time and place in which it was written. Create a technical visual presentation (such as PowerPoint or Flash) that fully explains their life, period in history, works, and more.
C	Create a board game to help others understand your playwright, their time in history, their works, and more.	Create a multi-sensory presentation for your playwright's place and time in history. What sights might one see? What smells and tastes were prevalent? What might the sounds or music of the day have been?	What role did costuming play in your playwright's productions? Either make one costume to present to the class, create a costume plot for eight characters from the play you read, or create a computer presentation depicting the costuming style of the period.

STUDYING CLASSICAL PLAYWRIGHTS

In addition to the time line, have each student become an expert on a classical playwright. The tic-tac-toe grid, like on page 129 of the Student Workbook, is a growing trend in theatre. It forces students to find more than one way to explore a topic. Use the same idea to encourage students to select various levels of thinking in your other projects.

The play evaluation in row A of the tic-tac-toe grid might be a report on a play based on your standards for student essays, or students may fill out the *Script Report* found on pages 206-207. They do not have this page in their workbooks, so you will have to make copies for them.

205

NAME ____ PERIOD _______ DATE ______________

SCRIPT REPORT

After you have read the play, answer the questions on this report thoroughly.
You may have to do some research to find some of the answers.

Title: ____

Playwright: ____

Date published: ___________________ Publisher: ________________________

Other plays written by this playwright: _______________________________

____

What type of play is this? (Circle all that apply.)

Comedy   Tragedy   Historical   Classic   Full-length   One-act   Musical

Other: ____

1. Where does the play take place?

2. What is the time period for the play?

3. List the main characters and tell a little about each of them:

4. What is the play about?

5. What is the climax of the play?

NAME ____________________________________ PERIOD _______ DATE ___________

SCRIPT REPORT - CONT.

6. How is the conflict resolved?

7. What did you think of the play?

8. If you were in this play, which character would you be and why?

9. What is the theme or message of the play?

10. Find a line that you think supports the general theme of the play and write it here. Indicate the speaker, the act, and the scene.

11. Choose a character who undergoes a great change from the beginning of the play to the end. Describe the change and the impact it has on the course of the story.

12. What events led to the beginning of the play?

13. What do you think might have happened after the conclusion of the play?

14. Find several examples of symbolism and explain them.

CHAPTER 4 NOTES:

CHAPTER 5
UNDERSTANDING AND WRITING SCRIPTS

VOCABULARY

UNDERSTANDING SCRIPTS

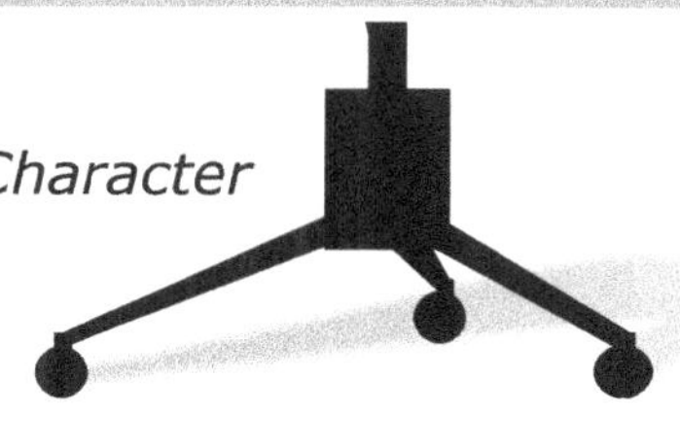

ADDITIONAL NOTES

VOCABULARY

In this chapter, you will learn about:

Act (as in sections of a play): A large division of a play.

Button: A term used to describe the feeling of satisfaction when a scene ends well.

Cast List: The list of characters and often the actors originally assigned to the parts.

Conflict: An obstacle that prevents or slows a character from reaching their goal.

Copyright Page: The page of a script with legal information.

Denoument: (DAY-new-ma) Another word for falling action, when the protagonist wraps up the story.

Dialogue: Spoken lines.

Play: The story written in dialogue form meant to be performed rather than simply read.

Production Notes: Vital information from the playwright and/or original director to those who may direct the play in the future.

Props List: Physical items needed to perform a scene or play.

Scene (as in sections of a play): Sections of acts within a play.

Script Cover: The outside part of a script book listing the title, playwright, and publisher.

Set Diagram: An aerial view of the original set or the suggested set for the play found in some scripts.

Stage Directions: Playwright's suggestions for character movement.

Story Background: Moments that influence the events in the play and may be mentioned but are not acted out onstage.

Story Foreground: The parts of the play including characters, relationships, etc., in the plot.

Strategies: The things a character does based on their personality to overcome obstacles and reach goals.

Suspense: A strong desire to find out what happens next.

INTRODUCTION

There are many wonderful scripts in this book that are not in this chapter. You and your students will enjoy reading and performing all of them. A list of additional scenes is provided on page 149 of the Student Workbook to help you find what you are looking for quickly.

Sometimes teachers expect that students understand what they mean when referring to parts of a script. To you, this is very familiar information, but the student may never have held a script prior to your class. Understanding scripts will teach your students how scripts are arranged, what is considered dialogue and what is stage direction, and how to approach the blocking that is included in some scripts.

UNDERSTANDING SCRIPTS

OBJECTIVE You will learn the parts of the script and their purposes in order to become more proficient as an actor and/or director.

If you've spent much time with scripts, you probably know how to navigate through them with ease. They are very well-organized, though they do not all look the same. Learning the parts of a script and their function will help you make sense of any script you pick up.

Script Cover: The front cover of every script will have the title, playwright, and publisher. It might also have the type of play (drama, comedy, etc.) and number of acts. If there is more information vital to any of these items, it will also be included, such as if a play is adapted from another work or translated. The back cover may have a summary of the script or an advertisement for another product.

Copyright Page: On the inside front cover or on the back of the cover page, this page contains the copyright information plus all of the legal information regarding the play, including how to secure permission to perform, how to credit the publisher and playwright properly, and how to contact the publisher or the literary agent for performance rights. It is important that actors, technicians, and directors understand the importance of taking this page very seriously, as failure to follow copyright stipulations can result in steep fines.

Cast List: This page is at the beginning of the script and lists all of the characters in the play. It is often arranged by order of appearance, though sometimes it's organized by group, such as by family or something like cowboys and farmers. Ideally, useful information like ages, characteristics, or relationships to other characters is also provided. (Occasionally, the original actors from the play's premiere will also be listed on the cast page or at the end of the script. This has no bearing on the play itself other than to honor the original cast.)

Props List: This attempts to list every prop that will be needed to perform the play, organized either by character or chronologically. However, rarely will a props list be totally complete, so additions might have to be made. The props list, along with the set diagram and other production notes, may be at the beginning of the script or at the end, depending on the publisher.

Set Diagram: This is a sketch of the set that fits the blocking in the script. Most directors use this as an idea, but they might need to formulate something slightly different based on their space. It's important to read the script and note special set needs before deviating from the diagram.

Production Notes: Playwrights use the production notes to convey additional tips to directors. These ideas might include lists of sound and lighting effects, music suggestions, double casting possibilities, and costume recommendations. Complicated sections of the script, such as chase scenes or scenes with special effects, might also be addressed in the production notes.

Play: This, of course, is the main part of the script. The play includes both the dialogue and the stage directions. Some playwrights include a little more information, such as a forward, suggestions for music or lighting, expanded character descriptions, or perhaps an epilogue.

Dialogue: The characters' spoken lines are the dialogue. Plays always indicate who's speaking by first indicating the character who says the line, though the style of how this is done varies by playwright or publisher. Whether the character's name is on the same line separated by a colon or on a completely separate line, the actor does not read the character's name before saying their line. Sometimes dialogue is broken up with stage directions, which are also not read. For rehearsals, actors highlight their lines so they can easily find them and work on memorization.

Stage Directions: These spell out how the playwright sees the characters moving onstage. Some, such as entrances and exits, are necessary so the play makes sense. Others are simply the actual blocking that was performed by the original cast. Unless a director builds a set in the same configuration as the original one, they will have to create their own blocking. Stage directions are

NOTES: _______________________________________

____

____

____

____

____

____

____

usually in brackets, parenthesis, or italics and are not read aloud.

Acts: The larger divisions of a play. There is no rule or formula to mandate how to divide a play. Some playwrights separate acts into chunks of time. Act I might be "the early years" and Act II "the later years." Some playwrights coordinate time-consuming costume or set changes with changes in acts since the curtains are generally closed between acts. For instance, when the second act opens in *Phantom of the Opera*, it is six months later and all the actors are in elaborate costumes for a masquerade ball.

Scenes: Acts may be divided into scenes. If so, it is usually to help the audience understand when the setting changes or there is a passage of time. Scene changes are usually indicated by a shift in lighting.

WRITING CHALLENGE

Write a few lines of dialogue below for at least two characters demonstrating the proper use of stage directions and clearly indicating the separation between character and dialogue.

DRAMATIC STRUCTURE

Whether performing, reading, or writing, all scenes and stories follow a basic configuration referred to as **dramatic structure**. Dramatic structure is how a story naturally evolves—or should evolve—to keep the audience interested. Knowing how the various elements work together to create suspense and drama will help you to become a better director, actor, and playwright.

As an actor, you will perform many scenes. Plays are stories, and in that regard, they follow dramatic structure. The audience craves entertainment, and the structure helps make the scene entertaining. When selecting a scene from a play, actors try to

their performance evolves in a way that hooks their audience from beginning to end.

The **exposition** (A) is the beginning. This is where we learn the setting and who the main characters (also known as the protagonists) are. We will get some inkling of what the problem is, and we will ultimately learn about the protagonists' goals.

Most importantly, the playwright will either convince the audience to tune in or give them a reason to tune out within the first few seconds of a story or scene. In other words, the exposition provides the first impression, and if a playwright can hook the audience immediately, they will stay hooked. The hook will almost always come from action and **suspense**. Suspense is *a feeling of eagerness to know or see more caused by the audience learning enough to get them interested but not enough to know for sure what will happen next*. A story with a suspenseful plot or storyline will hook the audience early with these elements and not give them the answers they seek until the climax or the falling action.

find scenes that start, build, and end like a complete story. But a scene is still only part of a larger story, so it will only contain bits of the overall structure. Consequently, actors must work harder to fill in some of the blanks when performing scenes, ensuring that

135

Dramatic structure is discussed in several places in this book because it is very important. The discussion in this chapter is the most in-depth, teaching the functions of the parts as well as the meanings of the words. It ends with a writing exercise that will get your students on the right path to writing a play.

Often the hook will come in the form of the inciting incident. In *Tortoise and the Hare*, the inciting incident occurs when the race begins between the tortoise and the hare. Think of it as the beginning of the action and not a part of the setup, which would be when the tortoise first challenges the hare to a race.

Following the inciting incident is the **rising action** (B). During this time, the protagonists will be faced with obstacles or antagonists that will stand between them and their goals. Protagonists use varying **strategies** depending on their individual personalities to overcome these roadblocks and get closer to their goals. The **climax** (C) is the high point of action in a story. It is where the main character either reaches their goal or does not. It should be the most energetic and interesting part of the story. During this part of the dramatic structure, there is usually a drastic change. In a good story, the climax is easy to spot. Consequently, if you are writing a story or play and cannot clearly identify your story's climax, it probably needs more work.

Following the climax is the **falling action** (D) or **denouement**. This is generally very short, allowing the characters just enough time to wrap up any loose ends. It is also where the moral of the story, evident throughout the plot, is generally restated by one of the main characters in a more concise but not overly obvious way.

Lastly is the **ending** (E), or "the hardest part" for playwrights. It is very difficult to end a scene because many playwrights do not understand the purpose of an ending. They associate it with everything being over. However, what do most people do when they reach a goal? They make the most of it. If a poor person finds sudden wealth, they begin a new life as a rich person. If a homely person is suddenly attractive, they begin a new life as a good-looking person. If a child is saved from a bloodthirsty wolf, they begin a new, more cautious life in which they listen to their mother. Rather than thinking of your "ending" as the end, think of it as the beginning of your protagonist's new life with goals achieved. Now that they have reached or failed to reach their goal, what's next?

Another way to think of your ending is as though it is the "off" button for your scene. Would you turn off a good show before the end? No! Think of the ending of your scene as a **button**. It must have a feeling of resolution and finality, and it must feel satisfying to the audience.

TIPS FOR ENDING A SCENE

- Don't start writing a scene until you have decided how it will end; otherwise, your action will seem pointless and ambling.

- Try a different approach: come up with a good ending, then think of a play to go with that ending.

- Your ending should come soon after your climax. The longer you make your falling action, the harder it will be to end your story.

- If your falling action appears to be rising, *stop!* It's possible that you ended your scene already and just don't recognize it because you started a new one on top of it. Keep an eye out for hidden endings.

- Don't try to make your ending bigger than your climax.

- Read what you wrote about the protagonist and their goal and take notes on everything related to that goal. Now that you are at the point of being able to wrap up your scene, some of those notes might help spark an idea.

- If your play "stops" rather than "ends," you may need to work on it a little more.

- Study how your favorite movies end and create an "Ending Journal." After a while, you will start creating endings before you have stories to go with them. This is how many playwrights get their best ideas!

ACTIVITY

Write a simple, two-minute, one-scene play. It must be meaningful to you, the playwright. It should be clear and understandable to readers, and it must have a definitive ending. Start with something that means a lot to you or perhaps an important incident after which you wished you had said something differently. Your short play might be serious or funny, but it should be visually interesting.

Suggested by Dr. Len Radin of Drury High School in North Adams, MA

Dr. Len Radin, suggests this activity:

Write a simple, two-minute, one-scene play. It must be meaningful to you, the playwright. It should be clear and understandable to readers, and it must have a definitive ending. Start with something that means a lot to you or perhaps an important incident after which you wished you had said something differently. Your short play might be serious or funny, but it should be visually interesting.

NOTES: ______________________________

CHAPTER 5 — UNDERSTANDING AND WRITING SCRIPTS

NAME _______________________________________ PERIOD _______ DATE ______________

WRITING WITH DRAMATIC STRUCTURE

Read the following story ending. Work your way backwards to create the rest of the story by writing notes in the spaces provided. Be prepared to write your story for a grade or tell it aloud.

A ————————————————————→ E

EXPOSITION:

RISING ACTION:

CLIMAX:

FALLING ACTION:

ENDING: Devin dropped onto the couch, threw open her arms, and plopped her feet onto the coffee table. She narrowly missed the large bowl of potato chip crumbs perched precariously near the edge. The music still filled the room, but she no longer heard it. Barbara the brat was hanging out, trying to act like she wasn't sleepy, but the eight-year-old could no longer stifle the yawns as she crawled onto her older sister's lap. Normally Devin would have resented her parents and sister being at her party, but this was different. "This party is the best birthday present," she whispered in Barb's ear, and she watched as her goofy father moon-walked for her friends on the patio. "Barb?" But there was no answer. "I take it back. You're the best birthday present ever." She placed Barbara on the couch and gave her a good-night kiss on the forehead. Her mom was doing the robot now, and despite everything that had happened, she couldn't let her parents upstage her at her own party. "Conga line anyone?"

NOTES: ____

____

____

____

____

____

____

____

WRITE YOUR FULL STORY HERE (use extra paper if needed):

____

____

____

____

____

____

____

____

____

____

____

____

____

____

____

____

____

____

____

____

____

____

Devin dropped onto the couch, threw open her arms, and plopped her feet onto the coffee table. She narrowly missed the large bowl of potato chip crumbs perched precariously near the edge. The music still filled the room, but she no longer heard it. Barbara the brat was hanging out, trying to act like she wasn't sleepy, but the eight-year-old could no longer stifle the yawns as she crawled onto her older sister's lap. Normally Devin would have resented her parents and sister being at her party, but this was different. "This party is the best birthday present ever," she whispered in Barb's ear, and she watched as her goofy father moon-walked for her friends on the patio. "Barb?" But there was no answer. "I take it back. You're the best birthday present ever." She placed Barbara on the couch and gave her a good-night kiss on the forehead. Her mom was doing the robot now, and despite everything that had happened, she couldn't let her parents upstage her at her own party. "Conga line anyone?"

Now, on separate paper, write your story in the form of a play.

NOTES: _______________________________________

____

____

____

____

____

____

CHAPTER 5 — UNDERSTANDING AND WRITING SCRIPTS

NAME _______________________________________ PERIOD ________ DATE ____________

DRAMATIC STRUCTURE WORD SEARCH

```
F  T  C  U  E  Q  A  C  E  E  B  A  B  A  F  E  D
S  C  D  E  N  O  U  E  M  E  N  T  T  N  A  B  E
R  P  I  N  K  C  M  V  A  P  R  S  D  E  L  S  X
B  L  I  T  Z  H  P  M  F  D  P  I  S  L  L  U  P
Q  O  B  S  T  A  C  L  E  S  S  N  E  A  I  G  O
U  T  A  R  Y  R  X  D  T  S  E  O  O  D  N  A  S
T  Q  I  T  C  A  O  W  E  P  T  G  B  U  G  P  I
C  U  B  S  M  C  N  I  S  M  T  A  P  B  A  I  T
I  O  P  I  D  T  G  U  F  O  I  T  E  U  C  K  I
L  K  L  L  M  E  S  X  A  N  N  N  T  T  T  H  O
F  C  C  N  T  R  I  S  I  N  G  A  C  T  I  O  N
N  K  D  A  D  S  B  Y  H  L  C  R  E  O  O  O  A
O  J  T  F  E  F  G  A  C  T  I  F  Z  N  N  K  D
C  T  N  E  D  I  C  N  I  G  N  I  T  I  C  N  I
S  I  A  T  S  I  N  O  G  A  T  O  R  P  E  F  C
D  J  C  I  F  E  N  D  I  N  G  C  H  C  A  G  D
```

1. The _ _ _ _ s _ _ _ _ _ is the beginning of a scene and generally introduces the characters and setting.
2. The problem around which the plot revolves is the _ _ _ f _ _ _ _.
3. The sequence of events in a story is called the p _ _ _.
4. An element of storytelling in which the teller, playwright, or player is able to end a story comfortably and satisfactorily without a feeling of being rushed, incomplete, or out of context is the b _ _ _ _ _.
5. D _ _ _ _ _ m _ _ _ is another word for falling action.
6. What makes the audience eager to find out more is _ u _ _ _ _ _ _.
7. The various methods are determined by a character's personality, setting, and situation, that they will use to overcome obstacles and to achieve goals are often referred to as _ _ _ _ _ _ g _ _ _.
8. The turning point in a story is the _ _ _ _ _ x; the protagonist either reaches or fails to reach their goal, and the energy and action peak.
9. R _ _ _ _ _ a _ _ _ _ _ is the development of the plot after the exposition and before the climax.
10. The character or force in a story that presents itself as an obstacle standing between the protagonist and his goal is the a _ _ _ _ _ _ _ _ _.
11. Where and when a story takes place is the _ _ _ _ _ n _.
12. The _ h _ _ _ _ _ e _ _ are the personalities in a story whose actions keep the plot moving toward the resolution.
13. The _ _ _ _ t _ _ _ _ _ c _ _ _ _ _ is the moment after the exposition that carries the story to the next point, the rising action.
14. The events in a story that keep the plot moving along are called _ _ _ _ _ n.
15. The final moments of a story where the "moral" or lesson is generally stated or revealed is the _ _ d _ _ _.
16. The things or people that stand between a character and their goals are the _ b _ _ _ _ _ _ _.
17. The main character in a story whose goal becomes the force that keeps the story moving towards the climax is the _ r _ _ _ _ _ _ i _ _, and contrary to popular belief, it is not always the good guy.
18. An element of storytelling that ensures either the reader or the audience will want read or hear more is called the h _ _ _.
19. The resolution of unanswered questions or tasks that need completing following the climax and before the ending is the _ a _ _ _ _ _ a _ _ _ _ _.
20. The things a character wants in a scene, and ultimately in a story or play, are called _ _ _ l _.

DRAMATIC STRUCTURE WORD SEARCH KEY

1. EXPOSITION
2. CONFLICT
3. PLOT
4. BUTTON
5. DENOUEMENT
6. SUSPENSE
7. STRATEGIES
8. CLIMAX
9. RISING ACTION
10. ANTAGONIST
11. SETTING
12. CHARACTERS
13. INCITING INCIDENT
14. ACTION
15. ENDING
16. OBSTACLES
17. PROTAGONIST
18. HOOK
19. FALLING ACTION
20. GOALS

You might want to use the *Dramatic Structure Word Search* to quiz or test your students on the vocabulary from the unit. While the puzzle is challenging, it could also be used independently, because the clues provided will allow students to find the words in the puzzle even if they are not certain of the answers, thus guiding them in self-discovery of essential vocabulary.

DRAMATIC STRUCTURE WORD SEARCH SOLUTION

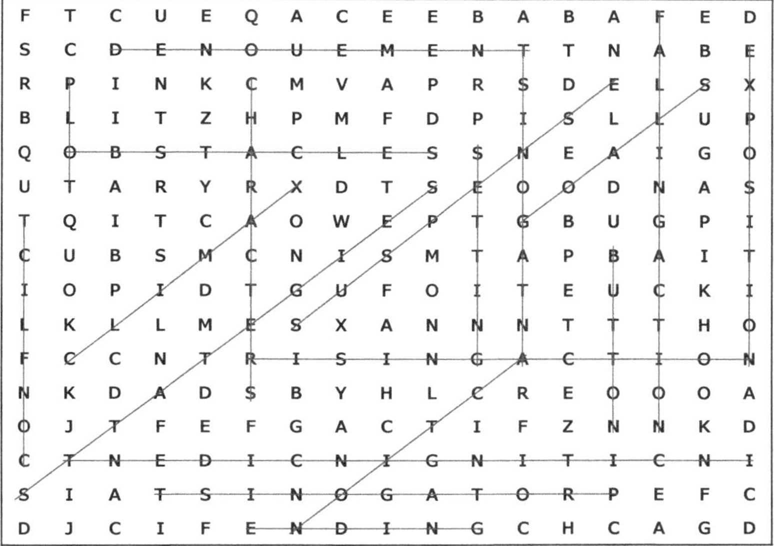

217

MOVING BEYOND THE FIRST DRAFT

This assignment has been adapted from the theories of Lindsay Price. Price is a writer with Theatrefolk, a Canadian play publishing company. Not only does she write, she also teaches workshops entitled *Moving Beyond the First Draft*.

Do you have a rough draft of a script in which the story is basically as you intend to tell it? Are your characters intact, and are you ready to move from rough draft to a better product? In her workshop, Price suggests investigating a few key areas. Will your draft benefit from doing any additional research? Is the story deep enough, or would it help to add a little background? Are the characters complex and interesting?

CHARACTERS

Scrutinize each character, writing a brief description for each one. Give each a secret, even if it is not in the play. Price suggests writing scenes about the characters' secrets. Even if you do not include the scenes in the play, the very activity will give each one additional depth and may help to build relationships.

Try the *Acre of Land* activity in the box above. It is another way to learn more about your characters and can help to you to discover new, key ideas and draw connections between unlikely personalities.

Create a profile for each character that includes: name, age, family makeup, favorite things, most hated things, best memories, worst memories, what makes them laugh and cry, and a favorite childhood memory. Create a list of personality and physical traits, look for inconsistencies, and decide if you have provided enough information about each character. Ask yourself if there is anything about each character that you would like to know. You may think of some other things that would also be beneficial to include.

STORY BACKGROUND

Write about all relationships and moments that are mentioned in the play but are not shown. Write the moment before the opening of the play. Again, you may not include any of this in your final draft, but it continues to create a stronger web from which your final draft will emerge.

STORY FOREGROUND

Work on the foreground of the play by asking questions. What is the main conflict? Who are the characters? How do they react to the conflict? Why am I writing this play? Allow others to question your work too. When others ask questions, Price suggests that there are only three answers: "I agree," "I agree but am not sure of the answer," or "I disagree," and then tell why. Questions should never be disregarded, because something in your text stood out enough to prompt each one.

ACRE OF LAND

Select one character from your draft. Imagine giving the character an acre of land. Write a description of what that character would do with the gift. You will not use the description in your play, but you will learn a great deal more about your character. Repeat this for other characters too.

CHARACTER DEVELOPMENT

Whether you are performing a scene that someone else wrote, playing improvisation games, or writing a scene, one of the first things you must focus on is character development. In scene work, much of this has been done for you, either in the script or by reading between the lines. But if every actor who played that same part depended only on those predetermined ideas, there would be a lot of similar performances, and that would be boring. It takes an extremely brave, talented, insightful actor to bring new life to a role.

One of your first jobs as actor or playwright is to determine each character's goal. What do they want immediately, by the end of the scene, by the end of the play, and in "life" after the play has ended?

Then, considering their personality, fears, skills, relationships to other characters, and so on, how will they reach that goal? Face it, it wouldn't be a story without obstacles to either stand in the character's way or to at least challenge them. What strategies will most likely be used based on what you know—or think you know—about the character to help them get around those roadblocks? And if your character achieves their goal, what is the likely outcome?

Let's start by focusing on character development from a comedy standpoint. Imagine writing a scene about three people shipwrecked on an island. Can you think of some funny things that might happen? If this is all you know to start, it will be a hard process. How do you make writing this scene easier? Focus on

REAL LIFE CHARACTERIZATION INVESTIGATION

Dr. Len Radin of Drury High School in North Adams, MA, suggests this activity:

Invite a guest to class who is unknown to the students. Seek someone who is interesting—perhaps an immigrant, an elderly person, or someone with a cool or unusual profession. The guest sits quietly in a chair, and the students sit on the floor around them in a circle.

You then prompt the students to describe the guest in great detail including both obvious and assumed traits such as:

- Skin tone
- Clothes
- Ancestry
- Confidence
- Specific health features
- Religion
- Intelligence
- Education
- Social skills
- Age
- Ethnicity
- Nationality
- Emotional health
- Talents (mechanical and cerebral)

Lindsay Price offers a few suggestions on writing a play. Your students will enjoy the in-depth character exploration ideas and hints on how to develop the background of a plot.

CHAPTER 5 — UNDERSTANDING AND WRITING SCRIPTS

four things: **characterization, goals, obstacles, and strategies**. If a character does not have a goal in a scene, there can be no obstacles. Obstacles are what make a scene funny, or in the case of a drama, "meaningful," and the more you know about a character's personality, the more you can deduce about what strategies they will likely use. It is from those strategies that your funniest moments will spring.

Now imagine the same island and the same three people. This time, however, you will know a little more about them. First is a toothless old man who has trouble saying certain sounds, so he is often misunderstood and is easily frustrated. The second is a snooty model, obsessed with finding her makeup bag, which has been lost in the wreckage. The final character owns a successful explosives company. He loves to blow things up, but he is also narcoleptic, meaning he falls asleep suddenly. Can you see how the story becomes more interesting when it involves fun, quirky characters?

TIPS FOR WRITING AND CHARACTER DEVELOPMENT

- Get at least a basic idea as to each character's personality before you begin writing, but don't limit yourself. Characters can grow in your mind as you write beyond your original expectations.

- Humor comes from putting characters in situations that are out of character for them. The more extreme, the better, especially when the characters can discover parts of themselves they did not know existed. Can you find an out-of-character situation for your protagonist or perhaps one of your supporting characters?

- Changes or evolutions in a character's personality can keep the audience attentive. For example, start with a character who is extremely vain, and by the end of your play, allow the events to transform the character into a selfless and humble person.

- Remember that characters in comedy are exaggerated. The monotone teacher in *Ferris Bueller's Day Off* is a great example, as are the outrageous characters in the sketch comedies of *Saturday Night Live*.

- Dramatic characters are more lifelike.

Remember the character chart you used for your storytelling project in Chapter 4? Use the same sort of table below to learn more about your characters as you begin your writing experience.

Character	Goal	Potential Obstacle	Physical Traits /Voice	Personality Traits / Quirks
1.				
2.				
3.				
4.				
5.				
6.				
7.				

 141

Whether your students are writing or acting, the "Character Development" lesson is extremely useful. You may want to create a character development bulletin board in your room and include all the helpful hints in this book, especially the tips from page 142 of the Student Workbook. Your students will appreciate easy access to such vital, helpful information.

After the students have completed the above investigation, allow the guest to move around the room. What can students learn from movement? Grace, sophistication, and confidence?

Ask the guest to share their name and a few short sentences about themself. Ask students what they can learn from speech patterns.

TIPS FOR SCENE WORK AND CHARACTER DEVELOPMENT

- Read the entire scene; if it is from a play, read the entire play. Few actors can do a scene justice without knowing its full meaning and context.

- Avoid watching the movie version of the play, as you will resort to imitation. After you have built a character, you may watch the movie to learn more, but never copy the way another actor plays your character. It would be better to try your own thing and fall short of the bar than to mimic. You might achieve success but will ultimately learn nothing.

- Highlight everything your character says about themself, everything the playwright says about the character, everything the other characters say about yours, and—if it is a historical character based on nonfiction—what has been said about your character throughout history.

- Get memorization out of the way early. Actors who are focused on what line comes next or whether a line is coming out correctly cannot put their energy into characterization.

- Think of your character as a real person. Stand like your character would stand, use gestures your character would use, say your words the way your character would say them, and so on. In other words, step into your character's skin and become the character.

- Use a copy of the *Role Scoring* form on pages 143-145 to further explore your character. This will allow you to learn things below the surface of your character's personality that the script may not address. Some of the things to consider are:

  ◇ How old is your character?

  ◇ What does your character want from this scene?

  ◇ What object do you associate with your character and why?

  ◇ What color do you associate with your character and why?

  ◇ What animal do you associate with your character and why?

  ◇ What animal traits from the above animal might my character possess and how can I realistically work those into my scene?

  ◇ What is my character's relationship to the others in the scene?

  ◇ What is my character's greatest strength?

  ◇ What has this great strength earned my character?

◇ What is my character's greatest weakness?

◇ What role has this weakness played in their life?

◇ What is my character's biggest secret?

◇ What are some obvious strategies my character would use to get what they want?

- What other questions can you think of to help develop your character?

If the scene has more than one character, should an actor learn about their acting partners' characters too? Explain.

How can you use the same type of character development when writing scenes?

NOTES: ____

____

____

____

____

____

____

____

CHAPTER 5 — UNDERSTANDING AND WRITING SCRIPTS

NAME ____ PERIOD _______ DATE _____________

ROLE SCORING

Answer the following questions in detail. Use any means available to find the answer. When you have exhausted all resources to find the answer, make one up. Explain any answer that you make up.

1. What play is your scene from?

2. Is it a monologue, duet, or a scene containing three or more characters?

3. What is the scene about?

4. What is your character's name? What are they like?

5. To whom is your character talking?

6. What happened just before the start of this scene?

7. What do you think will happen in the play after this scene?

8. When and where does the scene take place?

9. How old is your character? Are they mature or immature for their age? Explain.

Note that permission is granted to photocopy pages 143-145 of the Student Workbook so students can go through this exercise with every character they play all year. Make sure you copy them before the students write on them for this exercise.

CONTINUED ON NEXT PAGE

NOTES: ____

____

____

____

____

____

____

____

____

ROLE SCORING - CONTINUED

10. What does your character do for a living?

11. What are your character's hobbies?

12. How does the title of the play relate to your character?

13. What does your character want in this scene?

14. If your character repeatedly made a gesture in this scene, what would it be and why?

15. What color do you associate with your character and why?

16. What object do you associate with your character and why?

17. What animal do you associate with your character and why?

18. In real life, would you be your character's friend? Why or why not?

NOTES: ______________________________

____

____

____

____

____

____

____

CHAPTER 5 — UNDERSTANDING AND WRITING SCRIPTS

ROLE SCORING - CONTINUED

19. How is your character like you?

20. How is your character different from you?

21. What is your character's most positive trait?

22. What is your character's status in the world? Does your character have money or power?

23. What does your character want from life?

24. What does your character fear and why?

25. Who does your character admire and why?

26. What are/were your character's parents like?

27. If your character had one wish, what would it be and why?

     145

NOTES: ____

____

____

____

____

____

____

____

____

WRITING INTRODUCTIONS

OBJECTIVE You will compose effective, creative competition-style introductions that may be used with a variety of different types of performances.

There's an old saying: "You don't get a second chance to make a first impression." You might say the same rule applies to performances.

There are probably many schools of thought on how to do a good intro. Some directors teach their students to do introductions in character as extensions of that character's thoughts or dialogue. Others teach students to give background information on the play and playwright. For the purposes of this book, you will learn to write creative intros that are performed out of character and that attempt to draw a bridge between the audience and the piece.

THEME

Start by finding the theme of the piece. The theme is the main idea of the story, often referred to as the lesson or moral. The theme of *Snow White* might be that vanity is destructive. The theme of *Rapunzel* could be that no one is powerful enough to fully own another person. Can you match the themes to their famous fables below?

1.	*The Tortoise and the Hare*	_____	A. Always be kind, because you never know when you will need the kindness of another.
2.	*The Boy Who Cried Wolf*	_____	B. If you always want what you don't have, you'll never be happy with what you've got.
3.	*The Ant and the Grasshopper*	_____	C. Preparation is the foundation of success and survival.
4.	*The Lion and the Mouse*	_____	D. Pace yourself.
5.	*The Dog and His Bone*	_____	E. If you lie, no one will ever believe you when you tell the truth.

When you are confident you know the theme, you must somehow connect it to the audience. For example, if you are doing *The Boy Who Cried Wolf,* your first line might be, "Everyone has told a lie at some point or another in life." This statement is personal, and the audience will tune in because it applies to them. After the connection is made, expand on it some. Make it a little more personal: "Everyone has told a lie at some point or another in life. You think to yourself that one little lie won't hurt anyone, but then you get away with it, so telling a second one seems easy and maybe even fun! The problem is that it's easier to lose trust than to gain it." You must continue to draw connections between the audience and the theme, but be careful not to give the story away. Then, shift your audience's attention away from the theme and to the story itself. "A little boy thinks lying is fun, but what will he do when he needs people to believe him? *The Boy Who Cried Wolf,* by Aesop."

FINDING THE THEME KEY

1. D
2. E
3. C
4. A
5. B

USING INTRODUCTIONS IN THE CLASSROOM

You are probably using some type of introduction in your class for scene work. If not, it is a great way to gently warm students to the idea of performing. It serves as a soft transition from taking the stage to getting into character, and it also helps the audience to know what is happening in a scene.

The introductions in this book focus on theme and are relatively short, just four to six sentences—or about forty seconds—in length. They are the type generally used at drama competitions at the middle and high school levels. If your students are going to auditions for plays in the area or for area colleges, these are probably not the appropriate intros for that climate. Please consult the expert at the venue about how actors should introduce or slate themselves before sending them to auditions.

INTRODUCTION GUIDE

A GOOD INTRO WILL...	A BAD INTRO WILL...
Focus on a theme.	Focus on events in the story. The audience won't need to pay attention because they will have learned all they needed in the intro.
Be about 4 to 6 sentences long.	Be so long or so short that the audience loses or never develops interest.
Never use words or phrases that remind the audience they are listening to an introduction.	Say things like, "In this story, my monologue will," or "The piece i am performing..."
Flow into the title and author naturally.	Say things like, "Find out what happens in," as it leads to the title and author.
Mention the title and author at least once toward the end.	Not mention the title or author or will say something like "author unknown."
Fit the mood of the selection.	Not prepare the audience for the mood of the piece they are about to see.
Hook the audience, making them want to see the performance so they can find out more.	Not leave the audience wishing to learn more; either it did not set up the piece well enough or it gave away too much of the story.
Be memorable.	Quickly be forgotten.
Involve all group members as speakers or in some capacity.	Omit some group members.
Include interesting stage pictures, movement, sounds, levels, and teamwork.	Look and feel generic.
Be memorized.	Appear to be made up on the spot or not flow with ease.

NOTES: ____

____

____

____

____

____

____

____

____

CREATIVITY

Because you write the intro yourself, you have a little more room for creativity than you do with some of the other assignments you will do in theatre. Consider writing your intro as a song—either singing the entire intro or having one person sing while others, if working in a group, hum the background music. You can see an example like this in the readers theatre intro later in this chapter. Music can add a touching effect to a dramatic piece or humorous energy to a comedic piece. Movement is imperative and should hook the audience. If it works with your scene, try some fun stomping moves alongside an energetic rap.

INTRODUCTION CHALLENGE

Familiarize yourself with the five fables listed earlier in this chapter. Write an introduction for each one. At least one of your introductions should be written as though the piece was dramatic, and at least one must be written for two to six people. Follow the checklist below to ensure you are not forgetting anything. Select your favorite one-person intro to memorize and perform for the class. Either form a group to perform one of your group intros or join another group's intro to perform in. What were some of the traits that made the best intros? Why?

INTRODUCTION CHECKLIST

DID YOU...

☐ Focus on theme?

☐ Avoid using words or phrases that remind the audience they are listening to an introduction?

☐ Flow into the title and author naturally?

☐ Mention the title and author at least once toward the end?

☐ Hook the audience, making them want to see the performance so they can find out more?

☐ Involve all group members in some capacity?

☐ Write at least four sentences and no more than about six?

☐ Write the intro in a mood that complements the mood of the piece it is introducing?

☐ Write an intro that will be memorable?

☐ Include interesting stage pictures, movement, sounds, levels, and teamwork?

NOTES: ____
____
____
____
____
____
____
____

SAMPLE MONOLOGUES AND SCENES

OBJECTIVE You will explore the elements of production and various styles of acting through laboratory scenes.

Most of the following selections are laboratory or "lab scenes." These are short scripts written specifically for classroom study and intended to help students explore theatre, production, acting, and writing styles. They are a lot like the labs you do in science in which students learn a concept then put it to the test with some "hands-on" labs. Now that you know a little about theatre and acting, these lab scenes will be a great way to put the theories you have studied to the test.

What makes a lab scene different from other scenes is that it does not usually come from a play. When a scene comes from a play, the actor is encouraged to read the entire script before performing. This can be expensive in a large classroom if all the students are studying a small group of scenes. This is one reason why teachers have students find scenes on their own within scripts. This ensures that not everyone will have the same play and multiple copies will not be needed.

Reading the entire play is imperative. Dialogue within a scene can be very "cryptic," or mysterious, if the reader or actor has no idea what happened before the scene or what will occur afterward. On top of that, actors can study character development by reading the play from front cover to back cover. The key word here is development, meaning the way someone grows. The reasons for knowing the entire plot before studying a piece of it are numerous and all important.

So why do lab scenes? It would be easy to spend an entire semester studying one play, its characters, its subtext, the dramatic structure, the endless production possibilities, and so on. By the time you finished the unit, you would be an expert on the script and probably the playwright, but you would have only been exposed to one piece of literature. Lab scenes allow you to explore a variety of styles of writing and acting in the time it would take you to thoroughly understand one play. It is an excellent way to teach theatre, providing a broader exposure to a variety of selections.

A few of the pieces in this section did actually come from full-length plays. You can learn more about the individual scenes in the paragraphs preceding them. The first duet, from *Antigone*, by Richard Engling, is from a wonderful full-length published play. Unlike some versions of Sophocles's Greek tragedy, Engling's dialogue flows easily, like fluid song lyrics. You will enjoy the ease with which you understand the story.

ADDITIONAL SCENES IN THIS BOOK

Chapter 1: *The Environmental Adventures of Can Man*, various episodes

Chapter 3: Earth Day Public Service Announcement

Bicycle Helmet PSA/Commercial

Sample Newscast

Zombie High School Radio Theatre Script

Chapter 4: *Put Your Master on a Leash & Other Stupid Laws* Readers Theatre Script

Moose Mousse Sample TV Commercial Script

If possible, you should read the full play of *Antigone* prior to rehearsing and performing this scene. Attempting to understand a moment within a story without knowing the entire plot is like trying to finish a puzzle without knowing what it should look like upon completion. That same puzzle, when you know it as a whole, has light and shadows, subtext, and lots of small but significant prizes hidden in remote corners that actors can't know unless they study the big picture.

149

ABOUT SAMPLE MONOLOGUES AND SCENES

Each scene in this book was selected because it has the potential to teach a certain element. Some focus on the language while others focus on timing, characterization, or using theatrical devices. Some have lessons afterward that are informative, and some are challenging.

ANTIGONE

A NEW ADAPTATION OF THE TRAGEDY BY SOPHOCLES
Adapted by RICHARD ENGLING

Richard Engling is a playwright, novelist, actor, and director. He is artistic director of Chicago's Polarity Ensemble Theatre. The Chicago Actors Ensemble produced his first play, Ghost Watch, *in 1987. Penguin Putnam published his novel,* Body MortgageAntigone and Macbeth: Adaptations for a War-Torn Time, *in 2006. He holds a Bachelor's degree in theatre from Northern Illinois University and a Master's in creative writing from Indiana University. He has appeared in productions with Keyhole Theatre, Shakespeare Inc., Chicago Actors Ensemble, the American Institute of Barcelona, ImprovOlympic (now iO), and others.*

FROM THE PLAYWRIGHT

The private scene between Creon and Antigone does not exist in the original play by Sophocles. I worked on the script in collaboration with Ann Keen, who directed the first production. We felt the play lacked a scene in which Creon and Antigone could almost come together. In the original, neither character wavers from his or her position until Creon finally reverses his stance, but too late to save Antigone's life.

What might happen, we wondered, if they had a scene in private, where the public could not witness King Creon's deal-making. Creon and Antigone are uncle and niece. How might their family feelings pull them closer together? Which one of them might bend enough to avert disaster?

At the beginning of the play, we discover that Antigone's brother, Polynices, has attacked the city of Thebes where their brother, Eteocles, reigned as king. Eteocles and Polynices were to have traded off the kingship year by year. When Polynices's turn came, Eteocles refused to hand over the crown. Polynices went to neighboring city-states and raised an army to attack Thebes to force his claim for the crown. In the battle, however, the two brothers fought hand-to-hand and killed each other.

The crown of Thebes then went to their nearest male relative, their uncle Creon. Creon declared that Eteocles would be buried with full honors. Since Polynices attacked his home city, however, Creon declared that his body would be left on the field for the buzzards and dogs to devour. This was a horrible condemnation. The ancient Greeks believed that if one's body was not buried, the soul was doomed to wander and never find peace in the underworld.

Antigone would not allow this fate for her brother. She decided to bury him, even though doing so would mean her own death, according to her uncle's decree.

In the original play, Antigone never wavers from her decision to bury her brother. Creon never wavers from his position that anyone who breaks his edict must die, including his niece Antigone.

Antigone and Macbeth: Adaptations for a War-Torn Time can be purchased on amazon.com.

In the scene that follows, we see the two of them talk and negotiate in private. We get to see more of their inner emotions and thought processes. We even get to see them nearly come to an agreement. We see more of their human traits. We see them try and fail. And because of that, the final tragedy becomes all the more poignant to us.

ABOUT COLLABORATION

One of the joys of working in the theatre is that it is a collaborative art. It was a pleasure to work with Ann Keen on the adaptation of Sophocles's *Antigone*. Ann is an incredibly astute reader, and she contributed hugely to the vision of our Antigone. Volunteer actors and staged reading audiences also made their contributions to the script.

At the beginning of a script's life, it is common for many people to help give it shape by offering their critiques and suggestions to the playwright. After the script is in its permanent form, it still depends on actors, directors, and designers to bring it to life and to reinterpret it. Every performance of every production is a unique event.

—Richard Engling

NOTES:

CHAPTER 5 — UNDERSTANDING AND WRITING SCRIPTS

ANTIGONE

A NEW ADAPTATION OF THE TRAGEDY BY SOPHOCLES

Adapted by RICHARD ENGLING

PRONUNCIATION GUIDE

ANTIGONE—ann-TIG-uh-nee   HAEMON—HAY-mahn

CREON—KREE-ahn   ISMENE—IZ-muh-nay

ELYSIAN—ill-LIZH-uhn   OEDIPUS—ED-uh-puss

ETEOCLES—en-TEE-uh-cleez   POLYNICES—Pol-uh-NIGH-sees

HADES—HAY-deez   TARTARUS—TAR-ter-iss

CREON: Now answer plain: Had you heard my edict?

ANTIGONE: How could I not?

CREON: And you broke the law?

ANTIGONE: Let me ask you, Uncle, are you more high than Zeus? More profound than holy Justice below? Your mortal breath cannot overrule the laws of Heaven. Their jurisdiction is forever. Should I prefer your laws, I provoke the wrath of Hades and doom my brother's soul to wander. I knew that I must die. Had you not proclaimed it? Yet when one lives surrounded by sorrow, death is bliss. To leave my brother unburied, I would rather be dead. If you judge me foolish in this, it may be you are the fool.

CREON: Stubborn daughter of a stubborn sire, she glories in her wickedness. If she can flout the law unpunished, then she is king and I am the niece. Bring forth Ismene. I saw her in the palace, frenzied and distraught. A guilty mind oft betrays the doer. Go all and bring her. I would have a word alone with my sister's child.

ANTIGONE: Would you do more, Uncle, than execute me?

CREON: It is because I do not wish to see you die that I sent the others away. And Haemon means to marry you. I do not care to disappoint my son, either.

ANTIGONE: Perhaps your law is not so absolute

CREON: Perhaps you are not so stubborn when there is no audience.

ANTIGONE: What will you have of me, Uncle? In truth, I do not wish to be put to death.

CREON: Good. Then you must condemn your crime publicly and stay away from your brother's body.

ANTIGONE: I will do as you ask, but only if you allow Ismene or Haemon—or yourself—to give Polynices a burial.

CREON: I cannot show piety towards the one who attacked our city.

ANTIGONE: He is your nephew.

CREON: Did he show piety in killing his own brother?

ANTIGONE: It is not for us to judge his life. He deserves the rites of death.

CREON: Polynices died our enemy. He killed Eteocles.

ANTIGONE: And what of Eteocles? What about his vow to share the throne? If he had not refused to give Polynices his turn as king, neither one nor the other would lie low today. A year hence Eteocles would have been on the throne again.

CREON: Eteocles saw the weakness in divided power. And he was right. A leader must show strength. I offered Polynices my counsel in this dispute: I told him to be the power behind the throne, as I once was to Oedipus.

ANTIGONE: You abetted the arrogance of Eteocles? Then their blood is on your hands as well!

CREON: Eteocles was a stronger leader. A king makes decisions for the good of the realm.

ANTIGONE: Was it for the good of the realm that they are dead? I will not trade my brother's soul for the good of the realm. I will condemn my crime, as you ask, but only if Polynices is buried.

CREON: Antigone, I do not want to condemn you.

ANTIGONE: I cannot sacrifice his soul for my life.

CREON: But after a crime like his, can you hope that he will enter the Elysian Fields? Is it not more likely that your brother be condemned to Tartarus? Is it so much worse that his soul wander here?

ANTIGONE: You cannot know my brother's fate. His journey through Hades' lands is his alone. The one thing we know for certain is that he will never reach the Elysian Fields if left unburied here.

CREON: Perhaps it could be done. Many have fallen in this squabble. We could drag in some slave's body to replace your brother. I will let you do your rites in secret. In exchange, you must publicly condemn your crime and your brother's

     151

NOTES:

CREON: Think again. I offer you life.

ANTIGONE: At the price of betraying my brother's soul forever.

CREON: The gods will know what is in your heart.

ANTIGONE: The gods will hear the words from my mouth.

CREON: I give you the chance to save your life. Take it!

ANTIGONE: You think everyone can lie so convincingly? I cannot do it!

CREON: It is not a lie to remain silent. I ask for a simple act, and then you can live and marry Haemon. Don't you want to taste the fullness of life and grow old? Or if your devotions have become so strong, devote your life to the <u>temple of Hades</u>. But first you must correct your defiance of the law.

ANTIGONE: We are the last of a family destroyed by the gods. They will not accept an <u>approximation</u> of their due. If I condemn him, it will <u>contaminate</u> his funeral rites. Then what will be our <u>reckoning?</u>

CREON: You <u>sour</u> the love I feel for you. Go with your brothers to the <u>land of the dead</u> if you must. While I live, I shall not be overthrown by the <u>spawn</u> of Oedipus.

crime. You must give public support to my law and pledge that no one ever hear of our secret dealings.

ANTIGONE: I will do what you ask, except I cannot condemn Polynices at the same time I bury him.

CREON: You need not say his name. Merely gesture to the body of the slave.

ANTIGONE: I cannot take part in such a <u>conjurer's</u> trick.

CREON: I offer you life and your brother honor.

ANTIGONE: Public condemnation? A <u>clandestine</u> burial? Where is the honor in this?

CREON: The honor lies in doing the public good. Bury your brother in secret! It is our fate to rule. We cannot reveal everything we know! There are those in this city who would dispose of us now.

ANTIGONE: Words carry power. I cannot condemn him in public and bury him in private. Dark Hades would not accept his soul. Let me just condemn my crime. Let Ismene bury our brother.

CREON: Not even Ismene must know of this. And words do carry power. That is why you must condemn your act and your brother to the people. I cannot show a <u>wavering</u> hand.

ANTIGONE: I will not show a wavering heart.

NOTES: _______________________________

____

____

____

____

____

____

CHAPTER 5 — UNDERSTANDING AND WRITING SCRIPTS

NAME _______________________________________ PERIOD _______ DATE _____________

ANTIGONE —THE LANGUAGE MAKES THE SCENE

Most actors will see the complex and metaphorical language as the most challenging part of Richard Engling's duet between Antigone and Creon. However, simplify the vocabulary and change the sentence pattern to make it more comfortable, and you lose much of the poetry and passion. Engling chose each word very carefully and aid the words out in such a way that a captivating rhythm emerges early in the scene. Both characters become deep, intense, and layered due in great part to the words chosen for them by their playwright.

Look at the following lines in questions 1 through 5 below. Rewrite each line so that it sounds natural, the way you'd talk with your friends.

1. "Stubborn daughter of a stubborn sire, she glories in her wickedness."

____

____

____

2. "A year hence Eteocles would have been on the throne again."

____

____

____

3. "You abetted the arrogance of Eteocles? Then their blood is on your hands as well!"

____

____

____

4. "Don't you want to taste the fullness of life and grow old? Or if your devotions have become so strong, devote your life to the temple of Hades. But first you must correct your defiance of the law."

____

____

____

5. "You sour the love I feel for you. Go with your brothers to the land of the dead if you must. While I live, I shall not be overthrown by the spawn of Oedipus."

____

____

____

          153

NOTES: ____

____

____

____

____

____

____

6. If you had the chance to perform this scene either the way it is now or by using modern language, which would you choose and why?

____

____

____

7. You may have noticed that many of the challenging words in the scene were underlined. Use context clues (clues provided in the scene) to match the word on the left to the correct definition on the right by placing the correct letter in the box.

A. edict   ___ to cause
B. profound   ___ highly intellectual and emotionally penetrating
C. mortal   ___ punishment
D. provoke   ___ living and human
E. wrath   ___ formal command

A. sire   ___ mock, insult
B. flout   ___ often
C. frenzied   ___ distracted with worry
D. distraught ___ father
E. oft   ___ agitated

A. condemn   ___ in this context, "be dead"
B. piety   ___ religious-based respect
C. rites   ___ to declare disapproval
D. vow   ___ religious ceremony; in this case, the ceremony of burying the dead
E. lie low   ___ promise

A. hence   ___ advise
B. counsel   ___ disagreement
C. dispute   ___ supported or assisted
D. abetted   ___ self-importance
E. arrogance ___ from now

A. realm   ___ destiny
B. Elysian Fields ___ where the ancient Greeks believed the "bad" or condemned went after death
C. Tartarus   ___ in this context, "died"
D. fate   ___ where the ancient Greeks believed the "good" went after death
E. fallen   ___ kingdom

ANTIGONE KEY FOR #7

D (provoke) to cause
B (profound) highly intellectual and emotionally penetrating
E (wrath) punishment
C (mortal) living and human
A (edict) formal command

B (flout) mock, insult
E (oft) often
D (distraught) distracted with worry
A (sire) father
C (frenzied) agitated

E (lie low) in this context, "be dead"
B (piety) religious-based respect
A (condemn) to declare disapproval
C (rites) religious ceremony; in this case, the ceremony of burying the dead
D (vow) promise

B (counsel) advise
C (dispute) disagreement
D (abetted) supported or assisted
E (arrogance) self-importance
A (hence) from now

A. squabble   __ secretive
B. contaminate   __ disagreement
C. clandestine   __ uncertain
D. wavering   __ to ruin by making unclean or impure
E. due   __ something which is owed someone

A. approximation   __ in this case, the afterlife
B. conjurer   __ someone who performs tricks
C. reckoning   __ that which is born from something else
D. sour   __ what is owed to someone, almost like an invoice
E. Land of the Dead   __ to ruin something that would normally be likable
F. spawn   __ something that is close but not exact

7a. Which two words from the list above could be synonyms for argument?

____

7b. Find three terms that have to do with "the afterlife."

____

7c. In the last two groups of words, which two words are synonyms for something owed?

____

7d. In the last two groups of words, which two words mean to make a good thing bad?

____

      155

D (fate) destiny
C (Tartarus) where the ancient Greeks believed the "bad" or condemned went after death
E (fallen) in this context, "died"
B (Elysian Fields) where the ancient Greeks believed the "good" went after death
A (realm) kingdom

C (clandestine) secretive
A (squabble) disagreement
D (wavering) uncertain
B (contaminate) to ruin by making unclean or impure
E (due) something which is owed someone

E (Land of the Dead) in this case, the afterlife
B (conjurer) someone who performs tricks
F (spawn) that which is born from something else
C (reckoning) what is owed to someone, almost like an invoice
D (sour) to ruin something that would normally be likable
A (approximation) something that is close but not exact

7a. dispute, squabble
7b. Elysian Fields, Tartarus, Land of the Dead
7c. due, reckoning
7d. contaminate, sour

INTRODUCTION TO THEATRE ARTS 2

OVER THERE, HERE

Female Monologue

By LEVI CURTIS

Levi Curtis is a busy theatre teacher in Lamaline, Newfoundland and Labrador, on Canada's easternmost tip. With the island's lengthy and notable place in both the fishing and shipping industries' history, it is no wonder Curtis found inspiration for his characters and his stories. Just as colorful as his characters are the Newfoundland-Irish-Devonshire dialects with which they speak.

VERA is the town "know-it-all"; she's friendly but dearly loves to gossip. This scene takes place during World War II when all the men have left for the front, and only the women, children, and senior gentlemen remained in the small towns.

VERA: And so it was we sent parcel after parcel out of here on the steamer bound for the front. We sent mitts, socks, long johns, boots, cigarettes, photographs—those of us who had them—and letters... love letters. Oh, oh, I have to tell you this. Last week the steamer Glenco was coming to town with the mail and was going to take a bunch of our parcels out to the boys. Well, there we all was, standing on the wharf, all our parcels of food and clothes stacked up on this big box Helen Slaney was sending off to her Randall. I remember thinking *What in God's name was she sending off to Randall now?* It was only last week she sent him five parcels of food and clothes. I soon put all thoughts of Helen out of my mind when the Glenco started comin' into the dock. If you've never been in an isolated community, then you've no idea what it feels like to see the steamer comin' into the harbour. A lifeline to the outside world is what it is. News from outside, news from St. John's and news, please God, from the boys. Anyway, the Glenco off-loads her cargo and Herb Collins, the postmaster, started loading our parcels onto the ship. Well, that is all but Helen's. It was too heavy for seventy-five-year-old Herb. So the men from the Glenco come down and started to lift the box. Well, they started lifting, and lifting, but the box was right heavy. Then after much grunting and groaning they got the box up off the wharf, but just as they was about to head up the ramp the bottom of the box give way and out come Helen with not a stitch on, she was sending herself off to Randall. *(Pause.)* Helen was feeling stir crazy. What with her husband away... What? A whole year now. A whole year and the closest she ever gets to Randall is a letter or the packages she sends off every now and then. Well, I guess that would make anyone do silly things. I guess Helen just got tired of keeping the home fires burning and wanted to set a blaze burning with Randall.

NOTES: ____

____

____

____

____

____

____

____

CHAPTER 5 — UNDERSTANDING AND WRITING SCRIPTS

TRIFFIE

Female Monologue
By LEVI CURTIS

TRIFFIE is a "beach woman." They were female workers who turned fish to dry on the stone beaches in the early 1900s. Integral to the fishery, merchants depended on them to dry the fish for foreign markets before the invention of fish dryers.

TRIFFIE: Here's how it is. You get up early, real early, in the morning, makes the youngsters something to eat, gets 'em dressed for the day and you heads down to the beach. Most women dresses in full regalia, bonnet and all, before they leaves the house. Me, I hate that damn bonnet, can't stand the thought of wearing it. I tried going without once. All I remembers is looking down at the fish one minute and the next thing you knows I'm smacking lips with some ol' codfish. So now I knows the reason for the bonnet, I still hates it but I wears it. I puts it on when I gets to the beach. I works on Bishop's Beach. It's not called that now by ye crowd, but that's what we calls it. Bishop's Beach. I been working here now, what, four year. The pay's all right, forty dollars for the whole summer. Might not seem like a lot to ye but we certainly appreciates it, keeps the wolf from the door, if you knows what I mean. George, that's me husband, George Fudge, he worked on one of the schooners. Gone all the time he is. Gone for weeks on end. Sure the youngsters hardly knows him when he comes home in the fall. One time, after a particularly long time out on the banks, George come home with a face full of hair. Now George is a rather big man, some would say roly-poly, and he's ten year older than I. Anyway, George come home with his dirty clothes in an old gunny sack slung over his shoulder. Bridget, that's me youngest, she come bursting into the parlour just as George come in the front door. Well, you should have seen her face. The sun could not have shone no brighter. George was delighted, he dropped his bag and reached for Bridget. Bridget ran right up to him and kissed him on his long white beard and said, "Whatcha got for me, Santa?" George didn't know what to say but it wasn't long before he cleaned that hair off his face. I'm sorry, where was I? Oh yes, the beach, the beach where you breaks your back and burns your skin, just so some rich bugger can get richer, and the most you can hope for is enough credits to see you through the winter. So I hauls the bonnet on me head and goes and get a "yaffle" of fish from the pile and starts laying them out on the rocks. You got to keep your eyes on them fish and know the right time to turn 'em. You wouldn't want to blister the fish or ruin a batch. Your life's not worth that. Speaking of turning the fish, ol' Effie Martin, she must be, what, sixty, if she's a day. Well, Effie was a vain sort, her beach clothes was always the cleanest and her bonnet, just so. Well, Effie had poor eyes and, well, she needed glasses. If you ask me what she needed was a new set of eyes. And Effie never let on she needed them. Anyway, Effie was working away at the fish like she always done, layin' 'em out in lovely straight lines, waitin' a bit and turnin' 'em. She spent the whole day at that. Proud she was too. Effie was always proud of her work. The only thing was no one had the heart to tell her that she spent the whole day turnin' rocks instead of fish. I knows one thing when it was time to go home I was some happy. The other women and I would slowly "uncrick" ourselves and creep up the beach knowin' we still had supper to cook. There was this one time we was walking back from the beach when we heard a "jeesley" big racket comin' from the bridge. We couldn't figger out what was goin' on, was someone dead?

NOTES: ____

____

____

____

____

____

____

____

Was there a fire? Well, you never seen a faster bunch of women in your life then we crowd runnin' for the bridge. Well, I tell you... what a crowd of men was on the bridge. Yellin' and screamin', they was. "Down with this one" and "out with that one." The police was there and they was yellin' at the men and the men was yellin' back. Sure, it was like a riot. I heard someone say they wasn't payin' no town taxes. Next thing you knows there's men bein' arrested and hauled off and put in jail. And wouldn't you know it, my George would be right in the thick of it. And, yes, he was hauled off to jail like the others. He didn't get home 'til late the next day. The youngsters didn't know nothing 'cause it was no different than all the other times he was gone. I asked George what it was all about, he said he didn't have a clue. He was in Bungay's Barber Shop gettin' his usual when all hell broke loose and, well, George, being George, he charged out of the shop to see what was goin' on, he said he needed a bit of excitement, anyway. Michael, my oldest, he's ten, come into the kitchen, took one look at his father and started to laugh. Now, George didn't know what to make of this, his son laughing at him. I give George a smack on the chest and tells him why. There was a "gert" section of hair buzzed out right across his head. Oh, and ye crowd can thank George and barber Bungay for the Buzz Cut. Anyway, that's all I got to say right now. So remember when yous is out on the beaches round here, remember we crowd. Night.

NOTES: _______________________________

____

____

____

____

____

____

____

NAME ____ PERIOD _________ DATE _______________

OVER THERE, HERE AND *TRIFFIE* —
FOCUS ON SETTING AND CHARACTER

Both of the female characters from Levi Curtis's monologues are from Newfoundland. While they are separated by nearly half a century, both use the same dialect and appear to be in very similar settings. Unless you have spent time in the same type of setting—a fishing village near the coast in Newfoundland more than half a century ago—you may have to do some research to get a better grasp on your character and scene. You can also get some clues as to your setting and characters from the script. Read *Over There, Here,* look for clues to fit the following three categories, and write them in the spaces below.

THE PLACE	THE TIMES	THE CHARACTER

What are some words and phrases Vera uses that can help you to better understand her character? Explain your choices.

Research Newfoundland using whatever resources you can. Find five similarities and five differences to where you live.

Similarities: ____

Differences: ____

How are you and Vera similar or different? ____

NOTES: ____

Now read *Triffie* and look for clues to fit the following three categories, and write them in the spaces below. Place stars by the items that are the same in Triffie's scene as in Vera's scene before.

THE PLACE	THE TIMES	THE CHARACTER
________	________	________
________	________	________
________	________	________
________	________	________

What are some words and phrases Triffie uses that can help you to better understand her character? Explain your choices.

____

____

____

____

How are you and Triffie similar or different? ________________________

____

____

Use context clues (clues within the scene itself) or any other available resources to find the meanings of the following words:

Parcel: ________________________

Wharf: ________________________

Regalia: ________________________

Keeps the wolves from the doors: ________________________

Schooner: ________________________

Out on the banks: ________________________

Gunny sack: ________________________

Yaffle: ________________________

Jeesley: ________________________

Gert: ________________________

OVER THERE, HERE AND *TRIFFIE* VOCABULARY KEY

Parcel: A package.

Wharf: A place where ships may tie off or dock.

Regalia: Fancy clothing.

Keeps the wolf from the door: Pays the bills; keeps the collectors away.

Schooner: A type of sailing vessel.

Out on the banks: Refers to someone who is fishing in the Grand Banks area just off the coast of Nova Scotia where conditions are optimal. It was understood to be a lengthy trip.

Gunny sack: A large bag.

Yaffle: Newfoundland slang for "an armload."

Jeesley: Newfoundland slang used as a substitute for a curse word.

Gert: Newfoundland slang for "great."

CHAPTER 5 — UNDERSTANDING AND WRITING SCRIPTS

THE RETURN

Male Monologue

By LEVI CURTIS

It is 1692, and a stranger is on trial for healing a local woman of her blindness in Salem, Massachusetts. Judge Jonathan Parris has come to believe during the course of the trial that this stranger might be the Christ returned and has said so to Reverend Watkins. Watkins, fixated on the idea of convicting the stranger at all costs, kills Parris. This monologue is delivered shortly afterward, the court unaware of Parris's demise or Watkins's guilt.

WATKINS: Be seated. Mister Justice Jonathan Parris has asked me to speak with you, and seeing that this is a Church-sanctioned trial, I feel that it is appropriate that I, as the Church's representative, pass judgment. He had agreed with me. I have listened carefully to all the facts presented here today. I have considered everything carefully. We know for absolute certainty that Satan exists, as assuredly as we know that God exists. And we know He does exist. We know that evil exists, and that it manifests itself in many forms. We, here in Salem, have seen much evidence of this in the past number of months. Many of you have seen the trials of the creatures who disguised themselves as citizens of our town. We have dealt with them fairly and sent them back to their Father. This was just. This was right. Those men and women were eliminated. This case is no different. This man, this stranger, comes among us and does a wondrous thing. He cures Mrs. Smythe's blindness. Miraculous? I think not! *(Points at MRS. SMYTHE.)* This woman by her own volition says she is not a religious woman. Why, then, should she be favoured above all others to be granted such a gift? I'll tell you why! She has sold her soul. That's how the miracle happened. She sold her soul to *(Points at STRANGER.)* this man. The devil himself. This stranger. This Satan. *(To STRANGER.)* Beware, Satan, for we have found you out! *(Stands and adjusts himself pompously.)* It is the judgment of this court, this Church Court, that I sentence you, *(Goes to MRS. SMYTHE.)* Mrs. Smythe, to be blinded by hot pokers, so that you will always be reminded of the errors of your ways. And you, Satan, shall return home by the flames that created you. You will be burned at the stake.

     161

NOTES: ____

____

____

____

____

____

____

____

NAME ____ PERIOD ________ DATE ______________

THE RETURN — HISTORY ONSTAGE

Research the Salem witch trials. In the space provided, give statistics and facts that will help you to perform the scene, *The Return*.

1. Historical facts and statistics:

2. Why must an actor be aware of the connection between history and a play that is based on historical events?

3. Why do you think Reverend Watkins would go to such extremes to convict the stranger?

162   Photocopying this page violates federal copyright law.

NOTES: ____

____

____

____

____

____

____

____

HALF NELSON

A Scene for Three Males
By KIP PETROFF

CAST OF CHARACTERS

RON .... The oldest of the three; he has been put in charge

NELSON .... Ron's younger brother, and the better wrestler

SKIP .... Their friend, also a wrestler

The three boys, all wrestlers, are getting ready to leave their hotel room for a much anticipated wrestling tournament.

RON: Gear?

NELSON: In the trunk.

RON: Bags?

SKIP: I already put mine in the car.

NELSON: Me too.

RON: And I've got one of mine.

NELSON: I put your little one in the car with mine.

RON: So, I guess we're ready to go. Nelson. You call mom?

NELSON: Yup. She talked. I listened. My ear hurts from holding the phone while I was trying to clip my fingernails.

SKIP: *(Had been eating a pastry, but stops to pull something from his mouth.)* Um, Nel? Where'd you clip your nails?

NELSON: Over there. *(Indicates.)* Why?

SKIP: *(Relieved, returns object to his mouth.)* No reason. Anyone want the last donut?

RON: Can't. You eat it.

SKIP: Nellie?

NELSON: I'm good. Take it.

RON: Last chance for the bathroom. Anyone?

OTHERS: Nope.

RON: *(Checks his watch.)* We're early. Mom said we'd be sorry she didn't come, that we'd be lost without her, and here we are with our toothbrushes—

NELSON: Hang on! *(Runs to a vanity and grabs a toothbrush.)* Now I'm ready!

RON: Let's go. Nel, you got the room key?

NELSON: I already checked out, and the guy said to just leave it on the nightstand.

RON: *(Sees the key on the nightstand.)* Check!

SKIP: Let's go! *(The three leave the hotel room, closing the door behind them, and go to their car in the parking lot. All stand with their belongings in hand waiting for the others to unlock the doors.)*

RON: Nel, open the door, man! It's hot out here.

NELSON: Dude, lay off. Skip's got the keys.

SKIP: Sorry, dude. Beg to differ, but I gave them back to you.

RON: Okay, whatever. Just someone open the door.

NELSON: Skip, do I look like I have the keys? Where'd you put them after you put your suitcase in the trunk?

SKIP: I put them in your bag!

NELSON: My bag?

SKIP: Yeah. Your bag. *(Looks at the car.)* The bag you always carry to matches. *(Takes a step toward the car and peers in the back seat.)* That bag.

NELSON and RON: That bag?

SKIP: *(Suddenly realizes what he has done.)* Uh-huh. Oh, jockstrap! *(They check the doors just to be sure, but all are locked.)* Big stinking smelly pile of freshman jockstraps! Don't tell me... *(Thinks.)* What time is it?

RON: Ten till.

SKIP: What time's the match?

NELSON: We have to check in by 9:30.

SKIP: Spare! There's a spare key, right?

RON and NELSON: Spare? *(They look at each other with a glimmer of hope, then simultaneously.)* Mom gave you a spare! *(Pause.)* No, Mom gave you a spare.

RON: I don't have it. She gave it to you.

NELSON: Dude, why would she give it to me? You're the oldest.

RON: Yeah, but you're the one with the stupid driver's license.

NELSON: *(Gets frustrated.)* Ron, it was in the envelope in the side pocket of your—*(Turns to car, pointing.)*—that bag!

 163

NOTES: ____

____

____

____

____

____

____

____

INTRODUCTION TO THEATRE ARTS 2

RON: *(Realizes his mistake.)* Well, I didn't know there was a key in the envelope.

NELSON: You can read, right?

RON: I can read when there's something to read.

SKIP: *(Looks at the envelope through the window.)* "Spare k—spare key"! Hey guys, there's a spare key in that envelope! *(BROTHERS stare dumbly at SKIP.)* What?

NELSON: Why can't you just admit it, Ron?

RON: What?

NELSON: You're sabotaging the meet because you're afraid I'll do better than you.

RON: That's the kind of idiotic thing I'd expect you to say! You win one match against me in practice, and suddenly you're the golden child!

SKIP: Five.

RON: What?

NELSON: No, it was six. I got him on technical superiority that time, and he refuses to admit—

SKIP: Oh, yeah. I forgot about that. You're right, six.

RON: Five!

NELSON: I'll take five.

SKIP: Five it is!

RON: Will you two shut up?

SKIP: Sorry! Everybody's got to yell at the fat guy! *(Walks to the other side of the car.)*

RON: Skip, this is all your fault! Who puts car keys in someone's luggage?

SKIP: We wouldn't be having this conversation if you'd passed your driver's test the last time—or the time before that, or that time back in March, or that other time...

RON: Okay, it's only half your fault, then, half Nelson's.

NELSON: So, it's my fault? You're the one who's supposed to be in charge. You're the one Mom said to keep an eye on her car—which means the keys, too! *(SKIP has discovered that he can reach a stick through the slightly open window on one side of the car while BROTHERS argue with their backs to him on the other.)*

RON: I'm not the one who locked his luggage in the back seat with the keys in it!

NELSON: How was I supposed to know the keys were in it?

RON: Why'd you lock it if you didn't know where the keys were?

NELSON: I didn't want our stuff to get stolen! I assumed Skip had the keys.

SKIP: Drag me into it again. I'm an easy target. *(He is using the stick to pull the bag with the spare key closer to the window; BROTHERS pay no attention.)*

NELSON: *You got your cell phone?*

RON: Yeah. Why?

NELSON: I guess we're going to have to call for a taxi.

RON: But your gear? *(About this time, SKIP has retrieved the envelope with the spare key, opened it, and has opened his door and is sitting in the car, waiting for BROTHERS to stop arguing.)*

NELSON: We can beg, borrow, steal, rent, whatever. What time is it?

RON: Nine. Okay, we know enough guys there that we can borrow everything we need. Singlets, head gear, I've got clean socks for all three of us, shoes—

NELSON: They sell mouth guards at registration.

RON: Cool. Okay, we're covered, right?

NELSON: Straps.

RON: What?

NELSON: Dude. Jockstraps. I'm not borrowing a strap!

RON: I've got mine. I'm covered.

NELSON: What about us? You expect Skip and me to borrow some guy's strap? Where is Skip? *(Both turn to see SKIP sitting in the car. He waves, they wave back, they look at each other.)*

RON and NELSON: Skip!

RON: But how—

NELSON: Skip, Dude! How'd you—

SKIP: *(Holds up a torn envelope.)* Spare key. Used a stick. You guys done arguing?

RON: *(Gets in the car.)* Skip, you saved the day!

NELSON: Good escape, dude. *(Gets in the car.)*

SKIP: Thanks. Hey guys, all that arguing made me need to go. Let me run back in the room really quick. I'll only be a second.

NELSON: Sure. We'll wait.

SKIP: You got the key?

RON and NELSON: *(Look at each other.)* Key?

NOTES:

NAME _______________________________________ PERIOD _______ DATE _______________

HALF NELSON—CHARACTERIZATION STUDY

Complete the character study grid below using information from *Half Nelson*. You will find clues in what the characters say about themselves and others, the tone with which it is said, what the playwright says about the characters, and what they do. How can you use this information to create a funny character? Study the people around you, too, and the characters you see on TV and in the movies. You don't want to copy them because that would not be original; however, you can learn from them by working some of their more interesting traits into your character. Create your own character grid to use with other scenes.

	RON	NELSON	SKIP
Goal			
Potential obstacles			
Character clues from the script and what other characters say			
Based on what I know, I think…			
He reminds me of… (characters from shows/cartoons)			
And from those characters, I will use…			

165

NOTES: _______________________________________

____

____

____

____

____

____

____

INTRODUCTION TO THEATRE ARTS 2

THE LEGEND OF OLE CHARLIE WOLF

Male/Male Duet

By BUD LANG

Bud Lang is a collector and teller of stories. The Legend of Ole Charlie Wolf *is the true account of how he collected one of his favorite tales.*

CAST OF CHARACTERS

OLD MAN .... An old Cherokee recluse who lives on a small island and has a great deal to teach

BUDDY................................. A curious young relative who wants to visit the old man's wolf cubs

OLD MAN: Son, you got a very irritating way of showin' up at times and places where you ain't got no business and you ain't been invited.

BUDDY: I had to sneak. My daddy told me to stay away from here. He thinks—

OLD MAN: Your daddy's just looking out for you, son. Don't you see that?

BUDDY: He's just trying to be the boss of me, that's all. *(Looks to see if OLD MAN is going to continue his defense.)* Mama told me you was her uncle, and that makes you my uncle too. *(Sits on a log.)* Didn't think you'd mind family dropping in unannounced.

OLD MAN: This property's caused enough pain, enough so's folks keep their distance 'less'n they're invited.

BUDDY: I been thinking about them wolves an' how you told me they're as harmless as teddy bears. *(Looks around, moves to a different seat.)* Where are they?

OLD MAN: I put them in the cave when I saw you comin'. They're both sleepin' sound.

BUDDY: Both? There was six when I was here a couple of weeks ago. There's just two now? Where are they, Old Man?

OLD MAN: *(Stands, attempting to change the subject.)* Old Man, huh? Is that how your mama raised you to talk?

BUDDY: Sorry, I just—

OLD MAN: Those four you saw was their first litter. Understand, son... those puppies need to run free, and they can't do that here.

BUDDY: Oh. *(Disappointed, but not wanting to let it show; moves to a new seat, unable to stay still too long.)* Is it true what my mama and daddy said?

OLD MAN: Well, I don't know. *(Prepares for the worst.)* What'd they say?

BUDDY: They said them pups were symbols of freedom. *(Thinks, then with boyish innocence.)* Does that mean that if they're gone some of our freedom's gone too?

OLD MAN: Symbols, huh? *(Chuckles.)* They're symbols, all right. Our wolves are symbols of defiance, and we still have two *(Points to a cave.)* of the largest symbols right there. Those two can have four more symbols each. *Keeping* them pups don't mean *keeping* your freedom. It means we're defying the white man's need to keep taking what don't belong to him.

BUDDY: I thought wolves only had one or two cubs a year.

OLD MAN: You're changing the subject, boy. *(Looks to see if it's safe to continue his rant, but BUDDY is interested in reproduction now.)* Okay. In the wild, there's less food. These wolves know they're getting regular meals. They're *(Thinks.)*— conditioned! They can have more 'cause they can feed more. It's as simple as that.

BUDDY: Oh. *(Back on track.)* All right, so we can have a bunch more. That still don't tell me what happened to the others.

OLD MAN: They're on their way to Canada, son. *(Sits.)* I love the wolves. My daddy loved 'em before me, and his daddy before him. *(Pause, looks at BUDDY.)* Your daddy loves them too.

BUDDY: *(Looks up.)* My daddy's seen the wolves?

OLD MAN: *(Chuckles.)* He's the one who takes the cubs every year to Birmingham. To the zoo.

BUDDY: My daddy? I thought you said Canada? *(Gives a look of distrust.)*

OLD MAN: Yes, your daddy. Let's see here. 1938 to 1954. Yep. He's been taking them for sixteen

NOTES: _______________________________

____

____

____

____

____

____

____

years now. Canadian zoologists pick 'em up and move 'em up north.

BUDDY: Well, I'll be. You think you know someone... Sixteen years!

OLD MAN: Ever since the TVA flooded our land and tried to kill my daddy.

BUDDY: *(Stands, shocked.)* Then the Legend of Ole Charlie Wolf is about your daddy!

OLD MAN: *(Holds out for suspense.)* You want to know about the legend? Sit still. You're making me dizzy. *(Serious.)* The people along the river here all knew this was my daddy's land. His daddy acquired it when he returned home from the War Between the States. He'd been sent away to fight as a "substitute soldier" for the man that controlled the farms and people over there in Morgan County. Came home, everything was gone—his home, his family, his people. All the same. Cherokee, Creek, White Man. They come home to nothing, not even hope.

BUDDY: But he was a hero!

OLD MAN: Don't matter none. Never was any Cherokee celebrated by the white people.

BUDDY: My mama talks about him. I mean, she don't sit around fires telling stories or nothing, but I've heard her talking about Charlie.

OLD MAN: *(As if this explains it.)* Your mama's part Cherokee. *(Pauses to see if Buddy understands; he does.)* His daddy was twice a hero. He'd survived the Crash of Johnson's Landing back in 1838 when the Cherokee Indian Nation was trying any way it could to get its people to Oklahoma.

BUDDY: The Trail of Tears! The crash was so bad, only a few people survived, and barely!

OLD MAN: Just three. All young men, but they were strong. They were fished from the river by the Creek tribe of the great Chief Cataco, each taken in by a family, nursed back to health. My grandfather was one of them. He was sixteen.

BUDDY: Old Charlie Wolf.

OLD MAN: *(Not agreeing, attempting to continue.)* My grandfather was Charlie. His son was Charlie, the son of his son was—

BUDDY: Yeah, yeah. Spare me. I know. The son of his son, blah, blah, blah. *(Impatient.)* Which Charlie was *Ole Charlie Wolf?*

OLD MAN: *(Enjoys the tease.)* My daddy was always so angry. He'd tell campfire stories about the white government taking the land from the Cherokee Indian Nation and its people, 'bout how his daddy lost his wife and two daughters

fighting the White Man's war. He'd talk about hardship, 'bout how his own daddy built a new family and a new farm here, 'bout how he took over and tried to make the farm more what his daddy'd wanted. What he didn't talk about was the TVA coming, tellin' him he had to move off his land so they could bring in flood waters and destroy all that he was, all that he and his daddy had accomplished. Near seventy years of blood, sweat, tears. No, he didn't tell us about the TVA or the FBI. But we saw it. They tried to destroy the man, but they couldn't destroy his defiance. He walked back into the cave—*(Points.)*—that cave. Legend has it he never came out again.

BUDDY: Crazy! *(Picks up a pebble and skips it hard.)* Crazy!

OLD MAN: *(Light.)* Course, the reason the legend says he never came out again was because no one ever saw him come out again. Federal agents, Coast Guard, military—they all came to drag him out feet first, if that's what it come to, but they never found him.

BUDDY: And the wolves?

OLD MAN: The symbol of defiance. He mocked them at first, bringing the first two wolves in to howl and taunt. He built a small bonfire, up there, *(Points across a lagoon.)* kept it going, to let them know he was still here, defying them to come looking. And they did. For eight months.

BUDDY: Then they just quit?

OLD MAN: Yep. Quit coming 'round. Quit trying to make him leave; decided to flood him anyways. Daddy didn't come out to take nothing or move nothing. None of us did. It's what we believed Daddy wanted us to do—leave it all. There was wash hanging on the line. Scarecrow in one of the fields. Flood waters came in and just—took everything.

BUDDY: *(Stands to survey what was once a farm, imagining all he has heard, then slowly.)* Everything. *(Tries to resist the urge, but finally peeks over his shoulder at the cave, half expecting to see Old Charlie Wolf tending his cubs.)*

NOTES: ____

____

____

____

____

____

____

____

NAME ____ PERIOD ______ DATE ____________

THE LEGEND OF OLE CHARLIE WOLF —
INVESTIGATING THE ART OF TIMING

You may have noticed that there are a lot of pauses, cut-offs, and interruptions in *The Legend of Ole Charlie Wolf*. The two characters are constantly interrupting each other, and Old Man enjoys toying with the boy, creating even more room for creative timing.

A **cut-off line** is one in which a character is interrupted before he finishes. It ends with a dash, like this: "Sorry, I just —"

The dash indicates where the character is interrupted. However, it is a good idea to try to guess what they might have said and write it in lightly in the script, making it part of the character's line. This helps with timing. What if something happens and the person who is supposed to cut an actor off is slightly late with their cue? If Buddy doesn't continue to speak, it will be obvious that Old Man was supposed to interrupt but didn't.

The actor playing Old Man must also prepare a bit more, since he is the one to interrupt Buddy. Even though Buddy is ready with an assumed ending to the line, it would be helpful if Old Man would cut him off slightly earlier—to be safe. Old Man will interrupt Buddy on "I" and Buddy will continue until he is cut off or he has said a complete line — with a little ad lib at the end.

Fade-off lines, indicated most often by **ellipses**, create another type of timing issue for actors. In a fade-off line, a character's voice might trail off slightly at the end of the line, and he may pause a bit before he or another actor continues. Examples of fade-offs are: "Well, I'll be…" or "You think you know someone…"

Pausing may be indicated as **"beat"** or **"pause"** in a script, but actors can add pauses wherever they are justifiable. Mark your script by putting a **slash** between two words for a short pause, two for a longer pause, and three for a very dramatic pause.

Silence may be the best way of all to create intensity and suspense in a scene. Unlike a pause, which is quick and usually not action-filled, silence may last a lot longer, and it can be intense and filled with meaning. Young people tend to shy away from silence onstage because it feels like someone has forgotten a line. However, by maintaining strong energy and eye contact and staying in character, silence can be extremely powerful. Try this challenge: the next time you feel like a scene calls for yelling, try being very quiet instead. You will probably find that it can be even more intense than screaming.

Dramatic changes in pace can be extremely impactful in a scene. Speaking slowly and spacing words ever so slightly helps to draw emphasis. Increasing speed creates a sense of urgency, but be careful: some actors lose their clarity when trying to pick up the pace. You can use arrows to remind yourself to speed up or slow down, like this:

Decrease: Quit trying to make 'em leave.

Increase: Is that how your mama raised you to talk?

Even though it has nothing to do with timing, **volume** has a very similar effect on scenes. Many young actors get carried away with yelling and could learn a great deal from experimenting with stage whispers. Much like a ghost story told around a campfire, the actor lowers the volume but is still audible, draws the audience's attention, forces them to almost lean in, then, when the audience feels as though they are nose-to-nose with the actors onstage, SOMEONE YELLS, SHOCKING THE AUDIENCE!

168

NOTES: ____

Timing is not just for the voice. **Posture, body language, gestures,** and **movement** can also be developed as tools for creating dramatic timing. Buddy moves excitedly from one seat to the next, but Old Man rarely moves. The contrast shows the difference in their ages, their abilities, and maybe their health. At the same time, the slow deliberateness with which Old Man moves shows that he is sure. Buddy, on the other hand, appears fidgety, nervous, and unsure.

Explore timing in *The Legend of Ole Charlie Wolf* using the helpful prompts below to mark up the script. Become an expert—make dramatic timing and hooking the audience the foundation to all of your acting.

1. Cut-off lines:

   ☐ Find and underline all cut-off lines in the script.

   ☐ In pencil, finish any line that is interrupted.

   ☐ Circle a word just before the interrupt on that will be the new cue to break in.

2. Insert pauses using one, two, or three slashes. You must be prepared to justify pausing. Use pencil so that you can make changes as needed.

3. Find at least one place to give each character a long bit of silence. Mark it with brackets and the amount of time you want them to pause, like this: [15 seconds]

How is Buddy's silence meaningful? ____

____

____

What should Buddy be doing during his silence? ____________________________________

____

____

How is Old Man's silence meaningful? ____

____

____

What should Old Man be doing during his silence? __________________________________

____

____

4. Mark at least one place for each of the actors to pick up or slow down their pace.

     169

NOTES: ____

____

____

____

____

____

____

____

6. What physical traits can the actors incorporate into the two characters to add to their personal paces?

    Buddy:

    Old Man:

7. Now use what you know about dramatic structure to find the scene's climax and mark it with a star. Use all you know about dramatic timing to build to the climax and make a solid, satisfying ending.

NOTES: ____

____

____

____

____

____

____

____

DUET DUET

A Scene for Two Males and Two Females

By SUZI ZIMMERMAN

CAST OF CHARACTERS

DIA   KRISTIN

JACK   JACOB

The scene opens with KRISTIN and JACOB, a couple who work together, on one side of the stage in an office setting. On the other side of the stage, JACK, whose left arm is in a sling, sits alone at a restaurant table, waiting to meet DIA for the first time on a blind date. The two couples do not realize their linked history is very complex. JACOB and DIA are a former couple, as are JACK and KRISTIN. There is a sing-song symmetry as the dialogue switches back and forth between the two pairs. The scene flashes back in time occasionally. These flashback lines can be spoken with the actors' backs to the audience, if desired.

DIA: *(ENTERS and approaches JACK'S table, uncertain if she has found her date.)* Jack?

JACK: *(Stands.)* Dia!

BOTH: Hi.

DIA: I recognized the sling. *(Indicates his arm.)*

JACK: Yeah, the cat.

JACOB: He broke his arm on a cat?

KRISTIN: He tripped on the cat and sprained his arm stopping his fall.

JACOB: The black cat?

KRISTIN and JACK: *(Simultaneously.)* Little China Boy.

JACK: I hated that cat. I swear he did it on purpose. He was always jealous of me.

DIA: Jealous is a dirty word!

JACK: What about you? Any cats?

KRISTIN: A cat, two dogs, and fish. I love animals. But not him. He hated them all.

JACOB: Not an animal lover?

KRISTIN: I think he was trying to kill the cat. Serves Jack right, the big crybaby!

DIA: I'm not a pet person.

JACK: Me neither.

DIA: I mean—don't get me wrong—I love animals, but I travel so much, and I have a small apartment. It just wouldn't work.

JACK: It just wasn't working out.

DIA: He spent all his spare time at the gym working out.

KRISTIN: *(To JACOB.)* You been working out?

JACOB: Lifting weights.

KRISTIN: Looking good!

JACOB: *(Looks hopeful.)* Really? You can tell?

JACK: So how long were you together?

DIA: Thirteen months.

KRISTIN: Too long.

JACK: Three years.

JACOB: We were never really what you would call "together." She had issues.

DIA: Why'd you break up?

JACK: The animals!

KRISTIN: The complaining.

JACOB: The jealousy.

DIA: The lying.

JACK: I never lied to her. I told her from the very beginning that we were just dating. Nothing exclusive.

DIA: The cheating.

JACOB: I never told her we wouldn't see other people.

DIA: The secrets.

JACOB: Who goes through their boyfriend's things?

KRISTIN: So were you her boyfriend or not? I thought you were just dating.

DIA: The lack of trust.

JACK: I could never trust her again after that!

JACK: Wait a minute! You found a picture of his ex-girlfriend in the duffel bag you bought him, and he says he can't trust you?

KRISTIN: Jacob. Why did you have a picture of me in your bag?

DIA: He just couldn't get over her.

KRISTIN: Get over me, Jacob! You and I are over! I've moved on.

                                        171

NOTES: ____

____

____

____

____

____

____

____

____

JACOB: I know. I just liked the picture.

KRISTIN: I hope you liked it more than you liked your girlfriend. One of these days, you're going to be very lonely. Then maybe you'll realize how many good things you let slip between your fingers because you… You just need to learn to be honest.

JACOB: I know.

KRISTIN: With yourself, Jacob. It's after five, I'll see you tomorrow. *(JACOB takes out her picture and looks at it.)*

JACK: He let a good thing slip between his fingers.

DIA: Thanks. I guess.

JACK: I'm sorry he hurt you, but I'm not sorry you made the decision to leave. It's late. Can I see you again?

DIA: Call me.

JACK: I will. *(To KRISTIN.)* I will, I will, just stop nagging me!

KRISTIN: I'm not nagging, just reminding. They'll run out by the time we get home, and I don't want them to be hungry.

JACK: All right, already. I'll pick up cat food *(To himself.)* after I go to the cleaners and save Metropolis from the evil Cat Lady!

KRISTIN: *(From the next room.)* What?

JACK: Nothing. I may be a little late. I have a few stops to make.

KRISTIN: *(ENTERS.)* Watch out!

JACK: *(Trips over a cat.)* For crying out—stupid cat! Did something to my arm. He was trying to kill me.

KRISTIN: I'll get ice. *(EXITS.)*

DIA: *(To JACOB.)* What's that?

JACOB: *(Hides a picture.)* Nothing!

DIA: Nothing? Looks like a picture. Let me see. *(Grabs the picture.)* Oh. She's pretty.

JACOB: It's Kristen. My ex. But now it's history. *(Tosses the picture in a trash can.)*

DIA: Smart guy. Got to run. Remember, cleaning lady's coming today.

JACOB: I remember. You remember about the wedding planner, right? No cold feet this time?

DIA: I remember. *(Turns to JACK.)* Jack, what are you doing on the floor?

JACK: Remembering. Looking at old pictures from when we first started dating. *(Points.)* Remember our first date?

KRISTIN: Sure, I remember.

KRISTIN and JACK: The carnival, three years ago.

DIA and JACOB: Little Italy.

DIA: You were sporting the latest in hospital fashion. That was two years ago.

JACOB: That was years ago, Kristin. I've changed. Please give me another chance.

KRISTIN: Nothing's changed.

JACK: Everything's changed. I'm so happy now.

JACOB: I've changed.

DIA: Who's that?

JACK: That's Kristin, my ex-girlfriend.

DIA: That's Kristin? She looks like the girl in Jacob's picture, only prettier.

JACK: I heard she's engaged and moving out of state.

KRISTIN: I heard he's dating an art dealer.

JACOB: *(Looks up, surprised.)* Kristin, please don't go. Don't do this. I need you.

KRISTIN: What time is it?

JACOB: Just after five.

KRISTIN: I've got to go. I have a little packing and a plane to catch. *(Starts to leave, then stops.)* I hope you find happiness, Jacob. I really do believe you have changed. This is for the best.

DIA: *(A voice.)* You took her picture out of the trash can?

JACOB: Sir, it's after five. If there's something I can help you with quickly—otherwise, we open at nine tomorrow.

JACK: I'd like to look at your engagement rings. I'm going to ask my girlfriend to marry me.

NOTES: ______________________________

____

____

____

____

____

____

CHAPTER 5 — UNDERSTANDING AND WRITING SCRIPTS

NAME ____ PERIOD _______ DATE _____________

DUET DUET — USING THEATRICAL DEVICES

Duet Duet is not a duet at all. It is a four-person scene with some very tricky timing and blocking. Performed well, the actors can make the audience believe they are seeing the passage of time, flashbacks, and drastic segues from one setting to another and back again within just a couple of lines.

At no point in this scene should any actor leave the stage. At the same time, not all actors are always "on" or in the scene. How can actors be onstage without being "on"? Think of a lamp on a table. It is always there, but it isn't always on. Sometimes the bulb is turned off. Actors must find ways to be there without being in the picture.

One way to accomplish this is to use a theatrical device called a "freeze." When the actor is no longer "on," they freeze, usually in character, staying completely still until they are cued to un-freeze. This includes not moving the eyes, mouth, fingers, or even swaying. It is very difficult to master and requires a great deal of practice. However, done well, freezes can be very effective and extremely dramatic.

Another way to be onstage without being in the picture is to turn one's back to the audience. This is usually done away from the center of action, perhaps in the upstage areas or near the wings. Actors are generally still, if not frozen, so as to draw as little attention away from the action as possible.

Actors can become other characters, if needed. While this does not actually make them "out of the picture," it takes their old character out until that character is needed again. They can become props or set pieces, too. In one staging of *The Crucible*, the actors remained onstage as silhouettes in the upstage area for the entire show. No set pieces were used for the play, so when the characters met in the woods, the spare actors held branches and became trees swaying in the wind.

When working with any of these elements, consider the effect you want to achieve. Because there are no steadfast rules about what can be done, use creativity to make the device work for you. Take theme, rhythm, pace, and concept into consideration. Perhaps place actors who are not in the scene upstage, but have them evolve from one pose to another so slowly that the movement is almost imperceptible.

Try some of the different devices with *Duet Duet*. What works best and why? Record your thoughts below:

____

____

____

____

____

____

____

____

____

____

    173

NOTES: ____

____

____

____

____

____

____

THE LIGHTHOUSE

Female/Female Duet

By AUMNA IQBAL

Aumna Iqbal studies music and theatre at Stanford University, where she is preparing for careers in playwriting, theatre management, and the opera. The two scenes to follow are from playwriting projects, and she credits Cherrie Moraga and Kevin DiPirro for their instruction and guidance.

CADY works her way along the beach, talking to the rocks as she goes. GILDA is busily working at the lighthouse.

CADY: When I'm out here, I'm talking to Mom. In my head. I think she can hear me sometimes, but mostly it's just a way of thinking. I know that Mom is really just dead. But if she were here then maybe she would hear me and help. But I'd feel too stupid trying to talk to Mom out loud. So instead sometimes I'll talk to you, rocks, or a starfish I might see. But there never is anyone. Oh, well. If I get to the site maybe someone will let me help and I'll get free lunch.

GILDA: Cady! What are you doing here?

CADY: I wanted to help.

GILDA: You can't.

CADY: Why not?

GILDA: It's not allowed. You probably can't even get a working permit.

CADY: I don't want to be paid.

GILDA: It's dangerous.

CADY: I don't care.

GILDA: You'll get hurt.

CADY: You're doing it.

GILDA: Yeah, well. We haven't even started building anything yet.

CADY: What?

GILDA: There's no contractor.

CADY: But what about Dad?

GILDA: He won't do it.

CADY: That's silly. He just said—

GILDA: He won't do it. We'll find someone else.

CADY: Well, if there's no building, then it can't be dangerous and I can help.

GILDA: What? No, it doesn't work like that.

CADY: I can help you carry things. Get into smaller spaces than you. I'll get you coffee.

GILDA: How? You don't have a car. Just go home.

CADY: I want to help.

GILDA: You want to help? Get your father to get down here and do his job. And tell James that whatever he asked didn't work.

CADY: You talked to James?

GILDA: Yeah, kid, but we didn't go out.

CADY: Why not?

GILDA: It's not like you think it is.

CADY: I can get James over here again. You tell him what to tell Dad and—

GILDA: Listen. James and I... there's nothing between us. I don't know how much he told you, but it just won't work.

CADY: Oh.

GILDA: What I need I can't get from James. What I need is someone like your father.

CADY: To fix the lighthouse? But I don't see what that has to do with—

GILDA: It's just—it's complicated. I won't even begin to try and explain it to you.

CADY: Oh.

GILDA: It's nothing personal. I just need to talk to Patrick first.

CADY: Why? Every time I talk to you all you want to talk about is my dad. It's like you don't care about me anymore.

GILDA: No! That's not true at all. I care a lot about you.

CADY: Uh-huh.

GILDA: Don't be like that.

CADY: No. I'll just go home now.

GILDA: What? But I still need your help.

CADY: No, you don't. You know something? I always thought of us like sisters.

GILDA: Sisters.

The Lighthouse and *Typically American* are plays written by a young woman, Aumna Iqbal, when she was a sophomore in college. She spent a great deal of time and energy getting the scenes just right, and the reward came at the end when her shows were produced, starring her fellow Stanford classmates. Your students should be encouraged by Aumna's success. Find opportunities for them to practice writing plays or even scenes, and allow them to perform their work. It is from their performances that the real progress will come.

CADY: But I'm just an annoyance to you. Right?

GILDA: No. Stop. Has that been what Patrick's telling you, that I don't want to talk to you anymore?

CADY: See? It's always about Daddy!

GILDA: Cady, I... I don't think I should be the one to tell you this.

CADY: Tell me what. Tell me that I'm too young to know anything or to find out anything important?

GILDA: To tell you that—your father and I are fighting.

CADY: I know that.

GILDA: You do?

CADY: I'm not stupid. Or blind. I can see the way he acts when you're around.

GILDA: Oh. I'm sorry, then, I tried to keep it from you.

CADY: Well, now you know that I can handle it.

GILDA: So, you still want to help out at the lighthouse?

CADY: Not really. I just wanted to talk to you.

GILDA: To talk to me?

CADY: I miss you.

GILDA: I miss you too, sweetie.

CADY: So, I'll see you sometime soon?

GILDA: Yeah.

NOTES: ____

____

____

____

____

____

____

____

TYPICALLY AMERICAN

Male Monologue

By AUMNA IQBAL

TALIM is an Iraqi oil field worker disgusted with the anti-war protests. In this scene, he tries to convince AISHA to abandon her protest.

TALIM: Because what Saddam did doesn't follow the word of Allah!

Because there are people there

For whom a US victory will help.

Because I work in oil

And this will help me.

Sure there's soldiers

And they're dying

And there's civilians

And they're dying too.

But wouldn't that be happening anyways?

These deaths

This disrespect of civilians is on a personal level.

It isn't the fault of the war.

My brothers and I,

We've been working in oil

Probably from before you were born.

(Rising in volume to yell at the protesters again.)

Yelling at passing cars won't change anything.

That's why you should go home.

Calm down.

It'll all pass soon,

And then you'll be reaping the benefits.

You'll be grateful for me, okay?

Stop wasting your time.

(Back to AISHA, disbelieving, scoffing.) Am I really pro-war? You're too young.

Too naïve.

War is life.

NOTES: _______________________________________

____

____

____

____

____

____

____

VOCABULARY

In this chapter, you will learn about:

Acting Area: The part of the stage used for acting and visible to the audience.

Backdrop: Fabric that is suspended from battens and painted as scenery or background.

Backstage: The area behind the curtain or set that the audience cannot see.

Batten: A metal bar or piece of wood from which scenery, backdrops, draperies, and instruments are hung in the fly area above the actors' heads.

Border: Draperies that run the width of the stage above the actors' heads masking the rigging from the audience.

Cornerstone: Corner pieces that are glued to the stiles and rails on a flat and attached with hardware, giving additional support.

Costume: The clothing worn onstage to aid in the interpretation and expression of a character and situation.

Counterweight System: The systems of weights, ropes, and pulleys used to raise and lower draperies, scenery, and instruments onstage with ease.

Crew: A group of technicians assigned to a particular task (light crew, sound crew, costume crew, etc.).

Cut Drop: A backdrop with parts removed; what remains is reinforced with scrim, which is semi-transparent, giving the cut drop a three-dimensional effect.

Flats: Wooden frames with hinged braces on the back to help them stand.

Foundation: The base color of makeup that matches the actor's skin.

Grand Drape: The fancy front curtain onstage.

Groundrow: A piece of scenery designed to look like ground scenery which is often used to hide technical equipment.

Highlights: The raised or lighter places on a face that can be enhanced with lighter makeup.

Keystone: Slender pieces that are glued both to the stile and the toggle on a flat and attached with hardware, giving additional support.

Legs: Draperies that line the wings, masking from the audience actors awaiting cues.

Lighting: All of the devices and systems used to illuminate the show.

Luan: Another name for quarter-inch plywood, a building material common in set building because it is lightweight.

Makeup Morgue: A collection of faces and facial features that a makeup artist may reference to better understand how to apply makeup to resemble a desired effect.

Project: To speak with adequate volume onstage.

Proscenium: The vertical plane that frames the stage.

Rail: A top or bottom cross brace on a flat.

Scenery: The items used to create a location onstage.

Scrim: A type of loosely woven fabric that can be painted to match its background, making it almost transparent.

Shadows: Dark or sunken-in places on a face that can be enhanced with darker makeup.

Sound: The technical aspect of the production that encompasses all audio elements.

Stage Areas: Most stages are divided into nine or fifteen sections. These are denoted as C for center, L and R for left and right, and U and D for up and down. The letters define places on the stage; UC is up center, and so on.

Stile: A side piece on a flat.

Teaser Curtain: A type of drapery that reduces the height of the proscenium opening.

Toggle: A center cross brace on a flat.

Tormentor: A tall drapery that reduces the width of the stage.

Traveler: A curtain that moves horizontally from left and right, meeting in the center.

Wings: The area out of the acting area to the left and right where actors wait for their cues.

INTRODUCTION

Because every theatre space is so different, it is difficult to teach about the stage other than the most basic essentials. At the same time, it is frustrating as a director to tell students to "stand behind the second leg" and have them look at you like you are nuts! The same goes for costuming, makeup, and all the other aspects of theatre behind the scenes.

Each area of technical theatre is huge. As a result, none can be taught as a single lesson in a general theatre book. The lessons in this book do not claim to be all-encompassing or even to cover all of the basics. Instead, your students will learn enough to at least all be on the same page. You may already possess more information and can further enlighten them. The brief lessons in this chapter will, at the very least, give your students a taste of the world of technical theatre.

DRAPERIES AND SCENERY

Every stage is different. Some have a series of elaborate drapes that can be raised and lowered at the touch of a button. Others have **counterweight systems** on pulleys, and still others have tattered, paint-spattered, hand-me-down curtains that are permanently in place. Regardless of what you have, draperies are an important part of any stage. They have funny names, like "teasers" and "legs," but each has a very serious job.

When the audience enters the theatre, chances are the front curtain will be closed. Have you ever noticed how much fancier it is than those behind it? It is usually more decorative than the others, and it might be made of a very heavy velvet fabric. When closed, the fabric insulates the audience from the little sounds onstage. Of course, it is still only fabric, so the actors and crew must try to move about quietly. Do you know what this heavy, fancy curtain is called? If you guessed **grand drape**, you are absolutely right.

Another thing about grand drapes that makes them special is that they can be opened a number of ways. Most open horizontally, half sliding off to stage left and half to stage right. Curtains that move this way are called **travelers**. Some lift off of the stage vertically, flying up into the space above the stage. Some open diagonally, the two down center corners traveling along lines creating graceful folds in the fabric as they work their ways up toward the corners. Still others slide off to one side. Many can

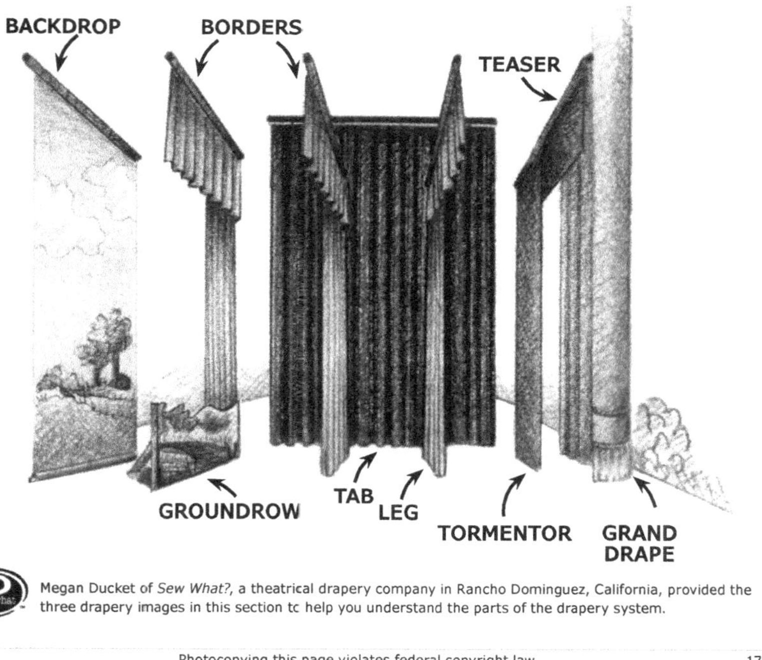

Megan Ducket of *Sew What?*, a theatrical drapery company in Rancho Dominguez, California, provided the three drapery images in this section to help you understand the parts of the drapery system.

179

DRAPERIES

This chapter introduces your students to the most common parts of the drapery system and their functions, and they will enjoy reinforcing their learning with a simple crossword puzzle. Take your students on a tour of your stage or any area theater and point out the same system parts there. The pictures provided by Sew What (www.sewwhatinc.com) clearly identify the various drapes, but nothing reinforces like seeing the different components for themselves. Allow students to touch the fabrics, discuss why certain fabrics are used and what characteristics each might possess that makes it ideal for the job, and how each piece is suspended. If you have a counterweight system, teach students to load it, then allow each to experience raising and lowering a batten.

open a variety of ways. How they open depends on the impression the director wants to make, the versatility of the space, and the budget.

The set of draperies behind the grand (see the large diagram on the previous page) are the **teaser** (the top piece) and **tormentors** (the side pieces). These are used to make the proscenium opening appear smaller. The **proscenium** is the frame through which the audience watches the actors onstage.

Most stages have several sets of **legs** and **borders** (see picture, left). The legs hide the actors while backstage, and the borders conceal the lighting and scenery rigging from the audience.

Groundrows are pieces built to represent ground-level scenery such as shrubs, rows of crops, or sand dunes. They are often placed strategically to hide equipment that must be on the stage floor.

Backdrops are scenery or backgrounds painted on fabric, weighted, and hung from the **battens**, or metal bars, above the stage. Backdrops are very versatile. If your crew is talented, they can paint a new backdrop over the old one for each show. Otherwise, you can rent them. Some backdrops span the entire back wall of the stage. Others hang in place of legs or reach only part of the way across the stage. **Cut drops** are backdrops that appear three-dimensional to the audience. Parts of the fabric are removed, and the remaining fabric is backed with **scrim** fabric. When the scrim is dyed to match what is behind it or when it is lit a certain way, it becomes nearly invisible. Layering the various drops that are designed to work together adds depth to a backdrop set.

Sew What? Inc., www.sewwhatinc.com; Artwork by S. Nelsen.

NOTES:

CHAPTER 6 — THEATRE BEHIND THE SCENES

NAME _______________________________ PERIOD _______ DATE _____________

DRAPERIES CROSSWORD

Find the answers to the clues below in the pages prior to this one. Fill in your answers in the crossword grid.

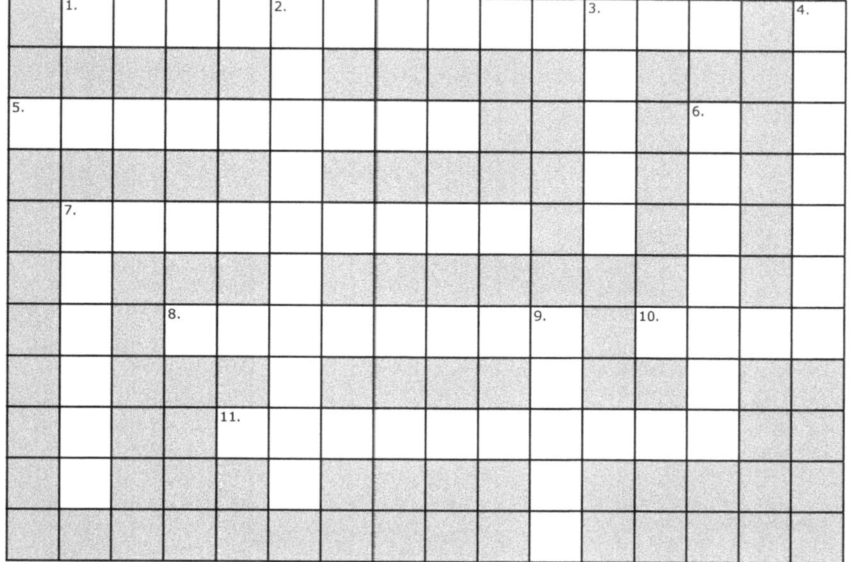

ACROSS

1. Systems of ropes, pulleys, and weights used to raise and lower draperies
5. Painted fabrics hung onstage to look like scenery or background
7. Curtains that travel horizontally along tracks
8. Backdrops with parts cut out, reinforced with scrim fabric (two words)
10. Drapes that hang alongside the backstage area, hiding actors awaiting entrances
11. These are designed to look like ground scenery and to hide equipment

DOWN

2. Draperies that reduce the width of the proscenium opening
3. The elaborate drape at the front of the stage
4. The bars from which backdrops and some draperies are often hung
6. Draperies that hang above actors' heads, hiding rigging and lighting
7. A type of drapery hung above the actors' heads that reduces the height of the proscenium
9. A fabric that can be painted or lit to blend in with whatever is behind it

　181

DRAPERIES CROSSWORD KEY

ACROSS

1. COUNTERWEIGHT
5. BACKDROPS
7. TRAVELERS
8. CUTDROPS
10. LEGS
11. GROUNDROWS

DOWN

2. TORMENTORS
3. GRAND
4. BATTENS
6. BORDERS
7. TEASER
9. SCRIM

DRAPERIES CROSSWORD SOLUTION

1.C	O	U	N	2.T	E	R	W	E	I	3.G	H	T	4.B
				O						R			A
5.B	A	C	K	D	R	O	P	S		A	6.B		T
				M						N	O		T
7.T	R	A	V	E	L	E	R	S		D	R		E
E				N							D		N
A		8.C	U	T	D	R	O	9.P	S		10.L	E	G	S
S			O					C			R		
E			11.G	R	O	U	N	D	R	O	W	S	
R			S					I					
								M					

FLATS MADE SIMPLE

Behind the set of a play, visitors are often surprised at what they see. Many are shocked to discover that the backside of the scenery is not similar to the front. Because scenery for plays must be lightweight, mobile, and durable while still resembling that which was intended, set pieces are built using nontraditional methods of construction.

Most school sets use combinations of pieces that include, among other things, **flats**. These are wooden frames with hinged braces on the back to help them stand. Look at the picture to the right. This is what the backside of a typical flat looks like. The fronts of the flats are often covered with a muslin fabric that is sized to fit and then painted. The frames may also be covered with cardboard, **Luan** (a thin wood), Masonite, or just about any lightweight material. Once each flat is constructed, it can be painted to look like just about anything and can be reused again and again with a simple paint job.

The corner pieces are called **cornerstones** (A), and smaller pieces on the ends of the center **toggle** (C) are called **keystones** (B). These are glued into place, then secured with heavy duty staples, nails, or screws. If a flat is taller than eight feet, you will want to use two toggles. As a rule, toggles should be spaced in increments of no more than four feet. This will give your flat the durability it needs while maintaining your flat's portability. And if you follow the exact same construction method, include dimensions, your flats will line up. You may then use something

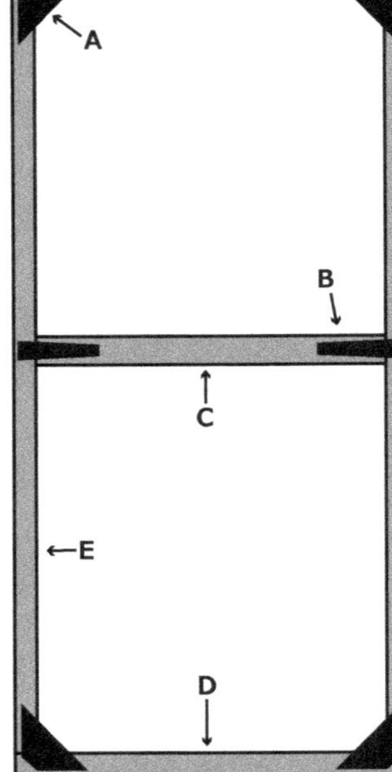

as simple as a bracket or hinge along the toggles to connect the flats to create larger walls or rooms.

The top and bottom pieces are referred to as **rails** (D). Note that they run the full length of the flat. The **stiles** (E) are the vertical pieces that connect the rails.

ASSIGNMENT

Find prices for the materials needed to build a flat four feet wide by eight feet tall. You will need approximately twenty-eight feet of one-inch by two-inch boards and a sheet of Luan or quarter-inch plywood plus an additional partial sheet for the cornerstones and keystones. Will the lumberyard sell scraps? If not, what is the smallest size of Luan they will sell? You will also need about thirty half-inch screws and wood glue. How much will it cost to build a flat at today's rates?

THINK ABOUT THIS

How many of the four-by eight-foot flats would it take to create a wall all the way across your stage? What if your teacher wanted the wall to have some angles? What if your teacher wanted windows and doors? How would you mask the backstage areas at these openings from the audience?

SIMPLIFYING FLATS

If you know how, building a flat is very easy. The simple diagram and description could guide most who know how to use a screw gun or power stapler through the process.

If you have flats on your stage, perhaps the best way to teach about them is to have students make repairs to those that need them. Gather all your flats and assign two students to be "quality control." These students will take blue painter's tape and mark all questionable parts of every flat in your shop. The rest of the class will follow these students and begin making repairs. By discovering what can go wrong

with a flat, students become more aware of how to construct a flat for durability.

Before your next show, purchase the materials needed to make all your flats and have your class make them. If you are not comfortable supervising the project, see if a parent with building experience will oversee the project, or contact your local college. They probably have students who need service hours who would be happy to lend a hand.

THE STAGE AND ITS AREAS

The diagram below will help you understand the stage and its areas. When standing center stage (C) facing the audience, up center is behind you, and down center is in front of you. Because stage directions are always from the actor's point of view, stage left is the actor's left and stage right is the actor's right when facing the audience. During rehearsals, keep a copy of this handy while blocking and you will have a quick reference for your director's stage directions. You can even draw scenery on it to remind you where to stand, enter, exit, and so on.

Remember the following tips and facts when doing stage work:

- Small- and medium-sized stages are divided into nine areas. Some medium and most larger stages have fifteen areas.
- The area closest to the audience is downstage (DL, DC, and DR), and the area farthest away from the audience is upstage (UL, UC, and UR).
- The terms "right" and "left" (R and L) refer to the actor's right and left, not the audience's.
- The **acting area** is the part of the stage used for acting and visible to the audience.
- When the actors are not onstage, they are **backstage**; this refers to the area that the audience cannot see behind the curtain or set.
- The **wings** are the areas out of the acting area to the left and right of the stage where the actors stand while waiting for their entrances.

A diagram of the stage is used for blocking and for set design. Practice set designing and learning the acting areas by completing the assignments or the next pages.

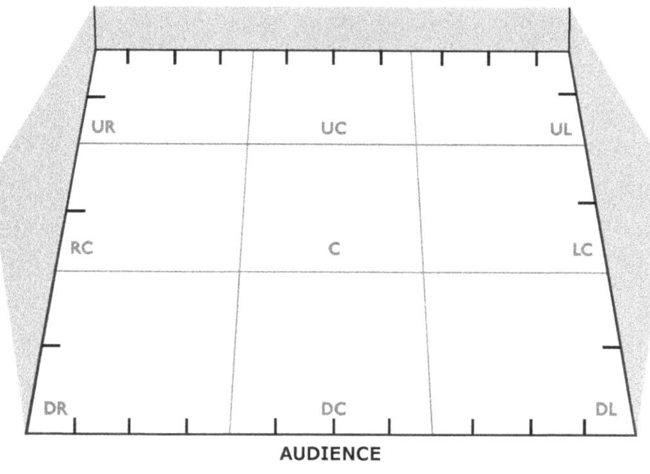

     183

STAGE LOCATIONS

Teach students to become comfortable on the stage listening to and following stage directions with this chapter. If they are actors, your students will benefit from learning what the stage areas are called and how to command focus by choosing strong areas. Your designers will learn to take maximum advantage of the space and to use weaker areas to their advantage.

You may want to make extra copies of the blank stage diagram on p. 263 for use in future lessons and to help you with set design.

Teach your students the difference between looking at the stage from the front (front elevation) and using aerial views (top elevation).

NAME _______________________________________ PERIOD ________ DATE _______________

STAGE DIAGRAM PRACTICE

The diagram on the next page is an aerial view of a stage, as if you are looking down on it from above. The scale is four feet for every one inch. Using a ruler and a pencil, mark where each of the set pieces goes on the stage diagram. You do not need to draw an actual sofa or bookshelf. Since this is an aerial view, you are simply marking the placement of each set piece with a rectangle or other shape. However, make sure you clearly label what each piece is.

1. Place a round rug with an 8 foot diameter center.

2. Put a sofa that is 6 feet long and 2 feet deep on the rug, facing downstage.

3. One foot to the left of the sofa, put a square end table, 2 feet by 2 feet.

4. Place a 1-foot by 3-foot bookshelf up right, facing down center.

5. Indicate with a "T" where you would place three silk trees upstage of the sofa.

6. Along the wall left center there is a 4-foot wide window.

7. Use an "X" to indicate a street lamp down right, removed from the living room set but not against a wall.

8. Add a 2-foot by 2-foot mailbox next to the street lamp.

9. Place a park bench, 4 feet long and 2 feet deep, in the down left area facing down left center.

10. Mark with a P where you would put two plants near this park bench.

Use the space below to determine the dimensions of each set piece using the scale 1 inch = 4 feet.

       ____ inch diameter = 8 foot diameter rug

       ____ inch x ____ inch = 6-foot by 2-foot sofa

       ____ inch x ____ inch = 2-foot by 2-foot square table

       ____ inch x ____ inch = 1-foot by 3-foot bookshelf

       ____ inch = 4-foot wide window

       ____ inch x ____ inch = 2-foot by 2-foot mailbox

       ____ inch x ____ inch = 4-foot by 2-foot park bench

NOTES: ____

____

____

____

____

____

____

STAGE DIAGRAM PRACTICE KEY

2 inch diameter = 8 foot diameter rug
1 1/2 inch x 1/2 inch = 6-foot by 2-foot sofa
1/2 inch x 1/2 inch = 2-foot by 2-foot square table (placed 1/4" stage left of sofa)
1/4 inch x 3/4 inch = 1-foot by 3-foot bookshelf
1 inch = 4-foot wide window
1/2 inch x 1/2 inch = 2-foot by 2-foot mailbox
1 inch x 1/2 inch = 4-foot by 2-foot park bench

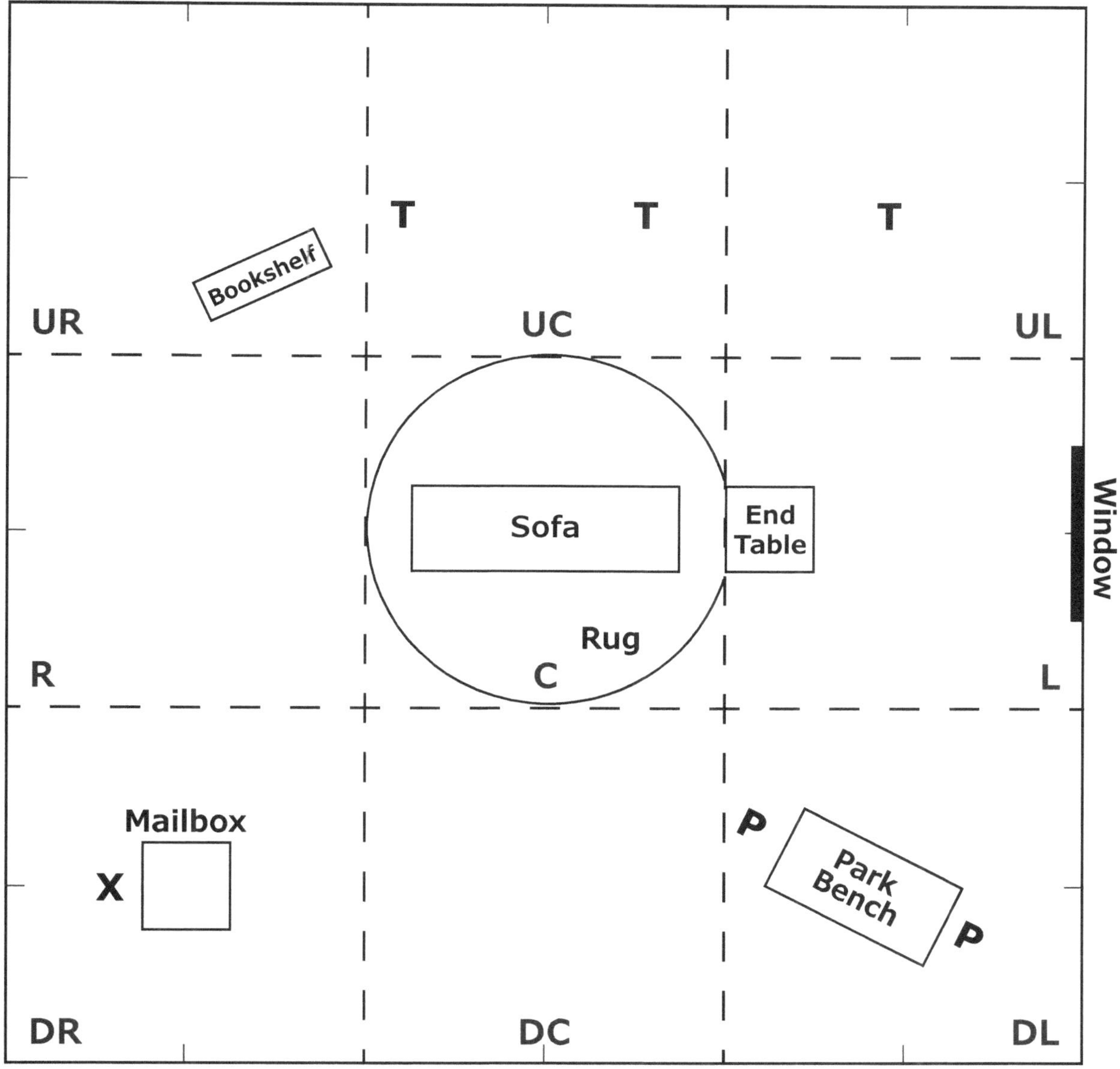

Note: Placement of the silk trees (T), plants (P), and street lamp (X) within the correct area of the stage is somewhat subjective.

Also appears as pages 185 and 186 of the Student Workbook

NAME _________________________________ PERIOD _______ DATE _____________

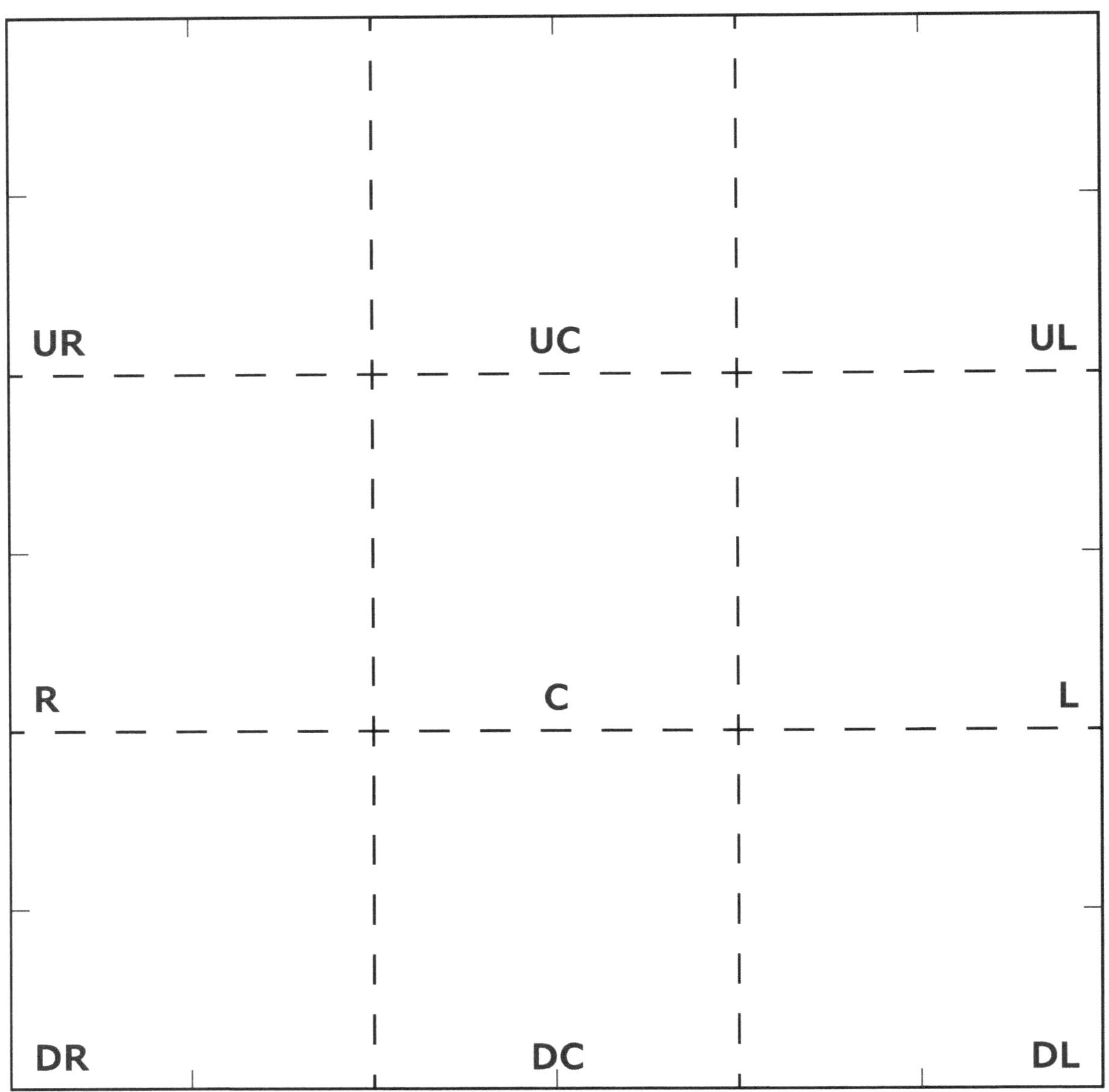

AUDIENCE

1 inch = 4 feet

CHAPTER 6 — THEATRE BEHIND THE SCENES

NAME ____ PERIOD _______ DATE _______________

STAGE DIAGRAM ADDITIONAL PRACTICE

Now practice finding the areas of the stage without the aid of the areas being noted on the diagram.

Follow the directions below for a special surprise.

1. Make a small dot right center.
2. Make a small dot left center.
3. Draw a straight line between the two dots.
4. Now make a small dot up center.
5. Place a dot down right center and another down left center.
6. Draw a straight line from your down right center dot to your up center dot.
7. Now draw another straight line from your up center dot to your down left center dot.
8. Connect your right center dot to your down left center dot with a straight line.
9. Complete the image by drawing a straight line from your left center dot to your down right center dot.
10. What is the image? ________________________________

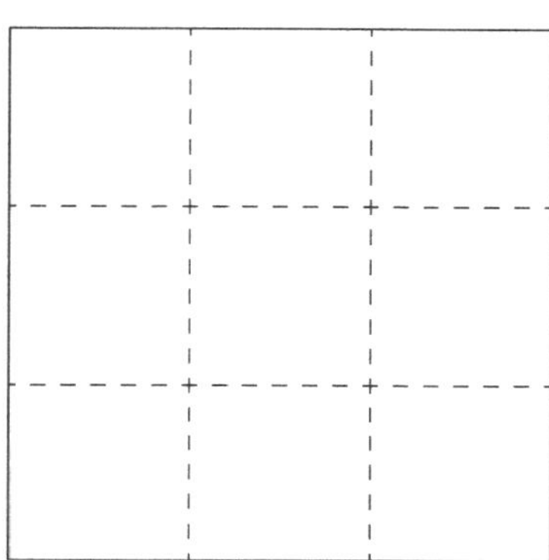

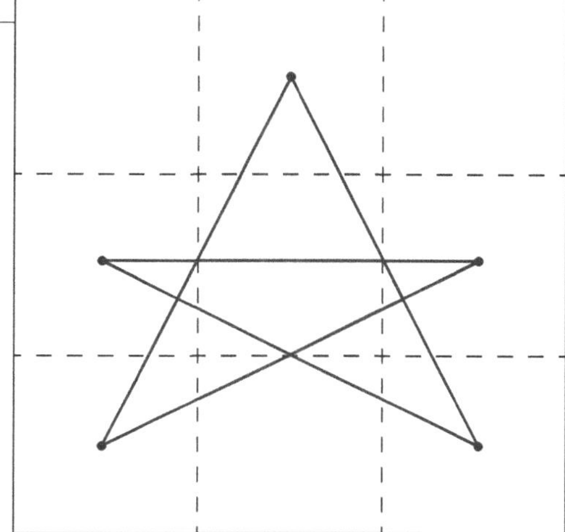

Think: What do you think is the strongest position onstage? Down center wins this honor because it is where one's eyes naturally migrate when prompted to look at the stage. As a rule, downstage is stronger than up, and center is stronger than left or right. Keeping this in mind, try to rate the nine areas in order from strongest to weakest. The first and last have been done for you.

Strongest								Weakest
DC								UL

PRACTICE KEY

DC	DR	DL	C	UC	RC	LC	UR	UL

Think: The areas closest to the audience are considered strongest, and center is always stronger than left or right. Because English is read from left to right, left draws our attention before right. But from the audience's perspective, stage right is to their left. Keeping all of this in mind, the order of stage area strength is generally agreed to be DC, DR, DL (areas closest to the audience are stronger), C, UC (center stage is stronger than right or left), RC, LC (of the remaining spaces, these are closer and in the order English is read), UR, and UL.

THE FUNDAMENTALS OF COSTUMES

Costuming is one of theatre's biggest complexities, but it is an area students often consider to be a lot of fun. Making costumes is something that requires a great deal of training, but on rare occasions costumers have been known to be self-taught. It is a very expensive craft, and unlike sets—which can be taken apart and recycled almost down to the nails, making the cost bearable—costumes are difficult to recycle. They are highly specific to the character and show, and they are made to fit the actor. So, if one cannot be reused—at least not right away—it must be stored, adding to the complexity. This requires added cleaning costs and storage space.

For educational theatre, there are a number of ways to costume shows. The method your director chooses probably depends a great deal on the requirements of the show, the budget, how long until opening night, and the sewing talents and availability of crew members. As you progress in theatre, chances are you will at one time or another be asked to costume a show or at least costume your own character. What is the best approach? The following list of suggestions should help narrow your choices.

COSTUME RENTALS

Probably the easiest way to costume a show is to let someone else do it for you. Rental houses have experts who are experienced in finding great pieces that come together to complement each other and to make your show look fabulous! For the most part, they offer special rates to schools and may even extend their usual rental period by a day or two, giving you additional time to return the costumes. If you are competing with your play and it advances to a higher level (meaning you may need to compete again in a week or two), many costume houses will waive additional fees or cut them considerably during the extended rental period.

RENTAL ADVANTAGES

- Less work for the director and cast.
- Professionally designed costumes.
- All that is required by the director or cast is to take measurements and send paperwork; costumes must be returned in the same manner they were received, usually the next business day after your show.
- Actors must pay for damage, so they tend to care for rented costumes better than they do for costumes they provide or make.

RENTAL DISADVANTAGES

- Renting can be extremely costly, especially if you have a large cast or a number of costume changes.
- Re-packing and shipping back the costumes takes considerable time and is another expense.

MAKING COSTUMES

Making costumes is more of an investment, especially if you go about the job with the idea that each piece should be reusable. By creating stock costume pieces that can be reused again and again, you are saving yourself both time and money in the long run, and if your students are sewing the pieces, they are learning a valuable skill.

As you create pieces, keep in mind that making each one slightly larger than the actor wearing it will give your pieces more flexibility. If it fits too well, only the actor for whom it is made or one slightly smaller will be able to use it in the future. Also, every movement will put stress on the seams, and by the end of your show, you may have to make repairs.

ABOUT COSTUMES

Ideally, you sew. Well, that may not be exactly true. Ideally, your students sew! On top of that, your ideal costume shop has plenty of uncluttered table space, several good sewing machines, and is well stocked and organized. If this is the case, you will probably have a number of stock costume pieces and beautifully costumed shows. If not, this lesson will help you and your students to understand additional options.

There are two challenges in the costume lesson. The first is a group project to be completed by the entire class. This can be super fun and very rewarding. Either have each student choose a character or assign characters for the students to costume. Consider creating a single slide show using all of the students' pictures (you will need to take pictures of the costumes modeled in class). This will be an excellent tool for teaching costuming to future groups.

As a follow-up to the *Costume Challenge*, consider taking your students on a field trip tour of a local costume house. Follow this trip with a stop at an area thrift store or vintage clothing shop. Tell students to bring spending money and enjoy finding some unique and unusual pieces that they can purchase. As a matter of fact, almost all of the costume houses also sell accessories and stage makeup. Your students will enjoy shopping at both, and if you spend enough

Use fabrics with a little give so that costumes last longer. Stick with one color palette for each show and use complementary color palettes across your various shows. That way you will be able to mix and match pieces while still giving each show its own look.

Lastly, make pieces as separates. Instead of sewing a fancy collar onto a dress, make the collar, top, and skirt all separate pieces so that they can be matched with other pieces later on. Learn to use Velcro and snaps instead of glue and tight stitches in order to make it easier to mix pieces.

ADVANTAGES OF MAKING COSTUMES	DISADVANTAGES OF MAKING COSTUMES
• Cheaper than renting.	• Very time-consuming.
• Can build an inventory of stock pieces.	• Requires a great deal of space to store costumes.
• Teaches a highly beneficial skill.	• Someone must be highly skilled, and others will need to be trained.
• Provides instant access to stock pieces rather than having to wait a week for rentals to arrive.	• Requires access to a number of sewing machines; one machine for every two students is best.
	• Homemade costumes might not be as durable, detailed, or fancy as rentals.

OTHER OPTIONS

You have probably discovered that there are many other ways to costume shows besides renting or sewing. You can change the time period of the show and use modern clothing, you can borrow from other schools, you can use combinations of methods, and you can take advantage of the greatest gift to middle and high school theatre teachers: the thrift store.

- If you are doing a period show or scene and do not have money to make or rent elaborate costumes, update the show or change it to a fantasy, "timeless" time period, like in the movies *A Series of Unfortunate Events* and *Nanny McPhee*. Even though the costumes in these films were not modern, neither did they fit particular time periods. They were almost "timeless," which appeals to viewers' imaginations. Use a lot of layers and accessories including tights, collars, jewelry, hats, gloves, belts, aprons and pinafores, wraps, and so on. Try to pull some influence from the original time period and meld it with more modern costumes.

- Actors can design and piece together their own costumes. If this method is used, the director should identify specific parameters from which students and parents can work. Hold a costume parade early to allow time to note what needs to be changed and make changes. An obvious benefit is your students' creativity—every costume will have special creative attention! At the same time, without a central designer, you may have issues with incompatibility, some students not trying as hard as others, or some students spending a great deal of money and making the other costumes look cheap in comparison. Students enjoy getting to keep their costumes, or they may choose to donate them to the theatre department.

- Your teacher can trade with or borrow from other schools or a community theatre. They can do the same with props and set pieces too.

money, you'll win the favors of the stores' managers and may receive special deals in the future!

The second assignment in the costuming section is for giant paper dolls. Paper dolls are an exceptional way to teach period costuming, and they are the perfect solution to displaying students' designs in your lobby prior to shows. Figure out a way to project the figures in the book onto Luan, Masonite, or heavy cardboard for easy tracing. You may want to have tech theatre students make the actual figures. That way you can have several of each that all match. Then have your design students make the costumes to go onto the figures.

If you select a play and color palette and instruct students to design their costumes using unit or stock pieces, you can demonstrate mixing and matching on the giant paper dolls. Consider starting with one-dimensional paper designs, but as students progress, have them make actual mini-costumes for their paper dolls. They can learn to sew, but because the costumes will be small, there will not be the expense, and your various scraps may be put to good use.

COSTUME CHALLENGE

As a class, familiarize yourself with a period play, something from before 1900. Read the play as a group and assign or choose a character for each student. It is important that all characters in the play are represented. If a character has more than one costume, assign each costume to a different student.

Study the costumes of the time period, paying particular attention to the accessories and small details. Next, discuss modernizing the play. Would it fit into a more recent period such as the roaring twenties, the Depression era, the fifties, or maybe even the future? Perhaps it would be a great play for the sixties—hippies versus conservatives? Or punk out your play with wild hair and makeup, fingerless gloves, and spikes.

Once you have narrowed your target period, study the clothing of that era. Note any similarities between the two periods and seek ways to integrate the two.

Next, select a color palette. This generally comes from clues in the play. Perhaps you are doing *The Ransom of Red Chief*—an obvious color to start with would be red. From there, you could add a few other colors, like yellow and navy, then build your palette around that. If your play does not offer clues, maybe the time period will. For example, if your play is set during the Revolutionary War, an obvious color palette would be red, white, and blue.

Decide on any additional information such as concept (minimalism, fantasy, etc.), audience (children, adults), or other influences, then begin your work as joint costumers for the mock show.

Your job is to create a costume for your character using what you have at home or what you can make or gather without spending a great deal of money. Remember to use layers—if that look fits your concept—and accessories. You should consider hats, hair accessories, jewelry, glasses, shoes, stockings or socks, and seasonal items. You may either bring your costume to class to model and explain, or create a slideshow of photographs of yourself modeling your costume (if the character is not your gender, you may select a different person to be your model). If you choose to take photos, you must include a shot of the front, back, and all details of the costume. All students must be prepared to discuss and explain their choices.

You may want to wear your basic costume with hair and makeup to an accessory shop. Ask the shop manager for permission to take photos with some of the accessories, and then experiment. Remember your parameters; just because something looks good doesn't mean it fits the show.

After all of the costumes have been presented, discuss what worked and what did not. Make suggestions about what you would do differently for each character, and compare characters side by side, especially those in the same scenes.

NOTES: _______________________________

NAME _______________________________ PERIOD _______ DATE _____________

COSTUMING PROJECT

Make a large cardboard doll of each of the silhouettes below or use your own original shape. Each must be between 12 and 24 inches tall. They must be free-standing and sturdy. Next, make a suitably-sized fabric or paper costume for each figure. They must be easily removable (using double-stick tape or sticky tack) so that different costumes may be applied. Use these large models to display your designs in the lobby of your auditorium during the run of your next show. Be sure to note the character, play, playwright, and scenes for which the costume was designed.

191

NOTES: ____

____

____

____

____

____

____

____

____

STAGE MAKEUP BASICS

Stage makeup has several purposes. First, it helps to establish a character by adding features such as age or a crooked nose. It also helps to define the actor's features so that the audience can see them and make out even minor facial expressions. Stage makeup can be corrective, making the tone of the skin even. For the most part, only a basic knowledge of makeup application is needed. Beyond the basics, books can do little to convey what a good class and plenty of hands-on experience can teach.

Most students use the stage makeup provided by their school or they use less-expensive street makeup. Theatrical makeup is more expensive, but the coverage is better and it is designed specifically for the stage. Regardless, each student should start by providing some of their own supplies.

Because your kit must move from home to stage and back again, it is important that it is mobile. Tackle boxes make great kits. They are sturdy, they have a convenient handle, and they have several compartments. Below are some items found in typical student makeup kits:

VARIOUS SHADES OF:	AN ASSORTMENT OF:	FOR CLEAN-UP:	OTHER ITEMS:
Foundation	Makeup Brushes	Cleanser	Shaver
Eye Color	Makeup Sponges	Toner	Shaving Cream
Cheek Color	Powder Puffs	Cotton Balls	Hair Brush and Comb
Lip Color	A smock for	Tissue	Hair Spray
Cream Liners	protecting clothes	Wash Cloth	Moisturizer
Pencil Liners	Hair bands or clips	Baby wipes for removing	Nail Polish Remover
Mascara	(even for short hair)	makeup quickly	Deodorant
Powder			Mirror

Look at the *Makeup Plot* on page 194. If you are designing your own makeup, use this to record the colors you are using. This will save a great deal of time and worry during the moments before the show, especially if you are sharing the class kit. You can also record how and where to apply the makeup by drawing lines onto the face or by actually applying the makeup onto the diagram. This is messy, but for those with a difficult application, this may help you remember what to do from night to night. Or you may want to simply diagram the makeup by drawing the application area and writing the color next to it. A sample has been done for you on page 193.

If you will have a makeup crew, the members of the team will diagram your makeup for their own use, and before each show, they will use it to gather what they need for each actor. The plots are usually taped to the mirror at the actors' stations so that the crew can quickly and easily refer to them as they make their rounds.

APPLYING STAGE MAKEUP

Before you get started, use your plot to record any information about your makeup application provided either by the script or in the lines. Research unusual requirements like those needed for aged or heavy characters. Keep pictures from magazines (called a **makeup morgue**) with your plot. You can refer to these if you get in a bind.

Learn to apply your own makeup long before you must do it with frayed nerves. You will get practice, see how your skin reacts to the makeup, and take inventory of your kit to make last-minute purchases.

Always start with a clean face. Then apply **foundation** using a clean sponge. You might have to custom mix your colors to get the right one for your skin tone. You will know when your foundation is applied correctly when the face and neck are covered thoroughly and evenly, and all excess makeup is blended. There should be no streaking or caking, and

ABOUT STAGE MAKEUP

It's a dirty job, but someone's got to do it—hundreds of dollars' worth of small pencils, pots, and sticks in a small, crowded case. Stage makeup is a large expense, a big mess, and a gigantic responsibility to maintain. It's enough to drive a theatre teacher to want to skip the unit. One tackle box of stage makeup could be valued at hundreds of dollars, but it only takes a few frenzied moments before opening night to ruin it all. The solution? Teach students how to care for stage makeup and require your students to purchase and use their own.

Stage Makeup Basics and *Applying Stage Makeup* teach the fundamentals of identifying and applying the most common makeup and organizing kits. The plot that is provided will assist students in preparing for each show.

If the mess frightens you, teach students to apply stage makeup by first using the practice sheet provided along with colored pencils. Then allow them to try it with the actual kit. It may be better to have them apply it to a friend first, as it is easier than trying to work backwards in a mirror. When they are comfortable with that, allow them to work on themselves.

Students enjoy making bruises, and they are easy to do. If you want to allow them to experiment but don't want a large mess, give each student a note card with a small dab of brown, yellow, white,

CHAPTER 6 — THEATRE BEHIND THE SCENES

STAGE MAKEUP TIPS

- Learn to apply your own makeup and remember to clean up after yourself.
- Avoid sharing makeup when possible, and never share mascara or eyeliner.
- Throw away outdated items and do not use makeup that causes severe skin reactions.
- Record the makeup you use and be ready to make changes to your application. What looks great in the dressing room might not look right under the stage lights.

any evidence of makeup lines means the coverage is probably too thick. Use a tissue to remove some of the excess foundation. Cover the lips, around the eyes, and up into the hairline. Do not cover your eyebrows.

Next, you will want to focus on your **shadows** and **highlights**. For example, an average actor who must play a thin, gaunt person should use a color several shades darker than their skin to give their cheeks, temples, and eyes a sunken look. They can use a cream several shades lighter than their skin to highlight the bone structure so that the bridge of the nose, cheeks, chin, jaw, and forehead appear bony and severe.

If your character has age lines or other features such as scars, you will apply these next. It is recommended that you get used to doing this with a brush and a cream makeup rather than a pencil. While some consider a pencil easier to control, the waxy makeup is actually harder to spread, and getting the definition is much more difficult. Using a cream

Photoc

red, and blue cream and a wedge sponge. Show them pictures of bruises (or allow them to display their own, as they enjoy comparing them), then try to use the stage makeup to copy the bruise on their arm or leg. Take plenty of pictures of real and fake bruises and see if your students can tell which is real and which is fake.

and a brush will allow you to have total control over the thickness, the texture, the blending, and the shape of the lines.

Next, you will want to define your features. A good rule of thumb for most is to showcase your existing features without making them appear fake. Use shadow on your eyes and blush on your cheeks, and line your brows, eyes, and lips. Then use loose powder on your face to set the creams. The best way to do this is with a large soft brush and very little powder. Apply powder everywhere you used a cream makeup, then brush off any excess. Some artists mist the powder with a very light spritz of mineral water, which sets it even more. Check your blush to make sure the powder did not conceal it. Now apply any non-powdered makeup such as mascara, lip gloss, and some eyeliners.

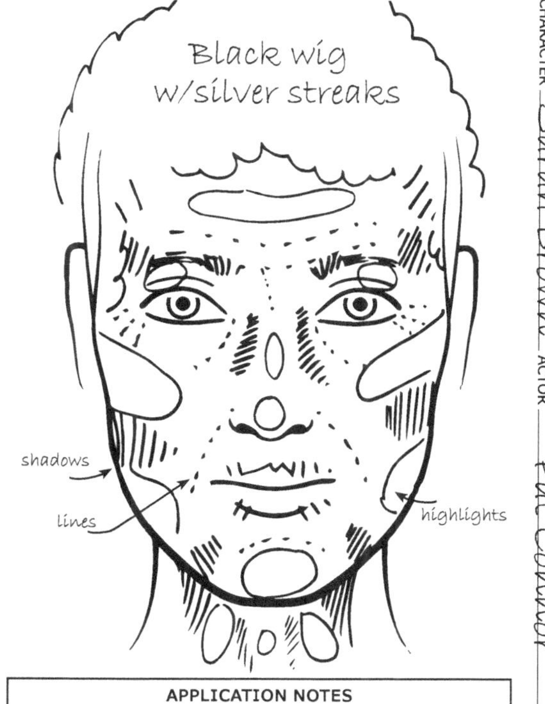

	BRAND	NUMBER	COLOR
FOUNDATION	BN	P-5	Old Age
LINES	BN	CS-3 (lighten w/P-5)	Char Brwn
HIGHLIGHTS	BN	CH-0	Ultra Lite
SHADOWS		DR-7	Char. Brwn/ Nat
ROUGE		LC-5	Coral
LIPS		CL-11	Nat.
EYES		DR-7 CH-0	Cin. Char. Brown
POWDER		translucent	
OTHER		silver gray liquid for 2 streaks	on wig

APPLICATION NOTES

Age-lines: crows-feet around eyes, lines on forehead (pic. #1) and around mouth (pic. 2) shadows on cheeks, temples, neck, nose, jaw for old age effect. Follow with highlights (pic. 3)

Mascara!!

Don't forget to line eyebrows with brown and gray

Also appears on page 193 of the Student Workbook

INTRODUCTION TO THEATRE ARTS 2

MAKEUP PLOT

	BRAND	NUMBER	COLOR
FOUNDATION			
LINES			
HIGHLIGHTS			
SHADOWS			
ROUGE			
LIPS			
EYES			
POWDER			
OTHER			

CHARACTER

ACTOR

MAKEUP ARTIST

APPLICATION NOTES

NOTES: ______________________________

____

____

____

____

____

____

____

____

CHAPTER 6 — THEATRE BEHIND THE SCENES

NAME ____ PERIOD _______ DATE _____________

STAGE MAKEUP PRACTICE

Using colored pencils, apply "makeup" on this figure for one of the following character types: cat, rabbit, a fairy that represents one of the seasons, a clown, or a devil. (Your teacher may offer some additional suggestions.) Cover the entire face, but some of the coverage may be skin-toned rather than a character color. Use the margins for notes and to indicate glitter, wigs, prosthetics, wax, fake eyelashes, and so on.

APPLICATION NOTES

          195

NOTES: ____

____

____

____

____

____

____

____

LIGHTING AND SOUND

Costumes, makeup, props, and set are all important, but in the typical public-school auditorium, perhaps the most essential theatrical elements are lighting and sound.

If an actor's primary objective is to be heard, then good sound is obviously a high priority. However, it is not just about microphones. Sound includes pre-recorded music and sound cues. Sound technicians must also know how to operate high-tech equipment with dozens of cables, buttons, knobs, lights, and an infinite number of variables. They must have very good ears so that they can sense when an actor's microphone needs to be tweaked. A good knowledge of acoustics is also important, as are a number of other factors.

In smaller theatres and in some schools, actors will not be able to use microphones and will rely on vocal **projection** instead. Because sound systems are very expensive, many schools do not own them. Sound systems can be rented, and technicians can even be hired to run them. A less expensive option is to use home stereo equipment for sound cues or to have actors create sound cues offstage using hand-held devices.

What good is sound if the audience struggles with trying to see the characters? The lighting team must make sure that each instrument is in good working order and that the lights are focused. They then add color gels to give the scene time, place, mood, and depth, but also to assure that the actors' features are visible and that the overall effect is what the director intended. Modern systems are computerized, and each show must be programmed individually so that the lights work in groups and each is assigned a cue number. Once the system is programmed, the light board operator must then follow the script at each rehearsal and cue the light board at the appropriate times. The light board operator also addresses any problems that arise during shows. For example, if an actor misses a line that is also a light cue, the operator must adapt. The lamps or bulbs inside an instrument may go out during a show, and the light board operator must know which instruments can be used to illuminate the area in an emergency situation.

One of the great things about lighting is that it can eliminate the need for expensive scenery. Colored lights can be used to create a number of backgrounds such as sunsets, evenings, and just about any surrealistic setting imaginable. By adding a small metal disc called a gobo to the instrument, stars, clouds, and other shapes can work with the color, creating wonderful effects. Robotic instruments, which can be programmed to move, can make clouds appear to drift past a sun as it sets, with stars beginning to twinkle on the horizon. Robotic equipment is rare in schools as it is very expensive.

Both lighting and sound are prone to sudden and drastic advancements in technology. A few years ago, both were controlled by large boards with sliding mechanical switches. Today, wealthier theatres may control both via a single computer, or perhaps two computers. Either way, computerization is the wave of the future.

But for most educational theatres, the transition is a bit slower, and for many reasons: some are not financially prepared for the full transition, and some who are purists choose to cling to the familiar. Still many more decide on a show-by-show basis. Students with an interest in lighting or sound should be prepared for the continuous need to learn new technology. If continued study does not interest you, perhaps costuming or makeup are more your speed, because in lighting and sound, things move at the speed of, well, light and sound!

BENEFITS OF LIGHTS AND SOUND

Lighting the stage isn't just about seeing the actors. It's also about creating settings, establishing mood, and eliminating the need for pricey set pieces. Sound can do the same when you create a soundscape for a location. For instance, a soundscape for a school cafeteria might include plastic trays clacking, silverware clinking, chairs scraping the floor, wrappers being opened, plus voices and laughter.

Become an expert on using these two tools to reduce the amount of time and money you and your students spend on building. Instead of building a jungle, use lighting and sounds to create one.

CHAPTER 7
PRODUCTION 101:
A PRIMER FOR LARGE-SCALE STUDENT-DIRECTED AND STUDENT-PRODUCED SCENES AND PLAYS

VOCABULARY

In this chapter you will learn about:

Audition: Tryouts for a play.

Author's Intent: What the author probably meant or had in mind when the play was written.

Blocking: The planned movement onstage.

Callbacks: A later part of auditions in which actors being considered for parts are asked to audition again.

Callboard: A bulletin board where actors and crew can count on finding updated information about rehearsals and shows.

Character Part: A part in which the actor is asked to be very different from themself.

Closed Auditions: Auditions limited to certain people.

Cold Audition: An audition for which the actors are purposefully not prepared.

Director: The artistic leader of a show.

Dress Rehearsal: A rehearsal in which everything is as it will be opening night, only there is no audience.

House: The audience part of the theatre including the lobby, seats, and anywhere the audience may come and go at leisure; the place where the audience sits to view the show.

Improvisation: A type of acting that is unscripted and unprepared; spontaneous acting.

Ledger: A form that is designed to track income and expenses.

Literature: In theatre, the literature is the selection of material or the script.

Master Director's Script: The script used by the director; this script is dissected and re-formatted to give more margin space for recording notes, stage directions, and blocking.

Minimalism: The practice of using fewer props, costumes, sets, etc., to reduce clutter and force focus.

Monologue: A scene with one person, or dialogue from a scene in which only one person speaks.

Musical: A play in which a large portion of the story is told in song.

Open Auditions: Auditions that may be attended by anyone.

Play Publisher: The company that prints, markets, and licenses play scripts.

Polishing Rehearsal: A rehearsal in which the director seeks to make the scene what it will be for performance.

Prepared Auditions: Auditions for which actors have been asked to practice/memorize a certain scene.

Pre-production: What happens in a show before the rehearsal process begins.

Production Calendar: The schedule that the cast and crew will follow throughout the production process.

Production Checklist: A running list of tasks to be completed as the performance draws nearer.

Production Contract: An agreement between the director and each participant. When the participants are students, their parents are often asked to join in the agreement.

Production Notebook: The notebook the director uses to organize the entire production; may become the stage manager's book as the show progresses.

Public Domain: In reference to a play, this is a script that no longer has copyright restrictions.

Publicity: Advertisement.

Read Through: A type of rehearsal in which the script is read, usually with the actors seated around a table.

Royalties: The payment performance companies make to the publisher for the rights to perform a script.

Script: The book in which a play is printed.

Sides: Small sections of scripts prepared for auditions.

Stage Manager: The person in charge of the backstage area.

Strike: To disassemble.

Technical Rehearsal: A rehearsal in which technical aspects are added; often lines are not run, but actors go from one cue to the next to ensure the technical parts of the show are properly functioning.

Working Rehearsal: A standard rehearsal as opposed to a technical rehearsal or a dress rehearsal.

199

INTRODUCTION

This chapter is for students who will be directing plays—the ultimate in teamwork experience. If your students are in high school, this is strongly recommended. If you have seniors who will be studying theatre in college, you will be doing them a great service allowing them to direct at least one show on your campus, because they will almost certainly be expected to direct at their new school. If you teach younger students, you can adapt this very lengthy project into a shorter one.

Even if you are not doing a student-directed play unit, consider doing a mock unit in which your students will experience many of the responsibilities of being in your shoes, from selecting a play all the way through to opening night, and even the tedious task of getting it all put away afterward.

One of the main topics of the *Production 101* project is being overly prepared. Talk to your students about times when your preparation paid off

PRODUCTION 101

OBJECTIVE You will experience directing a play or scene, from the selection of literature to performance. You will complete all phases: pre-production, casting, rehearsals, technical planning and implementation, costumes, props, publicity, and performance. (Your teacher will provide you with a rubric detailing your required duties.)

Have you discovered your place in the world yet? Are you a leader, a follower, an observer, or perhaps a philosopher? When you are a part of a group of students working on a team project, are you the one to take charge, do you encourage others to submit

A LITERAL APPROACH TO PRODUCTION

The play script itself is called "literature." It is important to consider your literature very carefully before making a final decision. What type of play will you do—comedy or drama? Will it be a period play or something with a social statement for modern teens? Many novice directors start with plays they have seen so that their first production isn't completely "from scratch." Taking all of this and your talent pool and the requirements of your assignment into consideration, what are some plays you are considering?

____

____

____

their ideas and encourage healthy debate, or do you enjoy letting others take the lead? As you begin making your own way in life, it will be important to your success to know how you fit into a team.

Not all teams are the same. Some need leadership, so a person who isn't normally one to take the lead may be placed in a take-charge position. This is not ideal, but it doesn't necessarily spell disaster. Some groups have too many leaders, so there is a great deal of arguing, and often the

most aggressive person rather than the best leader takes charge. Like the earlier scenario, it's not ideal, but the conditions still allow for a good outcome. Unfortunately, there are times when no one wants to take charge, and no one does. It is difficult to imagine that this type of group will ever band together without some semblance of leadership; the group is almost certainly doomed to failure (or at least mediocrity). The solution to each group's problems is to learn to capitalize on the strengths of the individuals; to establish a strong sense of teamwork.

An excellent way to learn more about teamwork is to be involved in a play or to turn a scene into a production project. If you have been a student director or a member of a student-directed production staff, you may have already shared this experience as an actor. However, if you are brand new to this experience, you may be in for a surprise. You are about to put on a very large, very busy pair of shoes—those of **director**.

This is especially true in educational theatre where the students and the director attend class all day and then must rehearse for several hours each evening. After rehearsals, the actors go home to study, and the director often has hours of costuming, set, props, publicity, and other production business still to be done.

While some directors are very good at making the job look easy, the truth is that producing a good school play usually means one person must do the jobs that a whole crew of people would do if the show was professionally produced. Even if the school is lucky enough to have two or more directors, that still means that both directors must be really good at multi-tasking.

Even when everything goes as planned, play production can become quite frenzied. However, most directors will agree that "going as planned"

in a show or when you wished you had been more prepared (see the example from the production of *Aladdin* in the Student Workbook on p. 201). What do you do to ensure that there are no disasters in your shows? How can your students use this information in their class scene work and in life?

The following pages assume that you are selecting just a handful of students from your class to be student-directors who will prepare their plays for a public performance, perhaps an evening of one-acts. If you want all of your students to have experience with directing, consider having them do student-directed scenes instead. By keeping scenes to ten minutes or less, many publishers waive the royalty fee, especially for in-class projects without an invited audience. There are also many books of royalty-free ten-minute plays, several of which even allow photocopying.

isn't something one can plan. One of the cornerstones of theatre is that it is live; therefore, it is always lively, if not a bit wild. Every show offers new challenges and unexpected dilemmas, and with every one of these comes the opportunity for the director to either become an emotional mess or shine like a superstar. Furthermore, if the director has done the job well, the crew is trained to handle the unexpected with calmness and poise.

Take, for example, one director's production of *Aladdin*. In this particular production, an entire scene revolved around a jeweled goblet into which a sleeping potion was to be placed. Because there were two goblets in the scene but only one with the potion, there was a great emphasis on the two goblets looking very different. Students worked for hours on the props, ensuring that one was dull and the other glistened in the light. Together, the pair was stunning, and the students were very proud of their creations. But on closing night, just moments before the goblet scene, their bejeweled prop was dropped and broke into several unusable pieces.

EXPECT THE UNEXPECTED

What are some "emergencies" your director has faced during a play production at your school?

How did preparation help make those emergencies manageable?

What skills do you possess that will help make you a more prepared and organized director? What are some of your organizational concerns?

The director, watching from the audience, was a little surprised to see the students doing the scene without their prized prop, but the audience seemed unaware that anything was amiss. The students handled it so well, the director's jolt of concern faded quickly. Afterward, the director learned that a quick-thinking **stage manager** had retrieved a plain wine glass from the costume room with only seconds to spare, and the villain changed the line from "jeweled goblet" to "crystal goblet" in an effort not to draw attention to the mishap. The stage manager had remembered the director saying that there was "no such thing as an emergency." Instead of panicking, the stage manager thought of the simplest solution and played a big part in averting chaos.

Perhaps the best way to be sure that the production and performances go smoothly and as close to "as planned" as possible is to be prepared. For those who are new to directing and producing, this can be difficult. Many actors are not aware of all the effort the director puts into a final performance. Consequently, when an actor makes the transition to director either as a student or as a first-time teacher/director, they can easily become overwhelmed without a little help. Hopefully this unit will assist you in organizing, prioritizing, and getting your performance off on the right foot.

NOTES: ____

____

____

____

____

____

____

____

____

PRODUCTION ELEMENTS

How prepared were you for the amount of work needed for your first show as a director? Were you surprised at how much was involved, or had you somehow already learned this? Hopefully your students will direct a play after this experience, and thanks to your guidance, they will be very prepared with knowledge, experience, and a sense of the materials needed to make the job much easier and more successful.

This part of the unit will introduce your young directors to some traditional tools directors have used for many years as well as some less traditional tools. All are designed to help your students achieve the highest level of success with the least amount of stress and oversight.

Several of these tools have been streamlined for the student-directed plays and are included in the Student Workbook. There are additional tools available at the end of this chapter.

The following section assumes that you are selecting just a handful of students from your class to be student-directors who will prepare their plays for a public performance, perhaps an evening of one-acts. If you want all of your students to have experience with directing, consider having them do student-directed scenes instead. By keeping scenes to ten minutes or less, many publishers waive the royalty fee, especially for in-class projects without an invited audience. There are also many books of royalty-free ten-minute plays, several of which even allow photocopying.

PRODUCTION ELEMENTS

OBJECTIVE You will learn the various smaller assignments that you will be expected to complete during the directing process and as a part of your student directing assignment.

Because you are now a director, you will soon start accumulating an assortment of materials, research, handouts, forms, scripts, audition applications, and a lot more. The worst thing you could do is to fall behind before you have even begun. Even the seemingly least significant bit of information could prove to be very helpful later, so knowing where to find it (and knowing beyond a doubt that you have it) will save you valuable time and energy. You need a system for keeping up with your production materials. A number of different methods will work, but most directors agree that a concise notebook with a lot of accessories like pockets, dividers, and tabs works best. It can be expensive to purchase everything needed for each and every show, so once your show is done, file the materials and reuse the binder and other items.

The following will help you get your **production notebook** organized. As you work with the notebook, you may find that you can tweak the system a bit to make it work better for your individual needs.

THE PRODUCTION NOTEBOOK

Because your student-directed scene or play is a very involved, complex project, start by getting organized. You will need a **Production Notebook**. For most productions, a two-inch three-ring binder with about twenty dividers will work best. Some three-ring binders have a clear plastic cover with a slit at the top. This allows the user to add a cover sheet and sometimes a back cover too. This is a great feature for a student production team: Insert your rubric into the front cover and your calendar into the back cover. You will also want a three-hole pencil bag with a couple of pencils, some highlighters, some sticky notes, and some paper clips.

Your teacher should provide you with a rubric. This is an important tool when working on any large project. It outlines the project, explaining how you will be graded, the standards the teacher will use, your deadlines, and so on. If you did not receive one, ask questions and note the answers in your production notebook. Once you know exactly what is expected of you, you can begin prioritizing and planning. If at any point you are uncertain about the expectations, it is your job to seek clarification. Later, saying "I didn't know" or "no one told me" is not an excuse.

Early in the project, create a **production calendar** that includes rehearsal dates, goals for each rehearsal (such as when memorization for each section is due, when to have props, and so on), conflicts for all participants, and performance dates. Give one to each member of your cast and crew, post one on the **callboard**, and provide your teacher with a copy and keep the teacher apprised of any changes. If your group is performing outside of the school day, you might also want to collect signatures from parents confirming that each student will be in attendance. You do not want to be surprised at the last minute by students who thought they were available for the performance only to learn their parents had other plans for them.

Another way to ensure that parents and students are all on the same page is to collect **production contracts** from each participant. This is also an ideal way to collect everyone's contact information, which is an important part of a production notebook. Remember to collect actors' measurements and sizes on this same form so that you will be able to costume your show, even if the students are responsible for their own costumes. You never know when you will need this data, and it is better to have too much information than not enough.

PRODUCTION NOTEBOOK

A very nice gesture from you, the teacher, to your student directors is to provide them with the three-ring binder that they'll need for their Production Notebook. Each notebook should include a copy of the *Production Project Rubric* found on pages 317-319 of this Teacher's Guide and maybe also a copy of the box office and publicity forms on the two pages after that. By helping your students get organized, you get them off to a strong start and establish your expectations from the beginning. Hopefully you have a classroom budget that will help cover the cost of these notebooks. You can even make a big production out of announcing who your student directors will be by making a grand presentation of the Production Notebooks.

Depending on your budget and the socio-economics of your student body, when you give the Production Notebooks to your directors, consider including:

One very handy tool, especially for those just getting started, is the production checklist (see pages 225-227). It is almost certain that your teachers use such checklists for their plays. However, many directors enjoy the ease of recycling the same one over and over so that the small items they "seem to always forget" are already printed as a reminder. There are spaces for you to write in items that are not provided for you, and you will want to cross out certain other items that do not pertain to your show or to your school.

The director's script will be the most important part of the notebook. You may use a legal copy of the playbook, or you may wish to make a **master director's script**. Your teacher will specify whether or not this is required in your rubric. The master script is easier to use because it gives you a great deal of extra margin space for writing in blocking and other important information. However, it takes a while to make. You will find directions for making a master director's script later in this chapter.

Other things to include in your Production Notebook are an ongoing list of props that can be checked off as the items are gathered, set and costume designs, all correspondence (especially your permission to perform from the publisher, if permission is required), receipts (including royalty payment, if applicable), purchase orders and any other paperwork that pertains to your production, copies of communication from the director to the cast or crew, rehearsal notes dated from each rehearsal with items that need the director's attention highlighted, a to-do list, a list of people to invite to the performance, publicity ideas, research, notes to yourself for future productions, and anything else that might be of interest or use throughout the production. Remember to keep a list of the people and businesses you want to thank. You can thank them in your program, with a thank-you note, or with a poster signed by the cast and crew. There are a number of creative ways to ensure that those who assist will feel appreciated and will be there for you the next time you need their help.

After your show is over, create a file of items in your notebook. Many directors refer to their old files time and time again to help them organize and prepare for future shows.

YOU THINK YOU ARE READY FOR AUDITIONS?

Before you can do anything, you should choose the right play or scene for your talent pool and the requirements of the assignment. There is a lot to consider:

- How many males will audition or are in your talent pool? How many females?

- Do you have to share this talent pool with other student directors or has your group been predetermined?

- What type of script will appeal to your audience and your actors? This is especially important if actors have several plays for which they may audition. You want the most qualified actors and technicians to be in your play, so you must choose a play that will attract those students.

- What type of play will appeal to your director? Remember, they would probably rather see you have greater success with an easier play than become stressed and fatigued trying to make a grander impression.

- Most importantly, what plays interest you? This will be your project for the remainder of the semester, and you have to start out loving it and love it through to the end. This would be difficult to do if you forgot to please the director (you!).

- Are there any restrictions that will limit your choices? Check with your teacher about the appropriateness of any play before investing your money in scripts or your time in reading and planning.

Read several plays before narrowing your choices; consider reading through the two best choices with friends and/or family and getting their feedback before deciding on one. You may even choose to ask your teacher's opinion, but again, you will be the one directing the play, so ultimately, the choice is yours.

Do not cast the play in your head, but instead make notes about which actors in your pool might be right for each character. If you have gaps (characters with no actors who will fit the part), consider selecting a different play, recruiting actors to come to the auditions, or being more flexible about casting. Let your pool of talent use their creativity to make the part rather than trying to find the actor who will play the part a specific way.

Have your scripts at the auditions. Making copies of copyrighted playbooks for any reason is illegal— even for auditions. Many directors make sides or photocopies of sample scenes for auditions, but according to Amy Langton at Dramatic Publishing,

- About 16 dividers (two packages of 8)
- Blank notebook paper or a spiral for rehearsal notes
- A three-hole zippered pencil bag containing pencils, a few highlighters, sticky notes, and paper clips

Your student directors should also be prepared to move several pages from their Student Workbooks to their Production Notebooks, including:

this is still illegal and can land you in a great deal of hot water. Do not fall prey to a common copyright myth: you are still committing a crime if you own a legal playbook but make a back-up copy, even if it is a small scene, and even if you are not making a profit. The only time it is legal to make copies is when you have specific permission *in writing* from the owner of the copyright or if the item is in the **public domain**. If you do not have a budget for buying scripts, select from scripts in your classroom or school library, find someone to buy an advertisement in your program that will pay for the scripts, ask your teacher to use classroom funds for the project (and your teacher will get to keep the scripts when the play is over), or ask the actors to pay for their own scripts. If these are not options, consider writing an original play, and then you will own the copyright.

NOW YOU ARE PROBABLY READY FOR THOSE AUDITIONS!

If you must have auditions, keep them very simple. You and your cast and crew will have a difficult enough time with the job ahead. Complicating things early on will only create problems. Your teacher may require that you hold auditions, but if not, simply talk to those students you feel would be most qualified. If this is allowed, it will save you a great deal of time. Furthermore, it may save you from disappointing a friend if they are not cast in the desired part. At your age, this is a situation you want to avoid if possible.

If you must audition, start with your main roles; you will probably be able to cast your bit parts from the actors who auditioned but did not get a main part. If not, hold a short second set of auditions to cast your remaining characters.

If you are still short of actors and if the publisher allows it, you might consider gender-bending roles.

This is the practice of ignoring gender in casting. This works especially well in children's plays, fantasies, and comedies, and it is a little easier if the part is a **character part** or *one in which the actor is asked to be very different from themself.* Consider carefully the views of your community before you gender-bend characters in romantic roles. You want to make choices that enhance or support the storyline, not distract from it.

Another option might be to double cast smaller parts, but avoid giving one actor two similar parts. Better that the two parts are quite different, though you have to make sure there is an appropriate amount of time for whatever costume and makeup changes may be necessary.

LET THE REHEARSALS BEGIN!

Almost. Before you begin rehearsing, ensure that your script isn't too long. If it is, cut it down. There is no need to rehearse lines and scenes that will not be performed. Some **publishers** require you to obtain permission in writing before making cuts. Be sure to add this correspondence to your Production Notebook.

When you have the script at the desired length, divide what remains into three to five parts. A part may be two short scenes, an act, or any logical section that would make a solid day's rehearsal. By rehearsing in parts, your actors can manage **blocking** and memorization in smaller chunks. It also allows actors to attend only those rehearsals for which they are needed, so it is nice to take stage time into consideration when sectioning your play. For your actors' sakes, try to section parts so that everyone gets a day off from having to be on stage, if possible. This improves morale and attendance.

Create a rehearsal calendar that specifies the rehearsal dates, times, and what will be done at each rehearsal. Distribute these to your cast, crew, and teacher, and post one on the callboard and anywhere else that may be a common area for your participants.

Try to get as much done in each **working rehearsal** as possible, but don't be too demanding. For example, if you are working part two and you have two hours of rehearsal, you might consider running through it one time with stops and starts for direction. Give the group a five- or ten-minute break, then run it again, this time straight through. Take notes and give them orally at the end of the run-through. Underline anything in your notes you think needs individual attention. After giving notes, give another very short break, then work on any of the underlined problem areas.

When possible, work with as few people as are necessary. If a participant will not have a significant amount of work and you feel you can do without them, allow them to miss rehearsal. If you give advanced notice, they can work in appointments, tutorials, lessons, line memorization, etc. This will improve attendance at rehearsals where actors are needed. It is important to let actors know that you are taking them off the schedule on that day so that they will

PREPARING FOR AUDITIONS

Have you decided if your students will hold auditions for their student-directed shows? This can be a very stressful part of the process, and it is stress that can easily be avoided.

First ask yourself this: how much of the work will be done in class and how much will you require them to do after school? If even part of the shows will be prepared in class, what will your students who are not in a student-directed show do? Will they be available to help with things like publicity and costumes? Will they have an alternate assignment?

Next, do your students know enough about each other to be able to cast their shows fairly without auditions? Non-audition casting is very easily justifiable and is common practice in professional theatre. As students, your directors may find surprising new talent by holding auditions, but in this case, it may be better just to let them choose without putting them in the difficult position of having to possibly turn away a good friend. Unlike scene work, where students are encouraged to say "no" to those who may not be up to the group's level, you are probably selecting very few directors, and they have probably already proven themselves to be capable leaders. Allowing these trusted leaders to hand-pick their casts and crews will allow each to include those who will make it the kind of memorable experience they will cherish.

not miss any other days. Do not set a precedent for "slacking off" by making them feel less needed than the others or by acting like missing rehearsals is "no big deal."

Stick to the rehearsal schedule. If you cannot do this for some reason, revise the schedule and alert every one of the changes. Early in the production, your schedule helps keep your cast and crew organized. The minute the director abandons the schedule, the cast and crew go adrift, not sure when they are needed or what they should be preparing.

SAMPLE REHEARSAL CALENDAR

RJ, Director 555-555-5555	**MONDAY**	**TUESDAY**	**WEDNESDAY**	**THURSDAY**	**FRIDAY**
November 1-5	3:30 - 5:00 block part 1	3:30 - 5:00 block part 2	3:30 - 5:15 block part 3	3:30 - 5:00 work part 1	Fall Social: no rehearsal
November 8-12	3:30 - 5:00 work part 2	3:30 - 5:00 work part 3	no rehearsal, memorize	3:30 - 5:00 work part 1, memorized	3:30 - 5:00 work part 2, memorized
November 15-19	3:30 - 5:00 work part 3, memorized	3:30 - 5:00 run part 1, memorized, props cue	3:30 - 5:00 run part 2, memorized, props due	3:30 - 5:00 run part 3, memorized, props due	3:30 - 5:00 run parts 1 & 2, no scripts on stage/add lights
November 22-26	3:30 - 5:00 run parts 2 & 3, no scripts on stage, add lights	3:30 - 5:00 run show, add sound	3:30 - 6:00 run show, stay late for notes	3:30 - 5:30 run show, photographer coming, bios due	3:30 - 5:00 wear work clothes, work on set
November 29 -December 3	4:00 - 6:00 tech rehearsal: ALL must attend!	3:30 - 6:00 run show with all tech, costumes due	6:30 - 9:30 dress rehearsal, places at 7 pm sharp!!	6:30 - 9:30 final dress, places at 7 pm sharp!!	Performance! makeup call at 5, costumes by 6, green room by 6:30, places by 6:50

COUNTDOWN TO OPENING NIGHT...

Keep a running list of what needs to be done:

- Delegate some of the work to responsible helpers, when possible.
- Do not allow your desire to control every aspect of your project drive you to exhaustion or depression.
- Become good at prioritizing.

Discuss call times with actors and with crew, expectations for performances, and any last-minute needs. Do not hesitate to ask crew and actors to help with final details.

Consider making or buying (or ask a club to help; National Junior Honor Society and Thespians are good places to start) small gifts for those who helped you. For example, if you are doing *Sylvia*, by A. R. Gurney, a comedy about a dog who is played by a beautiful, two-legged woman, invest in a keepsake dog tag for each participant. If that is too much, buy a cheap

205

The hardest part of doing a show for a new director might be budgeting. If your district does not have a policy regarding reimbursements, you can have your students save their receipts and reimburse them from the box office. However, most districts will not allow this. Many, in fact, will not allow you to give your students a budget at all. In this case, you can ask your booster club to set aside funds for your student directors. Most booster club funds are earned by students and can be spent on students with a vote.

Regarding copyright, be exceedingly careful to avoid doing anything that not only sets a bad example for your students, but also might cause you embarrassment or possibly put your job in jeopardy. Reproducing any part of a script that is copyrighted is illegal. This includes making sides for auditions, making copies because those you ordered have not come in the mail, making a back-up copy so you can write in it and keep your director's copy clean, and so on. There is never a situation in which reproduction of a copyrighted piece is allowable unless you receive written permission from the owner of the copyright. Possessing a copied script makes the bearer liable, so by putting a copy of a script in your students' hands, you are putting them at risk too.

Purchase a classroom set of your students' plays, number them, and check them out to the director

INTRODUCTION TO THEATRE ARTS 2

dog bone cookie cutter and make "treats" for those you want to thank. The simplest keepsake for those not in the play is a show poster autographed by each member of the cast and crew. Give each of your actors a small framed snapshot of himself in action alongside a cast and crew group picture in a simple paper mat or inexpensive frame. Remember your cast, crew, teacher, and everyone who did anything at all to assist in your play or scene. If you run out of time before your show, this is something that can easily be done in the less hectic weeks following the production. You may also use the "Bloopers" page later in this chapter as inspiration for cast and crew gifts.

POST PRODUCTION—WHEW!

- Return all borrowed items.
- Remove your production's items from the performance and practice areas before having to be told to do so.
- Turn in your Production Notebook to your teacher.
- Relax. You've earned it!

YOUR PRODUCTION'S "BRAIN"

OBJECTIVE: You will create a Production Notebook that will assist you with organization and will ensure that you are always prepared as a director and fully able to function as your team's leader.

The key to success for any large project is being organized. Some teachers roll carts or wagons to rehearsals each day so that they can have everything they need; others do just fine with a spiral notebook.

If this is your first play—or even if it is one of your first five plays—do not risk being too sure of yourself. Bring everything together in a sturdy, organized, portable binder. If you are directing a scene or something much less involved than a one-act play, a binder might be more work than it is worth. This concept is intended for student-directed one-act or full-length plays.

Think of your Production Notebook as "command central," the one source everyone can count on for answers. Your teacher may ask to see it so that your progress can be tracked. You will find yourself needing things from the binder throughout rehearsals, and if you allow them access to the binder (it can be "off-limits" if you desire), your cast and crew or perhaps your assistant director can also find needed information quickly. If you file things regularly, having a Production Notebook is a lot like having your desk at every rehearsal.

PRODUCTION NOTEBOOK ASSIGNMENT

- ☐ 1. Find a binder with rings large enough to hold all of your accumulated paperwork throughout your rehearsal. Bigger is better. Even if you do not have a lot of material to start, an organized director will eventually be able to fill (making use of everything) a two-inch binder.
- ☐ 2. Put your Production Rubric in the front of the binder. Your Production Calendar should be equally accessible. If your binder has the clear plastic sleeve cover, insert these items in the front and back covers, respectively. This will allow you to find your most frequently used items quickly.

- ☐ 3. Make dividers for your binder. A list of possible tabs is found below labeled "The Production Notebook Should Contain," but you will probably not need all of those. For example, you may be asked to direct your show without spending any money. If this is the case, you will not need item eleven, Finances. Your teacher may also take over all of your publicity. There are many reasons you may only need some of the tabs, but to be safe, keep extras in your binder. Even if others are helping, you may want to continue to document everything that is being done. After all, this binder will be a wonderful keepsake of your first show (or at least one of your firsts).

- ☐ 4. Keep your Production Notebook organized. As you complete required handouts, file them. Stay current with your production checklist too. You may want to keep a few sheets of hole reinforcers in your binder so that broken punch holes can be repaired; otherwise you run the risk of losing valuable research or other vital information.

- ☐ 5. Keep your Production Notebook with you at all rehearsals and during all classroom planning phases of your production. You are subject to having it checked at irregular intervals to ensure you are keeping it organized, up-to-date, and that you are making your own contributions to the notebook.

with instructions to keep track of who gets which script. After the show, have the director take up your scripts and return them to you. Students who lost or ruined their scripts can pay to replace them; if your student director fails to track the scripts properly, the director's grade can reflect the oversight. In general, students are allowed to highlight scripts and write in them in pencil only. Any abuse of a script that renders it unusable in the future would justify having the student pay to replace it.

Pay your students' royalties up front and provide them with copies of the receipt for their Production Notebooks. Non-payment of royalties or performing without permission are copyright violations. Producing a play without paying royalties and without paying for every copy of the script is stealing.

There are many cases where theatre teachers were caught violating copyright. Many were fined, and quite a few lost their jobs and suffered public embarrassment over the incident, which could easily have been avoided.

YOUR PRODUCTION NOTEBOOK SHOULD CONTAIN:

- ☐ 1. Rubric or grading standards
- ☐ 2. Production Calendar with rehearsals, deadlines, conflicts, and performances
- ☐ 3. Production Contracts or other documentation on all participants
- ☐ 4. Director's Master Script
- ☐ 5. 3-hole pencil bag with zipper and supplies
- ☐ 6. Production Checklist worksheet
- ☐ 7. Spare notebook paper
- ☐ 8. Ongoing list of props
- ☐ 9. Set and costume designs
- ☐ 10. Correspondence
- ☐ 11. Finances
- ☐ 12. Handouts, assignments, miscellaneous paperwork

- ☐ 13. Rehearsal notes
- ☐ 14. "To-do" list
- ☐ 15. Publicity, printing, posters, tickets, programs, fliers, announcements, etc.
- ☐ 16. Performance invitation list
- ☐ 17. Research
- ☐ 18. Reminders for future productions
- ☐ 19. List of people to thank
- ☐ 20. Miscellaneous
- ☐ 21.
- ☐ 22.

PRODUCTION NOTEBOOK GRADES

Your teacher may ask to see your Production Notebook at various stages throughout the production process. It is possible that your teacher needs to check a particular item or simply wants to be sure that you are not getting overwhelmed. Keep your notebook and the grading sheet on the next page with you at all rehearsals and any time you are working on your production in class.

PRODUCTION 101 FOR SCENE WORK

All of the forms in *Production 101* are useful for scene work projects as well as plays, depending upon how much time you are interested in investing in them. Consider using a simplified version of the student directing project in your beginner classes as a means of introducing them to the concept of directing, but with shorter scenes.

 207

As a teacher, you must model for your students legal and ethical standards for play production: use only legal scripts, pay your royalties, do not change the play or characters, make cuts only with permission unless permission is granted in the script itself, do not add anything, do not use images from the book or other productions in your publicity, and follow the guidelines for crediting the playwright and publishing company as cited in the script or by the publisher. When in doubt, contact the publisher. This is not intended to be legal advice and cannot attempt to encompass every aspect of copyright as it pertains to educational theatre.

INTRODUCTION TO THEATRE ARTS 2

DATE: _______________________ PRODUCTION NOTEBOOK GRADE: _______________

TEACHER NOTES: ____

____

____

____

____

____

____

DATE: _______________________ PRODUCTION NOTEBOOK GRADE: _______________

TEACHER NOTES: ____

____

____

____

____

____

____

DATE: _______________________ PRODUCTION NOTEBOOK GRADE: _______________

TEACHER NOTES: ____

____

____

____

____

____

____

LET THE REHEARSALS BEGIN

Remember that this is the students' first show as directors. Do not assume they know anything. Guide them through every process.

Even though you can produce a show in six or eight weeks, your beginner students will need either more time or less show. Many theatre teachers limit their student-directed performance time to under an hour, and some limit them to about a half-hour. If you choose to require a shorter script, your directors may be able to complete their shows in about eight weeks. Monitor progress closely, attending at least one rehearsal a week. If all is going well, you need not stay for the entire rehearsal.

You might also want to hold directors' meetings weekly for students to talk about their progress, concerns, and their production's needs. This will

CHAPTER 7 — PRODUCTION 101

PRODUCTION CALENDAR

OBJECTIVE You will create a Production Calendar for your show using either this template or any blank calendar or template.

The calendar will include all important dates; times; deadlines; locations, when different from the usual rehearsal space; which part will be rehearsed that day; what actors should have prepared, such as memorization, props, etc.; and any other useful information. Write the page numbers for each part (below last row) so that actors will be able to match the calendar to their scripts. Get approval for your dates, then make one or two copies per participant. You will want a copy for school and a copy for home, which will improve attendance and timeliness; a copy for your teacher; one for the callboard; a couple for the rehearsal area or other common bulletin boards; and at least one copy for the Production Notebook.

PRODUCTION CALENDAR

DIRECTOR: ____

NAME OF SHOW: ____

PHONE: ____________________ EMAIL: _______________________

	MONDAY	TUESDAY	WEDNESDAY	THURSDAY	FRIDAY	SATURDAY / SUNDAY
Week of:						
Week of:						
Week of:						
Week of:						
Week of:						
Week of:						
Week of:						
Week of:						
Week of:						

PART 1: _______ PART 2: _______ PART 3: _______ PART 4: _______ PART 5: _______

 209

be a prime time for you to take notes of things you and your spare students can do to help.

Check notebooks on a regular basis. If you are letting students handle money and correspondence, you are responsible for checking to be sure they have followed all the proper channels for paying their royalties and that they are using only legal scripts. Give grades for each notebook check.

If there are things you do for your directors like reserving the theatre, getting the air conditioner turned on, and so on, they need to know these things. If they continue directing, they should be fully aware of all you are doing on their behalf so that they can do it themselves when the time comes.

INTRODUCTION TO THEATRE ARTS 2

THE DIRECTOR'S MASTER SCRIPT

OBJECTIVE You will create a larger, legal version of your script that will make recording blocking, cues, and notes easier and more legible.

Many directors take notes in the margins of a playbook, but since the average script has less than an inch to the left and right and just over an inch in the center, below, and above, this can become crowded and messy. Because your director's script is almost always the only one in which all blocking and cues are recorded, it needs to be legible. That is why some directors create a master script. This is a regular script that has been cut and taped to copy paper giving the director twice as much margin for recording cues.

You will be making a master script for your play. Read the following instructions carefully to avoid damaging your playbook and creating extra work for yourself. Pay special attention to what is in italics, as there are strict laws regarding copyright to which you need to pay attention.

MAKING YOUR DIRECTOR'S MASTER SCRIPT

- Start with an actual legal script or book for the play you will be directing. Never make, possess, or allow your actors to use illegally photocopied scripts. If your script is stapled, remove the staple. If it is bound with glue, use an X-Acto or box knife to very carefully cut the pages from the playbook as close to the binding as possible. Count the number of pieces of paper you now have.

- Measure the text part of the page (just the words) from the first letter on the left to the last letter on the right and from the top line to just below the page number at the bottom (see sample, right). How tall is your text, including the page number? ______________ How wide is your text? ______________ Add one-half inch to each measurement (if your text is four inches wide, it will become 4½ inches; 6½ inches tall would become seven inches). Now, what is your new measurement? Height plus ½ inch = ______________ Width plus ½ inch = ______________. Now divide the width (left to right) by two for a half-width of ______________ inches. Save these measurements for the next step.

- Now take an 8 1/2- by 11-inch piece of paper and fold it left to right (see diagram, left). Using the last measurement from above (the width of your text divided by two), mark your paper that distance from the fold. In other words, if your final measurement above was two inches, measure two inches from the folded edge of your paper. Now mark your total height (height plus one-half inch), centered vertically on the fold, and use scissors to cut out the rectangle. Open the page, and you should have a piece of copy paper with the perfect sized rectangle to tape your pages from your script. Lay this on top of one of your pages, and if it is a good fit, use this page

◄——— 3.75" WIDE ———►

6" TALL

4: *(Dramatic.)* And, oh! The poor, poor chickens.
6: Wait. What about the chickens?
4: *(Dramatic.)* And, oh! The poor, poor chickens.
6: Wait. What about the chickens?
4: In Quitman, Georgia, it is illegal for a chicken to cross the road.
2: Why does a chicken cross a road?
1, 3, 4, 5, & 6: To get to the other side!
ALL: *(In vaudeville style.)* Da da da da da da!
6: It sounds like every state—
OTHERS: Every one.
6: —has its share of outdated laws!
5: That's right, and nowhere do they get any dumber than in the proud South!
1, 2, 3: *(Sing.)* Oh Susanna, don't you cry for me. I come from Alabama—
4: Alabama!
1, 2, 3: *(Continue song.)* —with a banjo on my knee.
4: Did you know that in Alabama, it is illegal to drive blindfolded?
OTHERS: No!
4: Yes!
6: Okay, I have heard that in Alaska it is illegal to whisper in someone's ear while they are moose hunting.
1: In Arizona *(Someone whistles "The Good, the Bad and the Ugly" theme music.)* criminals must be very color conscience. A misdemeanor committed while wearing a red mask—
4: Hmmmm. Should I wear the red *(Pantomimes a mask in the left hand.)* or the blue? *(Pantomimes a mask in the right hand.)*
1: —used to be considered a felony.

NOTES: ____

____

____

____

____

____

____

____

as a template to make as many as you need to complete your master script.

- Next, use clear tape to adhere your dissected script pages to the cut-out copy paper. Tape on all four sides of the page and on both sides of the paper so that vital information is not lost. Put the pages in the right order, then hole-punch the new pages. Because your script will be used a lot, put hole reinforcers on both sides of all three holes before you get started.

- You now have additional space on all four sides for writing, blocking, and notes (see sample, left).

- If the page numbers on the script are not visible after taping the new page to the paper, be sure to fill those in. It may sound cliché, but you want your director and actors to be on the same page! An easier way to do this is to tape strips of paper along the outside margin. This will only give you spare room on one side of your script, but it will also allow you to keep your script intact, and it will take less time.

Left: Fold paper in half from top to bottom, measure, and cut a 6" x 3.75" rectangle out of the fold.
Right: When opened, you have the perfect sized space for the pages from your script.

4: *(Dramatic.)* And, oh! The poor, poor chickens.
6: Wait. What about the chickens?
4: In Quitman, Georgia, it is illegal for a chicken to cross the road.
2: Why does a chicken cross a road?
1, 3, 4, 5, & 6: To get to the other side!
ALL: *(In vaudeville style.)* Da da da da da da!
6: It sounds like every state—
OTHERS: Every one.
6: —has its share of outdated laws!
5: That's right, and nowhere do they get any dumber than in the proud South!
1, 2, 3: *(Sing.)* Oh Susanna, don't you cry for me. I come from Alabama—
4: Alabama!
1, 2, 3: *(Continue song.)* —with a banjo on my knee.
4: Did you know that in Alabama, it is illegal to drive blindfolded?
OTHERS: No!
4: Yes!
6: Okay, I have heard that in Alaska it is illegal to whisper in someone's ear while they are moose hunting.
1: In Arizona *(Someone whistles "The Good, the Bad and the Ugly" theme music.)* criminals must be very color conscience. A misdemeanor committed while wearing a red mask—
4: Hmmmm. Should I wear the red *(Pantomimes a mask in the left hand.)* or the blue? *(Pantomimes a mask in the right hand.)*
1: —used to be considered a felony.

27

 211

NOTES: ____

____

____

____

____

____

____

____

INTRODUCTION TO THEATRE ARTS 2

CREATING A PRODUCTION CONTRACT

OBJECTIVE You will create a production contract with important information for participants, specifically what will be expected of them during the production process.

Imagine working hard on your play and coming to rehearsal on Monday of your production week. You are excited because everything seems to be falling into place. Then one of your actors walks up to you with a facial expression that tells you something is wrong. The actor says their parents didn't realize that the show was this particular weekend and bought nonrefundable plane tickets to visit a grandparent. The actor doesn't have a very important part and really wants to go and is dropping out. With only four days until your show goes up, what do you do? What could you have done to prevent this? And who gave the actor the impression that the part was less important than anyone else's?

There is not a great deal any director can do when a participant falls short of your expectations, but there is much that can be done beforehand to ensure it never comes to this. Of course, you can cast understudies, but that still doesn't prevent last-minute stress and added work. Instead, it is your job to make sure everyone is aware of what will be expected of them before you cast your show. If you use audition applications, why not make your production contract part of the application? That will ensure that every person auditioning for or seeking a part in your show knows the requirements ahead of time.

There is a great deal of information that needs to be distributed in most shows. However, since you are just learning how to do your job, keep it simple. If you give parents and participants too much information, they will feel overwhelmed, and many will not read it carefully. Instead, be thorough, be concise, and be neat!

YOUR PRODUCTION CONTRACT SHOULD COLLECT THE FOLLOWING INFORMATION:

- Thorough contact information for each participant including students' home phone numbers, cell phone numbers, email addresses, and home addresses. It will also be useful to get their class schedules and room numbers so that you may reach them during the school day in case of emergency. Do not overuse this privilege, and always seek your teacher's approval before interrupting another's class.

- Contact information for students' parents, including daytime phone, home phone, cell phone, and even potential weekend contact information (especially when a student lives with one parent but visits another in a different location); getting parents' emails will be an easy way to give weekly updates, request volunteers, and make changes to the rehearsal schedule.

- A parent signature saying the participant is available for performances and rehearsals and that the parent and student both understand all the parts of the contract.

- Any conflicts with the projected rehearsal schedule; get specific dates and times as well as the nature of the conflict (in some cases, these may be flexible, making rescheduling an option).

- This is also an ideal way to collect actors' sizes and measurements for costuming purposes.

- You may want to solicit parent volunteers for those areas in which your teacher said you could have help (especially for costuming, props, and set).

- If you will be ordering keepsake shirts, get a T-shirt size, inform parents of the projected cost, and request a volunteer to assist you with this particular job (the design, ordering, collecting money, and so on).

YOUR PRODUCTION CONTRACT SHOULD PROVIDE THE FOLLOWING INFORMATION TO PARTICIPANTS AND THEIR PARENTS:

- Information on how to reach you or your teacher.
- Projected rehearsal schedule (you may say something like Monday through Friday, 3:30 to 6:00, or you may provide a copy of your production calendar).
- Performance dates and times.
- Potential costs that parents and participants might incur (such as costume rental).
- Expectations for rehearsals, including behavior, attendance, participation, and meeting deadlines.
- Consequences for missed rehearsals (consult your teacher for this information).

NOTES: ____

CHAPTER 7 — PRODUCTION 101

PRODUCTION CONTRACT

Student: _________________________ Show: _________________________

Role/Position: ____

There is a production fee of $ __________ for this role. It is due by _________________

REHEARSALS

- Please mark all rehearsals on your calendar as soon as the schedule is posted.
- Attendance and promptness are extremely important. Please attend all scheduled rehearsals and be on time.
- If you must be absent or tardy, call _________________ at _________________ .

Rehearsals you are expected to attend: (circle one)   Few   Several   Most   All

Rehearsals begin: _________________ and will be _______ times a week.

Approximate rehearsal times: _________________ through _________________

Times: (circle one) Will / Will not run later during technical week and dress rehearsals.

The show runs _________________ through _________________

OTHER REHEARSAL RESPONSIBILITIES

- Pay attention to the rehearsal schedule and make all deadlines.
- Be of assistance when and where possible.
- Keep the rehearsal facility neat.
- Respect others' property.
- Respect fellow cast and crew members, directors, parents, and any other participants.

COSTUMES (check one)

_______ Students will need to provide their own costumes.
_______ Students will need to pay for costume rentals.
_______ Students' costumes will be provided.

PARENT VOLUNTEERS ARE NEEDED

Parents, please circle all areas with which you're able to assist.

Transportation	Snacks	Set Construction	Ticket Sales	_________
Errands	Drinks	Box Office	Publicity	_________
Design Poster	Design Program	Collect Props	Sewing	_________

PARENT INFORMATION

Name(s): _________________ Email(s): _________________

Phone(s): ____

I understand all that is expected of me and promise to abide by the above rules. My parents are aware of and support the rules of this contract.

_________________________   ________   _________________________   ________
Student   Date   Parent   Date

           213

NOTES: ____

____

____

____

____

____

____

____

BUDGET BASICS

Almost all student-directed plays are faced with theatre directors' most universally annoying challenge: no budget or a low budget. At the same time, you will probably get full access to more resources for free than you would be able to afford if you were on your own. Your teacher will discuss budget with you in detail, but for the purposes of this assignment, assume your entire play budget is $100.

It sounds a little daunting, doesn't it? Is it possible to produce a play for just $100? Let's put it to the test.

In 2021, a script costs between $6 and $10 per book. If there are four people in your cast plus a director, a stage manager, and one person each to run lights and sound, that equals eight scripts. That's already $80, over three-quarters of your budget! Royalties are going to be at least that amount on top of scripts. You're required to assemble a notebook, and then there are the turn-of-the-century costumes. Renting, even at a school rate of about $65 a costume, is out of the question. Luckily, the entire set is a living room, and you have access to the school's stock pieces, but there are a number of unusual props that will either have to be made or bought, and either way, that's going to cost at least $25. You have to print posters to publicize and programs for the guests, and you got a quote from a print shop of $125 for 50 posters and 100 programs. So how do you produce your show on just $100? You learn to make do with less.

- Get a sponsor to donate money to pay for your scripts in exchange for the back page ad on your program. If that won't work, borrow scripts from area theatre teachers or on your library's book loan program. This may take several weeks, so find your scripts well in advance of your show. Be advised that if you borrow scripts, students will not be allowed to write in them. You will need to put all stage directions and notes onto sticky notes and remove them when you return your scripts. Alternatively, ask your teacher to purchase the scripts so that the school will have a classroom set, or, as a last resort, ask each student to pay for and keep their own. Any one of these options will save you around $56 (plus shipping).

- Explain to the publisher that this is a student production. Ask if you are required to pay royalties or if there is a special rate. If royalties are required, consider a small fundraiser to pay for them, or sell an ad in your program specifically to cover that cost.

- Use an old binder for your production notebook and either make or use recycled dividers and other items.

- Again, you can borrow costumes from area theatre teachers, put your play in a time period for which you do have costumes, or update it to modern times and allow students to provide their own costumes. If that will not work, find a sewing club either at school or in your town and ask them to make your costumes. You will probably need to have fabric, notions, and patterns donated, but you'll have plenty of space for free ads in your program. Many organizations, including your church or the Rotary or Lions Club, will help. Sometimes they ask that you perform for them at their monthly meetings, volunteer to staff booths at fairs, or provide them with unlimited free tickets and dedicate your performance to them. Network with these organizations, and always return favors in greater volume than they were given to you. It is the sincerest form of appreciation.

- When possible, find a way to make props rather than buying them. It could cost $25 or more to buy a vintage suitcase, but you could have your woodshop class make one out of scrap lumber and hinges. You may have to purchase a handle or recycle one. Ask your art teacher if there is a student who would be willing to paint the prop to look authentic (providing a picture is always helpful), and then thank all of the students and teachers who helped in your program. Not only have you saved money, but you've also added a stock piece to your prop room.

- If you do have set needs, consider **minimalism**. *This is the practice of putting as little onto your set as possible.* For example, if your play is set in a living room and you are supposed to have a lot of fancy furniture, you might make more of a visual impact by having five plain white flats at various angles and depths with seemingly random spacing between them to serve as doors and windows. Backlight these and they'll almost glow! Add six large, black cubes to serve as chairs, a sofa, and a coffee table. With this simple black-and-white set, imagine the impact you can make with a prop as simple as a scarlet coffee cup or a girl dressed completely in black and white with red lipstick! Chances are your teacher has most of these materials or something similar already in stock.

NOTES: ______________________________

____

____

____

____

____

____

____

- Printing may not even be your job, but if it s, there are ways to get around this expense too. The most common way is to make the printing pay for itself by selling advertising space in your program. If that is not an option, keep the programs in a simple black-and-white design, and print them on a copy machine. You will have to fold and staple them yourself, if that is how they are designed. Since you will not need as many posters as programs, you can do several color posters directly off your computer's printer, then print the rest on a copy machine in black and white. There are color copiers, but they are not as affordable as the black-and-white option. If you do want a splash of color, print black-and-white copies on colored paper. You can reduce your print costs from $125 to about $15 by using these corner-cutting ideas.

Now you know how to work with a smaller budget. But you will probably still end up with some expenses. Here are a few questions to ask your teacher:

Do I have a budget? _______________________   If so, how much can I spend? ________________

What access will I have to the following:

- The theatre department's props?

- The theatre department's costumes?

- The theatre department's stock set pieces?

- Free or discount printing?

- Free scripts?

- Office supplies?

- What is the policy for making purchases?

- If I make the purchase, what is the procedure and time frame for being reimbursed?

- Do I have access to a tax-exempt number for purchases?

- Are there any other rules, restrictions, or guidelines regarding purchases?

     215

NOTES: ____

____

____

____

____

____

____

NAME _______________________________________ PERIOD _______ DATE ___________

BUDGET LEDGER

Use the ledger sheet below to track your budget. Record everything you spend in the debit column; incoming money will be recorded as a credit. If you want to keep your budget separated by individual categories (such as props, costumes, set, etc.), make several copies of this budget ledger and label each one accordingly. Then you can skip the second column unless you also want sub-categories.

SHOW: ____

DIRECTOR: ____

Is this the budget for the production or for a specific category? ______________

STARTING BUDGET

$ __________

DESCRIPTION	CATEGORY	DEBIT (money spent)	CREDIT (money collected)	RUNNING BALANCE
		–	+	
		–	+	
		–	+	
		–	+	
		–	+	
		–	+	
		–	+	
		–	+	
		–	+	
		–	+	
		–	+	
		–	+	
		–	+	
		–	+	
		–	+	
		–	+	
		–	+	
		–	+	
		–	+	
		–	+	
		–	+	
		–	+	

NOTES: ____

____

____

____

____

____

____

____

CHAPTER 7 — PRODUCTION 101

NAME ____ PERIOD _________ DATE _______________

PRODUCTION NEEDS LIST

As you direct your play, you will note and track your production's various requirements, including all props, costume features (pockets, suspenders, anything that affects the scene progress), specific set requirements, sound effects, and so on. If there is high danger of an item being damaged, mark the risk factor as "high."

ITEM NEEDED/ DESCRIPTION	SCENE/PAGE	RISK FACTOR	BORROWED FROM OR DONATED BY	DATE RETURNED
		HIGH MEDIUM LOW		
		HIGH MEDIUM LOW		
		HIGH MEDIUM LOW		
		HIGH MEDIUM LOW		
		HIGH MEDIUM LOW		
		HIGH MEDIUM LOW		
		HIGH MEDIUM LOW		
		HIGH MEDIUM LOW		
		HIGH MEDIUM LOW		
		HIGH MEDIUM LOW		
		HIGH MEDIUM LOW		

   217

NOTES: ____

____

____

____

____

____

____

____

INTRODUCTION TO THEATRE ARTS 2

PRODUCTION 101 JOURNAL

OBJECTIVE You will record a daily diary of your experiences and will answer various questions about your progress.

Directing a show, especially your first, can be a very emotional, exhilarating roller coaster ride. Hopefully you will direct many more—or at least be in many more—so having a journal today that you can enjoy reflecting upon for years to come will be a priceless part of your experience. Record your truest thoughts because this is for you, not your teacher. Your teacher will look at your journal but not read it unless you ask.

On the days you are asked to respond to a prompt, do so thoroughly, because prompts will be read to ensure you are continuing to make progress. On those days, writing in the journal is optional. If you choose not to record a journal entry, write "See Prompt # _____" largely in the journal space.

PROMPT #1:

If you were directing your show alongside the original playwright, how would the playwright expect you to costume your show? Whether you plan to use this style of costuming or not, begin gathering or sketching pictures of what you think the playwright intended for each character's costume.

PROMPT #2:

How do you plan to costume your show? How is this similar to or different from the playwright's intent? Justify your reasoning for your choices.

PROMPT #3: Select either A or B

A) If you are costuming as the playwright intended, will your actors or costumer face any unusual challenges? What are they, and how will you overcome them?

B) If you are costuming differently from the playwright's intent, in what ways might you blend the "original" style with your own?

PROMPT #4:

If money was not an issue and if you had a professional scenery staff at your disposal, how would your set or sets look? Either describe or sketch your ideas and explain them.

PROMPT #5:

Are there some elements of your dream set from Prompt #4 that you can implement into your actual set? How will you accomplish this?

PROMPT #6:

What are some of the music and sound effects you need or plan to use in your production? How will you get these?

PROMPT #7:

Pantomime can be an effective solution to a show with an unusual number of props. A form of minimalism, pantomime eliminates clutter from the stage, forcing the audience to focus more on action and dialogue and less on "things." Can you justify a show in which props are pantomimed? Would it change the way you envision your costuming, set, lighting, and sound? Explain.

PROMPT #8:

If you could invite five people who influenced you to come see your performance, who would they be and why? If they are living, your job is to let each of these five people know how they touched your life and invite them to attend your show. If they are not living, find someone to come in this person's place (such as a close family member). You will reserve ten seats of honor for these five individuals and their guests. If you are printing tickets, send two tickets to each, and remember to reserve the seats. Be sure to greet and thank these guests after your show.

PROMPT #9:

Regarding your production, what has been your greatest challenge so far? What has been your happiest moment? Have you had any memorable "bloopers" or unexpected funny moments? Explain.

PROMPT #10:

Assuming you direct another show, what would you do differently next time? Why? What has been your biggest success or milestone thus far? Do you plan to direct another show some day? Explain.

NOTES: ____

____

____

____

____

____

____

____

Also appears as page 219 of the Student Workbook

NAME ____

PRODUCTION JOURNAL, WEEK ____

MONDAY, _______ /_______ /_______

TUESDAY, _______ /_______ /_______

WEDNESDAY, _______ /_______ /_______

Also appears as page 220 of the Student Workbook

THURSDAY, _______ / _______ / _______

FRIDAY, _______ / _______ / _______

Permission to photocopy this page granted with purchase of book. Non-transferable.

CHAPTER 7 — PRODUCTION 101

NAME _____________________________________ PERIOD _______ DATE _____________

PRODUCTION PROGRESS REPORT

OBJECTIVE You will complete a column one day each week to keep your teacher updated on your progress.

Once a week, your teacher will ask you to complete one column of your progress report to ensure that you are where you should be in your production.

- Start by writing the dates for the week in the top row such as "Week of 3/6 to 3/10."
- Each row has an element or goal for your show; give yourself a reasonable deadline for completing each goal, and write the actual date in the square for that week (if your deadline is 3/7, write 3/7 under the Week of 3/5 to 3/10).
- It may help you to highlight each deadline; avoid putting deadlines too close together.
- Each week, code each row to let your teacher know how much progress you have made on that item.

	Leaving the space blank means no progress or have not started
S	Started but not halfway complete
/	At least half complete
	Almost finished
	The job is finished and ready for opening night

WEEK OF:												
Show is cast												
Legal scripts acquired												
Costumes designed												
Costumes ready												
Prop list complete												
All props ready												
Set designed												
All set pieces ready												
Rehearsing with set												
Blocking complete												
Lines memorized												
Technical crew fully staffed												
Light cues complete												
Run show with lights												
Sound cues complete												
Run show with sound												
Makeup/hair needs listed												
Programs complete												
Posters complete												
Tickets complete												
House staffed for performances												

221

NOTES: ____

____

____

____

____

____

____

____

INTRODUCTION TO THEATRE ARTS 2

UNDERSTANDING YOUR PRODUCTION'S VOCABULARY

OBJECTIVE All members of your company will understand and properly pronounce and use all vocabulary from the script as well as vocabulary not in the script, but which is directly associated with the genre, time period, culture, and other elements of the production.

Hopefully you have challenged yourself and your actors with a script that has at least a few new vocabulary words, or perhaps you are introducing them to a type of theatre that is new to your classmates. Either way, there will be a great deal to learn, and as the director, you have also taken on the role of teacher.

Not only is it extremely important to know what these words mean, but your actors must also be able to pronounce them *in character*. Unfamiliar words, phrases, dialects, colloquialisms (words unique to various regions), pop culture (such as vocabulary common to your generation but not your parents'), historical vocabulary, and even people, places, and ideas made popular by the news will crop up in plays and scenes. Actors must be able to say them as their characters would; if they do not understand what they are saying, it will show. If they are nervous, difficult words will get tangled in their mouths, and they will break character stumbling on them. It is the actor's job to learn what things mean, and they should do this outside of rehearsal time. But if they do not learn the vocabulary on their own, the director must be prepared to teach.

Even though words are familiar, phrases may mean something altogether different. Take this phrase: *"break the ice."* All the words in the phrase are very basic, but younger actors or those from another country may see that phrase and become confused. "Why 'break the ice'? There's no ice in this scene!" It is actually an older phrase out of the shipping industry that refers to the smaller boats that went ahead of the ships in cold climates and broke the ice that formed atop the waters. This allowed the larger vessels to pass without fear of becoming icebound, because getting stuck could result in a huge loss in business. Today, the phrase means to get to know someone or to ease the pressure among group members who don't know one another very well.

Improperly learning lines is another bad habit. One director recounts a very simple line from *The Ransom of Red Chief* by Anne Coulter Martens: "I'm going to burn you at the stake at dawn!" Early in the rehearsal process, the director thought the actor playing Red was saying the line wrong, but there were always so many other things of higher priority, the director never said anything. As the show progressed, it finally made its way into post-rehearsal notes as the director began hearing the other actors make the same mistake. Sure enough, the actor had simply learned the line wrong, and the other two actors picked up on the bad habit. When they realized the humor in their mistake, they all got a good laugh out of it, but frustration soon set in when they learned it was a hard habit to break. All three broke character repeatedly when they got to the line. Their director learned an important lesson: Make vocabulary an *early* priority.

Use copies of the worksheet on the following page both to learn and to teach your company the language of your show. Include words that you use in rehearsal or that they need to know in order to understand the play but that are not in the script. Keep a copy of the updated worksheet on the callboard or backstage and find ways to incorporate pronunciation issues and good habits into your warm-up activities before rehearsals.

NOTES: ____

____

____

____

____

____

____

____

CHAPTER 7 — PRODUCTION 101

NAME ______________________________________ PERIOD _______ DATE _____________

PRODUCTION VOCABULARY

Name of show: ____

Director: ____

All cast and crew are responsible for knowing the following vocabulary and its proper usage and pronunciation. If you have questions about a word or phrase in the script or one that is used in rehearsal but is not on this list, please add it. Let your director know when new words are added so that they may be taught to the rest of the company.

WORD	PAGE	SPEAKER	PRONUNCIATION and MEANING

  223

NOTES: ____

____

____

____

____

____

____

____

NAME ____ PERIOD _______ DATE _____________

BLOOPERS

Name of show: ____

Director: ____

Okay, enough of all that serious stuff. It's time to make memories! Every show has its bloopers—those funny moments when something happens and even your director "breaks character" and has a much deserved laugh. These little accidents, spoonerisms, and funnies are priceless, and long after your lead has forgotten a critical line or your lighting techs have figured out why that one light keeps slipping, you'll still get a kick out of your show's bloopers. So don't let them slip away! When a blooper happens, record it in one of these clouds.

NOTES: ____

____

____

____

____

____

____

____

CHAPTER 7 — PRODUCTION 101

NAME _________________________________ PERIOD ________ DATE ______________

PRODUCTION CHECKLIST FOR
STUDENT-DIRECTED SCENES AND PLAYS

SHOW: ____

NAME	JOB TITLE
	Director
	Lights
	Sound

BEFORE AUDITIONS	Major grade, Daily grade, None?	Assigned to	Grade
Create production binder; put this list at the front	M D N		
Seek administrative approval for play, if needed	M D N		
Secure performance date from teacher: ________________	M D N		
Reserve rehearsal space and times, if required	M D N		
Request permission to perform from publisher	M D N		
Purchase or gather scripts	M D N		
Advertise auditions	M D N		
Print audition applications	M D N		
Print audition numbers, score cards, etc.	M D N		
	M D N		

         225

NOTES: ____

____

____

____

____

____

____

____

____

INTRODUCTION TO THEATRE ARTS 2

AUDITIONS	Major grade, Daily grade, None?	Assigned to:	Grade:
Take pictures of (or collect pictures from) all who audition	M D N		
Collect and organize all paperwork	M D N		
Post cast	M D N		
	M D N		
	M D N		

REHEARSALS	Major grade, Daily grade, None?	Assigned to:	Grade:
Post and distribute Rehearsal Calendar	M D N		
Block show	M D N		
Gather props	M D N		
Publicize show	M D N		
Send personal invitations to show	M D N		
Design and print programs	M D N		
Design and print posters	M D N		
Design and print tickets	M D N		
Design lights; add to show	M D N		
Design sound; add to show	M D N		
Put fresh batteries in backstage and communication devices; Charge headsets, flashlights, etc.	M D N		
Have stage cleaned, if needed	M D N		
Complete set construction	M D N		
Take pictures of students in dress rehearsal for scrapbook or display	M D N		
Complete scrapbook or display	M D N		

NOTES: ____

____

____

____

____

____

____

____

CHAPTER 7 — PRODUCTION 101

PERFORMANCES	Major grade, Daily grade, None?	Assigned to:	Grade:
Make price signs for tickets	M D N		
Get change for box office ___$1, ___$5, ___$10 = Total $; prepare box office	M D N		
Sound check	M D N		
Prepare house area for guests • Who will have keys? ________________ • Music in lobby? Y N Title: ______________ • Unlock doors to lobby at _______________ • Open theater doors at ________________ • Check restroom cleanliness/supplies	M D N		
	M D N		
	M D N		

POST PERFORMANCE	Major grade, Daily grade, None?	Assigned to:	Grade:
Clean dressing areas	M D N		
Return or store costumes and props	M D N		
Clean additional areas:	M D N		
Secure lights, sound, etc.	M D N		
Secure proceeds	M D N		
Strike set	M D N		
Write thank you notes	M D N		
	M D N		
	M D N		

NOTES: ____

____

____

____

____

____

____

____

FROM THE DIRECTOR'S SEAT KEY

1. DIRECTOR
2. SCRIPTS
   PUBLISHER
   ROYALTIES
3. CREW
   PRACTICE
4. CLOSED
   OPEN
5. PREPARED
   COLD
6. SIDES
   MONOLOGUE
   MUSICAL
   IMPROVISATION
7. CALLBACKS
8. CAST
   CALLBOARD
9. REHEARSALS
   READ THROUGH
10. BLOCKING
    STAGE DIRECTIONS
11. WORKING
    SET
    POLISHING
    TECHNICAL
    DRESS
12. COSTUME
    SCENERY
    LIGHTING
    SOUND
    PUBLICITY
    STAGE MANAGER
    HOUSE
13. STRIKE

NAME ____ PERIOD ________ DATE ____________

FROM THE DIRECTOR'S SEAT

Use the clues below to complete the description of how a director prepares a play for performance, and then find the same words hidden in the puzzle.

1. The artistic leader or "boss" in a play production is the _ _ _ _ _ _ o _.

2. Before holding auditions, the director (or in professional theatre, the producer) reads many _ _ _ _ _ _ s in search of the perfect play. Once a play is selected, the director must request permission to perform from the p _ _ _ _ _ _ _ _. If granted, the director will pay _ o _ _ _ _ e _, although some plays do not require this fee.

3. The play's director is responsible for selecting both the actors and the technical c _ _ _. In school productions, the actors usually _ _ _ _ _ i _ _ to prepare for their audition. The crew is generally a specialized group selected from a highly trained class.

4. In professional theatre, a _ _ _ _ _ d audition means that only union actors may try out while an _ p _ _ audition allows both non-union and union actors to audition.

5. If actors are allowed to work on particular scenes in advance and then audition with those scenes, the audition is _ _ _ _ a _ e _. However, if actors are not told which scenes to practice, the audition is referred to as a _ o _ _ audition.

6. At auditions, the actors may read from s _ d _ _, from the script, or they may do a _ _ _ _ l _ _ _ _ audition. This is where they are given a slot of time to perform their piece and in some cases a song (if the production is a _ _ s _ _ _ _ or requires singing). There are other types of auditions, too, such as one in which _ _ _ _ _ v _ _ _ _ _ _ _ is used to test actors' abilities to work spontaneously.

7. If the director cannot cast the show after one audition, there will be _ _ _ l _ _ _ _ _, where the director will only bring back those actors still being considered.

8. Once the play is _ a _ _, the director will post a rehearsal schedule on the _ _ l l _ _ _ _ _. This is the place actors must train themselves to look every day. It will become the information pathway between the director and the actors.

9. One of the first r e _ _ _ _ _ _ _ _ will probably be a _ _ _ d   t h _ _ _ _ _ of the play. This gives the actors a chance to hear the play in its entirety with the cast reading their parts. At this time, the director will answer questions, offer corrections on pronunciations, and give insight into characterizations, plus much more.

10. Most directors make b _ _ _ k _ _ _ the play their next priority. Some will use the movement suggested by the s t _ _ _   _ _ _ e c _ _ _ _ _ in the script, but most have their own ideas. Still others will allow the actors to move about freely until they have established a comfortable pattern of movement. A combination of these blocking techniques is probably the most common method used.

11. The following few weeks will likely be devoted to w _ _ k _ _ _ rehearsals, during which actors can focus on their characters, the relationships between the characters, and getting comfortable with all the facets of the production. When props are added and the crew has almost completed the _ e _, it will be time for _ _ _ _ s h _ _ _ rehearsals. At this time, actors should be able to get through the play without calling for lines and while working with a basic set and all props. When the set is finished and lights, sound, costumes, and special effects are added, the director will want to do a _ _ _ _ n _ c _ _ rehearsal to combine all of the elements. It may take a couple of these rehearsals to get everything working the way the director wants. During this phase, actors must be patient. These rehearsals will focus on the tech crew and their many jobs. Lastly, in the days preceding opening night, the director

---

Without a word bank or preceding lesson, this puzzle could be the perfect challenge for a day when you need your students to be engaged, quiet, and focused. Remind students that they can seek combinations of letters (provided in the clues) in the puzzle to help them find the words if they get stuck.

will want to conduct at least one <u>d</u> _ _ _ <u>s</u> rehearsal. This should run just as the show will run when there is an audience. This will be the director's final chance to make any corrections, additions, or changes prior to opening night.

12. During the rehearsal process, a great deal has been happening behind the scenes. The _ _ _ _ <u>u</u> _ <u>e</u> crew has been busy making sure the actors have something to wear, while the set crew has been building the _ _ _ <u>n</u> _ _ <u>y</u>. The _ _ <u>g</u> _ _ _ _ _ and _ _ _ _ <u>d</u> crews have been working to make sure the audience can see and hear the actors in the director's artistic vision, and the _ _ <u>b</u> _ _ <u>c</u> _ _ _ crew has worked hard to ensure that there is an audience to see the show. All of the backstage jobs are managed by the _ _ _ _ <u>e</u> _ _ <u>n a</u> _ _ _, and the <u>h</u> _ _ _ _ manager makes sure everything runs smoothly for the audience's enjoyment.

13. Finally, it's opening night. The director's job is almost done. The director will get to enjoy the show, but after the run, will still have a few loose ends to secure. The crew (and in educational and community theatre, the actors) must _ _ _ _ <u>k</u> _ the set and store the costumes and props. The stage must be returned to its normal state so that the next production may begin.

D	L	O	C	O	L	R	O	Y	A	L	T	I	E	S	H	S	M	R	R
S	I	X	P	A	S	T	P	U	B	L	I	S	H	E	R	N	U	E	E
T	Z	R	R	S	I	D	E	S	I	D	O	G	R	U	N	O	S	A	C
G	R	Q	E	T	R	I	N	C	A	C	T	B	B	U	I	I	I	D	N
E	E	U	P	C	R	E	W	R	S	L	C	L	H	O	W	T	C	T	A
A	H	O	A	L	T	R	E	I	A	K	A	O	D	I	R	C	A	H	D
E	E	T	R	O	L	O	E	P	G	B	L	C	U	Y	M	E	L	R	G
T	K	H	E	S	O	E	R	T	H	G	L	K	I	E	R	R	B	O	N
E	R	I	D	E	K	S	K	S	N	S	B	I	C	S	E	I	R	U	I
C	P	L	R	D	B	U	Z	I	M	M	A	N	H	S	U	D	E	G	S
H	U	I	H	T	D	E	K	R	R	M	C	G	A	E	G	E	G	H	L
N	B	G	E	I	S	R	A	N	M	T	K	A	R	R	O	G	A	S	A
I	L	H	S	L	O	Y	C	G	A	T	S	E	A	D	L	A	N	M	S
C	I	O	U	W	S	R	E	H	E	R	S	E	L	C	O	T	A	U	R
A	C	S	O	U	N	E	E	A	U	D	I	T	I	O	N	S	M	T	A
L	I	G	H	T	I	N	G	A	N	S	T	A	G	U	O	E	E	S	E
I	T	L	W	E	A	E	T	U	H	O	R	R	E	I	M	R	G	O	H
G	Y	O	T	S	A	C	O	C	A	L	L	B	O	A	R	D	A	C	E
H	O	P	O	L	I	S	H	I	N	G	P	O	S	H	I	L	T	M	R
I	M	P	R	O	V	I	S	A	T	I	O	N	E	M	U	T	S	O	C

FROM THE DIRECTOR'S SEAT SOLUTION

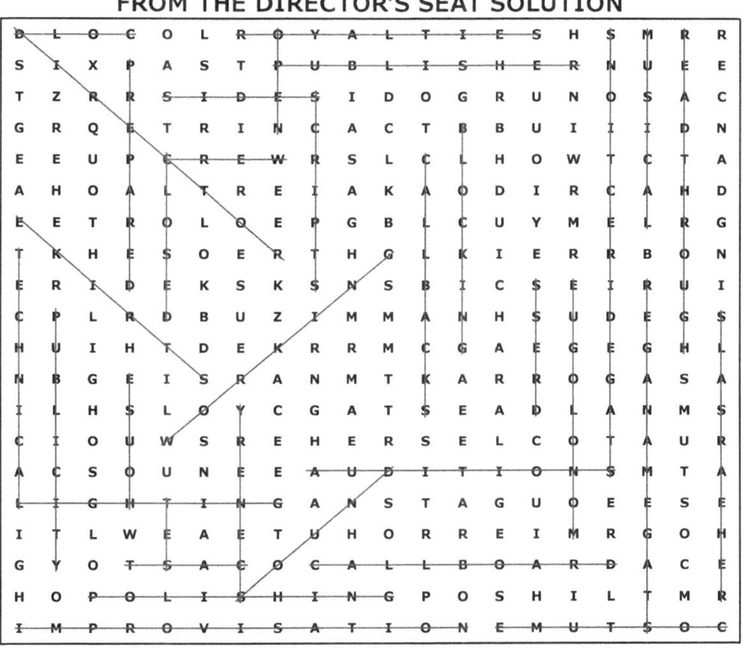

USING THE PRODUCTION CHECKLIST

It doesn't matter how many shows you direct, it is always a new experience. Even the most seasoned, expert, award-winning directors can become a little frazzled and frayed. It never fails that opening night is accompanied by several thoughts of "Oh, darn, I didn't do such and such," or "I wish I had thought to do so and so."

Every campus is different too. At one campus, an office manager may handle custodial requests, adding items to the calendar, or paying certain bills. A teacher gets used to this pampering and goes to another campus only to learn on opening night that the air coditioner was never turned on and that the bathrooms have no toilet paper. It is no particular person's fault; rather, it is just how things are done differently from one place to the next, and it's impossible to predict every possible need. The only way to ensure that everything will be as perfect as you desire is to know how to plan and be prepared for the unexpected. It is also vital to learn to accept imperfection and to learn to delegate.

It's likely that you will be directing a play in addition to teaching this class. The following *Production Checklist* is thorough and might be too detailed for most teachers. Before you begin to write on yours, make a copy and mark out anything you will not need. For example, if you do not plan to sell program ads, mark through anything mentioning them. Then use the extra spaces throughout the form to add other items as needed. Make another copy of this blank edited form and file it away. If these omissions and additions are items you would change with every play, you now have a master copy of a customized production checklist ready for other shows you direct in the future.

Once your play is finished, file the completed form away for future reference. When your next show rolls around, use the checklist to remind yourself of anything that might have caught you off guard. You'll also find your notes and time lines helpful if you ever direct the same play again.

Following this checklist are two other forms that will help you have a smoothly running show: *Box Office Instructions and Count* and *Publicity Checklist*. Feel free to work from copies of these pages and keep these as masters to help you with all your shows. You can also give copies of these forms to your student directors if they will have box office or publicity responsibilities.

After these two forms, the *Production Progress Report* and the *Production Project Rubric* will help you evaluate your student directors and monitor their progress. You will need a copy of these evaluation tools for each student director.

PRODUCTION CHECKLIST

Areas recommended for cast and crew members are in bold.
Areas recommended for parent volunteers are highlighted in gray.

SHOW ____ DATES _______________________

BEFORE AUDITIONS · ASSIGNED TO

		ASSIGNED TO
	Create master production binder or file; put this list at the front	
	Seek administrative approval for play, if needed	
	Put play on school calendar	
	Reserve rehearsal space and times, if required	
	Request permission to perform from publisher	
	Order scripts	
	Schedule and advertise auditions	
	Create sides for auditions, if necessary	
	Print audition applications	
	Print audition numbers, score cards, etc.	

AT AUDITIONS · ASSIGNED TO

		ASSIGNED TO
	Take pictures of (or collect pictures from) all who audition	
	Collect all paperwork	
	Explain audition expectations:	
	Behavior	
	How to audition (what director seeks from actors)	
	How auditions will be run	
	Call backs and other auditions, if needed	
	Discuss rehearsals:	
	Schedule	
	Attendance	
	Expectations and actor responsibilities	
	Discuss any fees actors will incur during the production	
	Discuss what actors will need to do themselves during production	
	Discuss what role parents/adults will be asked to play during production	
	Hold auditions	

AFTER AUDITIONS

		ASSIGNED TO
	Post cast list	
	Create rehearsal schedule	
	Create production packet:	
	Fees	
	Parent volunteers	
	Contract	
	Rehearsal schedule	
	Costume info	
	Program advertisement information	
	Bio worksheet	
	Other:	
	Order shirts	
	Schedule and announce parent meeting	
	Arrange for outside assistance or contractors where needed	
	Sound	
	Lights	
	Set	
	Costumes	
	Photographer	

PARENT MEETING

		ASSIGNED TO
	Collect Production Contracts if not already done	
	Collect fees for all participants	
	Collect program bios from all participants	
	Discuss ads for program	
	Discuss parent volunteers needed	

REHEARSALS

		ASSIGNED TO
	Memorization deadlines:	
	Pages _______ through _______ by ____________	
	Pages _______ through _______ by ____________	
	Pages _______ through _______ by ____________	

SIX WEEKS OUT · ASSIGNED TO

	SIX WEEKS OUT	ASSIGNED TO
	Have students make cuts in their scripts	
	Finish blocking show	

FIVE WEEKS OUT · ASSIGNED TO

	FIVE WEEKS OUT	ASSIGNED TO
	Collect program ads and ad money	
	Take pictures for program	

FOUR WEEKS OUT · ASSIGNED TO

	FOUR WEEKS OUT	ASSIGNED TO
	Create programs	
	Have cast and crew check name spellings	

THREE WEEKS OUT · ASSIGNED TO

	THREE WEEKS OUT	ASSIGNED TO
	Have all props gathered and ready	
	File news releases	
	Invite newspaper to dress rehearsal or other rehearsals	
	Request any performance arrangements needed for each performance:	
	Chairs	
	Air conditioner	
	Custodial attention	
	Administration's attendance	
	Security	
	Have stage cleaned if needed	
	Have programs printed	
	Have posters printed	
	Have tickets printed (and numbered if needed for reservations)	
	Send personal invitations and/or tickets to:	
	Administration	
	Staff	
	Superintendent and School Board	
	Previous students	

CONT. THREE WEEKS OUT   ASSIGNED TO

Other theatre teachers within the district	
Those who bought program ads	
Patrons	

TWO WEEKS OUT   ASSIGNED TO

Charge headsets	
Replace batteries on all battery-operated items (headsets, microphones, flashlights)	
Complete set construction	

WEEK BEFORE SHOW   ASSIGNED TO

Take pictures of students in dress rehearsal for scrapbook or display	
Complete scrapbook or display	
Begin ticket pre-sales	
Organize reservations, if needed	
Make price signs for tickets	
Get change for box office (___change, ___$1, ___$5, ___$10=Total $___)	
Buy/arrange for concessions	
Make price signs for concessions	
Get change for concessions (___change, ___$1, ___$5, ___$10=Total $___)	

OPENING NIGHT (DATE: ___________)   ASSIGNED TO

Prepare sound system	
Check to ensure all cables are secured, marked with glow tape if needed	
Check headphone power levels and reception	
Prepare microphones	
Prepare all music and sound effects	
Perform sound check	
Prepare box office ☐ Tickets ☐ Programs ☐ Cash box ☐ Reservations ☐ Seating for volunteers	
Prepare area for concessions ☐ Concessions ☐ Prices ☐ Cash box (with change)	
Set up table for other additional business ☐ Shirts ☐ Scrapbooks ☐ Club pamphlets ☐ Information on becoming a patron ☐ Fundraiser ☐ Keepsake items (programs, posters, photos)	
Prepare house area for guests ☐ Who will have keys? ☐ Unlock doors to lobby at ______ ☐ Open theater doors at ______ ☐ Check restroom cleanliness ☐ Provide seating for patrons with special needs before house opens ☐ Music in lobby Y N Title: ________________ ☐ Will concessions be sold before house opens? Y N	

CONT. OPENING NIGHT   ASSIGNED TO

	Start pre-show music at _______________________	

AFTER EACH PERFORMANCE   SHOW DATE: CHECKED BY

	Reset props for next performance						
	Properly store all costume pieces						
	Clean dressing areas						
	Clean makeup area						
	Clean following additional areas: _______________________ _______________________ _______________________ _______________________						
	Secure sound system appropriately						
	Secure light system appropriately						
	Secure money						
	Release students after final group roll call						
	Lock doors						
	Set alarm						

AFTER FINAL PERFORMANCE   ASSIGNED TO

	Count and deposit proceeds	
	Collect rented or borrowed costumes	
	Strike set	
	Return borrowed props	
	Properly store department-owned props	
	Sort and store lumber	
	Sort and store set pieces	
	Clean stage	
	Organize and store makeup	
	Collect scripts	
	Write thank you notes	

BOX OFFICE INSTRUCTIONS AND COUNT

Show: ____

Performance Date/Time: _______________________________________

Bank — Amount in cashbox prior to show: $ ______________   Source: _______________________

Final Box Office:

$100s and $50s _______________	Coins _______________
$20s _______________	Checks _______________
$10s _______________	Credit Cards _______________
$5s _______________	Other _______________
$1s _______________	Performance Total: _______________

Counted by: _______________   &   _______________

Box Office Information:

- Please make checks payable to _______________________________
- Any person handling box office money must be listed below for security purposes:

  _______________________   _______________________

  _______________________   _______________________

  _______________________   _______________________

- When in doubt about a reservation or comp ticket, please honor the request and put the patron's name and phone number on the bottom of this form. It will be resolved later.
- Any patron entering the show during the performance must have a ticket. Please continue selling tickets until the end of the show. If a patron does not wish to pay due to coming late yet insists on entering, allow them to enter only after taking their name and phone number so that the ticket may be settled later.
- Two people must count the money after each performance and sign off on this form.
- After the count, please return this form and the cashbox to _______________________

Complimentary Tickets at Will Call (or place tickets in envelopes with patrons' names):

  _______________________   _______________________

  _______________________   _______________________

  _______________________   _______________________

Notes or Concerns:

PUBLICITY CHECKLIST

Show Dates and Times: ____

Publicity Chairperson: ____

Publicity Committee: ____

Duty	Assigned to	Deadline	Completed?
Announce cast on school PA			
Cast news releases to papers			
Program design			
Student biographies for program			
Ads for program			
Print program			
Poster design			
Print poster			
Distribute posters			
Ticket design			
Print ticket			
Flyer design			
Print flyer			
Distribute flyers			
Invite newspapers to rehearsal			
News releases to papers			
News releases to radio			
Performance announcement on school PA			
Picture collage for lobby			
Invite administration/school board			

NAME ____ PERIOD _________ DATE _______________

PRODUCTION PROJECT RUBRIC

Congratulations! You have been selected to be a Student Director. This rubric will serve as your guide throughout the production process.

The following items are duties or jobs a director has. Some, though probably not all, will also be part of your job as a student director. Your teacher may have already indicated which will be part of your job. If not, do not be afraid to ask.

ASSIGNMENTS If an assignment will be graded, write the number of points or the weight of each part in the appropriate space to the right. Use the extra spaces for additional requirements.	Required for daily grade	Required for major grade	Required for notebook grade	Optional	Do not attempt	The best person to consult for assistance with this item	Check when completed
CREATE A PRODUCTION NOTEBOOK ☐ Follow the steps from the worksheet titled *Your Production's Brain* in this chapter. ☐ File items as they come into your possession. ☐ Take and use your binder at every rehearsal. ☐ Turn your binder in to your teacher after you have completed all of your post-production duties. ☐ _______________________							
MAKE A PRODUCTION CALENDAR ☐ Use the *Production Calendar Template* in this Section. ☐ Include all important dates and times including rehearsals, meetings, set construction, deadlines, and anything else that may be of importance. ☐ Remind cast and crew members what will be targeted at each rehearsal. ☐ Check with your teacher to ensure there are no conflicts with your dates. ☐ Give a copy to your teacher and to each participant in your cast and crew. Post several where students may easily find them including the callboard, backstage, and in the Production Notebook. ☐ _______________________							
SELECT YOUR LITERATURE ☐ Select a play and get your teacher's approval. ☐ Determine how to track students' scripts; if they are borrowed, do not number them; if they are yours or if your teacher allows, number each script and document who is using each one; collect these in the week following your show. ☐ Charge students for lost scripts PLUS shipping, if they did not purchase their own. ☐ _______________________							

ASSIGNMENTS If an assignment will be graded, write the number of points or the weight of each part in the appropriate space to the right. Use the extra spaces for additional requirements.	Required for daily grade	Required for major grade	Required for notebook grade	Optional	Do not attempt	The best person to consult for assistance with this item	Check when completed
PRODUCTION VOCABULARY ☐ Create a vocabulary and pronunciation list for your production using the *Production Vocabulary Chart*. ☐ Work with your company to ensure they understand each word and how it is used in your production. Make sure they are speaking with proper emphasis and pronunciation. ☐ _________________________							
MAKE A DIRECTOR'S MASTER SCRIPT ☐ Use the directions on the worksheet *The Director's Master Script*. ☐ _________________________							
CREATE A PRODUCTION CONTRACT INCLUDING: ☐ Thorough contact information on each participant. ☐ Sizes and measurements for actors. ☐ Performance dates. ☐ A parent signature saying their child is available for performance and rehearsals. ☐ Additional information as found in *Creating a Production Contract*. ☐ Your rehearsal calendar. ☐ _________________________							
PROPS ☐ Create a prop list. ☐ Complete *Production 101 Prop List*. ☐ Assign someone to be in charge of props backstage and during each rehearsal: _________ ☐ Return all props within of one week following your production. Properly thank all who a lowed you to use their items. ☐ _________________________ _________________________							
COSTUMES ☐ Design costumes for your show according to your color palette. ☐ Gather or make costumes or assign someone to do this for you. ☐ Instruct actors on the care of their costumes; ensure all borrowed or rented costumes are well cared for. ☐ Check costume room after your final performance to ensure students left it in good condition. ☐ If students provide their own costumes, assist them in achieving the look you envision. ☐ Return rented costumes the first workday following your show; return other borrowed costumes within a week, properly thanking those who assisted you. ☐ _________________________ _________________________							

ASSIGNMENTS If an assignment will be graded, write the number of points or the weight of each part in the appropriate space to the right. Use the extra spaces for additional requirements.	Required for daily grade	Required for major grade	Required for notebook grade	Optional	Do not attempt	The best person to consult for assistance with this item	Check when completed
SET ☐ Design your set. ☐ Build your set or have someone do it for you. ☐ Strike (break down) your set and clear the performance area following the final performance. ☐ Return all borrowed items; thank each donor for allowing you to borrow the items. ☐ _______________							
LIGHTING ☐ Design your lighting or have a lighting designer do it for you. ☐ _______________							
SOUND ☐ Design your sound or have a sound specialist do it for you. ☐ _______________							
PUBLICITY ☐ Create programs. ☐ Create posters. ☐ Create tickets. ☐ Make announcements. ☐ Film a "commercial" or record an audio commercial for the school's announcements. ☐ _______________							
PREPARE HOUSE AREA FOR THE AUDIENCE ☐ _______________ ☐ _______________							
OTHER ☐ _______________ ☐ _______________							

GLOSSARY

Act (as in sections of a play): A large division of a play.

Acting Area: The part of the stage used for acting and visible to the audience.

Action: Movement.

Ad-lib: To add lines to a scene "spur of the moment."

Advertising Revenue: Money made by the network or station from the sale of commercial airtime.

Antagonist: The people, things, or ideas that prevent or try to prevent the protagonist from reaching their goal.

Assignment: A short or simple task.

Audibility: The ability to be heard.

Audition: Tryouts for a play.

Author's Intent: What the author probably meant or had in mind when the play was written.

Backdrop: Fabric that is suspended from battens and painted as scenery or background.

Backstage: The area behind the curtain or set that the audience cannot see.

Batten: A metal bar or piece of wood from which scenery, backdrops, draperies, and instruments are hung in the fly area above the actors' heads.

Blocking: The planned movement onstage.

Body Language: The messages sent with one's body position, posture, facial expressions, and gestures.

Border: Draperies that run the width of the stage above the actors' heads masking the rigging from the audience.

Brainstorm: To write without censoring as you go, jotting every thought that comes to mind on the subject at hand.

Button: A term used to describe the feeling of satisfaction when a scene ends well.

Callbacks: A later part of auditions in which actors being considered for parts are asked to audition again.

Callboard: A bulletin board where actors and crew can count on finding updated information about rehearsals and shows.

Cast List: The list of characters and often the actors originally assigned to the parts.

Character Part: A part in which the actor is asked to be very different from themself.

Characters: The fictitious personalities in a scene.

Cheat Out: To turn out more toward the audience; similar to "opening up to the audience," only may be more involved, such as moving a chair or shifting one's whole body.

Choral Reading: Another way to say "readers theater."

Choreography: Planned dance movements.

Clarity: The quality of being easy to understand.

Climax: The turning point in a story in which the protagonist either reaches or fails to reach their goal.

Closed Auditions: Auditions limited to certain people.

Cold Audition: An audition for which the actors are purposefully not prepared.

Company: Team of actors working together on a show.

Confidence: Belief in one's self; in performance, confidence is "fearlessness."

Conflict: An obstacle that prevents or slows a character from reaching their goal.

Copyright Page: The page of a script with legal information.

Cornerstone: Corner pieces that are glued to the stiles and rails on a flat and attached with hardware, giving additional support.

Costume: The clothing worn onstage to aid in the interpretation and expression of a character and situation.

Counterweight System: The systems of weights, ropes, and pulleys used to raise and lower draperies, scenery, and instruments onstage with ease.

Creativity: Use of artistry and originality in a performance.

Crew: A group of technicians assigned to a particular task (light crew, sound crew, costume crew, etc.).

Cut Drop: A backdrop with parts removed; what remains is reinforced with scrim, which is semi-transparent, giving the cut drop a three-dimensional effect.

Dance: To interpret music or feelings with rhythmic and/or patterned movements of the body.

Delivery: The act of saying the lines; often the term used to describe the quality of how the lines are said.

Denoument: (DAY-new-ma) Another word for falling action, when the protagonist wraps up the story.

Dialect: A regional accent.

Dialogue: Spoken lines.

Director: The artistic leader of a show.

Dramatic Structure: The basic formation of a story; includes exposition, rising action, climax, falling action, and ending.

Dramatization: To turn something into a script so that it may be performed.

Dress Rehearsal: A rehearsal in which everything is as it will be opening night, only there is no audience.

Dropping Off: Allowing final sounds or words to become inaudible.

Echo Effects: To repeat lines, words, phrases, and sounds creatively onstage.

Ending: The final wrap-up of the dramatic structure.

NOTES: ______________________________

INTRODUCTION TO THEATRE ARTS 2—TEACHER'S GUIDE

Engage: Actively listening, understanding, and reacting.

Ensemble Reading: Another way to say "readers theater."

Event: An important bit of action in a play.

Exposition: The beginning of a play in which readers or viewers learn about the characters and setting.

Facial Expressions: The messages sent with one's face.

Falling Action: Following the climax, it is the short time when loose ends are tightened and any remaining questions are answered.

Familiarize: To learn a piece well enough that the performer must look at the script only occasionally.

Federal Communications Commission (or FCC): Government agency in charge of overseeing licensing and enforcing legislation regarding broadcasting in the United States and its possessions.

First Impression: The way the performer comes across the moment the audience sees him; can include appearances, confidence, timely set up, preparation, professionalism, and so on.

Flats: Wooden frames with hinged braces on the back to help them stand.

Focus: The actor's ability to concentrate on the moment and not be distracted by memorization issues, distractions, and nervousness.

Force Focus: To position actors, props, lighting, and scenery in such a way as to "command" that the audience look a certain direction.

Foundation: The base color of makeup that matches the actor's skin.

Fourth Wall: The imaginary wall between the performers and the audience.

Freeze: To be absolutely still onstage either for effect or to simulate being "off" or "offstage."

Gender Bending: To place an actor into a role that was intended for an actor of the opposite sex; to put a boy in a female part or a girl in a male part without changing the gender of the character.

Gestures: Hand movements that are expressive.

Gimmicks: Devices used to win the approval of the audience.

Goal: What a character wants in a scene or story.

Grand Drape: The fancy front curtain onstage.

Groundrow: A piece of scenery designed to look like ground scenery which is often used to hide technical equipment.

Habits: Distracting tendencies that can be corrected with practice such as shifting weight nervously or saying "um."

Highlights: The raised or lighter places on a face that can be enhanced with lighter makeup.

Historical Plays: Plays that teach about people, places, and events of our past.

Hook: A figurative term for getting the audience's attention and holding it.

House: The audience part of the theater including the lobby, seats, and anywhere the audience may come and go at leisure; the place where the audience sits to view the show.

Improvisation: A type of acting that is unscripted and unprepared; spontaneous acting.

In the Scene: Being an active, listening character; also "in the moment."

Inciting Incident: The bit of action that starts the characters on their upward journey toward the climax.

Inflection: A change in the pitch of one's voice.

Introduction: A small section written by the speaker at the beginning of some scenes that helps connect the piece to the audience and often gives the playwright and title of the piece.

Issue Plays: Plays about the modern challenges faced by young people today.

Jingle: The song used to advertise a product.

Karaoke: A form of entertainment in which people sing popular songs into a microphone over prerecorded backing tracks.

Keystone: Slender pieces that are glued both to the stile and the toggle on a flat and attached with hardware, giving additional support.

Knowing Your Audience: To understand as much as possible about the group to whom you will be performing (or who will read your material) including their maturity, interests, challenges, goals, and so on.

Ledger: A form that is designed to track income and expenses.

Legs: Draperies that line the wings, masking from the audience actors awaiting cues.

Levels: Taking advantage of various visual planes including height, width, and depth; changes in pace, pitch, or volume to add interest and draw audience's attention.

Lighting: All of the devices and systems used to illuminate the show.

Lip-sync: A type of performance in which an actor or actors act as though they are the ones singing a song by synchronizing their lip movements to the words of the song; also includes acting out the story of the song and/or dancing.

Literature: In theatre, the literature is the selection of material or the script.

Logo: The symbol used to identify a product for advertising.

Losing the Audience: Becoming so creative that it becomes a distraction or becoming so creative that the audience doesn't get it.

Luan: Another name for quarter-inch plywood, a building material common in set building because it is lightweight.

Lyricist: A person who writes song lyrics.

Lyrics: The words in a song.

Makeup Morgue: A collection of faces and facial features that a makeup artist may reference to better understand how to apply makeup to resemble a desired effect.

Manual Sound Cues: Sound cues made using various contraptions and devices and which were made "live" during broadcast.

320

NOTES: ____

GLOSSARY

Master Director's Script: The script used by the director; this script is dissected and re-formatted to give more margin space for recording notes, stage directions, and blocking.

Memorize: To learn a piece so that it can be performed without prompting or looking at a script.

Message: The lesson the playwright intends for the audience/readers to learn.

Minimalism: The practice of using fewer props, costumes, sets, etc., to reduce clutter and force focus.

Monologue: A scene with one person, or dialogue from a scene in which only one person speaks.

Morality Plays: Dramas that seek to teach people to make moral choices.

Motto: The short phrase that summarizes the product and/or what the advertiser wants the buyer to think of it.

Movement: In theatre, the way an actor uses their body for interpretation.

Musical: A play in which a large portion of the story is told in song.

Narrative: A story.

Networks: Groups of radio stations owned and run by the same company.

Obstacles: Things that stand in the way (often figuratively) of one's goal.

Old Time Radio: The term used to describe radio from its beginnings to the age of television (when radio was replaced by TV as the center of family entertainment).

Onomatopoeia: The term used to describe words that sound like what they mean, like "pop" and "drip."

Open Auditions: Auditions that may be attended by anyone.

Open Up to the Audience: To turn one's body out slightly toward the audience, usually by a simple shift of the foot.

Opposing Synchronization: Forces actors to work together to create movement that appears to be "cause and effect."

Pantomime: To act out a specific movement without the use of a prop (example: to act like one is holding a phone to their ear to tell a friend to get the phone).

Passion Plays: Dramatic presentations of the suffering, death, and resurrection of Jesus.

Perfect Synchronization: Two or more actors are doing the exact same thing for a sustained period of time.

Pitch: How high or low one's voice is.

Plane: A flat surface that is not always readily visible; may include Stage Left to Stage Right, Downstage to Upstage, and floor to ceiling.

Play: The story written in dialogue form meant to be performed rather than simply read.

Play Publisher: The company that prints, markets, and licenses play scripts.

Plot: The storyline or events in a story.

Podcast: A digital file that can be downloaded and enjoyed at the convenience of the listener.

Polishing Rehearsal: A rehearsal in which the director seeks to make the scene what it will be for performance.

Prepared Auditions: Auditions for which actors have been asked to practice/memorize a certain scene.

Pre-production: What happens in a show before the rehearsal process begins.

Pre-recorded Sound Cues: Sound cues played from CDs, tapes, or digital files.

Production Calendar: The schedule that the cast and crew will follow throughout the production process.

Production Checklist: A running list of tasks to be completed as the performance draws nearer.

Production Contract: An agreement between the director and each participant. When the participants are students, their parents are often asked to join in the agreement.

Production Notebook: The notebook the director uses to organize the entire production; may become the stage manager's book as the show progresses.

Production Notes: Vital information from the playwright and/or original director to those who may direct the play in the future.

Project: 1) A series of tasks that work together like a system. 2) To speak with adequate volume onstage.

Props List: Items needed to perform a scene or play.

Props: The things used by actors onstage.

Proscenium: The vertical plane that frames the stage.

Protagonist: The lead character.

Publicity: Advertisement.

Public Domain: In reference to a play, this is a script that no longer has copyright restrictions.

Rail: A top or bottom cross brace on a flat.

Rate: How fast or slow one speaks.

Read Through: A type of rehearsal in which the script is read, usually with the actors seated around a table.

Readers Theater: A piece for which actors use scripts onstage; other than that, it is very similar to other performances.

Rising Action: The development of the plot after the exposition and before the climax.

Royalties: The payment performance companies make to the publisher for the rights to perform a script.

Scene (as in sections of a play): Sections of acts within a play.

Scenery: The items used to create a location onstage.

Scrim: A type of loosely woven fabric that can be painted to match its background, making it almost transparent.

Script Cover: The outside part of a script book listing the title, playwright, and publisher.

Script: The book in which a play is printed.

Segue: (SEG-way) To make a connection from the current topic to the next topic for the purpose of flowing smoothly.

Selling the Performance: The ability to fully engage the audience in the performance.

NOTES: ____

____

____

____

____

____

____

____

INTRODUCTION TO THEATRE ARTS 2—TEACHER'S GUIDE

Set: Anything that indicates a place or setting or turns a non-traditional performance space into a suitable performance area.

Set Diagram: An aerial view of the original set or the suggested set for the play found in some scripts.

Set Up: The moments after the performer is called to the stage and before their performance begins; often the act of preparing the stage for the performance.

Setting: When and where a story takes place.

Shadows: Dark or sunken-in places on a face that can be enhanced with darker makeup.

Sides: Small sections of scripts prepared for auditions.

Sing-song Cadence: The effect of sounding like the lines have a musical quality; this is usually a negative effect caused when actors become too used to each other, and becoming "sing songy" replaces true interpretation.

Slapstick Humor: Exaggerated, very physical comedy in which the boundaries of common sense are often ignored to elicit a laugh.

Slate: To give one's name and other vital information prior to a performance, particularly an audition.

Slogan: The short phrase that summarizes the product and/or what the advertiser wants the buyer to think of it.

Sound Effects: Audio created to enhance a performance or used to indicate a bit of action (such as the sound of footsteps to indicate a person walking).

Sound: The technical aspect of the production that encompasses all audio elements.

Stage Areas: Most stages are divided into nine or fifteen sections. These are denoted as C for center, L and R for left and right, and U and D for up and down. The letters define places on the stage; UC is up center, and so on.

Stage Directions: Playwright's suggestions for character movement.

Stage Manager: The person in charge of the backstage area.

Stage Picture: A term used to describe each moment onstage as though it were a photograph; the desirable stage picture is one in which actors are focused, a story is being told, and there is a focal point.

Stealing Focus: To take the focus away from the performer who should be the center of the audience's attention at that moment.

Stile: A side piece on a flat.

Story Background: Moments that influence the events in the play and may be mentioned but are not acted out onstage.

Story Foreground: The parts of the play including characters, relationships, etc., in the plot.

Strategies: The things a character does based on their personality to overcome obstacles and reach goals.

Strike: To disassemble.

Suspense: A strong desire to find out what happens next.

Synchronize: To match or align two or more things exactly.

Tableau: Meaning "picture" and also meaning "scene," refers to creating meaningful pictures onstage.

Take Center: To make one's self the center of focus.

Teamwork: The result of more than one person using their assets and working together to reach a common goal; cooperation.

Teaser: A small section of the scene delivered in character prior to the introduction; after the intro, the scene continues where the teaser left off.

Teaser Curtain: A type of drapery that reduces the height of the proscenium opening.

Technical Rehearsal: A rehearsal in which technical aspects are added; often lines are not run, but actors go from one cue to the next to ensure the technical parts of the show are properly functioning.

Theme: The lesson the story is attempting to impart.

Timing: The effective use of pausing, pace and rate, silence, and building of suspense in scene work and performances; may also include movement.

Toggle: A center cross brace on a flat.

Tone: The sound of your voice.

Tormentor: A tall drapery that reduces the width of the stage.

Traveler: A curtain that moves horizontally from left and right, meeting in the center.

Unison: Together.

Upstage Hand (or Foot): The upstage body part is the one farthest away from the audience at that moment; it will change as actors move around on the stage.

Upstage One's Self: To poorly position one's self so that the audience's view will be obstructed.

Venue: Performance space or event setting.

Voice-over: A type of acting in which only the actor's voice is used; cartoons use voice-over, as does radio, and even many TV commercials are voice-over on top of action; narration is often voice-over.

Wings: The area out of the acting area to the left and right where actors wait for their cues.

Work Ethic: A strong impulse to do a job well; a belief that work should be done well.

Working Rehearsal: A standard rehearsal as opposed to a technical rehearsal or a dress rehearsal.

322

NOTES: ____

____

____

____

____

____

____

____

BIBLIOGRAPHY

"frenzied." Dictionary.com Unabridged (v1.1) Random House, Inc. 18 Jun. 2007. http://dictionary.reference. com/browse/frenzied

American Access. https://aaramps.com/resources/

Bailey, Sally Dorothy Wings to Fly: Bringing Theatre Arts to Children with Special Needs. Rockville, MD. Woodbine House, 1993.

Boyd, Lydia. "Brief History of the Radio Industry." https://guides.library.duke.edu/c.php?g=480747&p=3321106.

Clipsham, Jacqueline Ann. "Obstacles and Opportunities: Careers in the Visual Arts for People with Disabilities." http://artsedge.kennedy-center.org/forum/papers/clipsham.html

Daily Star, The. Wed. February 2, 2005, "In conversation with Mok Chiuyu," Ershad Kamol, http://archive. thedailystar.net/2005/02/02/d502021402115.htm

Hampton, Chris. "Preparing Public Service Announcements." http://ctb.ku.edu/tools/en/sub_section_ main_1065.htm

Hosking, Bev, and Christian Penny. "Playback Theatre as a Methodology for Social Change." October 2000. https://devnet.org.nz/

Mace, Ronald L. "Arts Access." https://artsedge.kennedy-center.org/forum/papers/mace.html

Nelson, Gaylord. "How the First Earth Day Came About." https://www.earthday.org/history/

Pepine, Arthur. "Disability and Training in the Arts." https://artsedge.kennedy-center.org/forum/papers/ pepine.html

Associated Press, "Actors with disabilities underrepresented, study says," https://www.backstage.com/ magazine/article/study-disabled-actors-underrepresented-18538/

Rhys, Will. "The National Theatre of the Deaf Professional Theatre School for Deaf Theatre Personnel." https:// artsedge.kennedy-center.org/forum/papers/rhys.html

NOTES: _______________________________________

ABOUT THE AUTHOR

Suzi Zimmerman was the youngest of three children and, admittedly, a bit of a troublemaker. Her siblings were good at sports and music, but she seemed to be flailing. She knew she was creative and loved to perform, but her community focused mainly on sports and music. Those who lacked a place tended to become bored, which led to unacceptable behavior.

She finally discovered theatre, but only because it was offered at the high school level. It was then that she vowed to fight for more accessible performance opportunities for all levels. After college, she founded a local theatre troupe, which eventually became a community theatre, fulfilling her dream of bringing performance opportunities to all. After twenty years in public education, she is now a full-time writer, artist, and businessperson.

Zimmerman has acted professionally in film and on the stage. She is the spokesperson for and director of New Hope Foundation, a nonprofit in northern Texas working to improve the lives of underprivileged families. She is married with five children, two of whom are successful in the film industry.